The Integrated Classroom

*The Assessment-Curriculum Link in
Early Childhood Education*

Sue C. Wortham
University of Texas at San Antonio

1996

Merrill,
an imprint of Prentice Hall
Englewood Cliffs, New Jersey   Columbus, Ohio

Library of Congress Cataloging-in-Publication Data

Wortham, Sue Clark, 1935–
      The integrated classroom : the assessment-curriculum link in early childhood education / Sue C. Wortham
          p.   cm.
      Includes bibliographical references (p.   ) and index.
      ISBN 0-02-326121-8 (alk. paper)
      1. Early childhood education—United States. 2. Child development—United States—Testing. 3. Handicapped children—United States—Identification. 4. Early childhood education—United States—Curricula. 5. Mainstreaming in education—United States.   I. Title.
      LB1139.25.W677   1996
      372.21—dc20   95-21526
                        CIP

Cover photo: ©Walter Hodges/Westlight
Editor: Ann Castel Davis
Production Editor: Alexandrina Benedicto Wolf
Photo Editor: Anne Vega
Design Coordinator: Jill E. Bonar
Text Designer: Mia Saunders
Cover Designer: Anne D. Flanagan
Production Manager: Patricia A. Tonneman
Electronic Text Management: Marilyn Wilson Phelps, Matthew Williams, Karen L. Bretz,
    Tracey Ward

This book was set in Bitstream Zapf Humanist and Bitstream Swiss by Prentice Hall and was printed and bound by Quebecor Printing/Book Press. The cover was printed by Phoenix Color Corp.

© 1996 by Prentice-Hall, Inc.
A Simon & Schuster Company
Englewood Cliffs, New Jersey 07632

Photo credits: pp. 2, 17, 51, 72, 104, 116, 132, 179, 201, 230, and 336 by Anne Vega/Merrill/Prentice Hall; p. 5 by Sandra Anselmo; pp. 24, 36, 107, and 173 by Scott Cunningham/Merrill/Prentice Hall; pp. 37, 76, and 156 by Todd Yarrington/Merrill/Prentice Hall; pp. 46, 48, 194265, and 303 by Barbara Schwartz/Merrill/Prentice Hall; p. 128 by Kevin Fitzsimons/Merrill/Prentice Hall; pp. 164, 260, and 326 by Tom Watson/Merrill/Prentice Hall; pp. 226 and 241 by KS Studios/Merrill/Prentice Hall; and p. 296 by Robert Finken/Merrill/Prentice Hall.

Printed in the United States of America

10 9 8 7 6 5 4 3 2 1

ISBN: 0-02-326121-8

Prentice-Hall International (UK) Limited, *London*
Prentice-Hall of Australia Pty. Limited, *Sydney*
Prentice-Hall of Canada, Inc., *Toronto*
Prentice-Hall Hispanoamericana, S. A., *Mexico*
Prentice-Hall of India Private Limited, *New Delhi*
Prentice-Hall of Japan, Inc., *Tokyo*
Simon & Schuster Asia Pte. Ltd., *Singapore*
Editora Prentice-Hall do Brasil, Ltda., *Rio de Janeiro*

To Marshal Wortham, my husband

Preface

The field of early childhood education is dynamic and is constantly evolving. There are many types of early childhood programs. However, all share commonalities. One commonality is that all are seeking to improve the developmental and learning experiences that are provided for young children. Another commonality is that all programs are seeking to improve how they address the group and individual needs of the young children that they serve. A reality in most types of programs and settings is that the children who are enrolled can be very diverse. The diversity can be developmental, cultural, linguistic, and in ability. In addition, children with disabilities or who are at risk for developing a disability or difficulty may also be members of the class.

This book was written to help teachers of young children prepare for diversity in their students. It was developed as a result of the concerns early childhood teachers have expressed about the needs of young children who enter preschool and primary classrooms. As children with disabilities are included into all types of early childhood classrooms, teachers and future teachers are becoming aware that they must broaden their knowledge base about similarities and differences in children and about ways to prepare quality programs for all children.

Another element in the decisions made as to the content of this text was the need to address how to determine the development, abilities, and needs of individual children who might be present in the program. It was thought to be necessary to establish the link between the evaluation of young children through assessment with the experiences that would be provided for them in the early childhood classroom. In addition, because the fields of early childhood education and early childhood special education have functioned somewhat separately in the past, it seemed important to discuss topics in linking assessment and curriculum in terms of the diversity in young children. In other words, another link was established between how to serve children with diverse abilities and backgrounds within the classroom that also serves children with more average abilities.

This text, then, is about integration: the integration of all types of children in the early childhood classroom; the integration of assessment and learning as an interactive process; and the integration of curriculum and instruction to be age appropriate, group appropriate, and individually appropriate. It is hoped that students using it will find information that will help them make connections between how children's development and backgrounds are both similar and different and how the early childhood teacher can prepare to work with each one individually and with a group of young children as a whole.

I am indebted to many people for the conceptualization and development of this text. The first ideas and planning came from conversations with John Cryan of the University of Toledo. Although he was unable to serve as coauthor, his perceptions and input were invaluable. Graduate students in various classes added needed information and ideas as did teachers in early childhood classrooms in the San Antonio area. My colleagues at the University of Texas at San Antonio were a source of resources and suggestions. I especially want to thank Suzanne Winter, Anthony Van Reusen, and David Katims for their help. Barbara Gilstad used an early draft in her class to try out the information with undergraduate students, and other colleagues have offered encouragement.

I also want to thank my editors, Linda Sullivan and Ann Davis, who were both patient and supportive. Reviewers provided important insights and suggestions. I am indebted to the following: John Chesky, Montreat-Anderson College; Suzanne E. Cortez, Northern Kentucky University; Robert G. Harrington, University of Kansas; Peggy Perkins, University of Nevada-Las Vegas; and Phil Wishon, University of Northern Colorado.

Sue C. Wortham

Contents

1

Introduction   2

Overview of Current Trends in Early Childhood Programs   3
Defining Early Childhood and Early Childhood Programs   6
Diversity in Young Children and Early Childhood Programs   7

Issues and Trends in Screening, Assessment, and Instruction in
    Early Childhood Education   10
Issues and Trends in Developing Programs for All Children   10
Issues in Using Standardized Measurement Instruments   12
Trends in Screening and Assessment of Young Children   14

The Relationship Between Screening and Assessment and the
    Early Childhood Program   16
Screening and Assessment for Initial Evaluation   16
Linking Screening, Assessment, and Instruction   17
Using Assessment Results to Plan Instruction   18

The Role of Federal Regulation in Screening and Assessment   18

2

Screening in Early Childhood Programs   24

Background on Screening in Early Childhood Programs   26
The Evolution of Early Childhood Programs for Populations at Risk   26

The Scope of Screening in Early Childhood Programs   *27*
Target Populations for Screening in Early Childhood   *31*

Selecting an Approach for Screening   34

Theoretical Influences on the Screening Approach   *34*
Possible Procedures for Screening   *35*

Selecting a Screening Instrument   38

Selecting Screening Instruments for Infants and Toddlers   *38*
Selecting a Preschool Screening Test   *39*

Setting Up a Screening Program   40

The Role of the Family in the Screening Process   41

3

Assessment in Early Childhood Programs   46

The Role of Assessment in Curriculum Planning   47

*Assessment for Children at Risk vs. Assessment for Children
    Not at Risk*   *47*
The Purposes for Assessment in Curriculum Planning   *49*
Assessment for Temperament and Learning Styles   *52*
Assessment for Instructional Grouping   *53*

Using Appropriate Assessment Strategies   54

Assessment Strategies at the Beginning of The Year   *55*
In-Depth Assessments at the Beginning of the Year   *58*

4

Initiating the Instructional Program   72

Preparing the Environment   74

*Understanding the Role of the Environment in the Early Childhood
    Program*   *74*
Understanding the Role of Play in the Early Childhood Program   *75*
Organizing the Indoor Environment   *78*
Organizing the Outdoor Environment   *83*

Planning the Instructional Program   89

Determining Goals and Objectives for Learning   *90*
Setting Up the Learning Environment   *92*
Planning Daily Routines   *93*

Guiding Children's Transition Into the Program   94
Teaching How to Use the Environment   94
Promoting Positive Classroom Behaviors   95

Conducting Initial Assessments   96
Strategies for Initial Assessment   96
Tips for Effective Initial Assessments   99

5

Linking Assessment and Curriculum Planning   104

Planning Appropriate Curriculum for Preschool and
    Primary Grades   106

Linking Assessment and Curriculum Planning   108
*How Does a Developmental Curriculum Reflect Assessment
    Information?   108*
Using Assessment Information to Plan Instruction   109

Planning and Managing Different Types of Instruction   113
Teacher-Directed Instruction   116
Instruction in Learning Centers   117
Balancing Teacher-Directed and Child-Initiated Instruction   117
Understanding Instructional Cycles   118

Planning Evaluation for Different Types of Instruction   121

Continuing the Assessment-Instruction Link   123
Ongoing Assessment and Evaluation   123
Regrouping Children   124
Record Keeping and Reporting Progress to Parents   124

6

Screening and Assessment in Early Intervention Programs for Young Children With Special Needs   128

The Background of Early Childhood Intervention Services   130
Legal Requirements of the Education of Handicapped Children Acts   133

The Screening and Assessment Process and Early Intervention
    Programs   135
Purposes for Screening and Assessment   135
Screening and Assessing Infants and Toddlers   138

Screening and Assessing Preschool and Primary Age Children   *139*
The Role of the Family in Screening and Assessment   *140*
Steps in Assessment and Placement in an Intervention Program   *142*
Goals for Intervention Programs   *143*
Models of Early Intervention Programs   *144*

Planning Intervention for Individual Children   148

The Team Role in Developing the Individual Intervention Plan   *148*
Steps in Developing the Individual Intervention Plan   *149*
The Role of the Family in Developing Individual Intervention Plans   *155*

The Issues of Integrating Children With Special Needs
    and at Risk   155

Issues Related to Inclusion in Early Childhood Programs   *156*
Issues Related to Inclusion in Public Schools   *159*
*Beyond Inclusion: Reforming Education and Special Education
    to Include All Children*   *160*

7

Linking Curriculum and Instruction for Young Children With Special Needs

164

Planning Instruction for Children With Disabilities   166

Linking Assessment and Curriculum Planning   *166*
*Using Assessment to Plan Instruction for Preschool and
    Primary Age Children*   *168*

Planning and Managing Different Approaches to Instruction   169

Curriculum Models for Early Intervention Strategies   *169*
Instructional Strategies for Early Intervention Programs   *171*
Developmentally Appropriate Instructional Strategies   *172*

Planning Instruction for Children at Risk   175

Linking Assessment and Curriculum Planning   *178*
*Using Assessment to Plan Curriculum and Instruction for Children
    at Risk*   *181*
*Planning and Managing Different Approaches to Instruction With
    Children at Risk*   *183*

Evaluating Curriculum and Instruction for Children With Special
    Needs and at Risk   189

Continuing the Assessment-Instruction Link   *189*
Evaluating Intervention Programs for Children With Disabilities   *190*
Evaluating Programs for Children at Risk   *190*

8

Cognitive Development   194

The Developmental Basis of Curriculum   196
Understanding Developmental Curriculum   196
Characteristics of a Developmental Curriculum   197
The Nature of Cognitive Development   198
Understanding Cognitive Development   198

Planning Instruction for Cognitive Development   202
Understanding the Teacher's Role   202
Understanding How Young Children Learn   203
*Understanding How Young Children Acquire Concepts in
    Mathematics and Science   204*
Organizing Curriculum for Cognitive Development   206

Assessing Cognitive Development   210
Strategies for Assessing Cognitive Development   214

Assessment/Learning Experiences for Cognitive Development   216

Planning Instruction in Cognitive Development for Children
    With Disabilities   218
Children With Communication Disorders   218
Children With Hearing Impairments   218
Children With Vision Impairments   219
Children With Learning Disabilities   219
Children With Mental Retardation   219

Evaluating Curriculum and Instruction for
    Cognitive Development   220
Formative Evaluation   220
Summative Evaluation   221

9

Language Development   226

The Nature of Language Development   227
Understanding Language Development   228
Components of Language   228
Components of Literacy   229
Theoretical Bases for Language Development   231
Implications of Theories for Development of Language and Literacy   233

Planning Instruction for Language and Literacy Development   233

Understanding the Teacher's Role   *234*
*Understanding Language and Literacy Acquisition in
  Preschool Children*   *235*
Organizing Curriculum for Language and Literacy Development   *237*

Assessing Development in Language and Literacy   246

Strategies for Assessing Language and Literacy Development   *248*

Assessment/Learning Experiences for Language and
  Literacy Development   251

Planning Instruction for Children With Communication
  Impairments   252

Planning Instruction for Children From Diverse Backgrounds   253

Evaluating Curriculum and Instruction for Language and
  Literacy Development   255

Formative Evaluation   *255*
Summative Evaluation   *256*

10

Social Development   260

The Nature of Social Development   262

The Role of Play in Social Development   *264*
Theoretical Bases for Social Development   *266*
Implications of Theories for Practices in Early Childhood Education   *269*

Planning Instruction for Social Development   271

Understanding the Teacher's Role   *272*
Organizing Curriculum for Social Development   *273*
Designing Goals for Curriculum in Social Development   *279*

Assessing Social Development   286

Observation   *286*
Anecdotal Records   *287*
Running Records   *287*
Time Sampling   *287*
Checklists and Rating Scales   *288*
Interviews   *288*

Assessment/Learning Experiences for Social Development   288

Planning Instruction for Children With Disabilities   289

Evaluating Curriculum and Instruction for Social Development   290
Formative Evaluation   290
Summative Evaluation   291

11

Physical Development   296

The Nature of Physical Development   298
Understanding Physical Development   298
The Role of Play in Physical Development   301

Planning Instruction for Physical Development   302
Understanding the Teacher's Role   302
Understanding the Role of the Environment   303
Organizing Curriculum for Physical Development   305

Assessing Physical Development   311
Observation   311
Motor Skills Tasks   312
Checklists   312

Assessment/Learning Experiences for Physical Development   313

Planning Instruction for Children With Physical Impairments   314
The Nature of Physical Impairments   314
Needs of Children With Physical Disabilities   315
*Adapting the Preschool Environment for Children
    With Physical Impairments*   315
*Planning Learning Experiences for Children With
    Physical Impairments*   316

Evaluating Curriculum and Instruction for
    Physical Development   318
Formative Evaluation   318
Summative Evaluation   320

12

Bringing It All Together   326

The Integrated Curriculum   328
Origins of the Integrated Curriculum   328
Integrated Curriculum Today   329

Understanding Integrated Curriculum   330
Integration From a Developmental Domain or Subject Area   331
Integration Through Topics   332
Integration Through the Early Childhood Environment   332
Integration Through Thematic Units   333

Planning Integrated Curriculum to Meet
   Developmental Needs   334
Understanding How Development and Learning Are Interrelated   334
Planning Integrated Curriculum That Is Group Appropriate   335
Planning Integrated Curriculum That Is Individually Appropriate   335
Planning Integrated Curriculum to Meet Cultural Differences   335

Planning Integrated Curriculum to Respond to
   Children's Interests   337
Teacher-Initiated Integrated Curriculum That Includes Input
   From the Children   337
Integrated Curriculum That Is Initiated From Children's Interests   337

Planning Integrated Curriculum to Understand Connections
   in Knowledge   338

Models for Planning Integrated Curriculum   339
The Project Approach to Integrated Curriculum   339
The Thematic Unit Approach to Integrated Curriculum   341

Planning for Inclusion of Diversity in the Integrated
   Curriculum   344

Evaluating Integrated Curriculum and Instruction   345
Assessing Children's Progress in Integrated Curriculum   345
Assessing Effectiveness of the Integrated Curriculum   346
Assessing the Teacher's Role   346

A Final Look at Early Childhood Programs   347

Glossary   351
References   355
Author Index   367
Subject Index   371
About the Author   383

 # 1

Introduction

➤ **Chapter Objectives**

As a result of reading this chapter, you will be able to

1. Describe the variety of early childhood programs
2. List key characteristics of diversity in young children who attend early childhood programs
3. Explain the role of screening and assessment in developing educational programs for young children
4. Discuss issues concerning the use of standardized measurement instruments with young children
5. Describe the relationship between screening, assessment, and planning instruction for individual children and groups of children
6. Explain the role of federal regulations in screening and assessment

OVERVIEW OF CURRENT TRENDS IN EARLY CHILDHOOD PROGRAMS

This book is about educational programs for children in the early childhood years. It is written for students who are preparing to teach in early childhood programs, as well as for teachers who are currently working with young children in various kinds of programs. The book focuses on how to develop quality programs for the diversity of children who attend early childhood classrooms—whether the classrooms be in public schools, private schools, Head Start centers, child care or child development centers, or children's hospitals. The children in such programs are a diverse population, including children with cultural or linguistic diversity and those with disabilities. All these children may be served within an **integrated classroom.**

A major concern at the present time is to provide programs that are suitable for young children. In the 1980s, early childhood classrooms from preschool through third grade were becoming more and more academic in focus to respond to measures for school reform designed to raise achievement. Teaching practices became more directed toward increasing scores on standardized achievement tests than on providing the best programming for young children. As a result, many children were not succeeding in their first years of schooling. The publication of *Developmentally*

Appropriate Practice in Early Childhood Programs Serving Children From Birth Through Age 8 (Bredekamp, 1987) marked a turning point; subsequently, teaching practices were revised to be more suited to young children's level of development. As a result of the guidelines for developmentally appropriate practices provided in that publication, there have been national efforts to develop quality programs for young children in all types of early childhood settings.

Congruent with this concern is the reality that there is a widening diversity in young children who attend early childhood programs. To meet the diversity, there has been an expansion in programs that provide varied services to children and families. In the effort to develop quality programs, early childhood educators must address the issues of development in young children and variations in development among individual children. The more diverse the children are, the more essential it is to know as much as possible about each child's developmental status so that instructional planning is suitable for the age of the child, as well as the needs of the individual child.

As children with extreme differences in development are integrated into early childhood classrooms, a new issue related to appropriate practices has emerged. The strategies used with young children with disabilities address their learning needs, which are somewhat different than those of children of more average ability. Children with mental retardation or behavior disorders require repetition of learning activities and focus on skill development, which may not be needed by all children. Teacher-structured and teacher-directed activities are used to provide children with disabilities with the repeated experiences using the skills that they need for daily functioning and learning.

As all kinds of populations are integrated into early childhood classrooms, the diversity in children must be accommodated. Early childhood educators must reevaluate what quality programming that is "developmentally appropriate" means in reality. Developmentally appropriate practices are constructivist in philosophy, based on the theory of development first proposed by Jean Piaget (1952). On the other hand, with children who need repetition and support in their learning efforts, instruction that is structured with the use of teacher-directed strategies supported with positive reinforcement has been used. This type of instruction has been identified with B. F. Skinner's (1972) theory of learning. The principles of developmentally appropriate practices have been founded on child-centered and child-initiated learning—a model that is based on the child's active interaction with the world. These principles have encouraged teachers to permit children to take a more active and responsible role in their own learning. In contrast, the practices used with children with disabilities have focused on adult-planned and adult-implemented intervention activities designed for individual children.

It is this author's position that we must broaden our vision of developmentally appropriate practices to include how best to serve all young children—including those with extremes in development. We must not view one or the other theoretical approach as the only appropriate one; instead we should evaluate how and when each should be used within a quality program. This is a complex task, but it is the reality that awaits future teachers. Throughout this book, we will be discussing the role of theories in curriculum and instruction for young children. We will also be

Young children experience all types of screening and assessment

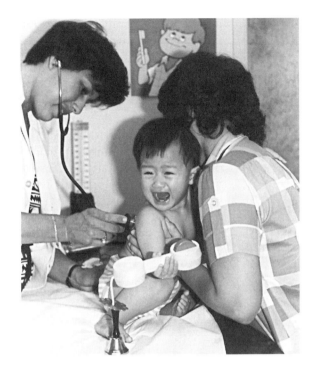

looking at how to organize the environment and learning experiences to meet diverse needs. The intent is to help teachers understand how to work with all young children who will be assigned to early childhood classrooms in the future. Not all programs include young children from diverse backgrounds and with disabilities, but it is likely that diversity will increase steadily in the years to come.

It is not the intent of this author to propose a return to the academic approach to early childhood education, which advocated practices that are now considered to be inappropriate for young children. It is this author's philosophy that the constructivist approach will need to incorporate a wider repertoire of strategies if the needs of all children are to be met in early childhood classrooms. Children with diverse needs will require teachers to be knowledgeable about variations in learning; moreover, teachers will need to be able to individualize for children whose developmental levels are outside the range of normal development. In the future, early childhood teachers and early childhood special education teachers will be working together to serve children of all abilities and with a variety of backgrounds. They will need to employ a variety of approaches and strategies to address the needs and potential of their students.

Before a program can be developed, teachers of young children must be able to determine what the developmental levels of children are and how their backgrounds affect their abilities, needs, and interests within the preschool setting. If a child exhibits significant developmental differences, a process of developmental **screening** may be initiated followed by more specific **assessment** of developmental categories. Screening is the process of evaluating general developmental indicators, while assessment is a more comprehensive and specific developmental evaluation. Results of screening and assessment are used as the foundation for designing the program for groups of children, as well as for the individual children within each group. Screening and assessment results are also used to decide the best type of program for children; and for some, they are used to design prescriptive plans for **intervention** that address a developmental or health problem. Intervention plans are designed and used with children who have developmental delays or disabilities that are serious enough to require early attention or mediation.

The intention of this text, then, is to guide the reader through the steps of assessment and instructional planning that ensure that all children in the early childhood years are engaged in curriculum approaches that facilitate their development and respond to their uniqueness as individuals. However, before we proceed further, we need to establish an understanding of the meaning of early childhood education, the nature of diversity in young children, and the diversity of programs that serve young children.

Defining Early Childhood and Early Childhood Programs

Early childhood, from this author's perspective, ranges from birth through the age of eight. Infancy and toddler years are the first stages of early childhood, while the years from three to five, prior to kindergarten, are the preschool years. Kindergarten and the three primary grades of elementary school are the latter stage of early childhood. Although definitions of the span of early childhood vary, the broadest perspective is taken in this text. This is particularly important when we consider the importance of early intervention in infancy for children who are at risk at birth and who need programs to support their development.

There are many types of programs that serve young children during the early childhood years. Although the history of early childhood education indicates that these programs have different origins, today they are similar in purpose and overlap in the services that they provide for young children.

Public school programs are obviously one environment for early childhood programs. Prior to the 1960s, public schools offered classes for kindergarten and elementary school children, typically serving children from the age of five and up. Special programs to support children from diverse backgrounds were not common. Since the 1960s, public school programs have been expanded to serve children under the age of five or six: these include bilingual programs, special education programs, and programs for children considered to be **"at risk"** for successful academic achievement—that is, there is some factor in the child's development, physical condition, background, or environment that might have a negative effect on successful learning. More recently, **mainstreaming** of children with disabilities and the movement toward integration, or **inclusion,** into regular classrooms have resulted in merging of programs rather than separating children with disabilities from other populations of young children (Deiner, 1993). The practice of mainstreaming involves moving children with disabilities from the special education classroom into the regular classroom for part of the day. Inclusion, on the other hand, is the practice of integrating the child into the regular classroom as much as possible and removing him or her to a special education environment only when necessary. Inclusion also means that there is a two-way integration of children from both the regular and special education classrooms. Not only do children from special education learn in regular classrooms, but children from the regular classroom also spend time in the special education classroom.

Child care originated early in this century to provide supervision and care for children of poor working parents in urban areas. Since the 1950s, child care has largely been supported through parental payment, often when a parent or both parents work, and the number of child care centers has greatly expanded. More recently, child care settings have been broadened: there are federally supported programs for some populations, and sometimes care is provided in the home during the day when parents are at work. Most recently, children with disabilities have been introduced into caregiving programs, adding a new dimension to the potential of child care centers to serve young children, as well as the new responsibilities and problems involved in addressing a variety of disabilities (DeHaas-Warner, 1994).

There are various other settings that serve young children. Private and parochial centers may serve children before they are eligible for public school, and many extend their services into elementary education, and in some cases, continue into secondary education. Programs for children under the age of six might be called nursery schools, preschools, early childhood centers, or other terms such as child enrichment centers. Head Start programs—initiated with federal funding for children from poverty backgrounds in the 1960s—continue today with expanded purposes to serve younger children and children with disabilities. There are early childhood programs for hospitalized children or medically fragile children, as well as centers that specialize in a particular type of disability such as hearing impaired children or young children infected with the HIV virus.

Diversity in Young Children and Early Childhood Programs

There is an increasing variation in the development, culture, and language of children in early childhood classrooms. This diversity can represent development that is outside the range we think of as "average." All children are unique and different. The differences in some children are more pronounced, and childhood itself is at risk in the society of the 1990s. Who are these young children, and how are they diverse?

We are a nation of many cultures and languages. We are, in addition, a large nation with many regions that are different in geography, economics, and the ethnic origins of people who live there. Florida has a large Latino population from the Caribbean and Central and South America, combined with native Floridians and retirees who have moved south to Florida because of the mild climate. Many states in the Central Plains reflect the immigrant populations that immigrated to the United States from Europe during the period of the nation's western expansion in the nineteenth century. Family farming has been a mainstay of these states, but corporate farming is transforming some of the areas. California has large Latino and Oriental populations who have contributed to the California culture, a state that has also experienced continued large influxes of populations from other regions of the United States.

Diversity at McDougall Elementary School

Patricia is a second grade teacher at McDougall Elementary School, which serves children of families that are apartment dwellers in a large urban area. Because the area around the school consists of mostly lower middle class families, there is a high turnover each year at the school as parents move from one job to another. The apartments in the neighborhood also serve as a low-cost source of housing for immigrants moving into the area.

Patricia's classroom reflects the diversity in the school. She has 22 students, equally divided between boys and girls. Seven of the children are Anglo, four are African American, and eleven are Hispanic in background. Five of the children are Spanish speakers, one boy has been categorized as emotionally disturbed, and two have learning disabilities. Although the school does not have enough children whose first language is Spanish to have a bilingual program, Patricia speaks Spanish and works with a bilingual consultant to plan how to incorporate Spanish into her teaching strategies. Special education specialists and the school counselor assist with the children with special needs, but Patricia is the primary teacher for all of the children.

The history of the United States began with the original settlers during the colonial period, and immigration has been a constant and important factor in the nation's history through the present day. As a result, the young children of this country represent a mixture of cultures, languages, ethnic groups, and regional differences that influence their uniqueness as they become part of early childhood programs. In addition, variations in economic and family conditions contribute to the diversity found in young children. Although many children grow up in two-parent, middle class or upper class homes, increasingly, young children are growing up in poverty, living in dangerous areas of the community where violence is rampant, or experiencing variations and changes in family composition that leave them with little permanence and security in their lives.

Many American children are born into poverty and violence. Their effects on young children are reported in shocking statistics. The Children's Defense Fund Annual Report (Children's Defense Fund, 1994, p. xxi) cites some of the effects of poverty and violence on young children in one year as follows:

208	children under 10 are killed by firearms
73,886	children under 18 are arrested for drug abuse
531,591	babies are born to teen mothers

928,205	babies are born to mothers without high school diplomas
1,047,000	babies are born into poverty
1,200,000	latchkey children come home to houses where there is a gun
1,213,769	babies are born to unmarried mothers
2,695,010	children are reported abused or neglected

While many of the numbers reported above are directly related to poverty, they include children from homes of all economic levels.

Separation and divorce result in families with single parents, as well as disruptions in living patterns for young children (Frieman, 1993). While not all children who experience divorce are troubled and insecure, a large percentage of children are negatively affected and the difficulties they experience can continue for a long period of time (Hetherington, Stanley-Hagen, & Anderson, 1989). Changing economic conditions, living conditions, and emotional trauma experienced by both parents and children result in young children who exhibit emotional problems that affect their ability to adjust and benefit from early childhood program experiences.

Diversity in young children includes diversity in educational abilities. A growing percentage of young children have disabilities that include mental, physical, emotional, and health-related differences (Spodek & Saracho, 1994). Mental disabilities can include **mental retardation**, a delay in intellectual growth, while physical disabilities can include visual, hearing, or motor disabilities as well as combinations of such disabilities. Emotional difficulties can have many causes and many effects on children's abilities in group settings. Extreme shyness, separation distress, and inappropriate behaviors are but a few manifestations of emotional differences in young children. Prenatal conditions can result in emotional problems. Children born to mothers addicted to drugs or alcohol can experience emotional disturbances, and in the case of **fetal alcohol syndrome**, permanent mental retardation. Emotional problems can cause children to be restless or excessively active, which can result in their having difficulty in participating in class activities. Extensive discussion of developmental diversity and disabilities will be incorporated into later sections of the book.

Children representing all types of diversity attend all types of programs from Head Start to public school early childhood programs, private, and parochial programs. Because of the growing number of parents from all economic levels who work, young children increasingly are entering child care, often beginning in infancy. The diversity of these children presents challenges to caregiving and preschool programs, as well as to public school programs. While child care settings must adjust to children with diverse abilities and backgrounds (Green and Widoff, 1990; Perreault, 1991), public schools also must expand their vision to respond to family changes and needs for child care, in addition to considering how to serve children's cultural, language, ethnic, and educational diversities (Coleman, 1990).

New early childhood programs have been established to respond to the need for early intervention for infants born with disabilities or conditions that cause them to be at risk. Although funding is available for programs to serve infants and toddlers who have disabilities, it is still not adequate. There is a shortage of trained early intervention personnel and programs for infants and toddlers, but such programs will be developed and expanded rapidly in response to federal legislation mandating services (Widerstrom, Mowder, & Sandall, 1991).

The challenges of meeting the diverse needs of young children in the early childhood years are numerous and significant. Early childhood programs will be expanded and transformed as they seek to make the changes and adaptations required for the inclusion of all children. These changes will not be easy. In the following section, some of the issues and trends involved in modifying programs and evaluating children to meet individual needs will be discussed.

ISSUES AND TRENDS IN SCREENING, ASSESSMENT, AND INSTRUCTION IN EARLY CHILDHOOD EDUCATION

The goal of settings providing early childhood programs is to meet the needs of the children who are enrolled and of their families. The major responsibility of early childhood programs is to determine the needs of the children and their families and decide how to organize the program to best develop each child's potential. In earlier decades, when children attending a program seemed to be more homogeneous, the practice was to design a program that reflected the perception that all children had similar needs and abilities. Programs serving children who were predominantly from homes that represented the middle class tended to take a single approach to curriculum and instruction. Children with disabilities were served in separate programs. Likewise, children who came from homes where the first language was not English were served in separate programs, called bilingual or English as a Second Language (ESL). Unfortunately, many bilingual programs are still separate, based on policies that discourage integration of bilingual students with students enrolled in other classrooms.

Because at this time the major effort toward instruction in integrated settings focuses on children with disabilities, the following discussion will address the issues and trends in serving children with disabilities in integrated classrooms. The issues to be discussed include the (1) concerns in developing programs that include children with disabilities, (2) issues in the measurement instruments that are used with young children, and (3) trends in screening and assessment for the purpose of identifying children who need early intervention and of determining the type of program individual children need to best develop their potential.

Issues and Trends in Developing Programs for All Children

U.S. Public Law 101–476, passed in 1990, mandated that special education services are to be offered in the least restrictive environment, a term that was originally described in P.L. 94–142 passed in 1974. Moreover, the Americans With Disabilities Act (ADA), effective January 1992, prohibits discrimination on the basis of disability.

This means that early childhood settings cannot prohibit children with disabilities from attending their program whether they be public, private, or parochial. The definition of least restrictive environment (LRE) means that if at all possible, the child should be placed in the educational environment in which he or she would have been placed if not eligible for special education and related services (DeHaas-Warner, 1994; Rose & Smith, 1993). Preschool programs now must attempt to serve all children, including those with physical and mental disabilities. While public schools must address inclusion or integration, private child care programs have more flexibility, but may need to make efforts to accommodate young children with special needs (DeHaas-Warner, 1994).

A Cooperative Venture in Early Intervention

Northwood School District conducts a large program in early intervention for preschool children with disabilities. Since the program is conducted for half days, many of the children are bussed in from area child care centers and then returned each day. Recently, the school district and some child care centers have entered into a cooperative partnership to eliminate some of the need to bus children back and forth. Instead of children going to the elementary school, teachers from the school come to the centers to work with the children. Parents have agreed to enroll their children in the centers that offer early intervention services within their program.

There were complications in getting the cooperative program started. Issues of who would pay teachers, the role of child care teachers, provision of meals, and provision for insurance for possible injuries on the part of children and adults all had to be resolved. Nevertheless, the satisfaction on the part of parents, teachers, and administrators at both sites resulted in the expansion of the program to other centers and schools for the second year of the project.

The nature of the child care field introduces specific difficulties in meeting these regulations and expectations. Since many caregivers and teachers in the child care field have not had access to training children with disabilities, they may not have the knowledge and skills to work with this population. The lack of quality in many child care settings is also an issue in relation to the inclusion of children with special needs. Bowman (1990) is especially concerned about the effects of poor-quality day care on children who are in a risk category. Lack of appropriate staff training is one of the major obstacles to providing quality experiences, especially in the light of high staff turnover in the field (Green & Widoff, 1990). This is even more significant given the need for continuity and long-range planning for children with special needs.

Intervention within an integrated setting raises the issue of possible philosophical differences in curriculum and instruction between early childhood educators and educators of children with special needs. The field of early childhood special education has developed from a behavioral perspective and has a strong teacher-directed orientation. In contrast, early childhood education places a strong emphasis on child-initiated learning that is developmentally appropriate. Although there are indications that children with disabilities who are integrated into regular early childhood settings make good progress, differences in philosophy and theoretical orientation must be resolved when programs for all children are developed (Diamond, Hestenes, & O'Conner, 1994). As teachers from both fields work together, similarities in philosophy and application of theories are being discovered. This issue will be addressed in more detail in Chapter 6, where the inclusion of children with disabilities in early childhood classrooms will be examined in detail.

There are other issues that cause barriers to mainstreaming or inclusion in preschool programs. One such barrier is the issue of turf—or losing influence in the education of children with special needs. Special education teachers may wish to keep children with special needs separated because they believe they can better serve the children or because they are concerned about their job security. Teachers of children with special needs may express doubt that teachers in the regular program can meet the needs of "their" children.

Classroom teachers may express concern about their own inadequacies. They are concerned that they do not have the resources and knowledge to work with children with severe disabilities. Moreover, they may have doubts about how the children will fit into their program.

Parental concerns about the adequacy of integrated programs can be another barrier. Parents of children in the regular program may express concerns because a majority of the time and attention will go to the child with disabilities. At the same time, parents of children with special needs fear that their child's individual plan and unique intervention strategies will be lost in the efforts of the teacher to address the program to the group of children (Rose & Smith, 1993).

The issues raised by the current approach of developing programs for all children are not insurmountable. Whenever new program approaches or strategies are introduced, differences between participants must be addressed and resolved. In this case, evidence already exists on the benefits to young children from mainstreaming or integration. It is clear that teachers serving different populations need to work collaboratively to develop programs that provide quality experiences for all children, regardless of the nature of their diversity.

Issues in Using Standardized Measurement Instruments With Young Children

Uses of Standardized Tests With Young Children   Programs that serve children in the early childhood years must conduct some type of screening and assessment of children, as well as evaluate the program itself. Standardized measurement instruments play a major role in the evaluation of children's development in the preschool years; in the primary grades, measurement of learning becomes significant.

There are appropriate uses of standardized tests with young children. Infants and toddlers are measured to determine if their development is normal. If developmental delay of some type is suspected, standardized measures may be used to determine if the child's developmental difficulty indicates a need for intervention. For example, if a child is found to be hearing or visually impaired, intervention services initiated as early as possible will enhance the child's adaptation to the condition.

Preschool children who are at risk for successful achievement in school might be measured to determine if they meet the qualifications for a preschool program. Children who speak a language other than English might be tested to determine if they have language limitations that can be addressed through a bilingual program or a preschool program that focuses on language development. Likewise, children with limited concept development can be identified through a standardized measurement instrument and served through a preschool program designed for children with like needs.

School-age children are given standardized tests to determine achievement in learning. If they exhibit poor achievement or difficulties in learning, standardized instruments are administered to diagnose the difficulty. Children with learning difficulties might be served through federally funded programs designed to help them stay up with their peers. Chapter 1 is such a program that is available in public schools. Children with more serious difficulties might be tested further to determine if they need special education services. Extensive testing might be conducted to diagnose the extent of the problem and to help in designing individual plans for the intervention services that the child will need (Wortham, 1995).

Concerns About Uses of Standardized Tests With Young Children   There is considerable dissatisfaction with the use of group standardized measurements with elementary school students. One concern is that too much testing is conducted in public schools. Another is that the measurement instruments are lacking in quality and that standardized measurement is inappropriate to evaluate children's progress and achievement.

These concerns are considered to be even more serious for young children. Tests designed for groups of students are thought to be inappropriate for young children. Further, early childhood specialists object to the use of achievement tests with children in the primary grades. They judge that these measures are unsuitable because they do not assess true learning and because they result in inappropriate instructional practices being used with children in order to prepare them for the test (Kamii & Kamii, 1990; Shepard, 1989).

Also subject to criticism are standardized measures used to place children in preschool programs. **Readiness tests** are frequently used to determine if children will be admitted to a kindergarten or first-grade program. Labeled "high stakes tests" (Meisels, 1989), readiness tests are considered inappropriate because important decisions such as retention, promotion, and admission to a program are based on the results of the test (Goodwin & Goodwin, 1993).

In contrast, measurement instruments administered to children for early screening of developmental, learning, and health problems are considered to be beneficial, particularly because they are administered individually to the young child. Needed intervention services resulting from this type of testing make their use significant for young children with special needs. Nevertheless, these tests have also been challenged as being poorly constructed or inadequate. One concern is that a majority of the tests being used are not technically adequate in terms of **validity, reliability,** and **norms** (Lehr, Ysseldyke, & Thurlow, 1987).

Many question the process of using standardized instruments with young children; nevertheless, such tests, when selected and used correctly, do have an important role in the evaluation of development and learning of young children. This is especially true when the tests are given for the purposes of screening and assessment of individual development. Moreover, federally funded programs for young children require the use of standardized measures to evaluate program effectiveness.

The issue is complex. Educators of children of all types in early childhood settings need to be knowledgeable about the benefits of standardized tests, but more important about the limitations and difficulties of the use of this type of measurement with children in the early childhood years (Wortham, 1995). Recognizing the complexities involved in the screening and assessment of young children, the trend today is to use a variety of strategies to ensure that children are measured appropriately. These trends will be discussed in the following section.

Trends in Screening and Assessment of Young Children

As a result of the widespread criticism of the use of standardized measures with young children, current efforts have focused on designing instruments that can give a more comprehensive, accurate picture of a child's development and learning. Before discussion of these alternatives, the meaning and uses of screening and assessment should be described.

Screening is conducted to identify children who are not developing normally in the early childhood years and who may need intervention services. There are screening instruments designed for infants and young children such as the *Denver Developmental Screening Test-Revised* (Frankenburg, Dodds, Fandal, Kajuk, & Cohr, 1975) and the *Early Screening Inventory* (Meisels & Wiske, 1983). These instruments provide brief measures of a number of categories of development to determine if a child is at risk. If a delay is found, more extensive investigation is conducted. While standardized tests are designed for screening purposes, other strategies are also appropriate, such as caregiver or parent observation. Pediatric examinations and informal developmental tasks can provide indicators of delay.

Assessment, on the other hand, is more comprehensive. Assessment of young children who have delayed or atypical development will be used to acquire comprehensive data on the developmental delays or disabilities the child displays. In addition, assessment can also be for purposes of linking development and learning. For this purpose, the assessment process is even more comprehensive and is used with all young children. Assessment is used to determine the child's developmental accomplishments or learning achievement. Further, it is conducted as an aid to instructional planning for a child or group of children and is an ongoing process. The assessment process can be conducted using all types of measures and strategies, in addition to or instead of standardized tests. Current trends are to use alternatives to standardized measures for assessment purposes.

One current trend for screening and assessment is the use of multiple strategies. Adult observation, developmental checklists and rating scales, play-based assessment, and other measures are used to gather the needed information about a child. A standardized test may be given, but it is supplemented with information collected by the caregiver or teacher. Parents are important partners in collecting information. Parents might record or relate their own observations, or they be interviewed to gather data. Whichever strategies are used, the purpose is to collect indicators of a child's development. If the purpose is for screening of development, information is collected to identify possible developmental delay. If the purpose is for assessment, the same strategies can be used to assess the child's developmental or learning progress accurately.

Another trend is to conduct **authentic assessment** or **performance-based assessment.** In this type of evaluation, the child's performance of a skill or developmental characteristic is documented in some fashion for assessment. Rather than the use of an artificial means to determine the child's progress, the child's actual performance of an activity becomes an indicator of achievement. An important advantage of using performance assessments is that assessment can be ongoing. For example, a child's ability to use fine motor skills is documented by collecting a series of drawings completed by the child over a period of time to identify the child's progress in using a writing instrument. The teacher or adult can also make anecdotal entries of a child's activity to document progress in language or cognitive development. Records of progress might be made by taking a photograph of a child at work in a center or on a group activity or by photographing the child's work. All of these assessments are considered to be authentic because the child is engaged in an actual activity. They can be described as performance-based because the child's work or activity is a demonstration of what a child can do, not just what a child might understand.

These alternative strategies are not themselves without critics. There is concern that these measures might lack validity and reliability. This means that it is difficult to establish the dependability of the information acquired with them. Moreover, the assessments are subject to teacher bias and are subjective rather than objective (Goodwin & Goodwin, 1993). Authentic or performance-based assessment will be addressed in more detail in Chapter 3.

The process of screening and assessment remains complex and imperfect; that is, there is no completely reliable, simple way to evaluate the development and learning of young children. Each type of screening and assessment can provide a piece of the puzzle about the child's development and learning. And because screening and assessment are an important part of developing curriculum and instruction that is appropriate for all children, early childhood educators need to develop a repertoire of such strategies, including ones appropriate for children from diverse backgrounds and with diverse abilities. In the next section, we will discuss more specifically how screening and assessment are conducted in early childhood programs.

THE RELATIONSHIP BETWEEN SCREENING AND ASSESSMENT AND THE EARLY CHILDHOOD PROGRAM

In previous sections, we have explored the nature of early childhood programs and how they are designed for the diverse needs of young children. We also reviewed the role of standardized tests in screening and assessing young children to identify developmental difficulties, disabilities, and other differences. In this section, we will survey how screening and assessment are related to how young children are served in early childhood programs.

Screening and Assessment for Initial Evaluation

So far in this chapter, we have discussed the importance and merits of measuring young children to determine their developmental status. This process is especially important for identifying young children who need early intervention. However, it is necessary to point out that for the majority of young children who are developing within normal expectations, screening and assessment prior to admission to a program is far less common or necessary. Children entering a child care setting, child development program, nursery school, or kindergarten generally are admitted on the basis of their age, although some private and parochial schools with limited enrollment may screen or conduct an assessment to determine selection. Typically the assessment conducted with children prior to or upon entry in a program is to determine the child's developmental status, and not to make decisions about his or her eligibility for the program. The initial evaluation of children is to assess where they are in their development and with this information to decide on the instructional program appropriate for them.

Initial evaluation of children who are suspected of having a developmental delay or other disabling condition is quite different. Children who are suspected or known to have a condition that puts them at risk or that requires specific kinds of intervention are screened and assessed very thoroughly prior to placement in an intervention program. Thus, initial screening is conducted to determine if a child needs an early childhood intervention program. Children who "pass" the screening process are served in classrooms where special intervention services are not required. Children who are identified as having a developmental problem are then assessed for extent of the handicap or disability.

Preschool children served under federal or state funding are screened and assessed prior to entry into a preschool program. If a school is using inclusion or integration, both regular and special education teachers are engaged in the screening process to identify children needing special services. Screening may be conducted for speech and expressive language, social and emotional development, hearing and vision, and gross and fine motor skills. Children who are identified as having difficulties in one or more of the developmental areas are then tested in those areas to determine how serious the problem is and to assess the child's strengths and weaknesses. Once the initial evaluation is completed, the next step is to determine the child's educational and intervention needs (Benner, 1992; Spodek & Saracho, 1994).

Frequently children are not identified as having learning difficulties until they have entered a program. In this situation, initial screening may evolve from teacher observation and documentation that indicates that the child is having difficulties. The child is then referred for further screening and diagnostic testing to determine if he or she needs additional services and what the nature of those services should be.

Linking Screening, Assessment, and Instruction

Once children have been enrolled into an early childhood program, screening and assessment information influences the instructional program that is to be organized for the classroom. For children who are enrolled in regular preschool and primary grade classrooms, the teacher may conduct initial assessments and ongoing evaluations as a guide to curriculum development. Regardless of the fact that the children in the group do not exhibit a special need, each child is developmentally different, and the teacher must conduct developmental or learning assessments to determine the individual status of each child. The assessment results determine how the teacher will plan instruction appropriate for the child.

More comprehensive information obtained from diagnostic testing may be available for children who have been identified as having special needs. Each child who is served in an early childhood special education program will have an **individualized education plan** (IEP), which describes the child's strengths and weaknesses, the goals and objectives that have been chosen for the child's improvement, and the intervention strategies that have been selected for the child's educational program. An IEP is a

The teacher uses assessment results to plan for the instructional program.

formal contract for the child's education that includes input from parents and is signed by parents. The assessment and testing needed to obtain information about the child is typically conducted by specialists who have been trained to administer the specialized tests used. Special education teachers who use the IEP for planning the child's program are also trained in suitable teaching and assessment strategies.

Using Assessment Results to Plan Instruction

The major role of initial assessment results is to serve as a blueprint for program development. Regardless of the diversity of the children in the classroom, some of the instructional activities will be designed for the group as a whole, while others are planned for small groups of children or for individual children. Children who have disabilities are likely to have a majority of their program designed for individual intervention; however, there will be group activities for these children as well. Children in a regular classroom program will engage in more whole-group and small-group activities. Nevertheless, each child's individual needs and progress will be accommodated with individual activities and experiences whenever they are needed.

If young children are being served through an integrated program, the regular teacher and special education teacher must work as a team to cooperatively develop the instructional plan. Both teachers must consider the needs and interests of the group as a whole, as well as the individual differences within the group. Although children with special needs require much individual attention, the intent is that the children function with their peers as much as possible. For children without disabilities, the goal of the integrated classroom is similar. Regardless of the fact that these children have fewer barriers to prevent participation in the group, their individual interests and developmental differences should be addressed. The higher the quality of the assessment results that are available to the early childhood educator, the more likely that instructional activities appropriate both for individuals and for the group can be planned.

THE ROLE OF FEDERAL REGULATION IN SCREENING AND ASSESSMENT

Early childhood programs that receive federal funding must follow federal regulations concerning program quality. Although each individual program has its own standards, there are common issues that all programs must address. Here are some of the areas in which there are federal requirements and which must be considered by all programs:

1. Who is eligible to be served by the program
2. How program participants are to be selected
3. The services the program will provide to participants

4. How the progress of children and success of the program are to be evaluated and documented

Screening and assessment are integral to following federal regulations. When children are screened to determine if they need intervention services in a special program, the issue of how participants are to be selected for a program is being addressed. Federally funded programs—whether they be bilingual, special education, or other type of program such as Chapter 1—require that standardized tests be administered to select children who are eligible for the program. Standardized or informal assessment strategies may then be used to determine individual needs within a program. Children who are bilingual may be administered language dominance tests for selection purposes. They may then take a series of language tests, combined with classroom assessment strategies, to determine their language strengths and weaknesses and their instructional needs. Children in a supplementary instructional program such as Chapter 1 are administered an achievement test to decide if they exhibit a delay in reading or mathematics that could be improved through Chapter 1 services. Formal and informal strategies can then be used by the teacher to assess individuals' strengths and weaknesses.

Assessment results are then used to determine program goals and objectives, which detail what the program proposes to accomplish with the children in it. The goals and objectives will establish expectations for children's improvement, and instructional experiences will be delivered to meet the goals and objectives.

Adams Elementary, A Chapter 1 School

Delilah teaches kindergarten at Adams Elementary School in a full-day program. Because a large percentage of the children enrolled in the school meet the income qualifications for the Chapter 1 program, it has been designated as a Chapter 1 school. Each year standardized testing is conducted to determine which children are in need of the program and how those currently being served are progressing. The test used at Adams Elementary School is the Iowa Test of Basic Skills.

Delilah has mixed feelings about administering the ITBS to her students. During the week of testing, she must cover all bulletin boards with newspaper to eliminate distractions and turn all center shelving to the wall. Testing is conducted each morning. Then in the afternoon, the room is restored to its normal arrangement. The routine is repeated each day that testing continues.

Delilah has concerns about the effects of testing on her kindergarten children. They are confused about the instructions and are frustrated and tired before the testing session ends. Although Delilah is not concerned about the performance of her children on the ITBS, she has doubts about the value of the testing process and its effect on five-year-old children.

Perhaps the most significant role of assessment is to document individual progress and program success. Federal regulations require that funded projects be accountable for the progress of the children being served and the overall success of the program. Standardized assessments are usually required to report the program's accountability. Assessments of the child's status after participating in the program serve as indicators both of individual and program success. The most common method used to provide information on individual and program success is standardized tests administered at the beginning and end of the program year. This means that the assessment instrument administered to diagnose the child's strengths and weaknesses at the beginning of the program is administered again at the end of the year to document progress.

Standardized achievement tests administered in public school programs serve similar purposes to those required in federally funded programs. Although there are no federal regulations that require how schools account for pupil progress, most states require standardized testing for program accountability. It is possible in the future that we will have a national assessment that will be administered to all children in public schools to evaluate individual and program success. And in spite of concerns educators have about the quality of standardized tests and whether or not they should be administered to young children, role of standardized tests in programs that are federally funded and for evaluation of public schools at the state level makes it probable that they will continue as key assessment tools in the near future.

⇢ SUMMARY AND OVERVIEW OF THE BOOK

The purpose of this chapter has been to introduce the reader to the goals and content of this textbook: how we can develop quality programs for children from birth to age eight through the process of determining their developmental progress and planning curriculum and instructional experiences to complement their development and interests.

There are many types of early childhood programs that serve children. Although they have different histories and original purposes, the programs now overlap in the services they provide to children and the ages of the children they serve.

The young children who attend early childhood programs represent diverse cultures, languages, family conditions, and abilities. Early childhood educators are challenged to plan programs that present curriculum and instruction that are developmentally appropriate for the individuals and groups in each program.

If programs are to adequately serve children who attend them, the children must be evaluated to determine their developmental status and potential for learning. There are many strategies that can be used to screen and assess young children: these strategies range from standardized tests to very informal measures, such as observation, checklists, and activities demonstrating the child's performance. While each of the available measures has weaknesses and strengths, a combination of strategies can best provide a profile of a child.

One factor in the servicing of children of diverse abilities is the trend toward the integration of children with disabilities into regular early childhood classrooms. This trend resulted from federal legislation requiring children with special needs to be placed in programs where they would have been placed had they not had a disability. The advent of teachers of early childhood special education working with other teachers of young children has introduced opportunities for cooperation as well as potential problems. Screening and assessment become essential to identify children who have special needs and to determine the nature of program they need. Teachers in integrated settings work cooperatively to screen and assess young children and plan instructional activities that permit children from diverse backgrounds and with diverse abilities to learn together.

Many programs available for young children who have disabilities and language differences or who are at risk are federally funded. These programs must follow federal regulations for screening, identification, planning for instruction, and evaluation of child progress and program success. Similar requirements are common in public school settings. Thus, there is an interrelationship between instruction and evaluation of instruction—a relationship that enhances development of programs of high quality for all young children.

The topics introduced in this chapter will be discussed in depth in later chapters. Chapter 2, "Screening in Early Childhood Programs," will describe how screening is organized and conducted in the initial developmental assessment of young children. Chapter 3, "Assessment in Early Childhood Programs," discusses the role of assessment once children are enrolled in a program. In this context, the interrelationship between evaluation and instruction, as well as assessment of progress of learning, will be examined.

Chapter 4, "Initiating the Instructional Program," provides a picture of how an early childhood program is actually implemented, including the environment, the role of play, and the steps that are taken to initiate the year with young children. Chapter 5, "Linking Assessment and Curriculum Planning," includes in-depth information on how teaching can implement a curriculum that is based on assessment of children. Management of different types and settings of instruction is described, as well as how ongoing assessment and evaluation continue the interrelationship between instruction and measurement.

Chapters 6 and 7 address the issue of inclusion more specifically. Chapter 6, "Screening and Assessment in Early Intervention Programs for Young Children With Special Needs," discusses the nature of early intervention programs and provides information on model intervention programs. Chapter 7, "Linking Assessment and Instruction for Young Children With Special Needs," explains the interrelationship between assessment and instruction for children with special needs, as well as the more extensive diagnosis and prescription that are entailed in planning instructional programs for children with some type of disability.

Early childhood curriculum and instruction are discussed in Chapters 8 through 11. Using a developmental approach, each chapter continues the approach of the text that assessment and instruction are interrelated and that the program must accommodate the diversity of young children. Chapter 8, "Cognitive Development," reviews the nature of development, theories of development, and the nature of the cognitive curriculum. Chapter 9, "Language Development," discusses the nature of language and literacy development and how the teacher supports their development. Specialized strategies for assessing language and literacy are included in this chapter. Chapter 10, "Social Development," describes the role of play in social development, the teacher's role in helping young children develop social skills, and how a curriculum for social development is organized and assessed. Chapter 11, "Physical Development," includes not only motor skills, but related content areas such as nutrition education, health education, and safety education. An important part of this chapter treats the use of indoor and outdoor environments to facilitate physical development for all children, including those with physical limitations.

Finally, Chapter 12, "Bringing It All Together," comprehensively explains how all types of children can be served in integrated settings and how an integrated curriculum can accommodate differences in children's development, interests, and background in the early childhood classroom.

⇝ STUDY QUESTIONS

1. Describe at least three different types of programs that are available for children in the early childhood years.
2. Why is it said that children in the early childhood years can be very diverse? Explain some types of diversity.
3. Why do we need to be very concerned about the effects of violence and poverty on young children?
4. What are some factors that cause children to be emotionally disturbed?
5. How do screening and assessment support the organization of quality programs for young children?
6. Explain how the process of screening and assessment is different for children who may have a disability.
7. What factors have led to the integration of children with special needs into all types of early childhood settings?
8. Why are there possible barriers to integration of all children? Describe some of these barriers.
9. Discuss some of the advantages of using standardized tests with young children and some of the criticisms of using this type of instrument.
10. What are "high stakes" tests? Why are they used?
11. What are the differences between screening and assessment?
12. Discuss why multiple strategies of assessment are more appropriate than using a single measure.
13. What are some advantages of authentic or performance measures and some possible weaknesses?
14. Describe the relationship between assessment and the instructional program.

15. How are initial assessment and ongoing assessment different? Where do they fit into the design of the instructional program?
16. How are early childhood programs that serve populations at risk affected by federal regulations?

⇢ KEY TERMS

assessment	mainstreaming
at risk	mental retardation
authentic assessment	norms
fetal alcohol syndrome	performance-based assessment
inclusion	readiness tests
individualized education plan (IEP)	reliability
integrated classroom	screening
intervention	validity

⇢ SUGGESTED ACTIVITY

Locate and read two current articles on the inclusion or integration of children with special needs in early childhood programs. What are the major points made by the authors?

2

Screening in Early Childhood Programs

✦ Chapter Objectives

As a result of reading this chapter, you will be able to

1. Describe how various types of early childhood programs use screening procedures to identify children who will benefit from program services
2. Explain how infants and toddlers are screened for developmental delay
3. Discuss how screening is used in early childhood special education programs
4. Define the meaning of the term *at risk* and children who may be in risk categories
5. List types of programs that serve populations at risk and how they use screening to identify children
6. Describe the difference between children who have disabilities and those who are at risk for developmental delay
7. List and define different types of atypical development
8. Discuss how screening instruments and other screening strategies can be related to developmental theories
9. Describe how to select a screening instrument and set up a screening program
10. Explain the important role played by the family in the screening process

As we discussed in Chapter 1, there is currently a variety of programs that are available at the preschool level, beginning with ones for infants. Such programs are designed to enhance the possibilities that young children will develop at their optimum capacity and be able to reach their full potential. Some of the programs have as their purpose to provide services to children who are at risk or have some type of physical, mental, or environmental difference that may result in delay or difficulties in learning. Research has documented that the earlier children are identified and placed in intervention programs, the more likely that they will be able to overcome the difficulty or show improvement.

In this chapter, we will discuss the identification process, generally called screening, that is used to determine if children are in need of an intervention program in the preschool years. First, however, we will look at the background of these early childhood programs and how and why they are funded.

BACKGROUND ON SCREENING IN EARLY CHILDHOOD PROGRAMS

The Evolution of Early Childhood Programs for Populations at Risk

In the 1950s and 1960s, the field of early childhood education became the focus of renewed interest because of new developments in child psychology and the national trend toward social and educational reform. New directions in child development research emphasized the importance of the early years for development and learning, as well as the relationship between environment and development. Changes in public education as a result of the civil rights movement and Head Start programs (developed in connection with the War on Poverty) had positive effects on early childhood education.

Cognitive psychologists developed new concepts of the relationship between environment and intelligence. Benjamin Bloom reported on the importance of the early years for intellectual development, as well as the influence of environment on development, in his book *Stability and Change in Human Characteristics* (1964). Jean Piaget's work (1952) also marked a shift in understanding about the importance of the child's experiences in influencing cognitive development. The efforts of these and many other scholars of the period were influential. The studies occurred at the same time as American society was looking to education to help eliminate poverty and improve the conditions of the poor. The tenet that the nature of the young child's experiences could make a difference in the child's intellectual development gave hope to a growing expectation that education could positively affect children living in poverty (Weber, 1970; Wortham, 1992).

For two decades, national attention was directed to the needs of children in poverty. The War on Poverty, part of President Lyndon Johnson's efforts to establish the Great Society, included funding for educational programs to put an end to the disadvantages experienced by poor children. A series of federal legislation acts established **compensatory programs** and **intervention programs** to address the needs of infants and young children who were at risk for learning as a result of a variety of conditions and circumstances.

At the preschool level, Project Head Start began as a summer program in 1965, and it was soon expanded into a year-long program. It included appropriate learning experiences for children, health care, meals, and parent education. It was joined by a Migrant Program to serve children whose parents migrated each year, following the harvesting of crops across the United States; a Home Start program that extended early education and parental participation into the home; and a variety of other programs with similar purposes (McCarthy & Houston, 1980). Outstanding leadership during these decades was provided by Edward Zigler, who headed the Office of Child Development from 1969 to 1972 and directed the early years of the new program initiatives (Hymes, 1991).

Kindergarten and primary grade programs were also affected by compensatory programs such as the migrant programs. The Bilingual Education Act in 1974 was funded to comply with a court-mandated ruling that school districts must establish special language programs for non-English-speaking children. A more comprehensive antipoverty approach was taken through the Elementary and Secondary Education Act of 1965, which provided funding to assist schools in the education of poor children.

At the same time that programs to serve children's individual needs were being funded and implemented, there were concerns about labeling children and putting them in special education programs. Large numbers of children were being channeled into special education programs because of difficulties they were experiencing in the regular classroom, rather than because of an identified disability. Biases in categorizing children as needing special education services resulted in large numbers of African American and Hispanic children being relegated to special education programs. Jane Mercer (1973) and Christine Sleeter (1985) researched and reported about poor and minority children who were trapped in special education programs, a practice that continues today (King, Chipman, & Cruz-Janzen, 1994).

The growing conviction that the separation and isolation of children with disabilities was inappropriate and that they would do better if they were educated alongside their peers led to passage of the Education of All Handicapped Children Act of 1975 (P.L. 94–142). The act mandated that handicapped students be mainstreamed as much as possible with their normal peers. Schools were required to screen, diagnose, and plan for the individual needs of each student (Deiner, 1993).

From these beginnings in the 1960s and 1970s, early childhood programs were established, expanded, and modified over the years to provide compensatory and intervention services to children beginning in the early childhood years. Studies of the programs documented their effectiveness in leading to more positive developmental outcomes for young children. Guralnick (1989) reported that intervention programs within the first three years of life may be significantly effective, while Hanson and Lynch (1989) proposed from their research that early intervention may remediate a primary handicap or prevent the development of a secondary handicap.

Studies of Head Start and early childhood special education programs demonstrated their effectiveness. One research finding was that children who attended Head Start might have improved developmental status (Lazar & Darlington, 1982), and children who attended preschool programs were less likely to need special education services later and were less likely to become delinquent (Barnett & Escobar, 1990; Schweinhart & Weikart, 1985).

As a result of the efforts at the national level and additional programs at the state level, preschool and elementary school children today may attend Head Start, prekindergarten, kindergarten, early childhood special education, bilingual, and migrant programs, as well as infant and toddler programs designed to serve children who will benefit from early intervention. Each of these programs has selection or screening processes to identify young children who are eligible for the program.

The Scope of Screening in Early Childhood Programs

The type and extent of screening that is done with young children depend upon the purpose of the screening and the severity of the condition that is being identified. The purpose of a program is a factor in selecting a screening process, as is the information needed about the individual. In the following sections, some of the types of screening that are conducted with infants, toddlers, and young children will be described, as well as the purposes for such screening.

Screening Infants and Toddlers for Developmental Delay and Disabilities   All infants and toddlers should be screened routinely. Newborns should be given developmental evaluations immediately after birth and at regular intervals by a pediatrician. If the child's development is normal, developmental progress is noted and checked again at the next scheduled appointment. If regular ongoing screening identifies the child is at risk for development or has a disability, more comprehensive assessment is indicated.

When it has been determined that an infant might have a **developmental delay** or **handicap,** evaluation procedures are needed to assess the child's strengths and weaknesses. The purpose of the assessment is to identify the area in which the child has developmental delays: cognitive, physical, language, social, or self-help development. Another purpose is to identify if there is a physical or mental condition that might result in later developmental delay or a medical or environmental condition that might result in delay if intervention is not provided (Smith, 1989; Widerstrom, Mowder, & Sandall, 1991). Because of developmental limitations in very young children, specially trained personnel are needed to conduct the procedures used in the screening process as well as to evaluate the child's responses to the screening items. Infants and many young children can only attend to a task for a very brief period; moreover, it is very difficult to obtain reliable results from tests used with the very young child.

Screening for Early Childhood Special Education Programs   A free appropriate education to children and youth was mandated in P.L. 94–142, the Education for All Handicapped Children Act of 1975. The Child Find Mandate within P.L. 94–142 requires that states locate, identify, and evaluate young children with **disabilities**. Amendments to P.L. 94–142—known as the Education of the Handicapped Act amendments of 1986, or P.L. 99–457—required that children from birth through five who have disabilities also be served. Compliance with these laws requires extensive efforts to locate, screen, and identify children with disabilities who need to receive intervention services. The screening process includes procedures to find children and determine if they need further evaluation or participation in an intervention program (Spodek & Saracho, 1994; Widerstrom et al., 1991).

Screening for special education intervention programs can be a lengthy process, beginning with the task of locating children who might need intervention services. Some children will be easily identified through referral from a pediatrician or other medical source. Others will be referred from local agencies that are working with families and are aware of infants and young children who demonstrate a developmental delay or disability. These strategies are not enough. Schools and agencies providing services must take other measures to locate preschool children. Announcements must be put in local newspapers, on television and radio stations, and in other sources. Children who can be screened also are located through examination of school records that include all of the children in a child's family. These families can be contacted to determine if preschool siblings are eligible for screening. Parents are encouraged to bring in their children for screening. The screening process includes evaluation of vision, hearing, intellectual development, motor development, social development, and self-help skills. Program planners must be prepared to handle large numbers of children on special days set aside for screening (Spodek & Saracho, 1994).

Screening in Programs for Children at Risk for Academic Success   Children who are at risk for academic success are also screened, but generally the process is less time consuming. The type of screening done to determine eligibility for a program varies depending upon the population of children targeted by the individual program. For example, children may be selected for Head Start based on the income level of the family. Public school preschool programs for populations at risk may follow similar guidelines. The family's income level or eligibility for the school lunch program may be the factor that determines the child's enrollment in such programs. Although screening may be conducted to determine the child's developmental status upon entry to the program, such screening—while important—may not be the determining factor for eligibility.

The Screening Process for Bilingual Classrooms in Auburn School District

Auburn School District serves a large population of Latino families. Each year a screening process is conducted to determine which students are eligible for the bilingual program, which begins in kindergarten and first grade. When children are enrolled at a school, parents are asked to fill out a Home Language Survey to find out the language spoken in the home. If parents indicate that Spanish is the language spoken in the home, they are asked to bring the child to the school for language screening before the beginning of the school year.

The Bilingual Syntax Measure (Burt, Dulay, & Hernandes, 1976) is administered to the child to obtain information about the child's language strengths. The child is asked questions in both English and Spanish. The child's responses are used to decide if he or she is a candidate for a bilingual classroom (in which instruction is conducted in Spanish), an English as a Second Language classroom (where instruction will be in English with support in Spanish), or a regular classroom.

During the initial weeks of school, teacher observation will be used to gather additional information about the child's language abilities. Some children may be moved to another kind of classroom setting, and others may be tested because their language abilities seem to indicate a need for bilingual instruction. Children who enroll during the school year may also be screened to determine whether they need bilingual or ESL services.

Parents have a choice as to whether their child will be served in bilingual or English as a Second Language classrooms. Regardless of screening results and teacher recommendations, parents determine whether they want their child in the special program or in a regular classroom.

Bilingual programs and programs to teach English as a Second Language (ESL) have specific screening measures to determine the child's strengths in both the home language and English. Screening serves the dual purpose of identifying children for inclusion in language programs and of helping with the decisions about the most appropriate language development program for that child.

Screening for Children Who Are Not at Risk   The programs described above are just a few of the many intervention programs that are available to children in the early childhood years. Each one has the purpose of serving children who need special programs of some type. But what of children who display no developmental problems? Are they screened, and if so, what is the nature of the screening used?

In fact, children who are attending regular early childhood programs may also be screened. The purpose for screening prior to, or upon, entry to a program is to determine the child's general developmental status. Program planners and teachers conduct screening to plan for the instructional program. Eligibility for the classes is usually based upon the child's chronological age. Screening helps the teacher find out about the child's family and experiences the child may have had prior to attending the program, as well as obtain developmental information that gives a fuller picture of each child.

Some school districts also require individual testing when there is doubt whether a child should be retained or promoted. In addition, proper preschool placement might require individual testing to ensure that the child is placed in the most beneficial program.

There are, however, screening practices in preschool, kindergarten, and elementary programs that are inappropriate—although widespread. It is common for public school programs to screen children for eligibility for programs based on developmental readiness. Unfortunately, such screening is for the purpose of denying children access to a program. It is conducted to determine if the child has achieved a developmental level that indicates that he or she is "ready" for the school program. The most frequent use of this type of screening is for entrance to kindergarten or first grade. Unlike the screening described in earlier sections, which is used to determine if the child is in need of the specific intervention provided in the program, readiness screening can result in denying children access to a program on the basis of developmental immaturity. There has been intense reaction to this type of screening: it is considered to be inappropriate in terms of the method of screening, as well as because it uses screening results for exclusion from programs and for retention and promotion (Meisels, Steele, & Quinn-Leering, 1993; Shepard & Graue, 1993; Wortham, 1995).

We can be more specific as to the populations of children that are identified and served as a result of the screening process. The next section describes these populations and the conditions the screening process seeks to assess.

Target Populations for Screening in Early Childhood

Throughout the first chapter and this chapter, reference has been made to children who are at risk. As a result, it would be helpful to describe different risk factors that are located through screening.

There are various causes and circumstances that cause children to be at risk. Infants and toddlers may be identified very early as being at risk because of a condition that was present at birth. Children who have a **genetic disorder** such as mental retardation or a condition such as **spina bifida** are at risk because of the limitations that the existing physical condition will cause for development. Other children may be at risk because of biological conditions that might result in developmental delay. An infant who was born prematurely or born to a mother with a physical condition such as **diabetes** or addiction to drugs has a high possibility of experiencing developmental delay. This type of risk is potential rather than present at birth.

Children can be at risk because of the effects of the home environment in the early months and years. This type of risk can overlap with the biological conditions cited above. Environmental risk can take many forms: from the effects of poverty, accidental injury, improper nutrition or nurturing, or neglect. Inappropriate parenting styles can put a child at risk as can living in a dangerous neighborhood or an area with environmental pollution (Spodek & Saracho, 1994). Not all children who are categorized as being at risk encounter developmental or academic difficulties; nevertheless, they have a higher potential for having problems (Deiner, 1993). Regardless of the source or extent of the risk, the purpose of screening is to locate the young child and provide intervention measures that will improve the child's potential for development and learning.

Children Developmentally at Risk   Infants and toddlers can experience developmental delay. Infants can give early signs that they are at risk. Common indicators that an infant will experience delay are failure to gain weight, commonly called failure to thrive, or feeding problems that prevent weight gain. Developmental delay can also result from prematurity or low birth weight.

Hannah

Hannah is six months old. She has an older sister who is almost three years old. When Hannah was conceived, her parents were in marriage counseling and had financial problems in addition to personal ones. Hannah was born with normal birth weight; however, her mother had problems during delivery and was confined to bed for several weeks.

Grandmothers and other adults took turns taking care of the family. Hannah was fretful during this period and cried much of the time.

When Hannah was taken for her first visit to the pediatrician at six weeks, she had regained her birth weight, but little more. The pediatrician diagnosed her condition as failure to thrive. Hannah's parents renewed their efforts to provide a nurturing environment for their children. Over the next few months, Hannah gained weight and by four months was within the normal range. Her mother had returned to work, and Hannah and her sister went to a family friend for care during the day. At six months, Hannah smiles easily and coos at friendly adults and her sister; nevertheless, her sleeping habits are irregular and she can be difficult to soothe when upset.

Delayed development or **atypical development** can be physical, sensory, or cognitive. Atypical physical development might result from a motor impairment obvious at birth. More frequently, motor development delay becomes apparent as the child fails to accomplish motor skills milestones in the early months of life. **Sensory delay**, a delay in the ability to use the senses to organize information about the world, can be caused by a biological or genetic condition at birth or become apparent during the first year. Children with suspected sensory delay or **impairment** (an established sensory disability) will be screened for visual, hearing and tactile development (Deiner, 1993; Widerstrom et al., 1991).

Delayed and atypical cognitive and language development can be the result of existing conditions, environmental circumstances, or a combination of factors. A child born with Down's Syndrome will have mental retardation that causes cognitive and language delay. Damage to the brain prenatally or during or after birth can cause cognitive and language delay.

When a biological or genetic cause is not present to explain atypical or delayed cognitive or language development, environmental factors are frequently a cause. Children who are reared in risk environments are screened to determine if delay or atypical development is occurring.

Delay in social and emotional development can be manifested early in life as the infant fails to form an emotional attachment with adults or is irritable and difficult to comfort. Many manifestations of emotional delay or atypical emotional and social development are difficult to identify because all young children exhibit some of the symptoms as part of normal development; however, behavior disorders that are serious are more obvious. Children who are aggressive, have temper tantrums, and are disruptive, can be more easily identified in the screening process (Deiner, 1993).

Children With Disabilities   Very young children with disabilities can have communication disorders, hearing impairments, visual impairments, physical disabilities, health impairments, emotional or behavioral disorders, and mental retardation. Infants and young children with evident physical and mental disabilities have established risk factors and do not have to be screened for delay or atypical development.

Instead, they are screened to determine the status or severity of the disability prior to undertaking the extensive diagnostic work needed to plan the intervention services.

Young children, especially those entering school settings, may be screened for a **learning disability**. The definition of learning disabled varies. Regardless of the explanations, children who have a learning disability are having difficulties that are blocking their potential to learn. Children with learning disabilities may not be able to use language successfully and may demonstrate limitations in their abilities to listen, think, speak, read, write, spell, or do mathematics. Behaviorally, learning disabled children may have difficulty in attending to activities and staying on task, have poor memory, and demonstrate perceptual-motor defects.

Just as the symptoms are extensive and vary from child to child, the causes can also be many. Learning disabilities can be caused by such factors as **brain injury, dyslexia, perceptual disabilities, emotional disturbances,** and mental retardation. Identification and diagnosis of learning disabilities is complex; as a result, the screening process is very important in identifying the individual child's difficulties and the appropriate instructional strategies (Meisels, Wiske, & Tivnan, 1984; Spodek & Saracho, 1994).

Children Who Are Linguistically and Culturally Diverse   Children who come from a home where a language other than English is spoken or a dialect of English is spoken represent the diversity of language that is present in the American culture. In the United States, children who are speakers of a language other than English or have limited English skills are considered to be at risk for learning because of environmental factors. Children who are from diverse cultural environments may be at risk in the school culture. Children with language differences are frequently served in early childhood intervention classrooms such as bilingual and English as a Second Language settings. Likewise, eligible for preschool programs that will focus on language and cognitive development are children from deprived environments where experiences important for school success have been lacking. Children who come from home environments that have language or cultural differences may be screened to determine if they have language and cognitive limitations that make them eligible for preschool programs.

Children Who Are Gifted and Talented   Some early childhood settings are able to provide programs for children who have atypical development in that their development is accelerated rather than delayed. Children who are gifted or talented may demonstrate high intellectual ability, creative thinking, aptitude in a specific academic area, or psychomotor ability. Early screening for programs designed to facilitate or support these talents and abilities is beneficial to young children. Programs are more likely to be available at the elementary school level rather than the preschool; nevertheless, intervention programs for this population of children is equally important, and screening procedures are used to identify and assess individual potential (Spodek & Saracho, 1994). The younger the child, the more difficult the process; and there is lack of consensus as to what comprises unusual ability and talent and how it is identified appropriately (Bloom, 1982).

SELECTING AN APPROACH FOR SCREENING

The approach that is used for screening infants and young children depends upon the type of risk factor that is to be identified, the nature of the intervention program, and the type of information that is sought from the screening process. The timing of the screening is also important. If the screening process is to locate children for a program, screening may take place within a limited period prior to the beginning date for the program. If children are already in a preschool or primary school setting, the screening might occur when the teacher and parents become concerned about possible difficulties that the child is exhibiting. The approach that is selected for the screening process is also defined by the goals and philosophy of the program that is to be used for intervention. It is likely that a combination of strategies will be used rather than a single method of identification and evaluation. In summary, screening can be a complex process that takes planning and thought prior to decisions about the approach that is to be used.

Theoretical Influences on the Screening Approach

The philosophy of the early childhood program and the policies under which it is realized affect the nature of screening that will be conducted. The type of population to be served can affect the goals of the program. Program developers and teachers, thus, need to use screening measures that will complement program objectives. Benner (1992) described three theoretical perspectives that programs commonly take as the (1) developmental perspective, (2) the cognitive stages perspective, and (3) the behavioral perspective.

1. The *developmental perspective* derives its philosophy from Gesell's maturational theory. Gesell (1925) described norms of development for chronological ages. Programs that seek to serve children with a developmental delay would use screening procedures that would seek to determine if a child has a developmental delay and the extent of that delay.

2. The *cognitive stages perspective* would use screening approaches compatible with Piaget's theory of cognitive development (Piaget, 1952). The sequence of stages of development and the emphasis on the importance of the characteristics of the child's environment on development would guide the screening process to determine the child's progress on Piaget's stages. Programs that base curriculum experiences on a cognitive-developmental approach would use screening measures that evaluate the child's developmental progress from a Piagetian perspective (Benner, 1992).

3. The *behavioral perspective* is based on the behavioral theory of development (Skinner, 1953). Programs that subscribe to the premise that all behavior is learned and the environment can reinforce appropriate learning behaviors would use screening measures that are compatible with that program philosophy. Programs based on

the behavioral perspective are common for children with mental retardation, behavior disorders, or sensory deprivations such as hearing disorders.

There is not always consensus as to which philosophy is appropriate; indeed, some programs use a combination of theoretical perspectives rather than a single perspective (Benner, 1992). For example, a preschool program may assess a child's development based on Gesell's developmental norms, but subscribe to a philosophy that the child's interaction with a quality environment is significant for addressing developmental delay. Likewise, a program for children with behavioral disorders might depend heavily upon the behavioral perspective for assisting the child to control his or her own behavior, but at the same time provide numerous opportunities for exploration of the environment within a developmental curriculum. Fewell (1991) cautioned that program developers must be informed as to the compatibility between the theoretical basis of a program and the practices that are used with children. This should also apply to the screening measures to be used.

Possible Procedures for Screening

If screening results are to provide a comprehensive picture of a young child's development, more than one procedure or measure should be used. Although the use of standardized tests is the most common tactic, the limitations of this type of measure with young children implies that other strategies should also be employed. Widerstrom et al. (1991) recommend four procedures to obtain a complete profile of the child's abilities and disabilities: (1) direct testing, (2) naturalistic observation, (3) reviews of records, and (4) interviews. Figure 2–1 includes a description of these measures.

Figure 2–1 Suggested Screening Procedures

Source: From At-Risk and Handicapped Newborns, by A. H. Widerstrom, B. A. Mowder, and S. R. Sandall, 1991, Englewood Cliffs, NJ: Prentice Hall. Copyright 1991 by Prentice Hall. Reprinted by permission.

PROCEDURE	DESCRIPTION
Direct testing	Objective measures of how the infant, toddler, or other individual responds to requests, instructions, standard stimulus, or set of materials.
Naturalistic observations	Direct observation by professional or parent of the infant, toddler, or other individual in natural situations. The observer records various behaviors and dimensions of behaviors.
Records review	Review of medical records, records from previous assessments, and developmental records from early intervention programs. This review provides additional perspective.
Interviews	Parent(s) and caregiver(s) provide their perceptions of the child's abilities and history and their concerns about the child.

Observation is an effective method of obtaining information about individual children.

Screening Instruments   Standardized measures are one resource for screening. They have the advantage of being objective and can measure all categories of development. However, there are also problems or limitations in the use of these screening instruments. More information about this type of approach will be provided in a later section.

Observation   Observation is the most effective type of assessment that can be used by teachers of young children, particularly children in the preschool years. This is because children's activities during work and play reveal their developmental status. The teacher or parent can observe the child's physical skills, language development, and cognitive strategies by watching the child while he or she is actively engaged with the environment, either alone or with others. Observation strategies can be preplanned or undertaken when a promising situation presents itself. Some possible observation strategies include anecdotal records, running records, time sampling, and event sampling (Gold & Abbott, 1989; Wortham, 1995). Further information on these strategies can be found in Chapter 3. Using a record-keeping strategy and developmental checklists that have indicators of physical, social and emotional, cognitive, and language development, adults can assess a child's developmental status and record interpretations of the information that is obtained.

Survey of Records   Earlier we described how school records could be examined to find children for screening for possible inclusion in intervention programs. Likewise, information could be obtained from organizations and agencies that serve young children and their families. The screening process should include review of all possible available records on young children. As mentioned before, medical records or medical referrals might be one source of information about a child's status. Social service agencies might be able to provide valuable leads as to a child's status and needs. Of course, all such information must be secured without violating a family's right to privacy. It is true, however, that parents themselves can be valuable in locating and obtaining records related to their child.

Interviews   Parents are a primary source of information about their young children. They can contribute their perceptions about their child's development and provide observational information that can be supplement to other sources of information. They can also add to available information by interpreting or giving explanations for a child's behavior. The skill of the interviewer is essential to secure appropriate information without alarming or alienating the parents. Likewise, examiners should be alert for limitations in objectivity that might affect parent reports (Abbott & Gold, 1991).

Other adults from the child's background can also provide needed information. Caregivers from a child care center, teachers in preschool programs, or program providers from an intervention program the child attended can describe their experiences with the child and their assessments of a child's development or difficulties. They should also be interviewed carefully to eliminate subjectivity and bias in the information that they report.

Parents can provide valuable information about their children.

SELECTING A SCREENING INSTRUMENT

There are numerous instruments available for screening young children from infancy through the early childhood years. Preschool instruments have been developed specifically to identify children with developmental delay or disabilities—a group of children who particularly need preschool intervention programs of one type or another. These instruments vary in quality, and cautions about their use, especially as the only measure of a child's developmental status, must be given.

When selecting an instrument for infants and toddlers, examiners should inform themselves of the purposes for the assessment and determine whether the instrument selected will provide appropriate information. Selection criteria should include review of the test manual to determine if the purpose of the test is suitable, if test design demonstrates that the test is meaningful or valid for the purposes of the screening, if the test has established reliability and consistency, and if the sample of children used to standardize the test was appropriate to provide confidence in test results. Examiners would also want to know if test administration requires extensive training and if scoring is economically feasible and time efficient (Wortham, 1995). A test selected to identify a child for a particular intervention program might not provide adequate information about the child's strengths and weaknesses nor include diagnostic information needed for individual program planning. Likewise, trained personnel should administer the instrument if results are to be depended upon for making decisions about the child (Fewell, 1991).

Preschool screening instruments can have similar limitations. Gold and Abbott (1989) expressed concern that preschool tests generally are designed to be used by persons not trained to be examiners, which may result in lack of consistency between testers. The tests themselves may have limited reliability, which can also affect consistency of test results over a period of time. The validity of preschool tests is also questioned in that tests may not measure what they say they measure.

An important problem with standardized measures is that children whose cultural background differs from white middle class populations are likely to score lower than average, for a variety of reasons. Consequently, test results can be difficult to interpret. Given that federal policies require that tests and other screening procedures be administered in the child's or parent's language or their preferred mode of communication, examiners should be alert and informed when selecting instruments for children whose culture and language vary from Standard English when assessing children for special education intervention programs (Fewell, 1991; Gold & Abbott, 1989).

Selecting Screening Instruments for Infants and Toddlers

Many scales of infant and toddler development are widely used and recognized as useful. Most infant and toddler scales reflect a developmental perspective; however, some can be categorized as being from cognitive or behavioral perspectives, as we will demonstrate later. Below are some of the better-known and respected infant-toddler screening instruments.

Bayley Scales of Infant Development (BSID) (Bayley, 1969)

Denver Developmental Screening Test (DDST) (Frankenburg, Dodds, & Fandal, 1975)

Developmental Activities Screening Inventory-II (DASI-II) (Fewell & Langley, 1984)

Developmental Screening Inventory (Knobloch, Stevens, & Malone, 1980)

Early Language Milestone Scale (Caplan, 1982)

Infant Intelligence Scale (Cattell, 1960)

Merrill-Palmer Scale of Mental Tests (Stutsman, 1948)

The Movement Assessment of Infants (Chandler, Andrews, & Swanson, 1981)

Ordinal Scales of Psychological Development (Uzgiris & Hunt, 1975)

Selecting a Preschool Screening Test

Preschool screening tests may overlap with infant-toddler tests. For example, the *Denver Developmental Screening Test* ranges from birth to six years of age. In this section, some of the scales listed are also useful for infants and toddlers. The tests listed below are organized by category of development.

Screening Tests for Cognitive Development

Griffiths Mental Development Scales (Griffiths, 1978)

Kaufman Assessment Battery for Children (Kaufman & Kaufman, 1983)

McCarthy Scales of Children's Abilities (McCarthy, 1972)

Screening Tests for Motor Development

Peabody Developmental Motor Scales (Folio & Fewell, 1983)

Screening Tests for Language and Speech Development

Preschool Language Scale (Zimmerman, Steiner, & Pond, 1979)

Receptive Expressive Emergent Language Scale (Bzoch & League, 1978)

Sequenced Inventory of Communicative Development, Revised (Hedrick, Prather, & Tobin, 1984)

Screening Tests for Social Development

Carolina Record of Individual Behavior (Simeonsson, Huntington, Short, & Ware, 1982)

Vineland Adaptive Behavior Scales (Sparrow, Balla, & Cicchetti, 1984)

Screening Tests for Multidomain Development   The most useful instruments for developmental screening in the preschool years are measures that include all categories of development. Some of these instruments, while originally developed for identification of children with disabilities, are also useful for other at risk categories and for general assessment of developmental progress of children who are not in a risk category. Below are some of the most commonly used instruments in this category.

The Battelle Developmental Inventory (Newborg, Stock, Wnek, Guidubaldi, & Svinicki, 1984)
Developmental Indicators for the Assessment of Learning—Revised (DIAL-R) (Mardell-Czudnowski, & Goldenberg, 1983)
Early Learning Accomplishment Profile (Glover, Preminger, & Sanford, 1978)

SETTING UP A SCREENING PROGRAM

When a group of young preschool children is to be screened prior to entering a program, administrators and teachers must make careful preparations to ensure that the screening is conducted in an orderly, supportive manner. Prior to the screening date, examiners need to be thoroughly trained if they have not administered the instrument previously or had specialized training. The training should continue until all examiners feel comfortable with the process. The area where the screening is to take place needs to be studied to determine where parents or adults will sit while the child is engaged in the screening process. Decisions have to be made about how the child will proceed through the process and how essential information will be obtained from the parents or adults accompanying the child. Prior to the screening date, the person in charge of screening needs to check to see that all needed materials are available and have been organized in the proper location in the screening area. On the screening date, examiners should arrive well before the time to begin and review procedures if necessary before working with the first child.

The DIAL-R, frequently administered to both populations at risk and groups of children who are entering regular programs, can serve as an example of the screening process. The instrument is administered at three stations: ones for motor development, one for cognitive development, and one for language development. In addition, there is a station where children may play with clay dough before visiting the stations and between testing periods. Children move from one station to another. The examiners at each station must be completely familiar with the tasks to be administered in their developmental category, as well as how to complete the scoring and record it on the child's individual record sheet. Adults are needed to work with the children at the activity table and assist in guiding individual children to the stations. There also must be a person available to greet and converse with parents, as well as an overall supervisor, available to solve problems and answer questions as they arise.

If the screening program is to be conducted as needed during the school year, the procedures may be quite different and more individualized. Classroom teachers and caregivers may initiate the screening process as a result of their concerns about a child or in response to parental concerns. In this type of process, observations and interviews may be the first step. Screening using a standardized instrument might follow and be conducted by the teacher or another examiner qualified to administer tests.

Other instances when a child might be screened individually would be when he or she enters school after the school year has begun. After discussing the child with the adult who is registering the child, the school director or counselor might determine that screening is necessary prior to assigning the child to a class or a program.

Regardless of the time and place, the screening process has the following goal: to identify if a young child has some type of condition that indicates that a particular program is needed or to determine if more extensive diagnostic testing is required before designing an individual intervention plan.

THE ROLE OF THE FAMILY IN THE SCREENING PROCESS

The family has a central role in the screening of the child who may be served in an intervention program. As was mentioned before, parents are a primary source of information about the child. They may seek help for the child initially and may have been referred to the program by a physician, friend, or colleague. Moreover, the parents may be able to provide details of the child's development that cannot be gathered from any other source; however, it should be mentioned again that parents may not be able to report objectively or accurately.

Parents play an important role in determining the child's needs for intervention or programming. Through interviews, parents can share what efforts have been made earlier to help a child with a disability or who is at risk. Because parents are involved in putting together the educational plan that is individually designed for children with disabilities or other special needs programs, they also play a key role in supporting the child's participation in the intervention program.

A Parent Interview

Carlos teaches second grade. He frequently uses an overhead projector to illustrate information that is being taught in a lesson. He sometimes has a student read part of the material that has been projected. He has noticed that Shana has difficulty focusing on the projected information. After other indications that Shana has visual difficulties, Carlos asks for a parent interview. Fortunately, both of Shana's parents are able to attend the meeting. Carlos asks about any indicators they might have that Shana has had difficulties seeing. The parents have noticed that Shana has learned to read more slowly than her older brother. They have also noticed that she tends to sit very close to the television set.

The parents agree to have Shana's vision screened by the school nurse. When the screening indicates that there is a vision problem, arrangements are made for Shana to visit an optometrist for a more extensive visual examination. Within a few weeks, Shana is fitted with glasses and is more confident in reading and in participating in class activities that require distance vision.

Because the family has a participatory role in the child's intervention, particularly in the infant, toddler, and preschool years, they must be active partners in the entire process, beginning with the screening process. Intervention services for very young children are individualized to include the needs and interests of the family and are not viewed as being conducted for the child alone; therefore, intervention is said to be family-centered, requiring that the family be involved in some manner. The nature of family activity varies depending on individual circumstances; nevertheless, parents and significant adults in the child's life need to understand their importance, as early as during initial screening (Sexton, Aldridge, & Snyder, 1994).

⇢ SUMMARY

Screening is a process used to identify and select children for programs in the early childhood years. While the majority of young children exhibit no developmental problems or disabilities, others may be at risk for developmental delay or have disabilities that are already present. There are screening procedures for each of these populations; such procedures provide needed information for selecting children for a program, planning the program, and designing individual intervention plans when necessary.

One source of the need to screen children arises from programs that are federally funded. The federal government requires that a screening process be used to identify children who are eligible for services provided in programs such as these: bilingual programs and early intervention programs for children with special needs or who are at risk for development or later achievement. Screening is conducted to determine if the child is in need of a program or would benefit from one.

Some programs that serve populations at risk, such as children from poverty homes, screen children through income level. The family's income level is a criterion for program eligibility, rather than an identified delay in the child. Nevertheless, in some cases, children may be screened to assess language and cognitive development to determine program eligibility or just to aid in instructional planning. Head Start programs are examples of programs that fall into this category.

Screening begins very early in the life cycle. Newborns, infants, and toddlers are screened periodically to determine if the child is beginning to exhibit delay in development. Mental retardation and delays in motor and social development can be identified during the first year, and such conditions may be improved with appropriate intervention. Children with disabilities are also screened during the preschool years so that it is possible to identify services that will improve the child's potential for development and provide therapy for existing handicaps.

Some young children may not present obvious handicaps, mental retardation, or other indicators of disabilities; however, they may be at a disadvantage for success in school because they have not had experiences that prepare them for school or they come from a home where the language spoken is not English. Children in these categories can benefit from educational experiences that will provide a foundation for successful learning in the primary grades. Screening for language differences, strengths, and weaknesses provides data about eligibility for programs, as well as information for program design. In addition, children who have limited concept development can be screened for preschool programs that focus on language and cognitive development, in addition to social and motor development.

The screening process used depends on the population to be identified and served. Screening for children with disabilities including mental retardation is conducted with instruments developed for the unique condition. In addition, other strategies, such as observations and interviews with parents and caregivers, are used to develop a profile of the child.

While instruments are available for many types of screening, there are cautions about solely using instruments to screen children in the early childhood years. Because of the limitations inherent with standardized tests and because of the difficulties in developing instruments that are valid and reliable for use with very young children, the screening process should use a variety of strategies to assess the child's developmental status. When standardized instruments are used, they should be selected using indicators of quality and appropriateness for the developmental levels; characteristics to be screened; and compatibility with the program's purpose, philosophy, and goals.

When a screening program is to be conducted for a large group of young children before the start of a program or term, test examiners and support personnel must be carefully trained and oriented to the screening process.

Finally, the input that can be provided by the family is crucial, reflecting the major role to be played by the family in meeting the child's needs. The screening process is a partnership between the family and program providers so that infants, toddlers, and young children in the preschool and primary years can be identified and served in programs well designed to meet their needs.

⇢ STUDY QUESTIONS

1. Why can the screening process used to identify and select children for early childhood programs be traced to federal programs initiated in the 1960s and 1970s?
2. Describe how the screening process can be important for all infants and toddlers.
3. How do federal laws governing programs for intervention programs for young children affect screening procedures?
4. Define the term *at risk* when used with children in the early childhood years.
5. Why are some screening practices inappropriate for use with preschool children?
6. Who are the children who are "at risk"? Describe target populations.
7. How can the environment result in risks for development?
8. What is the difference between atypical development and a known disability in terms of the screening process?
9. Describe why identifying learning disabilities is complex and uncertain.

10. What are the purposes for screening children who may use languages other than English?
11. How is the development of gifted and talented children atypical?
12. In selection of a screen instrument, why is it important to understand the theoretical perspective used in the development of the screening test?
13. Describe some of the strategies that are available for screening children in the early childhood years.
14. Why are screening instruments alone not adequate for identifying children who might need intervention services?
15. What problems can be encountered in selecting and using screening instruments?
16. What are the advantages of using a multidomain instrument? the disadvantages?
17. Explain how a screening program is conducted.
18. How is screening conducted differently before a program begins versus after a program is initiated?

➔ KEY TERMS

atypical development	genetic disorder
brain injury	handicap
compensatory program	impairment
developmental delay	intervention program
diabetes	learning disability
disability	perceptual disability
dyslexia	sensory disability
emotional disturbances	spina bifida

➔ SUGGESTED ACTIVITIES

1. Visit a public school program that serves children with disabilities with intervention services. Observe the class and interview the teacher about how the children were initially screened for the program.
2. Visit a Head Start program or public school classroom that serves children who are at risk for successful achievement in the primary grades. Find out the purposes of the program and how children are screened for the program.

3

Assessment in Early Childhood Programs

$\rightarrow$ Chapter Objectives

As a result of reading this chapter, you will be able to

1. Describe the purposes for assessment that is conducted at the beginning of the year in preschools and primary grades
2. List and explain appropriate assessment strategies in preschools and primary grades at the beginning of the year
3. Discuss how temperament and learning styles affect how young children interact and learn in early childhood classrooms
4. Explain how assessment is different in preschool and primary classrooms

In Chapter 2, we focused on the role of screening in determining a young child's developmental status and the existence of possible developmental delay or disabilities. We discussed programs that provide intervention services that can enhance children's development and learning prior to their entering school-age classrooms. The emphasis was upon developmental evaluation prior to children's entry into a preschool or kindergarten program. In this chapter, we want to take the next step and discuss how we gather additional information through assessment to plan appropriate instructional programs for young children. Although screening information will provide input about the child's developmental status, further assessment provides more comprehensive data about each child. The more information a teacher has about the children in the classroom, the more appropriate the curriculum planning process can be.

THE ROLE OF ASSESSMENT IN CURRICULUM PLANNING

Assessment for Children at Risk vs. Assessment for Children Not at Risk

From the first two chapters, we understand that when children are screened in the infant and toddler period and later during the preschool years, evaluation of the young child is to ascertain whether development is normal or atypical. Children with disabilities or who are developmentally at risk have special learning needs, and the programs developed for them address the disabilities or risk factors that are present. Children who are identified as having a developmental difficulty or disability will require extensive **diagnostic assessment** to gain comprehensive information about them and the kind of individual education or therapy plan they need. Diagnostic assessment conducted with these populations of children requires thorough training; therefore, this type of assessment is most likely to be administered by a diagnostician, psychologist, medical professional, or counselor, or a combination of examiners. The purpose of diagnostic assessment is to gather adequate information to develop individual plans for each child, and the process is a cooperative one between parents, teachers, and other professionals.

Assessment for children who are not at risk and do not have developmental disabilities is quite different. Assessment procedures are most likely to be conducted by the classroom teacher and parents using informal strategies. Although there is a need for information on individual development and achievement, assessment is more likely to be used for appropriate grouping and curriculum planning in the classroom. Teachers in regular classrooms are concerned with individual needs, but they are usually able to understand and address individual needs within the group setting. They typically use informal assessment strategies, rather than the type of diagnostic testing used for children with special needs. Curriculum planning for children who are not at risk is likely to be group oriented with accommodations for individual differences, while children with disabilities or at risk for developmental delay will have curriculum plans that are individual, with accommodations for group participation and group activities.

Chapters 6 and 7 will address the assessment process for children with disabilities or risk factors and how assessment guides curriculum planning for such children. Issues of mainstreaming and inclusion and of planning instruction that is appropriate

Classroom teachers need to determine the instructional needs of individual children.

and relevant for all children will be addressed in those chapters, as will how the teacher provides for the individual needs for children with special needs within a group setting. This chapter, in contrast, discusses the process of assessment and curriculum planning for children who are not at risk. It focuses on the purposes and processes for assessment and implications for instruction. While children with special needs might be part of the class, the content of this chapter will emphasize how assessment and curriculum planning are linked for children who are not at risk.

The Purposes for Assessment in Curriculum Planning

The obvious purpose for assessment of young children is to acquire information that can be used for program planning. While some children may have been screened prior to entry into the program, children who are not at risk for development and learning may not have been evaluated prior to the beginning of the program or school year. The teacher will have sources of information to draw upon, such as input from parents or from another early childhood program, but will need additional input to develop a profile of the child. The purposes of assessment will be slightly different for preschool and school-age children because of developmental differences and program differences at the two levels.

Purposes for Preschool Assessment

> Assessment involves the multiple steps of collecting data on a child's development and learning, determining its significance in light of the program goals and objectives, incorporating the information into planning for individuals and programs, and communicating the findings to parents and other involved parties (Hills, 1992).

As has been discussed previously, preschool screening and assessment have as their main goal to determine the child's developmental status. The preschool teacher is very aware that developmental changes are rapid in young children and there is wide variation between individuals on a specific category of development, as well as between an individual's development in different categories. A young child may be advanced developmentally in cognitive and language skills but less mature in social development and skills. Each child's developmental status is assessed after the school year has begun to determine the child's entry level and evaluated again periodically during the year to monitor progress. Evaluations provide information on the learning experiences that will be of the most benefit and interest to the child. It is important to remember that preschool screening and assessment should not be used for tracking, homogeneous grouping, or denying children access to a program. Children who are entering classrooms based on chronological eligibility should be assessed for curriculum planning purposes only (Shepard & Graue, 1993).

Assessment for Gross and Fine Motor Development.   Evaluation of motor development provides the teacher with information about what the child can do physically. What is the child's progress on basic locomotor skills? Can the child hop, skip, and climb and descend stairs with alternate feet? In the area of fine motor skills, can the child grasp a crayon and pencil appropriately? Can he or she cut with scissors, button clothing, and tie shoelaces? Motor skills abilities can reflect the kind of experiences the child has been exposed to, as well as his or her developmental progress.

Descriptors of developmental progress in motor skills can provide the teacher with ideas for the kinds of physical and motor development activities that are needed in the early weeks of the year by individuals and by the class as a whole. This information will guide the teacher in selection of motor skill activities for the learning centers and outdoor environment, as well as in the types of teacher-directed motor activities that should be included in the developmental curriculum. Examples of developmental and skills checklists are provided in later chapters, beginning in Chapter 4.

Assessment for Social and Emotional Development.   Social and emotional development is of primary importance in the preschool years. The child's emotional well-being and ability to engage in positive social interactions are developmental characteristics that affect the child's successful participation in the group. Assessment of social and emotional development will reveal the child's progress and help the teacher identify the kinds of experiences the child will be able accomplish and areas in which the child might need support. The teacher can, thus, be alert to assist the child in developing a sense of security and comfort in the group environment. Emerging leadership skills, as well as inability to enter a play group, are part of the characteristics of social and emotional development that can be addressed in the curriculum.

Assessment for Language and Cognitive Development.   Although motor and social development are significant areas of the preschool child's growth, language and cognitive development are areas that most heavily influence the child's later academic success. The child who enters a preschool program with a large bank of expressive and receptive language and extensive experiences that have fostered the development of concepts has a foundation for successful learning. Assessment of language ability and concept attainment provides major clues for the kinds of language and cognitive experiences that should be included in the curriculum. There is a wide range of variability among children in what may be considered normal language and cognitive development; nevertheless, the teacher will want to have a clear picture of each child's language facility and cognition to facilitate the child's progress in these categories during the program.

Purposes for Assessment in Kindergarten and Primary Grades   When children move from preschool to kindergarten and the primary grades, the assessment process gradually moves from measurement of development to measurement that is related to learning content of the curriculum. The child's developmental progress in acquiring necessary skills for learning becomes important. The purposes of assessment now include the child's acquisition of the tools for successful learning, such as the ability

Teachers use information about children's reading progress and interests when selecting appropriate materials.

to use a pencil and scissors or the ability to use word attack strategies to identify unfamiliar words. Particularly important in the primary grades are assessment of reading level, abilities in mathematics, and oral and written language skills.

Assessment for Reading Level. Teachers of elementary school children need to know the reading abilities of each child. Expectations that all children of a chronological age in a classroom can read the same materials are unrealistic. Children develop reading skills at different rates just as they acquire motor and social skills differently. In order to help the child select appropriate reading materials, the teacher will want to have a profile of the child's reading level, interests, and skills. The more information the teacher has about the child's reading progress and background, the better the match can be in finding books, magazines, and other reading materials that will interest each child and motivate the child to enjoy reading and progress in reading ability.

Assessment for Mathematics Ability. Mathematics is a content area that is sequentially organized, with cumulative skills. Each level of the curriculum is built upon an earlier foundation of concepts and skills. As the curriculum of kindergarten and the primary grades becomes more complex, prior learning is fundamental for continued progress. For example, the child who does not completely understand numerical value cannot apply that knowledge to the process of addition. Likewise, the child who does not understand the principles of simple addition cannot successfully move on to more complex addition or multiplication. The teacher assesses the child's level of attainment in mathematics at the beginning of the school year to determine where the child's understanding is complete and where the child needs additional work before making satisfactory progress in extending mathematical concepts and skills.

Assessment for Oral and Written Language Skills.   The assessment of oral language in kindergarten and the primary grades is an extension of how language is measured during the preschool years. The teacher wishes to know the extent of the child's receptive and expressive vocabulary and the child's ability to use syntax and descriptive language. Assessment of spoken language will assist the teacher in determining the type of language activities that will enrich and extend the child's language abilities. If the child's first language is one other than English, both languages can be assessed to determine strengths in each and how overall language development can be facilitated for the child.

Written language skills begin to emerge in the preschool years and become more established in kindergarten and primary grades. If whole language and emergent writing approaches are used, the teacher will assess the child's progress in writing using indicators of writing development. In the later stages of early childhood in the second and third grades, the teacher becomes more concerned with assessing grammar, punctuation, spelling, handwriting, and English usage in the writing process.

Assessment for Temperament and Learning Styles

In the sections above, we discussed the differences in assessing young children in the preschool years and in the kindergarten and primary years. We compared developmental assessment with content- or subject-related assessment. Now we turn to further types of assessment that add further dimensions to our understanding of the connection between assessment and learning. First, we will discuss the role of **temperament** and **learning styles,** and then we will follow with how assessment leads to grouping for instruction and learning experiences.

We are aware that children have different personalities and perspectives on the world. Children relate to others differently and approach new information differently. When we are assessing infant and toddler differences, we think about personalities in terms of temperament. In the preschool and primary years, learning styles complement and gradually replace temperament as a measure; however, personality differences continue to influence learning style.

Temperament can be identified in the early months of life. Chess and Thomas (1986) studied characteristics of temperament and proposed that there are three types of children: (1) easy to manage, (2) difficult to manage, and (3) slow to warm up. These characteristics can be identified as personality traits before infants reach six months. In the preschool years, these temperament traits affect how young children function in school. Children who are easy to manage tend to be optimistic, have low levels of distractibility, and tend to be adaptable to new situations. Difficult-to-manage children are more negative in outlook and more distractible. They have high activity levels, but short attention spans. They can be easily angered and may have temper tantrums. Children characterized as slow to warm up are very cautious. They find decision making very difficult and are slow to respond to new situations. They tend to be pessimistic and have difficulty in adapting (Machado & Meyer-Botnarescue, 1993).

Learning styles develop in the preschool and primary grade years. Two common classifications of learning styles are **field dependent** and **field independent learners.** Field dependent children require teacher assistance, need to be confident about a task before beginning, and prefer convergent tasks that result in a single response or solution to a problem rather than open-ended activities. They work well in cooperative group activities and look for structure in learning activities and are reassured when structural clues are present. Field independent children enjoy working alone, welcome new types of activities, and feel competent in addressing open-ended challenges without help from the teacher. They are comfortable with materials designed for individual effort and enjoy competing and finding their own solutions to problems. They also work well within structured activities, but look for possibilities for challenge.

Modality of learning is another perspective of learning style. Some children are **analytical thinkers** and prefer sequential activities. Other children are **holistic thinkers**; that is, they see information in a global fashion and later fit in details and organization.

Some children are **visual learners**, while others are **auditory learners** or **kinesthetic learners**. Young children are naturally sensory learners and use all of their senses to understand about the world. As they progress into literacy in reading and mathematics, learning through touch using concrete objects may be the preferred method for some students. Others move rapidly into a more abstract mode and can mentally solve problems in mathematics or decode unfamiliar words.

In the elementary grades, visual learners recognize words by sight in reading, think visually, and may engage in problem solving by writing their thoughts down or making lists. Kinesthetic learners learn by direct involvement in learning. They prefer stories with action and remember best when some kind of physical activity is involved rather than just seeing or hearing information. Auditory learners are likely to use a phonic approach to decoding, talk to themselves to solve problems, and are easily distracted by noise in the classroom (Barbe & Swassing, 1979).

There are various theories on the relationship of learning styles to success in learning. The concern is that teaching methods in schools are limited in addressing learning styles. A difficulty is that teachers tend to teach the way that they themselves learn best and are unaware of the complexities in how individual children process learning (Machado & Meyer-Botnarescue, 1993).

Young children might not yet have a strong preference in learning styles and need to be exposed to all methods of learning and practice. Because they have limited experience, they will benefit from opportunities to learn using different modalities.

Assessment for Instructional Grouping

Early in the year, teachers of young children begin to group the children in their classroom for different purposes. They might want to group children with similar learning needs for small-group instruction. As a result, they will form homogenous groups for some activities, particularly teacher-directed lessons. They might want to determine which children will work best on activities in independent learning center and assign groups to work at such centers on their own. This type of grouping is heterogeneous since the teacher selects children with complementary temperaments and learning styles to work together. Another type of instructional group is grouping for cooperative learning. In cooperative learning, groups of children work together to conduct a learning task. The group must include those with leadership skills and those who can contribute to the group effort in different ways.

In each type of grouping to be conducted in the classroom, the teacher considers the child's developmental progress and abilities as well as temperament and learning styles. In instructional grouping, the teacher forms small groups of children with like abilities and rate of learning progress. Children's current learning status in reading or mathematics determined as the result of assessment, for example, can be the primary factor in forming small instructional groups in those content areas. The process of linking assessment and curriculum planning will be discussed in more detail later in the chapter.

USING APPROPRIATE ASSESSMENT STRATEGIES

As we begin the discussion about how the teacher conducts assessment with young children, it is important to be reminded about guidelines that should be followed for appropriate assessment. Assessment is used to benefit young children and should be compatible with their level of development. It should occur as a natural part of the daily schedule and conducted in a supportive environment. It relies upon multiple sources of information including parents and should reflect cultural and linguistic diversity (Hills, 1993; National Association for the Education of Young Children and National Association of Early Childhood Specialists in State Departments of Education, 1991). Most important, the teacher should have a positive goal for assessment: to determine the strengths and progress of the child rather than what is wrong with the child. Assessment is ongoing and provides teachers with information about how they should pace teaching and when they need to teach information in a different manner or approach. In the current decade, curriculum and assessment reform efforts have assumed that performance assessments are being used. Such assessments measure what a child has achieved, including what he or she can apply or use, in addition to what he or she knows. Performance assessments include problem solving and group efforts and products (Pierson & Beck, 1993; Wortham, 1995).

In the beginning days and weeks of school, the teacher seeks to know students and to start an assessment profile for each child. This assessment process might be composed of two steps. At the very beginning of school the teacher makes a gross assessment based on information that is available from the child's previous school experiences. Next, but still early in the year, the teacher conducts more extensive assessments to form a more complete picture of the child (Kronowitz, 1992).

Assessment Strategies at the Beginning of The Year

Prior to the beginning of the year and in the beginning days of school, the teacher has an opportunity to find out some preliminary information about the children who make up the class. A combination of strategies can contribute to the collection of preliminary assessment information. Assessment information can include reports from standardized tests. In addition, it can include informal information such as (1) cumulative records, (2) curriculum continuums, (3) conferences and interviews, and (4) observations.

Cumulative Records   Whether the child is entering or continuing in an elementary school setting or participating in a preschool program, there are records that are available to learn about the child. In a preschool setting, there is information about the family, parents' occupations, siblings, and the child's medical history. The teacher can gain valuable information about the child's position in the family, as well as about other preschool and child care settings that the child has attended.

If the teacher works in a public or private elementary school setting, additional information might be available. The child's permanent record might include information from screening or some other type of testing. A child in the primary grades might have a portfolio from the previous year, which provides information about the child's work and progress.

There is some question about seeking information from cumulative records. Some teachers feel that they can be biased by information found in such records, particularly standardized test results. They would rather form their own opinions of the child's ability based on their own assessments. It is the individual teacher's decision whether to consult cumulative or permanent records before becoming familiar with the child. There can be important information in the folder, particularly about the child's background; however, there is merit to the position that the teacher should form an independent opinion about the child's status.

Harry and Larry: The Statler Twins

Harry and Larry Statler have entered the second grade, where they have been assigned to different classrooms. Abigail Bean, Larry's teacher, has been examining his cumulative folder. She notices that Larry was withdrawn from school during the first grade for several months and then reenrolled in March. Larry's parents were divorced and Larry went to live with his father, while Harry remained with his mother. In March, Larry's father returned him to his mother because of the extreme emotional difficulties the boy had experienced while separated from his mother and twin brother.

In looking at Larry's medical record, Abigail notes that Larry was born prematurely and suffered more lingering medical problems than Harry. He was referred for screening for special education services when he was three, but his parents did not want him in a different type of preschool program than his brother. Both boys attended a neighborhood day care center at ages three and four.

Larry's first grade academic report revealed that Larry was considered for retention in the first grade, but was permitted to enter the second grade at the insistence of his mother. Larry's teacher, Abigail notes the information about Larry and makes notes to herself to pay close attention to Larry's social and academic adjustment during the beginning weeks of school. She will use her own observations and beginning-of-school assessments to get a preliminary profile of Larry's current status and needs. Abigail also plans to visit with Larry's mother to get information on Larry's current status at home since he has returned from living with his father.

Curriculum Continuums   It is a common practice to organize the curriculum of a school based on a curriculum continuum. Preschools might use a developmental continuum organized into a checklist. Kindergartens can have a continuum that is developmental or organized by subject area. Primary grade continuums are usually organized by subject or content area. An example of a preschool curriculum checklist is found in Figure 3–1. It reflects a curriculum for emergent literacy. Figure 5–5 (in Chapter 5) is a checklist that reflects a portion of a curriculum continuum in mathematics.

Records of a child's progress during a school year might be found on the curriculum continuum that is used in a particular school. At the beginning of the school year, the teacher can learn much about the child's progress the previous year by looking at curriculum objectives that were included in the curriculum and how well the child was able to meet those objectives. There is currently growing interest in sharing curriculum and assessment information between child care settings and preschools and public schools so that receiving teachers can benefit from progress reports made by the teacher in the previous school.

Conferences and Interviews   Parents know more about their child than any outside sources. It is invaluable for teachers to have a conference with parents prior to the beginning of the school year. For many schools, a home visit to meet the child and parents serves this purpose. Teachers schedule visits to children's homes before the first week of school to become familiar with children and parents. During such visits, the teachers can explain the school program to the parent, and children can find out what to expect the first day of school.

A parent-teacher conference can also be accomplished by having parents visit the school before the beginning of school. In this context, the parents bring the child to school to meet the teacher and become familiar with the room where he or she will be assigned. The parents and teacher can also exchange information about the unique characteristics of the child and family circumstances that will be important to the child's success in school.

An Interview With Chad and His Mother

Helen Chandradotot makes home visits to every child that will enter her preschool class-room for four-year-old children. She makes an appointment to visit Chad and his mother in their apartment the week before the new session will begin. Chad answers the doorbell and is joined by his mother who invites Helen to come in. Helen is offered a cup of coffee and cookies. After chatting about plans for Chad's class in the coming year, Helen asks Chad about his interests and his friends. At his mother's suggestion, Chad takes Helen to see his room, which he shares with two older brothers. He shows her his toys and pictures he has drawn. Helen asks Chad about his favorite books. He shows her several books that his mother has purchased at the supermarket. Chad and his mother also share some pictures of the older brothers and pictures of the family.

In the course of the conversation with Chad's mother, Helen learns that she is separated from Chad's father who has moved to another community seeking work. Chad's mother works at night, leaving Chad to be cared for by the oldest brother, who is fourteen. A neighbor keeps an eye on the children and is available if there are any problems.

Before leaving, Helen takes an instant picture of Chad to put on his cubby at school. She describes what the first day of school will be like and what kinds of activities will be available. Chad tells her that a friend who lives in the same apartment building will be in a kindergarten class at the school. As Helen leaves, she tells Chad she will see him on the first day of school. Chad and his mother wave good-bye as she starts down the stairs to her car.

Observation   During the first days of school, teacher observation is a significant tool in conducting an initial assessment of young children. The alert teacher can quickly become aware of a child's social and emotional development, as well as how the child interacts with others. A teacher can make an initial assessment of a child's temperament and learning styles by observing how the child approaches classroom activities and assignments and how the child completes tasks.

Teachers of preschool children will observe children during their first experiences in learning centers to assess how well the child understands how to work in the center. Obvious developmental characteristics might also be noticed as children engage in art activities, teacher-directed instruction, and large-group experiences such as out-door play.

Primary grade children can also be observed during instructional activities to assess which children understand the work that is assigned and which children are hesitant or seem to be uncertain or confused. Likewise, children can be observed for their attitude and ability to adapt to the types of behaviors expected in the classroom.

Within the first two weeks of school, the teacher should have a preliminary pro-file of each child. From the information sought out before the beginning of school and interviews with parents and other adults, the teacher had an impression of the unique characteristics, interests, and needs of each child. Observations of children during the school day should provide initial supporting evidence of the nature of the child and how the child approaches the new classroom. After the period of adjustment to the new school year is over and children are comfortable with class routines, the teacher is ready to engage in more in-depth assessment, which will lead to grouping for various purposes and for planning curriculum that addresses the needs, abilities, and interests of the children.

Observing Tatiana and Keryma

It is the second week of school. Mike, a first grade teacher, has introduced the class to journaling at the start of every school day. He has invited the children to start with a picture and then to write a brief entry to describe the picture. Each day he circulates around the room observing the children as they work. His purpose is to learn how well they use fine motor skills and how they are progressing in expressing themselves in writing.

Today Mike is observing Tatiana and Keryma. Tatiana works meticulously at her picture. She is drawing a picture of her family and adds extensive detail to the drawing of each member. She writes a sentence about her father and mother and one about herself. Before she can add a sentence about her brother and sister, the journaling period has ended. Mike is able to identify a few words in her sentences and notes that most of her efforts are invented spelling.

Keryma rapidly draws her picture. She draws a picture of the school with a tree in the front. Her efforts to write about the school are very limited. She is still learning to form letters and must tell Mike what she has written. She struggles with two statements about going to school and asks Mike to write the words correctly. She dictates to Mike and he writes the dictation below her writing.

Mike uses his observations to plan future lessons and learning activities that meet individual progress and needs in his classroom. By observing and responding to children's journal entries, he is able to conduct ongoing evaluation of children's progress in becoming competent readers and writers.

In-Depth Assessments at the Beginning of the Year

After teachers and children are settled into the new school year and classroom management is well established, the teacher is ready to begin the process of in-depth assessments. Although many educators think of assessment in terms of skills and content, assessment should consider all types of development and learning. For the preschool teacher, this means assessment of children's physical, emotional and social, and cognitive and language development. Such assessment can help lead to curriculum that is developmentally appropriate. For kindergarten and primary grade teachers, added to developmental status is assessment of curriculum objectives in the content areas. These in-depth assessments help in designing curriculum and instruction that is suitable for the last stages of preoperational development and the transition into concrete operational learning. Chapter 8 has more discussion about Piaget's stages of development and how they are reflected in assessment and curriculum planning for young children.

The strategies described below meet the criteria for assessment that is appropriate for the development of children in the early childhood years. Such strategies are frequently described as authentic assessments because they reflect the child's active involvement in learning and are based on child performance rather than responses to a testing situation (Goodwin & Goodwin, 1993). They also are generic in that they can be used for various assessment purposes. Each type of strategy can be adapted for different assessment purposes. These strategies include (1) observation, (2) structured and unstructured interviews, (3) teacher-designed assessments, (4) diagnostic assessments, (5) checklists, and (6) portfolios. Each will be discussed in turn.

Observation   As described earlier, observation is a most flexible and useful form of assessment. Because it can be used throughout the school day for multiple purposes, it may also be the most accessible type of assessment. Observation in simple terms is the process of studying what a child or children are doing and interpreting what is happening for development and learning; nevertheless, there are distinct methods that can be used to gather information. Among them are anecdotal records, running records, timed samples, and event samples.

Anecdotal Records.   An anecdotal record is a written recording of a single event or happening that has been observed. The observer records objectively what is seen and heard. Interpretation of the recorded information is written separately. Thus, the anecdotal record includes both a description of the observation and interpretation of the significance of what was observed.

Observation of Jerome

Soshi Wong is a second grade teacher. She has been observing Jerome because he displays anger frequently and tends to become physical when he is angry. She decides to record incidents when Jerome is angry to try to determine what is causing his outbursts.

Today Jerome is unable to remain in his seat during silent reading. He fidgets and opens and closes his book without attending to the content. Soshi makes the following entry.

Anecdote

Jerome is sitting at his desk looking at his book. He closes it and opens it, but does not attempt to read. He looks at the students around him and then back at his book. He slams it on the desk and puts his head down. After a few minutes, he opens the book and then slams it even louder and puts his head down again.

Comments

Jerome is unable to participate in the reading activity. He behaves as if he is either unable to read the book, uninterested in reading the book, or upset about something that may or may not be related to the reading activity. Slamming the book seems to be an attempt to get my attention or to distract the other students and thus get their attention. I will first discuss the problem with Jerome and then talk to his mother if additional information is needed about sources of Jerome's behavior.

Running Records.   Running records are extensions of anecdotal records since they use the same process and format. The difference is that when a running record is used, the teacher wishes to record a sequence of behaviors or activities in the event that is being observed. The purpose might be to observe and interpret a series of actions or behaviors. The teacher continues recording changes in activities or interactions to get a more complete picture of the child's behaviors.

Timed Samples.   Timed samples are used when observations at regular intervals are important. The teacher might need to know how frequently an action or behavior occurs and decides to observe a child every five or ten minutes. A record is made of the time of the observation and the behaviors observed, and an interpretation is made of the observed behavior. For example, if a third grade teacher wished to know how well a student follows through on an assigned task, the teacher would record timed samples as to whether the child was on task or not during the times of observation.

Timed Samples of Learning Center Activities

Children in Rose's kindergarten classroom have been participating in center activities for several weeks. Rose is observing children engaged in center activities to assess the kinds of activities they enjoy and the length of time they remain at a center. She observes at 10-minute intervals for 30 minutes. She observes several children each day. She records the following for Ramon.

Timed Samples

8:30   Ramon asked to work in the block center. He takes out the blocks and dumps them on the floor.

8:40   Ramon is lining up blocks in parallel lines. He is working alone. No one else is in the center.

8:50   Ramon has used all of the blocks to make lines. Two other boys have come to use the blocks. Ramon leaves the center and goes to the manipulative center. He picks up a set of construction toys and begins putting them together.

9:00   Ramon has left the construction activity and watches Margaret working on a
            puzzle.

Comments

Ramon seems able to engage in center activities for some time. His timing in leaving the
block center may have been because the other boys came or because he had finished
using the blocks. In the manipulative center, he seemed less sure of what he wanted to do.
I need to remind him to put materials away before he leaves one center and goes to
another. He needs to be observed again to see if he chooses other centers or continues in
these two centers.

Event Samples.   Event samples have more components because the teacher is looking for the cause or motivation for behaviors. Timing of the observation is designed to
coincide with the setting or condition in which the behavior is most likely to occur.
The first part of the observation is to record the time and event that occurred, followed by the behavior that was triggered as a result of the event or behavior. Then
the teacher records what happened after the behavior. The components of the format
for this type of observation are called the antecedent event, behavior, and conse-
quent event. The teacher is seeking clues as to why behaviors, particularly undesir-
able behaviors, occur. Event samples are frequently used to discover the causes of
fighting or other conflicts between students in a classroom (Wortham, 1995).

Denzelle

Anita Black, a third grade teacher, is worried about Denzelle's social acceptance by his
peers. Denzelle tends to be a loner and does not participate in group activities in the classroom or on the playground. She decides to observe Denzelle to find clues to his behavior.

Event Sampling

The boys are on the playground choosing sides for a game of baseball. The boys choose
teams. Denzelle is asked if he wants to play. Denzelle agrees. After the teams are chosen,
the boys decide who will play in each position. Denzelle is asked to play third base. He
refuses because he wants to be the pitcher. Ben has already been selected to be the
pitcher. Denzelle leaves the group and sits down under a tree.

Comments

Denzelle made the choice not to participate when he did not get the position that he
wanted. He was not rejected initially by the other boys. He needs to be observed in other
situations to see if getting his way is a problem in other settings.

Structured and Unstructured Interviews   Teachers use interviews to acquire information about children's thinking and learning. In an interview, the teacher asks the child probing questions and uses the child's responses to assess the child's understanding of the topic being discussed. For example, a child might be having difficulty determining what mathematical process to use to solve a grocery shopping problem. The teacher questions the child to find out how the child is approaching the problem and then determines if the child can solve the problem with the approach or needs guidance in trying a different approach.

Interviews can be categorized as unstructured or structured. The informal interview is used when the teacher notices that a child is doing something unusual in an independent activity or seems confused when working on a group project. The teacher decides to engage the child in an interview to learn what is occurring in the child's thinking about the activity.

Structured interviews are designed with a specific assessment purpose in mind. The teacher plans the interview questions specifically to assess a child's understanding of a concept or procedure. Instead of administering a written test, the teacher uses the interview to determine if the child can explain the learning that occurred as well as provide the appropriate response (Kamii & Rosenblum, 1990; Seefeldt, 1993).

Graphing Lunch Choices

Students in Gloria's second class take turns taking the lunch count every day. Children have two choices for entrees or they might have brought their own lunch. Gloria has made a graph that is changed each day to reflect the lunch choices. She conducts interviews with the child in charge of the lunch count to determine the child's understanding of the graphing process. Children place their name next to the lunch choice that they are making that day. Then the child in charge makes a graph to report the results. On Tuesday, Jocelyn is in charge of the graph. The lunch choices are hot dogs, chicken nuggets, or lunch from home. After Jocelyn has graphed the names to correspond to their choices, Gloria asks Jocelyn which lunch was selected by the most children and which was selected by the least number of children. She asked her if more children selected hot dogs or chicken nuggets. Finally, Gloria asks Jocelyn to add up the numbers of choices in each category and compare the total with the number of children in the class.

Teacher-Designed Assessments   Teachers frequently design their own assessments of learning. The most commonly known teacher assessment is the written test used at frequent intervals in a content area such as mathematics. In the early childhood years, written teacher assessments must match the child's development in reading and writing. Written tests must be in line with the children's ability to read and write on their own. Regardless of the child's level of understanding of the objectives being tested, if the demands to read and write exceed the child's current abilities, the assessment may be invalid. Teachers must use caution in developing assessments that require children to read directions and write responses.

Of course, children who are in the early stages of literacy in reading and writing are not able to respond to a written assessment. As a result, tasks using concrete materials must be designed to assess their acquisition of concepts and skills. The teacher must organize hands-on activities and design the activity and directions to ensure that the child understands the purpose and process of the task and how to respond (Wortham, 1995).

Developmental Tasks.   In preschool and kindergarten classrooms, teachers design hands-on tasks, or tasks using concrete materials, for assessment. Because the child is preoperational in thinking and has possibly not yet developed reading and writing skills, the teacher devises activities to assess the child's developmental progress. Thus, to determine the child's understanding of the difference between zoo and farm animals, the teacher may have the child sort pictures of animals into the two categories. Likewise, the child may be asked to solve addition problems by making two groups of objects and then combining them to make a larger group.

Developmental tasks can be organized for motor skill assessment. The teacher might have the child throw a ball, walk a balance beam, or run from one point to another on the playground to assess gross motor development.

Written Tests.   As children enter the primary grades, teachers can begin to use written assessments. Such assessments can be introduced gradually as children develop a reading vocabulary. Using a paper-and-pencil assessment is a big step for beginning readers and writers; as a result, teachers begin with very simple written directions using only a few words. Responses from the children involve writing a single-word response to visual clues, circling the right answer, or drawing a line to match one item to another. As the children develop more advanced reading and writing skills and a larger vocabulary of words, the written assessments can be longer and more complex. When designing written tests, the teacher needs to keep in mind the normal developmental differences between children in the development of reading and writing skills. First grade children especially will vary widely in their emerging literacy abilities. Teacher assessments need to bridge the developmental differences between students. Children should be assessed on their understanding of the concept or skill, not whether they can read the instructions or give a written response on the paper-and-pencil assessment (Wortham, 1995).

Assessing Understanding of Words With Long Vowels and Silent e

Aghil teaches second grade. He wishes to determine which of his students understand the principle of the vowel having the long sound when followed by a consonant and silent e. He discusses the concept by giving examples on the board of words that have the long vowel and silent e and words that do not. He then presents a worksheet with an array of words with long and short vowels and asks the students to circle the words that have the long vowel and silent e. Aghil will later study the completed pages as an indicator of which students need additional instruction to understand the concept.

Diagnostic Assessments   Diagnostic assessments are conducted when the teacher needs information as to why a child is encountering difficulty in learning. A preschool child might be struggling with counting objects to match numerals up to 10. The teacher might have the child count groups of objects to determine if the child has mastered the prerequisite skills of number knowledge needed to match numeral and number. School-age children in the primary grades might be experiencing frustration and reading and mathematics. Primary grade teachers have numerous possibilities for conducting diagnostic assessment in reading and mathematics.

Reading Assessments.   When children in the primary grades encounter problems in reading, the causes may be easy or difficult to identify. The problem might be traced to a mismatch between reading materials and the child's reading level. Or the child may be unable to identify unknown words, and reading comprehension suffers as a result. Primary grade teachers have tools that have been developed for diagnostic assessment in reading. These include informal reading inventories, cloze tests, published diagnostic tests, interest inventories, and computer assessments.

Informal Reading Inventories:
Informal reading inventories are designed to provide a quick assessment of a child's reading level. These instruments contain graded word lists and paragraphs. They can be generic in nature or designed for a particular reading series used in classrooms. Basic instructions are included so that teachers can conduct the assessment quickly and accurately. Sulzby (1993) recommends that entire selections of literature that are part of the reading program be used with first grade children. She suggests that teachers use a modified informal reading inventory (IRI) and make a running record of the child's understanding of the material read. The following steps are suggested for a modified IRI (Sulzby, 1993, p. 31):

1.   Pick a story with a suspenseful narrative that the child has not yet read and that you think the child will like.

2. Read it and pick good spots for stopping for the child to confirm his or her pre-dictions and make new ones.
3. Pick two or three sections for the child to read aloud: one at the beginning of the story, one somewhere in the middle, and one at the end, so the child is the last reader. You will read sections in-between to the child.
4. Make a plan to end the reading by eliciting a summary of the story or sections read and the child's affective response to the piece of literature: Did you like/not like it? What did you like most? least?

The teacher evaluates the child's reading and responses to the questions to assess the child's reading level and his or her strengths and weaknesses in reading development.

Cloze Tests:
Even quicker than informal reading inventories for determining reading level are cloze tests, which are sometimes used with older readers. In cloze tests, words in a reading passage are omitted, typically every fifth word. Children are asked to provide the missing words. Progressively more difficult passages are used until the child is able to provide only 40 to 60 percent of the missing words. Cloze tests are simple to con-struct, but have less reliability than informal reading inventories.

Published Diagnostic Tests:
If teachers suspect that a child's difficulty stems from a problem with reading skills, they might use a diagnostic test produced by a publisher. Survey tests of various types can be used to assess the child's word attack skills or comprehension abilities. These might be provided by the publisher of a reading series used in the school or by an independent publisher.

Interest Inventories:
If reading materials are interesting to a child, the child is more likely to be motivated to read. When children have reached enough proficiency as readers to read books beyond the beginning levels, interest inventories provide a tool to match them with books that will be interesting to them. Interest inventories ask children about topics that are appealing to them. The results can be used to help the children locate trade books and magazines that they would like to read.

Computer Assessment:
A newer assessment resource consists of computer tests that help the teacher diag-nose a child's strengths and weaknesses in the reading process. Typically such tests are based on reading skills from a reading program or on a commonly accepted sequence and scope of reading skills. Computer reading assessments can be con-ducted to obtain a comprehensive profile of a child's reading skills. Programs to cor-rect a child's weaknesses are usually provided in conjunction with the assessment package.

Mathematics Assessments.   Diagnostic mathematics assessments are also used by primary grade teachers. These can include comprehensive instruments that assess a wide range of skills or assessments that focus on a single component of mathematics. Such assessments can be acquired from independent publishers or through the basal mathematics program used by the teacher, or they can be designed by the teacher. Computer assessments are also a possibility. As with reading, computer assessments are tied to individual programs to meet student needs. Although teachers will find all the types of diagnostic assessments mentioned above to be useful, the teacher-designed assessment might be the most helpful because the teacher can organize a test that suits not only the curriculum used in the classroom, but that also is matched to the needs of the children in that particular class.

Checklists   Checklists can be used at all levels of early childhood for in-depth assessment. Preschool checklists are developmental in nature and address the child's cognitive, language, motor, and social-emotional development. The most effective developmental checklists cover a range of development so that teachers get an overall picture of the child's developmental progress in relation to chronological age. They also permit the teacher to determine whether the child's developmental growth is different between categories of development. Moreover, although a teacher may have a group of children of one chronological age, the variance in the group can be extensive, with a wide range of development levels present.

Checklists in the primary grades are matched to reading skills and the hierarchy in which they are introduced or mastered. Checklists are most commonly available for mathematics, reading, and motor development, although lists geared to other content categories of the curriculum are also available. Figure 3–1 provides a checklist that bridges emergent literacy from the first stages in the preschool years through the ability to attend to print.

Assessment with checklists is combined with other assessment strategies. The purpose is to determine which skills a child can accomplish. The teacher can use observation, teacher-designed tasks, performance assessments, or instruments published for that grade level to identify checklist objectives the child has mastered or is having difficulties with during instructional activities. The checklist serves as a scope and sequence of skills and an instrument for record keeping (Wortham, 1995).

Portfolios   Portfolios are similar to checklists in that they are not in themselves an assessment, but a collection of materials that make up the assessment. Portfolios can contain examples of a child's work, results of teacher observations, completed checklists, scores on published tests, and other sources of assessment. Depending on the purpose of the portfolio, the contents can be selected by the child, the teacher, or both child and teacher. Portfolios can be organized by developmental categories, by content area, or to include all categories of the curriculum. They are particularly useful in sharing assessment results with parents or in developing a comprehensive picture of the child's abilities at the beginning of the year. Later, they can be used to follow the child's progress from one grading period to another (Tierney, 1992).

Broad Categories	Brief Explanation of Categories
Level 1 Attending to Pictures, Not Forming Stories	• The child is "reading" by looking at the storybook's pictures. • The child's speech is just about the picture in view. • The child is not "weaving a story" across the pages.

Level 2
 	
Attending to Pictures, Forming Oral Stories
	• The child is "reading" by looking at the storybook's pictures.
	• The child's speech weaves a story across the pages.
	• The wording and the intonation are like that of someone telling a story:
	  • like a conversation about the pictures, or
	  • like a fully recited story, in which the listener can see the pictures (and often must see them to understand the child's story).

Level 3 Attending to Pictures, Mixed Reading and Storytelling	• The child is "reading" by looking at the storybook's pictures. • The child's speech fluctuates between sounding like a storyteller with oral intonation and sounding like a reader with reading intonation. • To fit this category, the majority of the reading attempt must show fluctuations between storytelling and reading.
Level 4 Attending to Pictures, Forming Written Stories	• The child is "reading" by looking at the storybook's pictures. • The child's speech sounds as if the child is reading, both in wording and intonation. • The listener rarely needs to look at the pictures in order to understand the story. • The listener closes his/her eyes, he or she would generally think the child is reading from print.

Level 5
 	
Attending to Print
	• The child is attending to print as the source of reading in one of these subcategories:
	  • refusing to read based on print awareness,
	  • reading aspectually, with emphasis on words and/or letter-sound relationships and/or comprehension,
	  • reading with strategies imbalanced.
	  • reading independently (conventional reading).

Figure 3–1 Simplified Emergent Literacy Checklist

Source: From *Teacher's Guide to Evaluation* by E. Sulzby, 1993, Glenview, IL: ScottForesman. Copyright 1993 by ScottForesman. Reprinted by permission.

Portfolios are preferred in many school districts today because they complement the trend toward performance assessment, also known as authentic assessment. Examples and reports of children's applications of knowledge are best kept in a portfolio. For example, if a group of children engages in a project over a period of time, photographs and anecdotal records of the progress of their work could be included in their portfolios. A class working in cooperative groups to understand how wood is made into paper might record their research efforts, as well as photographs of themselves making paper samples. A final evaluation might be composed by the group and put into each child's portfolio.

Teachers like portfolios because of their flexibility. Unlike traditional report cards, portfolios permit a teacher and children to make decisions about what is significant information that should be retained as part of the evaluation process. Unless a school has established firm guidelines about portfolio contents and format, teachers and children can explore ways that they can document learning and achievement. There are many options to choose from, and innovative ideas for reporting information that accommodate learning differences can pique children's imaginations and interest.

➢ SUMMARY

In this chapter, we discussed how assessment supports curriculum planning for young children. The focus of the chapter was on children who are not at risk for learning.

In the preschool years, assessment is conducted to measure development. Gross motor, fine motor, social and emotional, language, and cognitive development are evaluated to determine what children need from the instructional program. In the primary grades, developmental assessment is combined with assessment of progress in content areas. For example, reading level and ability and mathematics ability can be assessed so that the teacher can determine what kinds of instructional activities are needed for groups of children and individual children. Assessment of oral language and language skills provides a similar type of information for curriculum planning in the language arts. This is especially helpful when planning instruction for children whose first language or dialect is not the language used in school.

The teacher also benefits from understanding the learning styles of the children in the class. Temperament categories are useful for teachers of very young children, and for teachers of preschool and primary school children, styles of working and learning become important. Children's temperament affects how they approach a task, how they engage in classroom experiences, and how they interact with others. During the kindergarten and primary grades, the child's personality characteristics and modalities of learning contribute to learning.

Children can prefer auditory, visual, or kinesthetic modes of learning. They can be field dependent or field independent, which influences their preference to work alone or in cooperative groups. The type of interaction they prefer with the teacher is also affected. And they can prefer analytic or sequential tasks versus unstructured or holistic approaches to learning.

Teachers also assess for instructional grouping. The type of assessment used depends upon whether the teacher desires to group children for individual instructional needs, cooperative learning groups, or heterogeneous combinations of students with different learning abilities.

Assessment in the first weeks of the year is conducted to develop an initial impression of each child. The teacher consults information from the previous year, discusses the child with previous teachers and parents, and observes the child in the classroom setting to determine how the child is adjusting to the environment and other members of the group and how the child is performing in classroom activities. Later in the beginning weeks, the teacher will conduct more specific assessments to develop a more comprehensive profile of the child's abilities and modalities of learning.

In the next chapter, preparing for the beginning of the year and preparing children to begin the year appropriately are discussed. How to organize the classroom, the outdoor environment, and the curriculum is described. Another focus is on curriculum planning and how assessment information is actualized in designing curriculum and instruction for the children in a classroom.

✈ STUDY QUESTIONS

1. Why is assessment of children with disabilities or who are at risk different from assessment of children who are not at risk?
2. Why is preschool assessment described as developmental assessment?
3. Why does the preschool teacher assess the development of children?
4. How is assessment different in the primary grades? What kinds of information are now useful in planning curriculum and instruction?
5. Why is it important to assess children's oral and written language skills?
6. How is language assessment different from assessment in reading?
7. Describe three different approaches to understanding learning modalities or styles.
8. How does understanding temperament help teachers to understand how school-age children learn differently?
9. Should instructional grouping be conducted to organize children by ability? Describe different types of grouping and how assessment is useful in the process.
10. Define characteristics of appropriate assessment strategies.
11. What assessment strategies are used for initial assessment at the beginning of the year?
12. How do initial assessments at the beginning of the year contribute to the more comprehensive profile of children also developed early in the school year?
13. Describe appropriate assessment strategies for in-depth assessment at the beginning of the year.
14. How is observation useful for determining learning styles in young children?

15. Why are teacher-designed assessments for preschool children different from assessment in the primary grades?
16. What are the differences between inventories and diagnostic tests? Explain.
17. Describe the dual purpose for checklists.
18. Why is assessment of young children at the beginning of the year a key to successful teaching and instruction?

→ KEY TERMS

analytical thinker	kinesthetic learners
auditory learners	learning style
diagnostic assessment	modality of learning
field dependent learners	temperament
field independent learners	visual learners
holistic thinkers	

→ SUGGESTED ACTIVITIES

1. Compare and contrast two instruments for assessing development of preschool children. Evaluate their strengths and weaknesses, including ease of administration and effective use of time for assessment.
2. Study two sources of informal reading inventories. Evaluate their strengths and weaknesses, including ease of administration.
3. Interview two teachers from different schools. Find out what kinds of assessments they conduct at the beginning of the year and the purposes for the assessment.

4

Initiating the Instructional Program

→ Chapter Objectives

As a result of reading this chapter, you will be able to

1. Discuss the importance of careful planning for ensuring a positive beginning to a new school year
2. Explain the role of the indoor and outdoor environment in the young child's play and learning
3. Describe the role of play in the early childhood program
4. Explain how to adapt play for the diversity in children
5. List the characteristics of a quality indoor and outdoor environment for young children
6. Develop a plan to design and arrange the indoor and outdoor environments to facilitate children's development and learning
7. Develop a plan for play experiences in the indoor and outdoor environment
8. Describe strategies for designing a safe outdoor play environment
9. Establish goals and objectives for an instructional program
10. Assess curriculum resources for the instructional program
11. Develop a plan for daily routines for the instructional program
12. Describe how to prepare for the beginning days and weeks of school
13. Discuss how to conduct initial assessments with young children

In previous chapters, we discussed the role of assessment with preschool and primary grade children, both children with disabilities and ones potentially at risk for succeeding at school, as well as for children who are not at risk. We have also explored different types of formal and informal assessment strategies that are appropriate to use with young children.

In this chapter, we will describe the process of beginning an instructional program with a new group of children at the beginning of the school year. Before teachers are ready to welcome children into the classroom, they have to address several important considerations. Teachers must make decisions about how the indoor and outdoor environment will be used to promote children's development and learning. Concurrently, they must begin to plan for the instructional program that will be implemented. Most important, teachers will want to consider his or her role in guiding development and learning for the needs of individuals and the unique group of children who will be participating in the classroom experiences.

Once teachers have planned the program for the children, the next step is to prepare the children to participate in the program. The first task is to help children make a successful transition into the school or center setting. Each child brings different background experiences and perspectives about what "school" is going to be. Teachers will want to guide each child's adjustment during the first days and weeks of the program so that the experience is positive and the child encounters as few problems as possible.

After children are settled and comfortable with the school and classroom setting and their fellow classmates, teachers are ready to begin assessing each child's development, needs, and potential for learning. Children who have special needs or are at risk for successful learning will possibly already have undergone comprehensive assessment. If a child has an Individualized Education Plan (IEP), the teacher will want to review the plan to determine how the goals and objectives in the child's plan can be addressed in the program. Children who have been identified as being at risk for successful learning may need assessment strategies that can identify their specific needs. Although learning experiences have been in progress since the day the children first entered school, as teachers become acquainted with the children and become more knowledgeable about the children's needs and potential, more comprehensive curriculum and instructional planning can evolve.

PREPARING THE ENVIRONMENT

Understanding the Role of the Environment in the Early Childhood Program

> The *environment* is the sum total of the physical and human qualities that combine to create a space in which children and adults work and play together. Environment is the *content* teachers arrange; it is an *atmosphere* they create; it is a *feeling* they communicate. Environment is the total picture—from the traffic flow to the daily schedule, from the numbers of chairs at a table to the placement of the guinea pig cage. It is a means to an end. (Gordon & Browne, 1993)

The classroom and outdoor environment has an important influence on the play, development, and learning of young children; it can have a positive or negative effect on the quality of the child's experiences and success in the program. The environment where young children live, work, and play when they are in an early children program reflects the philosophy and approach to early childhood education that is used by the teacher and preschool or early childhood center. An environment that lacks centers or areas where children can interact and explore may indicate that the teacher and school perceive that all learning is directed by the teacher, who distributes materials, toys, and games at appropriate times. The classroom with activities and toys that are scattered on shelves or that are dusty from infrequent use may indicate a lack of understanding of the need to organize the indoor environment into areas of interest or of the child's need for organization and order in the environment (Trawick-Smith, 1992). In a quality program, both the indoor and outdoor environments are designed and organized to promote children's development and learning through a wide range of possible experiences and activities.

The indoor environment is the part of the child's world where much of a child's physical, socioemotional, and cognitive development occurs through daily interactions with materials and experiences that have been prepared by the teacher. The quality of the child's growth and development in the preschool and primary grade program is influenced by how well the teacher has planned and organized the environment to implement the educational program.

The outdoor environment is also important for development and learning. Although we often think of the role of outdoor play in terms of physical exercise, the outdoor environment can be organized to promote all categories of development and play. The outdoor areas can be described as a playground or playscape because we understand outdoor activities take the form of play, or we can perceive it more broadly as the outdoor environment where the natural world becomes part of the child's growth and development through play (Frost, 1992).

The outdoor environment that is equipped with only a few pieces of traditional play equipment reflects the philosophy that outdoor activities are primarily for physical exercise. Exploration, discovery, and creative expression are not understood to be significant when children are outdoors. When the outdoor playscape has a variety of play structures but lacks facilities for sand and water play, gardens and animals, or toys and construction materials, it fails to provide the variety of experiences that an outdoor environment can offer. Such a facility reflects a belief that play structures are the essential elements of outdoor experiences. The concept that zones or areas can be organized for different types of development and play is lacking. In contrast, the best outdoor playscapes are designed and constructed from the philosophy that children develop and learn equally outdoors and indoors. The outdoor playground is, in fact, another classroom where young children's play has the same benefits as indoor play.

Whether the teacher is planning the organization of the indoor or outdoor environment for preschool and primary grade children, a preliminary step is for the teacher to become knowledgeable about the role of play in the young child's development and learning. That understanding, in turn, permits the teacher to develop indoor and outdoor environments that will facilitate children's developmental progress.

Understanding the Role of Play in the Early Childhood Program

When given the opportunity, young children spend many hours in play each day. During play, they engage in a wide range of activities that involve physical exercise, socialization when other children are present, exploration and discovery, experimentation, pretending, and construction. Between the ages of three and six, they use their emerging development to engage in increasing complex play. Progress in one developmental category can facilitate higher forms of play in other developmental categories. For example, as language skills improve, young children engage in more frequent verbal interactions with other children. These interactions, in turn, lead to more group play. As children become comfortable in play groups, they use their social and communication skills to plan sociodramatic play activities, which result in increased physical activity and more frequent verbal communication.

Cognitive development also benefits from play experiences. When there are materials in the play environment that permit the child to encounter and explore new information, repeated opportunities to explore the materials lead to a deeper understanding of concepts and their relationship to the child's existing knowledge. At the same time, ongoing play experiences with other children using the same materials broaden the child's exposure to other children's thinking about, and understanding of, the same stimulus (Frost, 1992; Johnson, Christie, & Yawkey, 1987). For example, children in a preschool classroom had an array of seashells in the science center. The children were encouraged to play with the shells during center time. A group of children extended possibilities for exploration by tracing around the shells with a pencil. Two boys picked out a shell that had a shape that they liked and found all the shells that were similar to that shape. After the teacher conducted activities to examine weight and texture of different shells, some children were observed using more complex categories for classification of the shells.

Teachers who understand the importance of play in the development and learning of children in early childhood programs can set up environments that facilitate

Young children develop cognitive, physical, language, and social skills through play.

play experiences. Such experiences include opportunities for (1) social play, (2) socio-dramatic play, (3) physical play, (4) opportunities for language and cognitive development, and (5) creative expression.

1.   Social play occurs when two or more children are able to interact in a play activity. This ability emerges gradually in very young children, who first engage in play by themselves or as observers of the play of others. As social development advances, children are able to play alongside others and move toward tentative play interactions. Finally, they are able to fully engage in interactive play with other children and plan together for play events (Frost, 1992).

2.   Sociodramatic play is related to the emergence of social play. When cognitive development permits the child to use symbolism, the child is then able to engage in fantasy or pretend play. For example, when the child is able to pretend to bathe a baby or prepare a road to use for play with small cars, pretend play is present. When the child is able to pretend to take the role of a parent or a pet, dramatic play occurs. Sociodramatic play, however, requires interaction in pretend or dramatic play among two or more children. When a pair of children or small group of children can play and carry out a pretend play activity together, sociodramatic play is being used (Trawick-Smith, 1992).

3.   Physical play is part of all play activities. Whenever the child is using fine motor and gross motor skills in play activities, he or she is engaging in physical play. Physical play can occur indoors and outdoors; however, gross motor play is experienced more fully outside, where there is ample space for free movement. Fine motor skills are more predominant in indoor play, where materials for manipulative activities, art, and writing are more likely to be available. Space limitations in the indoor environment also help determine that more fine motor activities than gross motor activities will be possible.

4.   Language play occurs when a young child verbalizes to himself or herself during play. When children engage in group play that includes ongoing communication, there is rich potential for language development.

Play encourages cognitive development as the child encounters new materials and items in the indoor and outdoor environments. The presence of butterflies during warm weather or falling leaves in October provide natural opportunities for new cognitive experiences. New materials in centers and the presence of books and other sources of information encourage children's cognitive development during indoor play periods.

5.   Creative expression can take place both indoors and outdoors. When the teacher supplies a rich variety of media for exploration and experimentation in the indoor and outdoor play areas, the child is able to use creativity as part of the play experience.

Teachers recognize that to facilitate higher levels of play requires ample time, resources, and materials. When teachers plan the daily routines, scheduling, and program planning, they should place appropriate emphasis on time and supporting materials for play (Christie & Wardle, 1992).

Play and Children With Diverse Needs   Children who have special needs or who reflect language, ethnic, and economic diversity have unique needs for play experiences. Although the need for play for all children is recognized, there may be theoretical differences between early childhood and special educators over the issue of the role of play. Special educators may view play as a skill that must be taught (Widerstrom, 1986), while early childhood educators consider play to be a necessary component of development and learning (Association For Childhood Education International/Isenberg & Quisenberry, 1988; Bredekamp, 1987). Nevertheless, with increasing integration of children with special needs into early childhood programs, adults will need to understand how best to assist children with disabilities to engage in natural play that is developmental in nature (Bordner & Berkley, 1992).

Research indicates that children with disabilities progress through the same social and cognitive play levels as other children, although the level of sophistication varies (Malone & Stoneman, 1990; Rogers, 1988). Nevertheless, these children may not achieve social integration without some type of intervention (Honig & McCarron, 1987). Children with disabilities may need help in learning social play skills. Within a natural play environment, adults may need to use direct instruction, modeling, and positive reinforcement to help some children learn how to engage successfully in play activities. Nondisabled children may likewise need intervention strategies to help them understand and accept diversity in their playmates. Adults can reduce children's misconceptions or fears about children with disabilities by helping children learn about one another and answering their questions honestly (Derman-Sparks & A.B.C. Task Force, 1989).

Children who come from poverty homes have needs for play that are different from the needs of middle class children. Children from low-income environments will have had different play experiences. Because they might have lacked toys and opportunities to visit local sites such as a zoo or library that provide informational sources for play, their play behaviors may be less developed. Not only do these children need ample time for play, but they may also need assistance from the teacher in developing more advanced developmental levels in play.

Organizing the Indoor Environment

Role of the Indoor Environment   The importance of the indoor environment for young children can be described from more than one perspective. The indoor environment is where children explore and play; in addition, it is their "home," where they live during the day and the place where learning takes place. The role of the classroom in the early childhood program is as significant as the role of the teacher. It is a key element in a quality early childhood program.

One role of the indoor environment is to facilitate the child's growth toward autonomy and independence. The environment should be organized so that the young child is able to become responsible for making choices, using materials, and master personal care. Gordon and Browne (1993) describe this role as facilitating self-help. Interacting with the environment permits the child to become confident and competent.

The indoor environment can also be set up to facilitate self-directed learning. From this perspective, the teacher plans, organizes, and arranges materials that support the curriculum. The child then selects and conducts experiences within the classroom that will allow growth and learning based on individual interests, needs, and level of development. Beaty (1992) proposed that the self-directed environment is the curriculum. The teacher arranges the environment for teaching and then serves as the coordinator for learning by working with individuals and small groups within learning centers.

The environment has a role in responding to the unique group of children that it serves. That is, the environment must be tailored to the population of children who will be using it for a specific period of time. Just as each family organizes its home to respond to the needs, culture, and lifestyle of family members, the classroom needs to be organized to reflect the needs, cultures, and lifestyles of the children. In order to accomplish this, the environment will have a **multicultural** perspective, in order to help children understand and appreciate the backgrounds that they bring to the group as a whole. This approach could also be called an **antibias** environment (Gordon & Browne, 1992). For example, a dramatic play center in an antibias environment would have dolls that reflect a diversity of ethnic groups. Clothes for role playing would represent clothing worn by members of children's families or the working roles held by children's parents.

What, then, are the characteristics of a quality indoor environment that meets the standards of self-help, self-directing, and antibias?

First, it has been planned for the developmental level of the children that will live there. It provides experiences for all categories of development and is sensitive to children's developmental differences, learning styles, and interests.

Second, the environment has a rich collection of materials that attract and challenge the young learner and that provide a balance between types of experiences. Greenman (1988) classifies experiences as being on the following continuums: active/quiet, social/solitary, novel/challenging, open/closed, simple/complex, and realistic/nonrealistic. For example, open activities are those that are divergent and without a single response, permitting the child to be creative. There is no one way to engage in the experience. The closed activity, on the other hand, has a clear solution or point of completion, such as a puzzle. The difference between simple and complex could be described by contrasting the simple experience of looking at books with the complex experience of engaging in dramatic play episodes. An appropriate environment provides balanced and rich opportunities for all types of activities.

Considerations for a Good Indoor Environment   When young children enter an early childhood classroom, they are immediately affected by the atmosphere they perceive. They can feel that the environment is warm and welcoming or cold or unattractive. They can sense that the atmosphere is calm and soothing, or hectic and disorganized. The environment will influence children's behavior and their sense of security and curiosity. The teacher needs to take into account a number of physical characteristics in planning an environment to influence children's play and learning. The characteristics include size, density, lighting and color, hard and soft areas, noisy and quiet areas, wet and dry areas, and spaces for exploration and learning.

Size.   The size of the classroom affects how children play. Children in small areas engage in more social interaction and engage in elaborate fantasy play (Bruner, 1980; Moore, 1986). More running and chasing occur in large play spaces, and children engage in less socialization and cooperative behaviors (Clarke-Stewart & Gruber, 1984; Smith & Connolly, 1980). Large space may be more difficult to organize and maintain, while, on the other hand, small space may limit the number of learning centers.

Density.   Although the information cited above would make it seem more desirable to have a small classroom space, a high concentration of materials, equipment, and people in a small space can be a negative. Young children are more likely to be involved and use cooperative behaviors when social density is appropriate. Because smaller groups create feelings of comfort and safety, classrooms designed for optimal teacher-child ratios and square footage per child will be more likely to foster peer interactions, verbalization, fantasy play, independence, and social competence (Trawick-Smith, 1992).

Lighting and Color.   The feeling of the classroom is affected by the type of lighting and color. Natural lighting is preferred so that children can see outside and experience changes in time and weather. The color of the classroom also affects the overall ambience of the area. Moderate variation in color is recommended; moreover, an overabundance of bright colors, pictures, and displays on the walls can contribute to overstimulation. The room should not be sterile and drab, and it should stimulate the senses without overwhelming them (Olds, 1987; Trawick-Smith, 1992).

Hard-Soft and Noisy-Quiet Areas.   Children need a contrast between hard and soft areas in the classroom. Because textures and tactile stimulation are an important component of sensory development, young children are sensitive to the textures that are present in the environment and benefit from experiences with both hard and soft materials. Soft materials can include stuffed toys, carpets, finger paints, and clay (Jones & Prescott, 1978; Prescott, 1987). Children likewise need a balance between noisy and quiet areas.

   Block construction and workbench activities produce noise, while a manipulative center, art activities, and library nook are conducive to quieter activities. Normal classroom noise is not a problem for most children; however, children need quiet places where they can be alone or seek quiet within the classroom arrangement (Olds, 1987; Weinstein, 1987).

Designing and Arranging the Indoor Environment   After considering the characteristics of a quality classroom environment and factors in space and arrangement that can affect the overall effectiveness of the classroom, the teacher can determine what measures need to be taken to optimize the environment that is being planned for children. The problems with less-than-perfect classrooms can be offset if appropriate modifications are made. Large spaces can be partitioned to reduce children's tendency to run in them and engage in inappropriate behavior. Smaller areas can be organized within the larger area to promote children's sense of security and warmth. Small areas can be adapted by simplifying the types of areas or centers that will be included. A feeling of clutter and too much density can be reduced by carefully selecting and displaying fewer materials and rotating centers and materials more frequently.

Keeping in mind the modifications that might be necessary for organizing an appropriate environment, early childhood teachers will also consider how they want to approach organization of space, equipment, and materials. Two options to consider are a developmental approach and a curriculum or content area approach.

Arranging From a Developmental Approach. Many teachers in early childhood programs think about classroom areas in terms of the child's play and development. The room is organized for large and small motor play, socialization activities, dramatic or fantasy play, creative expression, and areas for cognitive development, which include opportunities for language and concept development. With this developmental approach to arrangement, there might be a block center, writing center, large motor development area, creative area that includes art activities, and the dramatic play or housekeeping center.

Some early childhood educators prefer to limit the arrangement with a few large areas, particularly if they have a smaller space. Spaces might be organized by function, such as wet and dry and quiet and noisy. The housekeeping and block area would be located within a noisy area, while the art activities and sand and water play would be located in a wet area. The space for the library and other language development activities, including a writing center, listening center, and computers, would be located in a quiet, dry area. Manipulatives and science and mathematics concept activities would also be located in a quieter setting.

Arranging From a Content Approach. Another perspective for classroom arrangement is from a curriculum content approach. The learning centers or areas are conceptualized and arranged to facilitate the early childhood curriculum. Beaty (1992) proposes this method to arrange classroom centers by curriculum subjects:

Curriculum Topic	**Learning Center**
Language Arts	Story Center
	Writing Center
	Computer Center
Social Studies	Block Center
	Dramatic Play Center
Science	Science Center
	Computer Center

Mathematics	Manipulative/Math Center
	Computer Center
	Block Center
Physical Activities	Large Motor Center
	Manipulative/Math Center
	Block Center
Art	Art Center
	Writing Center
	Computer Center
Music	Music Center
	Large Motor Center (p. 4)

Whatever the approach to organization that is selected by the teacher, each individual classroom is planned and arranged to fit the needs of the teacher, children, and philosophy and goals of the program. The important point is that the teacher needs to plan how the environment should be best organized to facilitate the kind of early childhood learning program that is to be conducted. For specific ideas for all types of classrooms, the reader is referred to an excellent resource: *Caring Spaces, Learning Places: Children's Environments That Work* by Jim Greenman.

Tips for Effective Arrangement of the Indoor Environment

1. Learning centers should be arranged logically. Centers with quiet activities should be located away from noisy, active centers.

2. Furniture and equipment can be used to define a center. Low shelving should be used for young children. Physical arrangement of furniture should provide a feeling of clear organization of an area rather than a feeling of clutter. Areas should be defined to allow visual and physical separation without losing a sense of openness.

3. If the room is very small, consideration can be made to combine centers or areas. In a very large room, provision can be made for small, cozy areas and places where children can retreat to be alone.

4. Organization of materials in centers should be orderly, with toys arranged by some type of classification. Small wheel toys might be arranged by size, blocks by shape, and so on. Labels should be provided on shelves as guides for where items should be returned when children are through playing with them.

5. A large, open space should be arranged for large-group activities. This area might be defined by a large rug and be combined with a block or construction area.

6. Avoid crowding the classroom space with excess furniture and materials. If storage space is available, store materials and equipment that are not being used.

7. Consider the use of lofts, platforms, and sunken areas, to give variety to the environment. Lofts are particularly helpful in extending space in small classrooms. A center in the loft can share space with another center below.

8. Keep the arrangement and materials flexible. Study the use of centers and make adjustments in room arrangement if traffic patterns or center arrangement

needs improvement. Evaluate how interested children are in the materials that are available in centers. Materials that are no longer of interest or have not been selected should be replaced to maintain variety and challenge.

9.   Be sensitive to the spatial needs of the children in the class. Some children may require more privacy or space. Boys feel comfortable in larger spaces than girls (Johnson, Christie, & Yawkey, 1987). Children with physical disabilities may have special space requirements. Wheelchairs, walkers, or other apparatus must be accommodated so that all children can have access to centers and areas.

Organizing the Outdoor Environment

Role of the Outdoor Environment   Since the turn of the century, playgrounds for young children have reflected the influences of various movements in early childhood education. They also have been affected by the nature of the setting where the program is located. These influences have resulted in playscapes that have broader or more restricted roles for the play of young children.

One role the environment can play is to nurture physical fitness. This role arose early in the history of playground development when equipment became available from commercial manufacturers and was installed at public schools and parks. Smaller equipment for younger children that echoed the design of larger apparatus was frequently included on the playground. The role of physical fitness is still the only purpose for outdoor play in many public and private settings today. Traditional swings, seesaws, jungle gyms, and merry-go-rounds have remained on some playgrounds, while more contemporary complex climbing structures have complemented the older equipment in many locations (Frost, 1992).

A broader role for preschool and primary grade playgrounds is reflected on playscapes that are based on a developmental approach. Such outdoor environments reflect the evolution of different movements in early childhood education such as the nursery school and progressive education movements. The value of free play was advocated by early leaders of both nursery schools and kindergartens. Information from child development studies that burgeoned during the first decades of the century supported the notion that young children benefitted from opportunities to engage in extended outdoor play periods enriched with equipment, toys, and other materials (Parker & Temple, 1925). The influence of early childhood educators beginning in the early decades of the twentieth century have resulted in the playscapes of today that are designed to nurture all categories of development.

Early childhood playgrounds of today also reflect this expanded view of the role of outdoor play for young children. Attention is given to children's social, cognitive, and creative development. The early childhood playscape includes not only climbing structures and other apparatus that facilitate physical development, but also areas or zones that nurture all types of play, incorporating a changing array of toys, art media, construction materials, and wheel toys.

A slightly different, but complementary approach is taken by Esbensen (1990), who perceives the outdoor environment to be a classroom. In Esbensen's view, the outdoor play area is equally rich in opportunities for learning through play as the indoors. He proposes that the outdoor environment should be considered a learning environment designed to carry out curriculum objectives through play activities that are both child- and teacher-initiated. The teacher needs to give as much thought to the provision of appropriate areas for learning and play outdoors as indoors.

Considerations for a Good Outdoor Environment   If you watch young children on their way outside to play, they are excited about the opportunity to be outside. It is difficult to restrain them as they get to the door and they may start to run to begin the process of exploration in the outdoors. The characteristics of their playscape will affect how they play and how rich their play activities become. When planning for the outdoor playscape for young children, teachers should consider variables such as the site, types of play to be included, zones or play areas, and safety.

The Site.   The outdoor play site needs to be considered as carefully as the indoor classroom. If one is lucky enough to have the opportunity to develop a new playground, preserving the natural features of the site is an initial consideration. As much of the existing trees, shrubs, and other features should be retained as possible. If there is an existing playscape, some minor, or even major, modifications might be needed before a quality outdoor environment is a reality.

Other site features to be considered are fencing for the perimeter of the playscape, drainage, and provisions for maintenance. A fence should not only protect young children from wandering into dangerous streets, but should also protect them from intrusion from people who have no association with the center. Appropriate drainage is needed to prevent the playground from becoming unusable after wet weather. Provisions for outdoor maintenance are needed, just as for indoor spaces. Equipment, grounds, and portable and temporary features of the environment need to be repaired, maintained, and replaced when necessary to ensure that quality experiences are available for the children.

The size of the available play space is important, although it is difficult to establish optimum figures because of variations in individual sites (Frost, 1992). One guideline that is commonly considered is 75 to 100 square feet per child (Esbensen, 1990; Frost, 1992). The total number of children using the playground during the course of a day makes a difference on the wear and tear on natural features such as grass and other ground covers.

Safety.   A prime consideration for the outdoor playground is safety. Although a comprehensive discussion of all of the elements of playground safety cannot be included here, it would be remiss not to emphasize its importance in discussion of a quality outdoor play environment for young children. Injuries from falls, inappropriately sized equipment, poorly maintained equipment, and multiple hazards found on playgrounds are well documented (Frost, 1992). Playground standards are available to alert playground designers how to develop safer playgrounds for young children. Common hazards that can be prevented include entrapments, excessive heights, pinch and crush points on moving equipment, inappropriately constructed protective railings, and toxic materials and plants. The reader is urged to consult *Play and Playscapes* by Joe L. Frost for a comprehensive discussion of elements of playground safety that must be considered in the design of the outdoor play environment.

Planning for Play Experiences. While most teachers are familiar with the need to provide for a variety of play experiences indoors, they might be less familiar with how the outdoor playground can provide experiences for all types of development. The early childhood teacher needs to consider opportunities outdoors for social play, cognitive play, and creative or expressive play, along with physical play. In order to provide these types of experiences, the teacher considers how the outdoor environment contributes unique experiences for development that are not possible indoors.

Physical play includes exercise that promotes development in both the upper and lower body, as well as fine motor and gross motor skills. Equipment, materials, and experiences planned for the outdoor environment should allow for a variety of kinds of movement. In addition to play structures that present possibilities for use of a variety of motor skills, natural features such as horizontal tree trunks, rope structures, and temporary arrangements for physical challenges broaden the possibilities for play activities (Jambor, 1990). Sand and water play, complete with pails, shovels, and other accessories, introduces endless opportunities for filling, forming, and patting—which entail the use of fine and gross motor skills.

Social play includes possibilities for interactions with other children, as well as opportunities for sociodramatic play. Complex play structures, vehicles, and playhouses or forts support social and sociodramatic play, but large cardboard cartons, large construction materials, and props provided for a current theme are equally effective (Rogers & Sawyers, 1988). Preschool children are in the important process of moving from egocentrism to becoming more socially aware. The outdoor playscape provides them natural occasions for trying out new social skills. Playground apparatus that encourage togetherness and cooperation positively influence socialization. Sliding down together on the wide slide and working together to make a dam in a puddle during water play enable children to learn how to socialize as part of a small or large group. Sociodramatic play themes emerge spontaneously when children have adequate time to engage in extended play. As children learn to play together and extend symbolic play to include others in their sociodramatic play, their attempts become more complex as they experiment and explore fantasy and role-playing themes. A large area, with its wider range of play possibilities, enables young children to engage in expansive role play as they utilize the entire play area for their play event (Johnson, Christie, & Yawkey, 1987).

Cognitive play is also nurtured through outdoor play. Significantly, the child encounters the world firsthand when outdoors. Nature is experienced through weather changes, gardening, observing trees, animals, and birds, and exploring natural play materials such as sand and water. Sensory experiences can be provided through a scent garden that contains plants with leaves that have various aromas such as geraniums, mint, and other herbs. This is especially pleasurable for children who are blind or have limited vision. Although many parents and teachers dismiss the value of play as irrelevant for learning, preschool children especially learn best in this mode of experience. Children's involvement in outdoor play as they engage in problem solving, building, observing, and manipulating validates the value of play for cognitive development (Rogers & Sawyers, 1988).

Finally, creative play is also enhanced through outdoor play. Chalk drawing on a hard surface, painting different surfaces and textures with large brushes and water, or finger, arm, and foot painting on plexiglass panels and other surfaces—all contribute to the child's expressive nature. Messy creations using mud and water or exploring the sounds made by hitting different found junk objects can only be freely done in open, unconfined spaces. Group dancing, circle activities performed to music, and story reenactments acquire additional meaning when experienced under a tree or in an outdoor amphitheater. Rhythm band experiences, singing, and movement to music are experienced differently outdoors.

When planning the outdoor play environment, the teacher thinks about all of the possibilities for development and learning that can occur in open space. If an existing playground is to be organized as a space for development and learning, the teacher will want to plan how to arrange the space for developmental experiences. If a new play space is to be developed, plans can be made to design the space to accommodate different kinds of development and play in a fashion similar to what is used for the indoor environment.

Zones or Areas for Play.   While the indoor environment can be thought of in terms of learning centers or areas, the outdoor environment lends itself to play areas or zones for play. Factors to be considered are the categories of developmental play and making the best use of the available space. Although all types of play can occur in all zones of the outdoor playscape, areas can be designated for creative play, motor activities, sociodramatic play, and so on. Zones thus arranged can overlap and extend into other areas. Creative activities are located near a water source, while, large, open areas are included for large-group play and possibilities for more vigorous running and tumbling. The playground designer thinks of the playscape space in these terms and thoughtfully considers the types of play opportunities to be provided in each portion of the environment.

Designing and Arranging the Outdoor Environment   Unlike an indoor classroom, much of the outdoor play space is constructed to be permanent. Once the layout for play structures and zones has been designated, little can be done to modify the basic plan. However, many elements can be varied and changed as needs and interests change. The combination of permanent and temporary arrangements to facilitate children's play can be considered from the same perspectives as the indoor environment: arrangement from a developmental approach or from a curriculum approach.

Arranging From a Developmental Approach.   When thinking of arrangement of the playground from a developmental perspective, playground designers develop zones or play areas designed specifically for physical, cognitive, and social development. For physical development, a central zone for complex climbing structures, swings, and other equipment that facilitate physical exercise is combined with a large, open area or zone for active, group play. Paved vehicle trails provide opportunities for riding wheeled vehicles, and craft areas and loose parts zones—with a wealth of materials to manipulate—foster large and small motor skills.

Cognitive play also utilizes similar zones. Construction play occurs in the loose parts zone where lumber, tires, boxes, and other materials can be used much like large building blocks. Symbolic play results from play structures that suggest the forms of a house, boat, or space station. The introduction of dress-up clothes, small vehicles, and push toys broaden possibilities for symbolic and sociodramatic play. The inclusion of a garden area and animal cages support cognitive development through nature study.

The creative zone can contain a changing array of possibilities for expressive play. Easels, a low table for clay constructions and other art media allow for personal expression. Musical chimes made from junk and introduction of colorful flags and banners or hanging baskets with flowers add to the aesthetic enjoyment of the environment. A workbench with scraps of wood and tools provides for both motor skills and creative expression.

All zones support social play. The construction zone, climbing structures and other equipment that are arranged for physical play, the area for expressive activities, and provisions for sociodramatic play—all support social development. Within each of these zones there are possibilities for children to play alone, alongside other children, or in group activities. The zones are arranged to facilitate development: permanent elements are supplemented with materials and props that enrich the possibilities for play in the same manner as learning centers are equipped indoors.

Arranging From a Content Approach. The description of playground arrangement using a curriculum approach results in areas or zones that are similar to those for indoor arrangements.

A manipulative/creative zone can be perceived as a location for quiet and concentrated activities.

The physical zone is for more active, noisy activities such as climbing, running, rolling, sliding, and balancing. Because of the active, boisterous nature of the motor and play activities that are encouraged in this area, it should be located away from the manipulative or creative area.

The social-dramatic zone includes permanent or temporary facilities for sociodramatic play that can include housekeeping and other dramatic play equipment, as well as loose parts, household utensils, and other props as play themes and interests dictate. If a wheeled vehicle path is nearby and the physical zone is accessible, sociodramatic play can flow into other zones and areas (Esbensen, 1990).

Whether the outdoor environment is arranged from a developmental or curriculum approach, certain practical features need to be included. The outdoor space will need a storage facility for vehicles, art materials, and portable equipment and resources that are used interchangeably. Frost (1992, p. 144) suggests materials and supplies for a rich outdoor environment that promotes development and learning for young children. See Figure 4–1 for these suggestions.

Wheeled Vehicles
tricycles
wagons
wheelbarrows
fire engines (pedal cars)
road signs
spare parts

Sand and Water Play
shovels
rakes
assorted containers
screens
cooking utensils
water hoses
funnels
soap bubbles

Assorted Toys
hula hoops
lemon twist
can stilts

Construction
assorted wood blocks
interlocking plastic blocks
Coke crates
lumber
saw horses
wood
cable spools
plastic electrical spools
packing crates
assorted tires

Dramatic
folding chairs and table
sheets of plastic
dress-up clothes
refrigerator boxes (folded)
puppets
puppet stage
parachute
mats
folding screens

Nature
animal feed
bird feeders
nets
magnifying glasses
binoculars
gardening tools
seeds
watering hose

Creative Arts (optional
indoors and outdoors)
paints
brushes
art paper
clay
pottery wheel
handicraft materials
assorted art supplies
rhythm band instruments

Carpentry
hammers
saws
screwdrivers
nails, nuts, washers, bolts
wrenches
carpentry table
vise
paint and brushes
scrap lumber
clamps
brace bits
sandpaper
portable tool kit

Figure 4–1   Equipment and Materials for Preschool Outdoor Play Environments
Source: From *Play and Playscapes* by J. L. Frost, 1992, Albany, NY: Delmar. Copyright 1992 by Delmar. Reprinted by permission.

Tips for Effective and Safe Arrangement of the Outdoor Environment

1.   Approach the design and furnishing of the outdoor environment to address the developmental needs of young children. Include possibilities that the natural outdoor environment can contribute to the child's learning experiences.

2.   Evaluate the experiences available on a regular basis. Change and add materials when children's interests and the curriculum indicate such a need.

3.   Provide enough materials and equipment to accommodate the number of children who will be using the playscape.

4.　Observe safety guidelines when organizing and maintaining the playground.

5.　Consider the range of social and cognitive development of preschool children when planning outdoor play experiences.

6.　Arrange play zones to encourage play both within and across zones. Organize the playscape so that transition from one area to another is inviting.

7.　Be aware of special physical needs of children who use the playground. Make needed modifications for safe accessibility for children with disabilities.

8.　Integrate indoor and outdoor activities whenever possible. The outdoor play environment should complement indoor experiences and vice versa.

9.　Plan for frequent safety review of the play areas to determine if maintenance and repair are needed.

10.　Provide ample time for outdoor play. Provide time for children to plan and carry out play experiences, creative activities, and projects.

PLANNING THE INSTRUCTIONAL PROGRAM

Experienced teachers understand the importance of getting off to a good start at the beginning of the school year. The success of the beginning weeks and months can be attributed to how prepared the teacher was the day children entered the classroom. Beginning teachers who have just completed their first or second year of teaching invariably describe how they will begin the next year differently based on their experiences, which have convinced them that preparation and organization at the beginning of the school year is predictive of how smoothly the year will proceed. Moreover, teachers of preschool children learn quickly that it is very difficult to undo mistakes in teaching children routines than it is to take enough time to orient children carefully and correctly during the first weeks. Comprehensive planning for initiation of a quality early childhood program includes establishing one's philosophy and goals for learning and using that foundation for determining goals and objectives for the instructional program, organizing instructional resources, setting up the learning environment, and planning daily routines.

The first important step before taking any action is to consider one's own philosophy of how young children develop and learn. There is a tendency for teachers to become so involved with the process of teaching and managing children that they lose sight of why they are a teacher and what they believe about the best kind of program for young children. After completing courses that include theories of learning and appropriate methods of curriculum and instruction, teachers commonly become preoccupied with new curriculum materials and teaching strategies promoted in workshops and inservice training. They may need to stop to reflect upon their own basis for planning experiences for the children they are guiding through development and learning.

Recently there has been much concern about schools that place demands for learning and performance that is beyond the developmental capacity of children in the early childhood years. The effort to improve schooling in the United States resulted in an emphasis on academic performance that put pressure on preschools to accelerate curriculum and instruction for young children. The negative effects of academic pressures included delaying certain children's entry into preschool programs, placing children into pre–first grade classrooms after kindergarten, and retention. Such negatives led to a movement for reestablishing developmentally appropriate programs for young children (Bredekamp, 1987). Teachers who had felt that they had to respond to the expectations of parents, administrators, and the general public to accelerate curriculum and instruction with young children now were urged to reconsider the characteristics of quality programs for young children.

Thus, at the beginning of a school year, teachers, both inexperienced and experienced, need to reflect upon what they understand about the education of young children and the implications that their belief will have on how they plan their program. A review of the best knowledge we have about how young children develop and learn will give significant direction to help each teacher translate an individual philosophy into a program for a classroom of diverse children.

Determining Goals and Objectives for Learning

On what goals for development and learning will the teacher plan the instructional program for children in preschool and in the primary grades? What kind of instructional framework will be used to organize activities and experiences during the year? After reflecting on how the program should be consistent with the developmental levels of children and how the program can best guide their learning, the teacher next determines what goals and objectives will best give direction for curriculum and instruction.

Establishing Sources for Goals and Objectives   There are extensive resources upon which preschool and primary grade teachers can form the educational program. Some teachers follow a single source to organize the instructional program, while others select from several possibilities to design their own program.

Public schools in many states have state-mandated curriculum goals and objectives. Teachers in the public schools are generally expected to follow the state goals and objectives in planning their instructional program. In states where kindergarten is the first level of the public educational system, the state curriculum begins with that level. In states where public preschool programs begin earlier for children at risk, the state objectives might begin at a level prior to kindergarten. Because the state-mandated curriculum objectives and guidelines may be set at a minimum level, the teacher may have the latitude to supplement with additional goals in an individual classroom or school.

Some teachers rely upon developmental checklists or inventories as the framework for curriculum and instruction. Some assessment resources provide a developmental instrument along with suggested teaching resources. Examples of standardized developmental inventories with related instructional resources are the *Battelle Developmental Inventory* (BDI) (Newborg, Stock, Wnek, Guidubaldi, & Svinicki, 1984), the *Brigance Diagnostic Inventory of Early Development* (Revised Edition) (Brigance, 1991), and *The Learning Accomplishment Profile*—Diagnostic Edition (LAP-D) (LeMay, Griffin, & Sanford, 1978). These instruments are particularly useful because they can be used for all preschool children, including those with developmental delays.

Less structured approaches to curriculum objectives can also be taken. The emergent literacy approach to language development and language arts might include indicators of development in emergent reading and writing for preschool classrooms. The teacher can use indicators of development in a checklist form to guide planning for child-initiated experiences and activities and for the materials and resources that need to be available in the environment.

Goals and objectives can be derived totally from teacher planning. As the teacher designs integrated, thematic units of learning, goals and objectives for children's development and learning within unit experiences can be specific to the unit. Goals and objectives can also be drawn from commercial curriculum resources. Curriculum kits and guides developed for preschool and primary grade classrooms include stated goals and objectives. The teacher can use the objectives from the guide as they are or modify them to better reflect his or her individual program. An example of such a resource in mathematics is *Mathematics Their Way* (Baratta-Lorten, 1976).

Many teachers rely on a combination of resources for their instructional program. They use and modify objectives from several resources and add their own when needed. Sometimes a school district or preschool center will design objectives for the whole system or for an individual preschool center. Whatever strategy is used for designing program goals and objectives, they become the link between teaching philosophy and instruction, as well as the link between instruction and the evaluation of children and the program.

Inventorying and Organizing Instructional Materials   Part of the process of planning for curriculum and instruction is to assess what resources are available for the teacher and children to use, as well as the condition of such resources. The teacher needs to be reminded of what is available in the classroom from the preceding year. If the teacher is returning to the same school setting, he or she should survey the quality and quantity of games, toys, instructional materials, and so on. When teachers do not inventory their resources frequently, they sometimes forget or overlook resources that have been stored away for a time. This is similar to the situation of a young child who rediscovers a favorite toy that has been tucked away in the closet or at the bottom of a toy chest. The toy now seems new as he or she begins to play with it again. The teacher who locates forgotten puzzles, materials for mathematics, or a kit with lovely pictures rediscovers items that can be used in centers, for instruction, or outdoors for a new or different purpose. Keeping goals and objectives before him or her, the teacher takes inventory of what is available in the classroom for teacher-directed, child-initiated, and center activities for each instructional goal and its related objectives. Lists can be made of relevant resources, and materials can be reorganized and shelved according to the purpose for which they will be used.

If the preschool has a resource or curriculum center, the teacher will wish to extend the inventory or survey to such resources. An example is a preschool center in San Antonio, Texas, that has a well-arranged resource room that is organized by content area or learning center category for infants through five-year-olds. Here teachers can check out everything from aquariums to cooking equipment. There are shelves of prop boxes for the dramatic play center and materials for art activities and projects. Teachers can find taped music, unit ideas in file cabinets, and collections of natural objects for the science center.

A school recycling center can be a resource for materials. Children and teachers may bring materials from home, which are then organized and inventoried in the recycling center. Teachers and children can then borrow or take items that they need in the classroom and return them so that the items can be used again. A recycling center not only is a source of needed materials, but can be used to help children understand why recycling is important in preserving the environment.

Part of the inventory process is to ascertain the condition of available center materials. The teacher checks puzzles for missing pieces and looks for large wooden blocks that might need sanding. Storage containers are surveyed to see if they need replacing; and dress-up clothing is reviewed to see if it is becoming bedraggled and needs sprucing up with new items. As materials are inventoried, the teacher notes where there are not enough materials and lists materials that can be added to enrich the curriculum. The objective is for the teacher to become aware of what is available, what needs replacement and repair, and what needs to be acquired for the program for the current year, particularly for the first month or two of classroom and outdoor experiences.

When the inventory is complete, the final step is to identify how and where the materials and resources are to be used. They can be identified by center, curriculum topic, or both. Kits with multiple resources inside can be labeled with an inventory on the outside of the box. Teachers can never have enough storage space; however, no matter if there is an abundance of both space and materials, if materials are not organized and stored in a logical manner, they are likely not to be remembered or used when they are most needed.

Setting Up the Learning Environment

The final step in preparing to begin the instructional program is to arrange the learning environment. Having planned for the first few weeks of school, the teacher is ready to prepare the environment for the children. The first consideration is to arrange the centers according to the plan that was designed earlier. Equipment is placed first and then materials are arranged in the centers.

The teacher determines the best arrangement for toys and materials and decides how to communicate to the children where objects belong. Picture clues on shelf surfaces or the back of the shelves can provide information as to where items belong. If manipulative toys are stored in a basket or box, an outline on the container can communicate where such toys should be returned. Containers and materials can also be coded by color or shape to help a child know where items are to be returned after use.

After each center or area has been arranged, the teacher thinks through how the children are to use the center and materials that are stored there. A list will be made of all of the directions children will need to select, use, and replace materials in a center. These instructions will be taught systematically during the first weeks of school. For example, in the manipulative center, are the materials to be used while children are seated on a rug or at tables? How are puzzles to be removed from the shelf, carried to the rug, and then replaced after use? Are plans made to teach children that materials must be put away after use in one center before moving to another center? Will the child know that a puzzle must be put in order before it is returned to the shelf? How are art products to be displayed when they are completed? Teachers need to carefully think out the procedures for each center and prepare a list of instructions for using that center prior to the beginning days of school.

Planning Daily Routines

A similar process is used to plan for the daily schedule and routines. First, the teacher reviews the daily schedule. Then the routines that accompany each component of the schedule are considered. Questions are asked about the behavior that the teacher expects of the children throughout the day. What are the children to do when they first enter in the morning? Are they to indicate to the teacher that they have arrived and then find an activity in a center? Are they to get a book from the library center until all have arrived, or will they do some other activity they can select on their own?

During circle time, how are children to sit on the rug? In a assigned spot, or may they choose? What other routines are observed during circle time? How do they indicate they would like a turn to participate in a discussion?

What procedures will be used for using the bathroom for toileting and washing hands? If a bathroom is adjacent to the classroom, are children free to use it whenever they need to without asking permission? If restrooms can only be used at certain times during the day, what provisions have been made for flexibility for individual needs that vary from the set routines for toileting?

Teachers need to remember that young children are just learning procedures and routines. Because practices in each home will be different, the teacher should never assume that children enter school knowing how to flush the toilet, dry their hands using a paper towel or hot-air blower, or how to carry a chair properly. All of the routines and desired practices should be taught explicitly so that very young children feel secure in what is expected of them. Children who understand routines may need assistance in being consistent in observing them. Children who do not understand routines have to guess what is expected. It is harder for them to use appropriate behaviors throughout the day if they have to learn what is expected by trial and error. Sometimes new teachers need to be made aware of how important it is to guide children into mastering and observing classroom routines. Even experienced teachers frequently have to be reminded that children sometimes misbehave because they don't know what is expected. If daily routines are analyzed prior to the beginning of school and taught during the first days and weeks, both children and teacher will feel more successful and confident that they are getting off to a good start.

A final consideration in preparing for the children is to evaluate the unique needs of the children who will be served in the classroom. What diversities will be represented in this particular class of children? Are there children whose first language is not English? What provisions need to be made to make the transition from home to school smooth and comfortable for them? Are there children with mental or physical disabilities? What preparations need to be made to ease their adjustment to the group setting? Are there children who are experiencing an unusual family situation that needs special understanding or consideration? Are there unusual circumstances concerning individual children that warrant preparing the other children in the class? Teachers may not always know ahead of time about the diversity in the children that will be in their classroom; nevertheless, teachers will want to be alert for children with special needs and be prepared to make each child equally welcome.

GUIDING CHILDREN'S TRANSITION INTO THE PROGRAM

Prior to the opening of the school year, the teacher prepares the environment and plans for the instructional program. When the children actually enter school, they must be prepared to use the learning environment and manage themselves throughout the day. During the first days and weeks, the teacher concentrates on orienting the children to school procedures and facilitating their successful transition into the group.

The first days in a new classroom can be both exciting and frightening for very young children. If it is their first experience in school, their biggest adjustment may be to leave their parent or adult caregiver and embark on a new kind of experience. Young children who have had previous experience in a child care or preschool center are still apprehensive when entering a new situation. It is important for the child to feel comfortable and secure during the first day and the days that follow.

On the first day, the teacher will want to follow a very simple schedule. Toys and books are made available for the children to use. Much of the first day is spent in simple group activities such as listening to stories, coloring with crayons and paper, and learning basic classroom routines such as using the restroom, washing hands, going outdoors to play, and using individual cubbies. The initial schedule is followed for several days until children are familiar with the indoor and outdoor environments and begin to feel comfortable with the teacher and one another. Once children understand how to follow the daily schedule and routines, they are ready to learn how to use the environment.

Teaching How to Use the Environment

During the first days of school, the teacher concentrates on teaching daily routines and makes materials available as they are needed for planned activities. Using the instructions developed prior to the opening of school about how children are to use each center or learning area, the teacher introduces children to each center separately and instructs them on what activities are available in the center and what their responsibilities are for using center activities. Although not all possible problems can be avoided, the teacher tries to anticipate difficulties students might face while working in the centers and tries to eliminate or minimize them before children begin work.

The teacher first has to determine how many centers to introduce at one time. Some teachers prefer to set up one center and limit children to use of that center until children are comfortable with the required procedures. Other teachers prefer to organize the entire classroom, introduce the children to several centers, and rotate use of the centers until all are mastered. Opportunities need to be provided for children to practice center procedures under supervision. Children who demonstrate mastery are then allowed to work independently while the teacher gives individual attention to children who are still having difficulty. After children are familiar with center activities, the teacher may solicit their input on how center use can be refined or guidelines be changed.

Orienting children to the learning centers is never a completed process. Each time new materials are placed in a center, the teacher must orient the children to their proper use. Also, after a period of time, the students sometimes gradually slip into inappropriate behaviors. In this case, the teacher should "recycle" the children through instruction for proper center use until the correct behaviors are again in evidence.

Similar procedures are used to acquaint children with the outdoor environment, although children typically need fewer directions on how to use equipment and materials. The most important element of outdoor play that the children need to understand is related to safety. The children must understand what play behaviors are dangerous and must be avoided. They will also need specific direction on how to use certain equipment and tools such as the workbench or art media. However, too much direction can restrict children's play in the outdoor environment. Therefore, instruction should be limited to teaching children how to use the playscape safely, particularly the climbing structures and other fixed equipment. Otherwise, children should be free to explore freely and focus their attention on play activities.

Promoting Positive Classroom Behaviors

The purpose for establishing and teaching classroom routines is so that children can become self-directed and responsible. The more the children feel that they have the opportunity to make choices and decisions, the more likely they are to demonstrate positive classroom behaviors. The teacher's responsibility is to guide the children into taking initiative for their own learning through development of positive self-management of their own work and play. The more informed and skilled the children are in appropriate ways to act in the school environment, the more their behavior will reflect their sense of belonging in the program.

Each time the teacher shows children how to function independently, in a self-directed manner, children are learning how to accept responsibility. The more students accept responsibility for their involvement in daily activities, the more the teacher is released from imposing disciplinary measures on them. The goal is a smoothly functioning community where positive interactions between the members have developed from the practices the teacher has taught the group to use.

CONDUCTING INITIAL ASSESSMENTS

Once children have learned how to function with some independence in the classroom environment, the teacher can begin initial assessment of children's development. Depending on the instrument or developmental guide being used, assessment can be accomplished through individual or group activities or by observation of students rather than by administering an assessment. The following sections give an overview of initial assessments using strategies that were introduced in Chapter 3. Example of developmental sequences for language and physical development are included. Chapters 5, 8, 9, 10, and 11 contain additional examples of resources for developmental assessment.

Strategies for Initial Assessment

Motor and Social Development   The key to successful assessment that is not overly time consuming is to keep it as simple as possible. For some categories of development such as motor and social development, observation during indoor or outdoor play offers the best type of evaluation. While children are engaged in center or other play activities, the teacher observes behaviors for a few minutes as part of her or his interaction with the children.

For assessment of social development, the teacher picks two or three children to observe and notes the desired behavioral characteristics. What kind of play does the child prefer? Does the child share and take turns? Which relationships are in evidence? Which relationships are not in evidence? The teacher marks the behaviors of the children being observed on a given day. On succeeding days, the teacher will in turn observe other groups until all children have been observed; then the process is repeated. If there are aides or parents available, they can assist in the observation process. At all times, the teacher is observing without interfering with ongoing activities.

Gross and fine motor development can also be assessed through observation. Many of the gross movements occur naturally during outdoor play. Again, the teacher selects several children to study and spends a few minutes observing those children during the play period. In some instances, an activity may have to be staged so that motor skills can be observed. For example, the teacher may have to stage activities with balls in order to observe the child's skills in throwing and catching. With a few minutes of observation each day, the teacher is able to determine the progress of motor development for each of the children. Figures 4–2 and 4–3 show chronological sequences of gross and fine motor development.

2 Years (24–35 Months)	3 Years (36–47 Months)	4 Years (48–59 Months)	5 Years (60–71 Months)
Runs well straight ahead	Goes around obstacles while running	Turns sharp corners while running	Runs lightly on toes
Walks upstairs, two feet to a step	Walks upstairs, one foot to a step	Walks down stairs, one foot to a step	
Kicks a large ball	Kicks a large ball easily		
Jumps distance of 4 to 14 inches	Jumps from bottom step	Jumps from height of 12 inches	Jumps distance of 3 feet
Throws a small ball without falling	Catches a bounced ball, using torso and arms to form a basket	Throws a ball overhand	Catches a small ball using hands only
Pushes and pulls large toys	Goes around obstacle while pushing and pulling toys	Turns sharp corners while pushing and pulling toys	
Hops on one foot, 2 or more hops	Hops on one foot, up to 3 hops	Hops on one foot, 4 to 6 hops	Hops 2 to 3 yards forward on each foot
Tries to stand on one foot	Stands on one foot	Stand on one foot 3 to 8 seconds	Stand on one foot 8 to 10 seconds
Climbs on furniture to look out of window	Climbs nursery-school apparatus	Climbs ladders	Climbs actively and skillfully
		Skips on one foot	Skips on alternate feet
		Rides a tricycle well	Rides a bicycle with training wheels

Figure 4–2 Sequence of Gross Motor Skills Development

Source: From *The World of Children* (p. 280) by C. Etaugh and S. A. Rathus, 1995, Fort Worth: Holt, Rinehart, and Winston, Inc. Copyright 1995 by Holt, Rinehart and Winston, Inc. Reprinted by permission.

Cognitive Development   Strategies used for assessment of concept or cognitive development may vary. For mathematics, the teacher may assess specific skills. The teacher gathers a set of activities related to a sequence of skills and works with one child at a time to ascertain what kinds of mathematical experiences the child is ready for. Then children with like levels of development can be grouped for instruction.

However, for the best use of time, group assessment is desirable and should be conducted whenever possible. Some concepts can be assessed as part of group activi-

2 Years (24–35 Months)	3 Years (36–47 Months)	4 Years (48–59 Months)	5 Years (60–71 Months)
Builds tower of 6 cubes	Builds tower of 9 cubes	Builds tower of 10 or more cubes	Builds three steps from six blocks with model
Copies vertical and horizontal lines	Copies circle and cross	Copies square	Copies triangle and star
	Copies letters	Prints simple words	Prints first name and numbers
Imitates folding paper		Imitates folding paper three times	Imitates folding triangle from square paper
Paints on easel with brush	Holds crayon with fingers, not fist	Uses pencil with correct hand grip	Traces around diamond drawn on paper
Places simples shapes in correct holes	Strings 4 beads with large needle	Strings 10 beads	Laces shoes

Figure 4–3 Sequence of Fine Motor Skills Development

Source: From *The World of Children* (p. 283) by C. Etaugh and S. A. Rathus, 1995, Fort Worth: Holt, Rinehart, and Winston, Inc. Copyright 1995 by Holt, Rinehart and Winston, Inc. Reprinted by permission.

ties. While conducting a series of activities for a given concept or while observing groups of children working on projects related to the concept, the teacher notes which children can successfully complete activities and which children are unsure of themselves. When the results are unclear for some children, group activities may be followed by individual assessment.

Language and Literacy Development   Observation of children's natural language is the most effective method to assess language development. The teacher can use an instrument or checklist of the progression of acquisition of oral language skills as a guide to trace the child's current status. Figure 4–4 provides a chart of development of language skills during the preschool years. Caution should be used in initial language assessments with young children because they may be hesitant to speak during their adjustment period to school. This point is particularly relevant for children who speak a language other than English at home. Their actual ability to use the home language and English may both be masked by their reluctance to speak during the beginning weeks of school. They may need more time than English speakers before their language abilities can be measured accurately.

Age	Characteristics	Typical sentences
2 1/2 Years	Rapid increase in vocabulary with new additions each day No babbling Intelligibility still not very good Uses 2–3 words in sentences Uses plurals Uses possessive Uses past tense Uses some prepositions	Two cars Adam's ball It broke Anthony in bed
3 Years	Vocabulary of some 1,000 words Speech nears 100 percent intelligibility Faulty articulations of *l* and *r* frequent Uses 3–4 words in sentences Uses yes-no questions Uses *wh* questions Uses negative Embeds one sentence within another	Will I go? Where is the doggy? I not eat yucky peas. That's the car mommy bought me.
4 Years	Vocabulary of 1,500–1,600 words Speech fluent Articulation good except for *sh, z, ch,* and *j* Uses 5–6 words in sentences Coordinates two sentences	I went to Andi's and I had cookies.

Figure 4–4   Sequence of Language Skills Development
Source: From *The World of Children* (p. 328) by C. Etaugh and S. A. Rathus, 1995, Fort Worth: Holt, Rinehart, and Winston, Inc. Copyright 1995 by Holt, Rinehart and Winston, Inc. Reprinted by permission.

Emergent literacy development can be assessed through observation of children engaged in reading and writing activities or through collection of examples of children's initial attempts in the writing process. Portfolio collections begun during the early weeks can be extended throughout the year.

Tips for Effective Initial Assessments

The biggest difficulty teachers have in conducting assessment for the first time is that it becomes too time consuming. They get discouraged because the task seems endless and instruction is delayed. Here are some strategies teachers can use until they develop shortcuts of their own.

1. Avoid overassessing at the beginning of the year. Initial assessments should be conducted to obtain a general understanding of the child's level of development.

2. Assess in groups whenever possible. Assess individually only when an individual response is necessary.

3. Incorporate assessment during other activities and use small blocks of time for assessment. Use nap time or the end of a group activity for bringing records up to date.

Developing a Student Profile   As the process of assessment progresses, a picture of each student begins to emerge. The teacher is able to determine how various components of the child's development affect and interact with each other. As the teacher compares the child's progress in various aspects of development, strengths and weaknesses become clear and suggest the kinds of experiences that will be most helpful in facilitating the child's learning and growth. Instruments such as checklists and other strategies used to observe and record a child's progress can be collected in a portfolio or file for each individual child. This can serve as a reference for planning for curriculum and instruction.

Incorporating IEPs and IFSPs in Initial Assessments   Children entering the preschool program who have disabilities may have previously been served in an early intervention program. If the child has been served through an Individualized Family Service Plan (IFSP), the services provided to the child have tried to address the needs and desires of the family for services. Depending on individual family circumstances, the child may have been served through Head Start, a child care program, or a home-based setting.

Some preschool children will come to the new program with an Individualized Education Program (IEP) plan, particularly if they were served in a public preschool setting. Services were provided to the child through an individualized plan based on goals and objectives set for the child as a result of diagnostic testing to determine the child's need for intervention services.

Regardless of which type of plan or prior services the child has received, children with disabilities entering a new program have special needs. They come also with extensive information about their progress as a result of previous intervention efforts. A major concern is to assist these children in making the transition from one program to another. In addition, continuity in their individualized educational program is important, as well as success in including them in programs with other children of their age who do not have disabilities. When initial assessments are being conducted, the teacher also evaluates the special needs of these children and determines their progress within the new setting. The teacher uses assessment and evaluation activities to become familiar with the child's potential and limitations and to determine how to update the individualized plan with the team of adults who will be collaborating on further services with the child (Deiner, 1993).

⇥ SUMMARY

There is much planning needed prior to beginning a new year with children in early childhood programs. The teacher needs to plan for the environment and the instructional program, as well as how children will be introduced to the program during the beginning days and weeks.

Both the indoor and outdoor environments are important for children's growth and development. In planning them, the teacher takes into account the important role of play for young children and evaluates how the indoor and outdoor environment can be organized and furnished for optimal play experiences. In the indoor environment, the teacher considers the size, density, lighting and color, and areas that are to be arranged for various types of play. In the outdoor environment, the teacher utilizes the size of the site in arranging zones for play and must keep important safety features in mind.

In both the indoor and outdoor environments, the teacher organizes and plans for the development of the whole child, and provides spaces and materials for social development, sociodramatic play, physical development, cognitive development, and aesthetic development. The environments can be arranged from a developmental or curriculum subject approach; nevertheless, all materials and experiences are selected with the children's developmental needs and interests in mind.

The instructional program is planned along similar lines. The goals and objectives for the instructional program can be derived from various resources ranging from state guidelines, commercial sources, or from the teacher, but they need to be compatible with the developmental levels of the children to be served. The teacher reviews materials that are available and organizes them to support the instructional program that is planned.

Before the children enter the program, the teacher sets up centers, reviews daily routines, and establishes procedures for all elements of the daily schedule that will need to be taught to the children. During the first days and weeks of school, children are gradually and carefully introduced to the environment and routines so that the year will proceed smoothly and the children feel secure and comfortable. Children need to understand the teacher's expectations and feel that they belong.

Once the children are adjusted to their new school experience, the teacher can actively engage in assessing the children. This part of the program is begun after the children are comfortable with school routines and adults in the environment so that accurate information can be obtained about each child. Initial assessments for physical, social, cognitive, and language development are obtained as much as possible from informal observations and samples of children's work to eliminate extensive use of time for individual assessments. Once the assessment process is well under way, profiles of individual students begin to emerge, and individual portfolios can be organized to contain ongoing information about children's progress throughout the year.

⤏ STUDY QUESTIONS

1. Why is planning prior to the beginning of the school year critical for the successful entry of children into the program? Give examples.
2. How does the environment have a major role in preschool children's development and learning in a program? Why is the environment particularly important with young children?
3. What do teachers and parents need to know about the role of play for development and learning?
4. How do the indoor and outdoor environments have a similar role in developmental play and learning? a different role?
5. Describe some considerations that need to be addressed in understanding play possibilities and needs for children who have disabilities.
6. Explain some of the physical considerations that need to be addressed when preparing the indoor environment and the outdoor environment.
7. Why is it appropriate for teachers to approach the organization and arrangement of the environment from a developmental or curriculum approach? How are they both similar?
8. How are learning centers and areas in the indoor environment similar to outdoor zones or areas for play?
9. Why is safety important in the outdoor environment? What steps can the teacher take to ensure safety in the outdoor environment?
10. How does the teacher establish goals and objectives for the instructional program?
11. Why is the teacher's philosophy about development and learning important in designing the instructional program?
12. Describe some key elements in organizing and arranging centers for young children.
13. How does the teacher mentally prepare for introducing children to routines and the environment when they enter school?
14. Why is it important that children get a good start during the first days and weeks of the program?
15. When does the teacher initiate assessments of children's development at the beginning of school?
16. What are some cautions teachers should remember about timing and conducting initial assessments?
17. Why is observation the most useful form of assessment of young children? Give examples of how observation can be used for assessment of language development, cognitive development, social development, and physical development.
18. How does the teacher assess children who may have disabilities?
19. Why is the daily schedule kept very simple during the first weeks of school?
20. How do the environment, instructional program, and assessment contribute to a program that is appropriate for the development of individual children in the program?

⇢ KEY TERMS

antibias   multicultural

⇢ SUGGESTED ACTIVITIES

1. Visit a preschool classroom. Observe children during center activities. Try to determine what practices children have learned for using a particular center.
2. Observe children in outdoor play. What provisions have been made for development? Make a list of equipment and materials that are present for cognitive, physical, social, and aesthetic development.
3. Design an indoor and outdoor environment. Draw a general scheme for how you would organize areas or zones for children's play and learning.
4. Describe an individual learning center such as the art, manipulative, or dramatic play center. List the practices you would establish for children to use the center.

5

Linking Assessment and Curriculum Planning

✦ Chapter Objectives

As a result of reading this chapter, you will be able to

1. Describe how assessment facilitates the design of a curriculum that is appropriate for individuals and for the group
2. Explain how the teacher uses assessment information to plan appropriate curriculum and instruction
3. Discuss how individual assessment profiles are linked with curriculum planning
4. Explain how to use different modes of learning experiences such as teacher-directed instruction, learning center–based activities, and child-initiated activities in curriculum planning
5. Define instructional cycles and their use in curriculum planning
6. Differentiate between process evaluation and skill evaluation and explain their appropriate uses
7. Describe how to conduct ongoing assessment and record keeping

In Chapter 3, we discussed assessment that is conducted before the beginning and during the first weeks of a new school year. We also described how assessment is first an evaluation of the child's developmental status in the preschool years and later also includes assessment of progress and skill development. In Chapter 4, strategies for assessing development and skills were described as part of the process for preparing for the beginning of the year. Within that context, information was presented on how to organize the indoor and outdoor environments and how to establish routines for children to use those environments.

The assessment process described in Chapter 4 as part of preparing for the beginning of the year included the construction of individual student profiles. In this chapter, we will continue discussion of the relationship between assessment and curriculum and instruction with young children. We will explore how to use individual student profiles to plan curriculum and then how to plan and manage different types of instruction. First, however, we need to review what we mean by appropriate curriculum and instruction in the early childhood years.

PLANNING APPROPRIATE CURRICULUM
FOR PRESCHOOL AND PRIMARY GRADES

In earlier chapters, we have referred to assessment strategies suitable for the development of young children. We have also mentioned that curriculum and instruction in early childhood classrooms should be appropriate for developmental, cultural, and linguistic diversity, as well as differences in abilities. In this section, we will explore in more depth what a developmentally appropriate curriculum implies.

A stumbling block in designing suitable curriculum in the past has been the different teaching practices used by preschool and kindergarten teachers on the one hand and primary grade teachers on the other. While the preschool teacher encouraged play and exploration of the environment, primary teachers frequently used workbooks and other paper-and-pencil activities for reinforcement of learning. The different approaches resulted in teachers encountering frustration with many of their students. Preschool teachers were puzzled by students who were bored or did not respond to the kindergarten curriculum, while primary teachers were confronted each year with students who were unable to work successfully because the curriculum seemed too difficult. This situation was exacerbated in the late 1980s when school reform efforts resulted in the increased emphasis on academics in all levels of early childhood programs.

An understanding of how young children learn provides some clues to the problems teachers encountered and continue to address. We mentioned in Chapter 1 that the period of early childhood can refer to the age span between birth and eight years of age. Children between the ages of three and eight share similarities in how they learn. The child who is in nursery school, a child care environment, kindergarten, or primary grade is at some stage of early childhood. However, each child's development is different, depending partially on the kinds of experiences that have been available in his or her own world. Because children do not develop by chronological age alone, children at each age level are at various points on the developmental continuum. As a result, there can be a wide disparity of development among children at each chronological level.

The teacher designing curriculum needs to be aware of normal developmental differences in the children in the classroom in order to design instructional activities that will challenge each student, but also facilitate success. As a result, instructional practices in preschool, kindergarten, and primary classrooms should be more similar than different.

In the past, preschools were characterized by informal or open environments. Children spent time each day in learning centers exploring with puzzles, manipulative materials, and other discovery activities. There were opportunities for formal group instruction, but large blocks of the day were devoted to relaxed interaction between teachers and children as different activities took place. In the primary grades, the environment was more structured, with children spending long periods of the day being instructed formally by the teacher or occupied with written assignments to be completed at their desks. There was a sharp difference between the environmental settings and learning activities for preschool versus primary grade children.

As the school reform movement of the 1980s put more pressure on schools to increase the academic achievement of students, more difficult curriculum and increased amounts of curriculum content were introduced in lower elementary grades, including kindergarten. Preschool teachers felt the pressure to provide more academic activities to "get children ready for first grade." As a result, many preschool programs became more structured, emphasizing academic activities that mimicked primary grade practices. The ultimate goal was to prepare young children to do well on the standardized achievement tests that were ahead in the primary grades.

As early childhood specialists became alarmed at the shift in practices in early childhood programs, steps were taken to restore sound practices that complemented the development patterns of young children (Bredekamp, 1987). With the new awareness of the conflict between actual practice in curriculum and the knowledge about how young children learn in the early childhood years, teachers in early childhood programs have taken a new direction in order to plan curriculum that is developmentally appropriate for young children.

Teachers are now realizing that there is a great need for continuity between the preschool and primary grade curriculum. Children in all early childhood years require an educational program that matches their development, regardless of their chronological age. Teachers in preschool and early elementary programs have a responsibility to structure the curriculum so that their students can move through the early childhood years with learning opportunities that are compatible with their ability to learn.

The student in early childhood needs to be an active, involved learner, with real experiences and many concrete materials available to explore and manipulate to stimulate the process of cognitive learning. If the teacher understands this, the curriculum at all levels becomes somewhat altered. Preschool environments, while retaining a child-centered, informal approach, reflect the fact that, although children are chronologically the same age, developmentally they are different. More diversi-

Young children need real experiences with concrete materials to facilitate learning.

fied activities are provided to accommodate differences in learning style, readiness, and interests.

Thus, for some children, more advanced learning activities previously delayed until first grade are available within an environment that is designed to promote active, child-directed learning. Primary grade classroom teachers, also recognizing the need of their children for active, hands-on learning in later stages of early childhood, are expanding their use of concrete learning materials to provide children with opportunities to plan and carry out exploration and inquiry. They, too, are planning more diversified curriculum and instruction to complement different developmental rates and stages in their students. The links between development and curriculum and instruction will be discussed more specifically and comprehensively in Chapters 6 through 9.

LINKING ASSESSMENT AND CURRICULUM PLANNING

How Does a Developmental Curriculum Reflect Assessment Information?

If teachers are to develop curriculum and instruction experiences that meet the needs of the diverse backgrounds and the levels of development of their students, they must rely on screening and assessment information they have gathered. The initial and ongoing assessment information on each student becomes the source for the curriculum and for instructional strategies and experiences implemented for individual students, for small instructional groups, and for whole-class activities. This requires that the teacher plan for variety in learning experiences to match the diversity of students within the class. It is assessment data that informs the teacher about developmental status of the students. Obviously, the practice of planning curriculum for students based on chronological expectations alone cannot continue; rather, curriculum should be organized based on the progress and abilities of the students. Nevertheless, much of the curriculum can continue to address the group as a whole, with activities to complement individual differences. In other areas, the curriculum will have to be planned specifically for individuals and groups of students within the larger group.

Beginning the Year in Thelma Goodson's Second Grade

Thelma Goodson teaches second grade in Honeygrove School. Her new class of students this year consists of 15 girls and 11 boys that represent three ethnic groups in the community. It is the second week of school.

During the first week, Mrs. Goodson worked with the children on learning classroom routines and establishing procedures for appropriate behaviors. Two learning centers for language arts and mathematics were introduced. The children had several opportunities during the first week to use center materials and demonstrate their ability to use the centers appropriately. Whole-group activities to review mathematics and reading and writing were conducted to enable Mrs. Goodson to obtain a general picture of individual status in those content areas.

Now, on Monday of the second week of school, Mrs. Goodson has planned assessment activities to determine where instruction should begin in mathematics. Working with groups of five children at a time, she presents a series of addition and subtraction activities that are curriculum objectives for the first six weeks. She provides counters and worksheets for the children to use. She observes individual children as they work the problems and notes which children can solve the problems with little difficulty. After all of the children have been assessed, she organizes instructional groups for children who need instruction in addition and subtraction and conducts further assessment on simple fractions with students who were able to master the addition and subtraction objectives.

By the end of the second week, Mrs. Goodson has conducted assessment activities on three objectives in mathematics and has completed the process of organizing small groups for instruction in mathematics. During the third week of school, she will conduct assessment in language arts using the same process.

Using Assessment Information to Plan Instruction

During the beginning weeks of school, when children are learning about the environment and daily routines, the teacher is conducting initial assessments. Using the strategies described in previous chapters, the teacher collects information on each child. At the same time, instruction is conducted for the whole group. When adequate information has been accumulated to develop individual profiles, the teacher is ready to use assessment information for program development. In the sections to follow, we will discuss individual profiles for two children whose development is different. Then we will describe how individual profiles can be analyzed from a group perspective to find common areas of need.

Using Developmental Profiles to Plan Instruction   When developing a profile of individual children, the teacher uses some source or guidelines on which to base the assessment, often a developmental checklist of some type. The checklist from *Beginning Milestones* (Sheridan & Murphy, 1986) is an example of one that can be used at the preschool level. In the portion of the checklist below, the teacher has used observation, interviews, and concrete tasks to evaluate children in mathematics, science, and social studies on the first 10 checklist items. (Items labeled *M* are mathematics; *S,* science; and *SS,* Social Studies.) Categories could have been just as easily labeled as social development and cognitive development. Using one child as an example, the following information emerged for Bert. Figure 5–1 shows a part of Bert's profile. The items with a plus indicate Bert has demonstrated mastery, while items with a minus indicate that Bert has been introduced to the concepts or observed for appropriate behaviors, but needs time and further learning experiences to master them. Blank items have not been observed or assessed.

STUDENT_____Bert_____TEACHER_____Felipe_____

UNIT	OBJECTIVE	I	E	M
1M	Sorts concrete objects into groups			+
2SS	Identifies acceptable/unacceptable behavior			+
	Understands consequences of behavior			+
3M	Uses accurate vocabulary to compare sets/groups	−		
4SS	Identifies potentially dangerous situations			
	Observes safety rules	−		
5S	Obtains input through sight, smell, taste, sound, feel			
	Describes sensory input			
6M	Sorts and re-sorts objects by different characteristics	−		
7SS	Uses may I, please, excuse me, thank you appropriately			+
8S	Uses sensory input to determine if two stimuli are alike/not alike			
9M	Uses objects to repeat a simple pattern			
10SS	Says name, age, sex			

Figure 5–1   Part of an Individual Student Profile

Source: From *Beginning Milestones* (p. 32) by S. Sheridan and D. B. Murphy, 1985, DLM Teaching Resources. Reproduced with permission of McGraw-Hill, Inc.

Figure 5–2 shows a group profile. The teacher can determine which children need experiences or lessons to understand a concept and which children are ready for experiences in another area. Such a checklist would be designed to record information for an entire class. More on this checklist will be discussed in Chapter 6.

Checklists can be used to develop a profile of social development for children at all stages of early childhood. The Social Attributes Checklist developed by McClellan and Katz (1992) can be adapted for a class profile. Figure 5–3 shows this checklist, adapted to record initial assessment and further progress of the same group of students as in Figure 5–2.

Bert's teacher now has some indications of Bert's accomplishments and needs for instruction. His profile will include additional information on language and literacy development and motor development. In the category of cognitive development, the teacher has indications from the checklist that Bert needs language to express what he understands about concepts and is making progress in his ability to sort and classify. The teacher can work on classification experiences and vocabulary while conducting further assessment to find where learning experiences are needed for Bert's cognitive development. In the area of social development, Bert has some social skills, but seems to be sensitive about being accepted by his peers. He has some difficulty in interacting with peers in that he does not affirm his own desires and interests in play situations and can be intimidated by others, especially those who are aggressive. Bert needs some assistance in communicating and making contributions during play activities so he will not become frustrated and discouraged by negative social interactions.

Bert's teacher will consult observations that Bert's parents have made of his motor development and put them into portfolio form for his profile. The teacher will continue to evaluate Bert through observation, checklists, and performance to add to the information compiled at the beginning of the year. The teacher will study Bert's needs as compared to other children in the class to form groups for instruction and child-initiated activities.

Using Reading and Mathematics Assessments to Plan Instruction As children move from kindergarten into the primary grades, developmental assessment continues. In language, emergent reading and writing gradually develops into conventional reading and writing. In the second and third grades, word attack skills and comprehension skills complement the child's natural acquisition of literacy. In mathematics, a similar process occurs. The child's concept development becomes organized more formally into mathematics, social studies, and science. Assessment profiles in the primary grades tend to include specific assessments in reading and mathematics because

UNIT	OBJECTIVE	Mario	Lisa Marie	Jeanelle	Liu	Emory	Bert
1M	Sorts concrete objects into groups	+	+	+	−	+	+
2SS	Identifies acceptable/unacceptable behavior	−	+	+	+	−	+
	Understands consequences of behavior	−	+	+	+	−	+
3M	Uses accurate vocabulary to compare sets/groups	+	+	−	−	+	−
4SS	Identifies potentially dangerous situations	−	+	+	+	−	+
	Observes safety rules	−	+	+	+	−	−
5S	Obtains input through sight, smell, taste, sound, feel						
	Describes sensory input						
6M	Sorts and re-sorts objects by different characteristics	+	+	−	−	+	−
7SS	Uses may I, please, excuse me, thank you appropriately	−	+	+	−	−	+
8S	Uses sensory input to determine if two stimuli are alike/not alike						
9M	Uses objects to repeat a simple pattern						
10SS	Says name, age, sex						

Figure 5–2 Example of a Group Profile
Source: From *Beginning Milestones* (p. 32) by S. Sheridan and D. B. Murphy, 1985, DLM Teaching Resources. Reproduced with permission of McGraw-Hill, Inc.

I. Individual Attributes The child:	Mario	Lisa Marie	Jeanelle	Liu	Emary	Bert
1. Is usually in a positive mood						+
2. Is not excessively dependent on the teacher, assistant, or other adults						+
3. Usually comes to the program/setting willingly						+
4. Usually copes with rebuffs and reverses adequately						−
5. Shows the capacity to empathize						+
6. Has positive relationships with 1 or 2 peers; shows capacity to really care about them, miss them if absent, etc.						+
7. Sometimes displays the capacity for humor						+
8. Does not seem to be acutely lonely						+
II. Social Skill Attribute The child usually:						
1. Approaches others positively						+
2. Expresses wishes, preferences clearly; gives reasons for actions/positions						−
3. Asserts own rights and needs appropriately						−
4. Is not easily intimidated by bullies						−
5. Expresses frustrations and anger effectively and without harming others or property						
6. Gains access to ongoing groups at play and work						
7. Enters ongoing discussion on the subject; makes relevant contributions to ongoing activities						
8. Takes turns fairly easily						
9. Shows interest in others; exchanges information with and requests information from others appropriately						
10. Negotiates and compromises with others appropriately						
11. Does not draw attention to self						
12. Regularly gains access to ongoing groups at play and work						
13. Interacts nonverbally with other children with smiles, waves, nods, etc.						
14. Accepts peers and adults of other ethnic groups						
III. Peer Relationship Attributes The child is:						
1. Usually accepted versus neglected or rejected by other children						
2. Sometimes invited by other children to join them in play, friendship, and work						

Figure 5–3   Example of a Social Development Checklist

Source: From "Assessing the Social Development of Young Children" by D. McClellan and L. G. Katz, Fall 1992, *Dimensions of Early Childhood, 21*(12), p. 9. Adapted by permission of the authors.

the more complex operations and skills they require build on the foundations that are developed earlier. Thus, in reading, for example, as the child moves from emergent reading into conventional reading, the teacher needs a profile to evaluate student progress during the transition.

Suriah is in the first grade. Her teacher has developed an individual profile for her, using checklists, observation, interviews, and performance. From Suriah's participation in language and reading activities, her teacher has recorded her progress on a checklist. Study of Suriah's progress on a part of the checklist reveals that she has some understanding about print, but is just beginning to address how to gain information from print in a book. She is developing comprehension skills, but needs frequent experiences with story readings followed by participation in discussions. Figure 5–4 shows Suriah's profile in reading as recorded on a portion of an emergent literacy checklist. A complete representation of the checklist will be found in Chapter 7.

A checklist can be used to develop a profile of progress in mathematics. Because the mathematics curriculum is sequential, a checklist will have a hierarchy of simple to complex, with succeeding objectives based on understanding of earlier objectives. One checklist that serves as a portion of a master list of the mathematics scope and sequence is the checklist for subtraction of whole numbers. Figure 5–5 demonstrates a sequence of objectives for subtraction. Suriah's name could be added to the list of children and her progress on the objectives recorded.

PLANNING AND MANAGING DIFFERENT TYPES OF INSTRUCTION

When using assessment information to plan curriculum and instruction, the early childhood teacher needs to have a sound perspective of how learning occurs. Curriculum and instruction should focus on the child's inquiry and reconstruction of knowledge; that is, the child learns through an internal system of acquiring knowledge. The mode of constructing understanding is through encountering information and fitting it into knowledge that is already part of that child's repertoire from previous experiences. The child has a system for learning that is intrinsic. Developmentally sound curriculum and instruction is planned to enable this kind of learning to occur.

Further, learning is **integrated.** The child does not learn merely through internalizing pieces of information that are taught through teacher instruction followed by drill activities. Learning is integrated when language, cognitive, and psychomotor development is promoted through a **thematic curriculum** that presents information across the curriculum in a meaningful context. The teacher considers concepts to be presented to children and plans a variety of experiences that allow children to use the concept in exploration and inquiry activities and to demonstrate their emerging understanding through activities that reflect what is being learned. Children can use painting, construction, role-playing, writing, making models or murals, and various other activities to illustrate learning. In this framework, assessment information using authentic or performance strategies permits the teacher to document what children

Student: Suriah	Always	Sometimes	Never
Comprehension of Story			
Retells familiar stories using the pictures in the book to help recall the details	+		
Retells a story without the help of the book and demonstrates knowledge of details		+	
Retells stories with reading like intonation			+
Includes elements of story structure in story retellings: setting (beginning, time, place, characters)			
theme (problem or goal of the main character)			
plot episodes (events leading toward the solution of the main character's problem or the attainment of his or her goal)			
resolution (problem solved, goal achieved, story ended)			+
Responds to story readings with literal, inferential, and critical questions and comments		+	
Responds to story readings with inferential and critical questions and comments			
Participates in story-reading behavior by reciting or narrating stories as the teacher is reading them		+	
When read to, fills in words of a story according to knowledge of syntax and context		+	
	Always	Sometimes	Never
Concepts About Print			
Knows that print is read from left to right	+		
Knows that oral language can be written down, then read	+		
Knows what a letter is and can point to one on a printed page	+		
Knows what a word is and can point one out on a printed page	+		
Is aware of environmental print and can read some signs and logos		+	
Recognizes some words by sight in book print		+	
Can identify letters by name		+	
Associates some sounds with letters		+	
Asks questions about letter names, words, and sounds			

Figure 5–4 Example of a Reading Checklist

Source: From *Literacy Development in the Early Years* (p. 185) by L. M. Morrow, 1989, Englewood Cliffs, NJ: Prentice Hall. Copyright 1989 by Prentice Hall. Reprinted by permission.

Skill	Child's Name							
	Enrico	Joel	Jon	Katy	Emma			
1. Demonstrated knowledge of basic subtraction facts								
2. Subtracted one-digit number from two-digit number, no regrouping								
3. Subtracted one-digit number from two-digit number, with regrouping								
4. Subtracted two-digit number from two-digit number, no regrouping								
5. Subtracted two-digit number from two-digit number, with regrouping								
6. Subtracted two-digit number from three-digit number, no regrouping								
7. Subtracted two-digit number from three-digit number, with regrouping from tens to ones only								
8. Subtracted two-digit number from three-digit number, with regrouping from hundreds to tens only								
9. Subtracted two-digit number from three-digit number, with regrouping in both hundreds to tens and tens to ones								
10. Subtracted two-digit number from three-digit number, with regrouping across zero in tens place								

Figure 5–5   Example of Part of a Mathematics Checklist
Source: From *Science and Mathematics in Early Childhood Education* (p. 269) by D. M. Wolfinger.
Copyright © 1994 by HarperCollins Publishers. Reprinted by permission.

have accomplished. How to design and use an integrated curriculum will be discussed in Chapter 12.

Assessment information is also used for more specific kinds of instruction, such as development of skills in mathematics and language arts. Although many skills are acquired through natural, child-centered activities such as emergent writing and reading, there are more specific skills that children need to learn and use. Thus, assessment information that informs the teacher about a child's ability to use word attack skills in reading or to use computation skills in mathematics provides information that can be used to pinpoint specific instruction for individuals and groups of children.

As has been discussed above, the teacher needs assessment information for various types of curriculum and instruction. In the sections that follow, we will discuss differing ways that teachers can plan for instruction using assessment information that is suitable for children's evolving development in preschool and primary grades.

Teacher-Directed Instruction

The teacher has the major responsibility for children's learning—whether the role is as facilitator or guide or as instructor. Although a major focus of learning is child-initiated or child-directed, there is a place for teacher-directed instruction. The latter type of learning experience can be defined as an activity when the teacher is introducing or extending information.

Teacher-directed instruction can be planned for the entire class, for a small group of children, or for individual children. A whole-group activity can be a formal lesson, a group discussion, a music activity, and any other examples of experiences that are conducted by the teacher with all students. Small-group activities also have an important role. Small groups can be organized from assessment information that indicates that particular children need, or would benefit from, a lesson or activity. For example, if a teacher determines that a group of children need to have opportunities to use descriptive language, the group can be scheduled for a series of activities that will focus on expressive language experiences. Small groups can also be created because clusters of children work well together. This type of grouping can emerge from assessment information on social skills and evaluation of styles of interaction that children exhibit during observations. Individual instruction occurs when assessment indicates that a single child has a unique need for instruction.

The teacher has the major responsibility for guiding learning.

Figure 5–2 provides possibilities for instructional grouping for teacher-directed instruction. Suppose the teacher wanted to focus on classifying. If the teacher was planning an activity in which children described groups of objects that have been sorted by some characteristic, three students—Jeanelle, Liu, and Bert—might work in a small group with the teacher. Beforehand, however, the teacher should give Liu individual instruction on sorting concrete objects into groups since Liu was unable to understand simple sorting or classification. In other cases, the entire class might engage in making patterns because the teacher has not introduced the concept nor conducted an assessment to determine which children understand patterns.

Grouping for each type of teacher-directed instruction is dynamic in that as children's progress and needs change, grouping for instruction is modified.

Instruction in Learning Centers

Children's learning can evolve from activities that take place in learning centers. Again, assessment information provides data needed for organization of centers. When curriculum and instruction are center based, the teacher organizes the center and materials to support children's learning. Activities are placed in the centers to reflect the information or skills that children need based on prior assessment conducted by the teacher. For example, if a first grade class is engaged in single-digit addition, and observation has made the teacher aware that some students need addition practice, games and activities that involve single-digit addition would be put in the center for those students.

Center materials could be used for both teacher-directed instruction and child-initiated activities. The teacher could work with small groups at the center, using materials provided there for students needing experiences with single-digit addition. For example, the teacher could begin with an activity to review single-digit addition, using counting bears in the center to ensure that children understood the process of combining groups to make larger groups. Then the teacher could engage in an addition game with the children or monitor the group as they try out their skills with different center activities. The same materials could be made available for other members of the class, who might be able to solve more complex addition problems but would still enjoy working with the games and activities.

Center activities can meet the needs of individuals and the needs of the entire class. For example, the teacher might have several shelves of mathematics activities at different levels of difficulty and challenges. Children might freely select among the activities or be directed by the teacher to engage in a specific activity for reinforcement of a skill or for problem solving.

Balancing Teacher-Directed and Child-Initiated Instruction

If learning is to be developmentally appropriate for young children, the teacher must help maintain a balance between teacher-directed and child-initiated learning activities. Earlier in this chapter, we discussed historic differences between preschool classrooms in which the focus is on play, exploration, and child-centered curriculum and primary grade classrooms, where teacher-directed instruction predominated. Teachers tend to feel very responsible for student learning and feel that their responsibility is best fulfilled in teacher-directed activities. To the contrary, child-initiated learning is equally valuable in the early childhood classroom. Thus, whatever the grade level—from prekindergarten through third grade—the teacher must be alert for opportunities for including child-initiated learning each day.

The teacher, however, must maintain balance between teacher-directed and child-initiated learning. To that end, curriculum and instruction would include working with the same concepts through teacher-directed instruction and through center activities that incorporate the targeted information or skill. In addition, an integrated curriculum based on a theme topic permits students to apply the new information or skill in a meaningful context. Assessment of progress or mastery could also be conducted with the same experiences.

Understanding Instructional Cycles

The link between assessment and curriculum and instruction can also be demonstrated through the use of **learning cycles**. Learning cycles describe the process used by the teacher and children to acquire new concepts and information. Learning cycles typically have four steps: (1) selection of an objective, (2) sequence of strategies to provide instruction related to the objective, (3) activities to help children to integrate and apply new skills or information, and (4) follow-up assessment to determine children's progress or mastery.

The instructional objective is selected from new material that is to be introduced to children or from assessment information that suggests that the objective is needed by some or all of the class. The first step in the cycle, then, is the selection of the objective to be learned. The second step in the cycle is introduction of the objective through teacher-directed instruction or through a child-centered exploration or discovery activity. The teacher conducts a lesson and perhaps follow-up lessons, using concrete, hands-on experiences to ensure that children have some confidence in their understanding of the objective or processes inherent in the objective.

The teacher then supplements teacher-directed activities with activities that are child-initiated or assigned. The purpose of the activities is to help children internalize and use the new information. The follow-up activities could be located in centers and be chosen by individuals or group, be conducted in cooperative groups, or involve projects related to a thematic unit. They could also include opportunities for older children to complete assignments designed to facilitate their understanding of the objective and demonstrate their ability to apply the knowledge in a meaningful context. Ongoing monitoring of student activities would provide the teacher with data on which students might need more instruction and which students need the opportunity to engage in more practice or other experiences related to the objective.

The final step in the learning cycle is to determine children's progress on the learning objective. Assessment is conducted to determine if the individual or group of children is ready to move on to another objective or needs additional experiences or extensions of the same topic. Figure 5–6 provides a visual scheme of a learning cycle,

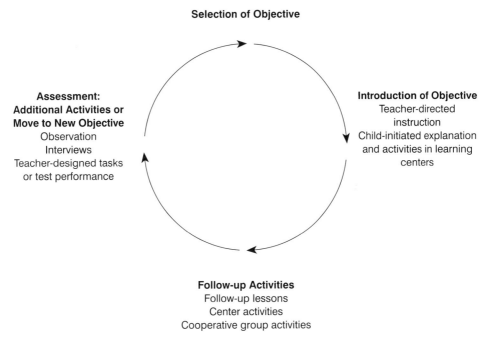

Figure 5–6   The Learning Cycle

while the lesson on coins in the next section demonstrates how elements of the cycle are incorporated in planning for instruction.

The learning cycle should incorporate the philosophy of curriculum and instruction that is appropriate for young children in the early childhood years. It should accommodate for individual differences, provide a variety of experiences and activities that complement individual interests and needs, and promote active learning. Therefore, the learning cycle would also reflect a balance between teacher-directed and child-initiated learning. It would include concrete experiences and opportunities for children to demonstrate their learning through representational activities and projects. It would include provisions for children to show their understanding through performance activities and would provide opportunities for children to apply what they have learned in a practical or meaningful context.

Using the Learning Cycle   The learning cycle can be applied in a single lesson, in weekly or biweekly planning, or as part of an integrated, thematic unit that is conducted for several weeks. If used for an individual lesson plan, the cycle might be charted through the following lesson components:

Lesson Objective
Lesson Activities (to include both teacher-directed and child-initiated activities)
Lesson Evaluation

A kindergarten—first grade lesson on identification and using coins can serve as an example of using the learning cycle for one day's activities to meet the learning objectives.

Lesson Title: Learning the value of coins
Lesson Objectives:

> Students will be able to identify a penny, a nickel, a dime, and a quarter.
> Students will be able to name the value of coins in terms of the number of pennies in each.
> Students will be able to trade pennies for an equivalent coin.
> Students will be able to buy objects marked as costing 1 cent, 5 cents, 10 cents, and 25 cents.

Lesson Activities:
Teacher-Directed Activities:

The teacher will begin the lesson with a counting activity using fingers and toes. Next the relationship between numbers of fingers and toes and coins will be discussed.

The teacher and students will review identification of coins. Students will be asked to find a coin named by the teacher until all students have identified a coin. The teacher will then write numbers on the board identifying the number of cents in each coin, and students will be asked to find the coin that corresponds to each number. Finally students will be given the opportunity to trade the correct number of pennies for a designated coin.

Learning Center Activity (Child-Initiated):

A store is set up in the dramatic play center. Items for sale are marked at 5 cents, 10 cents, and 25 cents. During center time, students are encouraged to use play coins to buy items from the storekeeper.

Additional Reinforcing Activities:

In a teacher-directed lesson, children will take turns buying classroom items, using pennies and equivalent coins. Each student will be asked to count the appropriate number of pennies for an item and then find the equivalent coin.

In a center-directed activity, the teacher will conduct small groups in the dramatic play center and ask students to take turns buying an item in the store. More advanced students will buy two or more items and count out the number of coins needed.

Lesson Evaluation:

Students have had previous experiences with the identification and value of coins. The teacher has evaluated students' understanding of the identification of coins and their value in terms of pennies. Evaluation of lesson activities will be conducted by documenting children's verbal responses and their ability to identify the coins with the number of cents corresponding to numerals on the board. Also, children will be observed using coins in the dramatic play center.

In the activities on coins, the teacher will use observation of student performance and verbal responses for assessment of student learning. Identification of individual student understanding and need for more practice will be determined through ongoing monitoring of individual students' responses in lesson activities. Students still needing more experiences following the series of teacher-directed and student-initiated activities will be recycled into another series of activities on coins. Use of coins will continue for all students as subsequent lessons incorporate more complex combinations of coins.

The learning cycle can be readily adapted for a thematic unit. In this context, teachers plan a variety of activities that include numerous opportunities for children to work with concepts through both teacher-directed and child-initiated experiences. In addition, different domains of development and curriculum can be incorporated into the learning experiences. For example, a thematic unit on trees could include a series of activities on identifying trees and measuring trunk circumferences. Students could write stories about trees, read stories about trees, make a graph of trunk circumferences, paint a mural of trees, and learn a poem about trees. These and many more activities could be designed to fit a learning cycle for the objectives of the tree unit.

PLANNING EVALUATION FOR DIFFERENT TYPES OF INSTRUCTION

In Chapters 3 and 4, we discussed several types of assessment, which included both formal evaluation such as standardized tests and informal evaluation such as observation, checklists, teacher-designed assessments, and performance assessments. The strategies to be employed by the teacher depend upon the type of evaluation that is needed. Keeping in mind that all assessment should be appropriate for the intended purpose and for the developmental level of young children, the strategies that are selected should also be suitable for the type of curriculum and instruction that is prepared for children in the early childhood years.

We are proposing that the evaluation of young children's learning can be divided into two categories: **progress evaluation** and **skill evaluation.** Most of the assessment purposes will be to determine progress, while skill evaluation is used least in the preschool levels and gradually becomes more important in the primary grades.

Progress evaluation refers to assessment related to development of some type. Curriculum and instruction that is related to a child's development is evaluated from a developmental approach. The teacher wants to know how the child is progressing within a developmental continuum. Thus, the preschool child's development in social or physical areas is assessed to determine changes and progress. In the primary grades, emergent reading and writing are evaluated from a developmental perspective. The teacher monitors children's progress in writing and reading using indicators of the sequence of development in emergent literacy.

Progress evaluation is also appropriate for evaluation of student learning in an integrated thematic curriculum. The teacher looks for indicators of the student's understanding of learning objectives through the activities and projects that the student engages in during theme. Each student might have learned differently, depending upon the activities chosen or assigned. Performance or representation of the learning as reflected in completed individual or group projects, artwork, writing, or a dramatic performance could serve as the sources of assessing students' progress in understanding unit concepts.

Learning in content areas such as social studies and science lend themselves to progress assessment. The nature of inquiry and research in these areas, even with very young children, is best assessed through progress evaluation. The teacher can observe and document children's experiences in mixing colors or tracking temperature changes to determine progress in understanding science concepts. Likewise, student social studies projects related to types of merchants in the nearby neighborhood can be assessed through progress evaluation.

Skill evaluation is conducted when the teacher needs to know if students have mastered a specific skill or concept. While a teacher might conduct progress evaluation to understand how a child goes about solving a mathematics problem, skill evaluation would be used to determine if a child has mastered a specific numerical operation.

Mastery of spelling certain words or correct use of simple punctuation can be assessed through skill evaluation. However, if a teacher is interested in learning what words are being used correctly in the child's emergent writing, progress evaluation is used. In this case, the teacher is evaluating the words that are being included in child-initiated writing activities. On the other hand, when children are learning specific spelling words, for example, words illustrating a principle such as two vowels together in a word take a long sound or words are changed from singular to plural by adding s or es, then assessment is for mastery of those specific words.

Teachers need to be aware of the type of evaluation that they desire to accomplish—whether progress evaluation or skill evaluation. The strategies discussed in Chapter 4 can be used for either or both types. For example, teachers can use observation to perform either progress evaluation or skill evaluation, or they might use checklists and performance assessments. Nevertheless, the teacher needs to be informed as to whether the assessment being used is appropriate for the development of the children. Very little skill assessment is needed in preschool classrooms. Very young students are not evaluated to determine if they have performed to a previously set standard for skills. Instead, progress evaluation is more suitable for young children since it assesses developmental growth. It is true that the teacher might evaluate skills such as buttoning, tying shoes, or using zippers; however, it is hoped that most assessment will be to track progress toward developmental goals.

Skill assessment should not be the only type of assessment in the primary grades. Although specific skills in mathematics and language arts can facilitate progress in developing children's competence in those content subjects, much of the primary grade curriculum and instruction is developmental in nature and should be evaluated to determine progress. A child's reading accomplishments can be evaluated through the kinds of books that the child selects to read and his or her overall progress in fluency and comprehension. The manner in which a child chooses to measure ingredients for a cooking experience in the third grade is as significant as the child's ability to multiply and divide. Thinking skills in mathematics are assessed through progress evaluation rather than skill evaluation. The process used by the child in approaching the problem is as significant as his or her ability to correctly solve a page of multiplication problems.

Achievement in basic skills in the primary grades is measured through skill assessment. There are important purposes for evaluating each child's achievement in basic skills. It should be remembered, however, that this type of assessment only measures a small portion of young children's learning. Progress evaluation provides a broader picture of the child's development and understanding.

CONTINUING THE ASSESSMENT-INSTRUCTION LINK

Throughout Chapter 4 and at the beginning of this chapter, we have discussed assessment in terms of developing an initial picture and then comprehensive profile of a child's development and learning. Then we discussed how the profile is translated into planning for instruction for the children as groups and as individuals. The same process is used during the rest of the school year to continue the assessment and instruction link.

Ongoing Assessment and Evaluation

Assessment of children should be continuous. As a result of the development of a variety of assessment strategies, the teacher is able to maintain instruction to meet the individual needs of children throughout the year. Ongoing assessment and evaluation mean that, once the teacher has completed an initial assessment, developed individual profiles, and grouped children for instruction where indicated, assessment of their progress will be continuous.

Assessment does not mean that instruction ceases when evaluation is needed; continuous diagnosis is built into ongoing direct instruction or child-initiated activities. Essentially, the teacher uses all of the experiences planned for children to keep tabs on what progress the children are making. Some of the following conditions can provide the teacher with ongoing diagnosis and assessment.

1.   Culminating activities that are planned in a structured lesson directed by the teacher. As a final assessment, after a series of experiences over a period of time, the

teacher involves the children in an activity that will allow her or him to determine whether the children exhibit mastery of a concept.

2.   Observation of or interviews with children working in centers. Children may be working with materials to which they have been assigned or doing self-selected activities involving the concept being studied.

3.   Activities designed in a game format. These are partially conducted by the teacher or other adults and require that children use the targeted concept or skill for successful participation in the game.

4.   Formal assessment at the end of instruction of a single objective or a series of objectives

5.   Collection of student work into a portfolio that can be used for documentation and evaluation of progress

The process of ongoing assessment and evaluation should be conducted within the normal activities of the day and not require large amounts of time taken away from instruction and learning activities. The teacher may want to use an occasional instructional period to conduct assessment activities to verify a child's understanding of a series of objectives that have been checked off as a result of informal assessments over a period of time. Such a formal approach to assessment can be used infrequently so that assessment is not time consuming. Using natural interactions with children would be more productive in the long run and is always a preferred evaluation strategy.

Regrouping Children

As a natural process of instruction and ongoing assessment, children will typically be regrouped. The grouping of children at the beginning of the year usually is a very temporary arrangement. Children tend to be inconsistent in their pace of learning. In addition, young children attending school for the first time succumb to colds, viruses, and childhood diseases that result in frequent absences. Consequently, grouping of children must be flexible and will frequently change, as some children advance more rapidly than others and some children for one reason or another need more experiences with a concept. Some children will also demonstrate the need for a slower-paced progress more comfortable for their style of learning. Whatever the cause for indicated changes, the teacher will regroup whenever necessary. Occasionally, when it is warranted, some children may be working in more than one group. The teacher's expectation that frequent regrouping is a natural part of instruction will do much to make flexible grouping a little-noticed part of classroom routines.

Record Keeping and Reporting Progress to Parents

With the trend of increasing accountability to parents, school administrators, and state and federal agencies, record keeping becomes a necessary task for teachers, who may be required to, or desire, to have individual assessment records on children.

Records are useless if they are not kept up to date. In some districts where records of individual progress are kept for parent conferences or visits by local administrators or official representatives of state and federal programs, up-to-date record keeping lends validity to the teacher's effectiveness in providing for individual needs and to the teacher's knowledge of the children in the classroom. Parents who drop in for an informal or scheduled conference are reassured when the teacher can explain the curriculum being used and give specific examples of how the individual child is mastering specific concepts.

Teachers who are determined not to let record keeping become unmanageable invent strategies to keep them from getting behind. One method that has proved successful is to have master profiles of the class accessible during work periods. As the teacher is conducting lessons, working with children, or observing the children, changes in progress that need to be recorded are noted immediately at the end of a lesson or during a transition period. Other teachers prefer to keep a small pad and write down items to be recorded at the end of the day. Regardless of the method used, teacher who have successful record-keeping systems track progress as frequently as every day and update individual student records once a week, or no less frequently than every other week.

When record keeping is implemented as a natural part of the teaching process, it becomes a powerful tool for short- and long-term planning. As more teachers adopt strategies for record keeping and share its advantages with their peers, teacher are becoming less apprehensive about including it as part of their instructional responsibilities.

⇢ SUMMARY

Assessment information about individual children is useful when it is used for planning the instructional program for the year. Individual profiles and group profiles enable the teacher to form instructional groups and also to attend to individual needs.

A major purpose for developmental assessment in early childhood classrooms, particularly preschool classrooms, is to ascertain the developmental progress of the children. This is particularly important as a result of the trend toward focus on academics in early childhood education over the past years and the need to ensure that curriculum and learning experiences are appropriate for children's development. In the primary grades, assessment is also developmental, but expands to include content-oriented skills in reading and mathematics.

The link between assessment and curriculum development is extended into the types of instruction and learning experiences that the teacher implements. Although teacher-directed instruction is the most familiar mode, the teacher who considers the importance of child-centered learning incorporates learning centers and child-initiated learning experiences into the planned curriculum. Teachers work to balance teacher-directed and child-centered activities in keeping with the understanding that the child's construction of knowledge through active interaction with concepts is as valuable as the teacher's role in introducing information and modeling modes of learning with the children.

Instructional cycles serve as a tool for planning curriculum and instruction. Through instructional cycles, the teacher can develop connections between instruction and assessment, both before and after learning experiences. Instructional cycles include the objective to be learned, the experiences planned for learning, opportunities to apply learning, and assessment of learning before moving on to another objective. Learning cycles can be used for a single lesson, for a series of objectives and lessons, and for content curriculum or integrated curriculum units of study.

A variety of assessment strategies is used by the teacher in linking assessment with curriculum planning and evaluation. Assessment can be organized into two categories: process evaluation and progress evaluation. Process evaluation is appropriate for all types of developmental progress by children where the process of learning is as important as the product of that learning. Skill assessment is used when specific skills or abilities are evaluated. Reading comprehension and word decoding skills and mathematical concepts and applications are the most common skills that are assessed in the primary grades.

The ongoing cycle of assessment, learning, assessment, and introduction of new curriculum continues throughout the year as the teacher continues to track progress of individuals and groups. Ongoing assessment and regrouping of children is accompanied by ongoing record keeping to document growth and development. In this manner, the initial assessments made as school began are maintained and extended to record the progress of each child throughout the school year. Such evaluations can be shared periodically with parents and serve as the profile of the child's development and accomplishments.

✧ STUDY QUESTIONS

1. How does using assessment profiles enable the teacher to develop curriculum and instruction that is suitable for the children in the classroom?
2. Why do early childhood educators need to be aware of the need for developmental assessments as tools for planning appropriate curriculum and instructional experiences?
3. How does teacher use individual assessment information to develop group profiles and ultimately group children for instruction?
4. What is the difference between developmental checklists and content skills checklists? Explain.
5. Why is teacher-directed instruction only one of several learning modes? Why is it not the most significant mode in early childhood?
6. Describe how learning centers can be used to implement curriculum and instruction.

7. What are some instructional strategies that permit children to initiate and direct their own learning? Describe them.
8. How does the teacher maintain a balance between teacher-directed learning and child-initiated learning?
9. How does the instructional cycle help the teacher organize a framework to link assessment and learning? Describe how to use an instructional cycle.
10. Discuss the roles of process assessment and skill assessment. How does understanding the differences in the two help the teacher in designing appropriate assessment strategies for children's learning?
11. Why does the teacher need to maintain strategies for linking assessment and curriculum design throughout the year? How do ongoing assessment and record keeping promote this process?

→ KEY TERMS

integrated learning
learning cycles
progress evaluation

skill evaluation
thematic curriculum

→ SUGGESTED ACTIVITIES

1. Develop a learning cycle to be used with a preschool objective. Develop assessments to be used before and after learning experiences. Develop learning opportunities for the objective, including teacher-directed activities, learning center activities, and child-directed or group-directed activities.
2. Develop a learning cycle to be used with a mathematics or reading objective. Develop assessments to be used before and after learning activities. Develop learning opportunities for the objective, including teacher-directed activities, learning center activities, and child-directed or group-directed activities.

6

Screening and Assessment in Early Intervention Programs for Young Children With Special Needs

→ Chapter Objectives

As a result of reading this chapter, you will be able to

1. Describe the history of early intervention programs for young children with disabilities

2. Explain the process used to determine if children are eligible for intervention services

3. Define different models used for early intervention

4. Discuss how individual plans are developed for young children with disabilities.

5. List and explain the issues concerning inclusion programs in preschools and public schools

Throughout this text, we have discussed the need to address the differences among children in early childhood programs. In earlier chapters, we considered the importance of including children who are at risk for development and learning and children with disabilities into all types of programs for preschool and primary grade children. In Chapter 2, we presented information on the evolution of services for young children who need early intervention. In this chapter, we will further discuss the history of programs for children with special needs and the types of programs that are available to provide intervention services. Topics include how these children are identified, screened, and assessed to specify their developmental and learning needs and how individual plans are developed for infants, toddlers, and young children with disabilities. We will again discuss the practice of including or integrating these young children into regular classrooms and the benefits of such a practice and issues that are of concern to parents and educators.

First, we will look at the historical background of how programs especially designed for children with disabilities and with other risk factors became a part of early childhood education. Then we will see how legislation regarding services for these populations of young children has expanded to include more children and improved expectations for programs that provide intervention services.

THE BACKGROUND OF EARLY CHILDHOOD INTERVENTION SERVICES

Early childhood education and early childhood special education have a common history in that the efforts for both types of programs included serving the needs of the poor, the disadvantaged, and those at risk for development and learning. While some early efforts focused on health issues and providing care so that parents could work, there were concerns in all programs for promoting positive development in young children.

The first formal early childhood program established in the United States for preschool children was the kindergarten, as described in Chapter 1. It was based on principles and methods established by Friedrich Froebel in Germany in the early 1800s. Support for the kindergarten program in the United States came from churches, private agencies, and philanthropic groups in an era of immigration, industrialization, and urbanization. Kindergarten became a part of the public schools in the latter half of the nineteenth century. Other early childhood programs such as nursery schools and child care initiatives had the primary purpose of serving very young children and their families. None of these original programs focused on children with atypical development.

Montessori schools, first established in Italy by a physician, Maria Montessori, were originally designed for children with disabilities. Incorporating methods used by Froebel and by Edouard Seguin—an educator of children with disabilities from France—she designed a program that focused on sensory education. When adopted in the United States, the Montessori method was first implemented in schools for children without disabilities (Spodek & Saracho, 1994).

These early programs for young children prior to entry in the primary grades established a precedent for intervention services for very young children with disabilities or at risk. Indeed, Meisels and Shonkoff (1990) propose the following:

> Early childhood intervention services have been influenced significantly by our history of education of young children prior to traditional school entry. The central features of these early programs that have become firmly embedded in current intervention efforts include a child-centered curriculum focus; an emphasis on early socialization of the child outside the family, an enhanced understanding of child development and the practical applications of developmental theory; and a belief in the importance of the early years as a foundation for later social, emotional, and intellectual competence. This conceptual legacy, in conjunction with the wealth of materials, resources, and techniques that have been refined over the years, is woven throughout the day-to-day activities of contemporary early intervention programs. (p. 7)

Concerns for the health and welfare of infants and young children led to the establishment of other measures and programs that would set precedents for early intervention programs. The high infant mortality rate and concerns for appropriate medical services for children in the eighteenth century led to the establishment of pediatrics as a medical specialty. In addition, steps were taken to establish milk stations where clean milk and advice for mothers was available (Public Health Service, 1976; Wortham, 1992).

At the turn of the nineteenth century, efforts were begun to end child labor and to improve conditions for children. The Children's Bureau was established by Congress in 1912 to address the exploitation of working children, but it also investigated the causes of infant mortality and childhood accidents and diseases. Through the Children's Bureau, the federal government published information on infant care and child development, which gave practical advice for mothers. The bureau studied day care, the health of preschool children, institutional care, and mental retardation and crippled children. The safety of school environments was a national concern, as was better training of doctors and nurses (Meisels & Shonkoff, 1990; Public Health Service, 1976).

During the 1930s, legislation was passed that affected child health and welfare. The Social Security Act of 1935 initiated federal responsibility for children of the poor. Part II of the act created a federal program to deliver services to crippled children. The law established a comprehensive service system with the goal of preventing crippling diseases and treating handicaps. In addition, the Social Security Act promoted the health and care of mothers and children through prenatal care, well baby clinics, immunization, public health services, school health services, and health education. Child welfare services of the act established funding to states to provide services for homeless, dependent, and neglected children (Meisels & Shonkoff, 1990).

The 1960s were the decade of the initiation of programs for children with special needs. Nevertheless, the government programs and services established prior to the 1960s were significant and joined the educational, caregiving, health, and medical fields in addressing the needs of children at risk for development and children with disabilities. Although not all of the efforts were interactive, all were concerned with the need of children and families for economic, health, medical, and educational services.

By 1960, significant advances had been made in child health and services to children. Control of communicable diseases had been made possible through the availability of penicillin, sulfa drugs, and antibiotics. It was now possible to treat tuberculosis, mastoiditis, meningitis, osteomyelitis, and pneumonia. Poliomyelitis was almost eliminated through the Salk and Sabin vaccines. Voluntary organizations that focused on the health needs of children included The National Society for Crippled Children and Adults, United Epilepsy Association and National Epilepsy League, The Allergy Foundation of America, The American Hearing Society, the National Society for the Prevention of Blindness, American Optometric Association's Committee on Visual Problems of Children and Youth, United Cerebral Palsy Association, and Muscular Dystrophy Association (Public Health Service, 1976).

Advances in early childhood education affected educational services for young children. Emerging research on child development that pointed to the importance of the early years resulted in new directions for early childhood education. The work of Benjamin Bloom (1964), J. McVicker Hunt (1961), and Jean Piaget (1963) led to the understanding that the early years are critical for development and that the experiences of the early years make a significant difference in development. These new sources on development and learning coincided with a changing view on civil rights, which brought a concern for the education of poor and minority children and awareness of the needs of children with disabilities (Wolery & Wilbers, 1994).

The Head Start movement was the most significant educational program for young children developed from the newer theories of development and learning. As a federal initiative to eliminate the disadvantages of children from poor families, it provided medical, dental, parental involvement, nutritional, and educational services for preschool children. A variety of Head Start models based on emerging theories and practices in early childhood education were designed and implemented throughout the United States to provide intervention services for children who were at risk for optimum development and learning (Spodek & Saracho, 1994; Wortham, 1992).

Advances in intervention programs for children with disabilities came through litigation and legislation. Families of children with disabilities initiated legal suits to secure the rights of individuals with disabilities. Professional organizations that included the Council for Exceptional Children, Association of Retarded Citizens, and American Association on Mental Retardation served as advocates for the needs of children with disabilities (Wolery & Wilbers, 1994). These efforts in the 1960s, combined with federal funding for intervention efforts in early childhood and public education programs, led to initiatives for early childhood intervention programs for children with disabilities (McCollum & Maude, 1993; Meisels & Shonkoff, 1990).

In 1963, Public Law 88–156 provided funding under the Social Security Act for projects for children with mental retardation, while Public Law 90–538 passed in 1968, the Handicapped Children's Early Education Assistance Act, provided funds to develop model programs for the education of infants and preschoolers with disabilities and their parents. Thus, the Head Start movement and initial funding for early intervention models laid the foundations for the major achievements in early intervention that were accomplished in the 1970s, 1980s, and 1990s.

Early intervention programs are beneficial for many young children with disabilities.

Meisels and Shonkoff (1990, p.11) cite Caldwell's description of three major historical periods in the education of children with disabilities. The practice of the first half of the century was labeled "Forget and Hide," when children with disabilities were kept out of public schools and public view. The second period of the 1950s and 1960s was called "Screen and Segregate" because children were identified and tested and served in separate facilities and programs. The third period beginning in the 1970s was labeled "Identify and Help" because children were identified and served as early as possible to minimize the handicapping conditions and maximize the potential of young children with disabilities.

The War on Poverty and civil rights movement had benefits for children at risk for success in learning beyond Head Start. Antipoverty measures to provide equity in education were addressed in the Elementary and Secondary Education Act in 1965, which funded compensatory education programs in public schools. The Bilingual Education Act passed in 1974 provided funds for special language programs for non-English-speaking children. Funding was also provided for migrant children and schools affected by desegregation. All were designed to assist low-income, minority, and low-achieving students improve their chances for success in school learning (Wortham, 1992).

Beginning in the 1970s, attention was given to children with disabilities, their social status, and their legal rights. Funds from the Bureau of Education for the Handicapped and the Division of Maternal and Child Health were used to implement training programs to prepare professionals to work with children with disabilities. Special certification for teachers became a goal as the demand for preschool teachers to work with children with special needs grew. The growing conviction that children with disabilities would do better if they were educated alongside their age mates in the public schools led to passage of the Education of All Handicapped Children Act of 1975 (P.L. 94–142). The law asserted that handicapped children had a right to an education in the **least restrictive environment** that would meet their individual needs. Schools were required to screen, diagnose, and plan for the individual needs of each student. This landmark legislation initiated federal legislation and funding that survived federal policies in the 1980s that all but eliminated the War on Poverty. The interest has continued in the 1990s with an expansion of services to include infants and families (McCollum & Maude, 1993; Meisels & Shonkoff, 1990; Wortham, 1992).

Legal Requirements of the Education of Handicapped Children Acts

A number of laws have been passed to establish and strengthen services for children with disabilities. Wolery and Wilbers (1994) summarized that legislation as follows:

P.L. 90–538 (1968) established the Handicapped Children's Early Education Program (currently known as the Early Education Program for Children with Disabilities). This law authorized funds for the development, evaluation, and dissemination of model programs for serving infants and young children with disabilities. Programs funded from this act have been and continue to be a major force in developing knowledge about services for young children with disabilities and their families. This law and the action that resulted from it can legitimately be called the birth of early childhood special education.

P.L. 93-644 (1974) amended previous Head Start legislation and required that 10% of the children served by Head Start programs must be children with disabilities. This act established the first nationwide mainstreaming program for preschool children. Recently, the regulations governing the provision of services to young children with disabilities in Head Start have been revised.

P.L. 94–142 (1975), The Education for All Handicapped Children Act, established a national policy related to the education of children with disabilities from ages 3 to 21. The major impact of this law was for children 6 years of age and older: special education. For example, this law formalized use of the Individualized Education Program (IEP).

P.L. 98–199 (1983) authorized funds to help states plan and develop early intervention services for children from birth to age 5.

P.L. 99–457 (1986) effectively mandated the provisions of P.L. 94-142 for preschoolers (children ages 3 through 5) and provided incentives to states to serve infants and toddlers who had disabilities or were at risk for having disabilities. The framework specified in this law for serving infants and toddlers acknowledges the ecological perspective of services and requires an Individualized Family Service Plan (IFSP).

P.L. 101–576 (1990) reauthorized the Education for All Handicapped Children Act (P.L. 94–142) and renamed it the Individuals with Disabilities Education Act (IDEA). It also established two new categories: autism and traumatic brain injury.

P.L. 101–336 (1990), known as the Americans with Disabilities Act, is major civil rights legislation that extends beyond educational issues. Specifically, it requires that individuals with disabilities have equal access to enrollment in early childhood facilities. This act prohibits discrimination against individuals with disabilities because of their disability. (pp. 18–19)

The laws cited above have specific provisions for children with disabilities. Several features are consistent throughout the sequence of legislation, but many have been modified in later laws. These features are described below:

1. *All preschool children, regardless of their disability are entitled to free, appropriate public education. No child can be excluded because of a disabling condition.* As a result of this provision, Head Start programs were required to include children with disabilities, beginning in 1968. Under P.L. 94–142, public schools were funded to serve children with disabilities from age 3 to 21. However, these services were not mandated until the passage of P.L. 99–457.

2. *Each individual with a disability must have an Individualized Education Plan (IEP). If the child is younger than 3 years of age, there must be an* **Individualized Family Service Plan (IFSP).** The provision of services for children with disabilities as required in P.L. 94–142 included requirements for the IEP. Under P.L. 99–457 services for infants and toddlers were initiated. The importance of earlier intervention and the role of the family was acknowledged in P.L. 99–457 in that a plan was required to meet the needs of the family as well as the infant or toddler.

3. *Children must be placed in the least restrictive environment.* The early provisions for this component of legislation encouraged mainstreaming, whereby children were placed in special education classrooms for part of the day depending on individual circumstances. P.L. 99–457 modified this requirement to the expectation that children would be included or integrated into an environment as close as possible to the environment where the child would have been placed if no disability existed. Deiner (1993) developed a diagram to describe the least restrictive environment or level of inclusion as described in Figure 6–1.

4. *Parents have a right to be involved in developing and planning the child's IEP or IFSP, as well as in the development and planning of local and state policies.* Parents also have the right to challenge actions taken by a school. This provision addresses the important role of the family. Not only does it require that families have an opportunity to be involved in planning and implementation of their child's education, but the families' needs should be supported as part of the intervention process.

5. *Procedures used to identify, screen, assess, and place children should be nondiscriminatory.* Parents must be notified prior to any evaluation of their child. Their consent must be obtained for testing and assessment procedures. Further, tests and other assessment measures used should be administered by people who are properly trained, and they should be administered for the purpose for which they were designed and developed. (Bailey, 1994; Deiner, 1993; Spodek & Saracho, 1994; Wolery & Wilbers, 1994).

THE SCREENING AND ASSESSMENT PROCESS AND EARLY INTERVENTION PROGRAMS

Purposes for Screening and Assessment

In Chapter 2, purposes for screening were discussed comprehensively, with the goal of understanding screening and how it differs for children who have no developmental problems and for children at risk or with disabilities. That chapter also discussed types of screening and screening instruments. In this section, we want to look more closely at the screening process for children with disabilities, who often will need early intervention. Because the process is different for infant and toddlers as compared to preschool children, each group will be described separately.

Benner (1992) summarized the principles for screening children with definite developmental problems:

1. Screening assumes that the condition can be improved through the intervention.
2. Early intervention will improve the condition more than would intervention at a later date when the problem becomes more obvious.
3. The condition screened for can be specifically diagnosed through further application of measurement procedures.

Most Inclusive – – – – –▸– – – – –▸– – – – –▸– – – – –▸– – – – –▸– – – – –▸– – – – –▸

Setting	Child care, preschool, regular kindergarten	Child care, preschool, kindergarten with consultation	Regular setting with itinerant teacher/therapist
Children typically served	Children who haven't been identified, children with mild speech and language delays, conductive hearing losses, mild behavorial and emotional disorders, and health impairments	Identified children with mild to moderate disabilities and some children with severe impairments	Children with visual, hearing, physical, or communication impairments
Teacher's role	Teach all children in the classroom, make referrals	Teach all the children, receive some training in disabilities, are part of the intervention team, implement IFSP or IEP	Teach all children; accommodate and work with itinerant teacher/therapist on intervention team
Specialist	No specialist	Early childhood special educator (ECSE)	Itinerant teacher (for visually, or hearing impaired, and others)
Specialist's role	Child may receive therapy outside of setting	Model, demonstrate, and provide technical assistance, writes part of IFSP or IEP	Visits classroom, provides specialized materials and program, teaches child in regular classroom, may pull child out for specialized instruction, helps write IFSP or IEP
Features	Teacher meets child's needs; may be unaware of problem, rarely part of team for services outside the setting	Teacher teaches all children; ECSE provides technical assistant and consultation	Child is with peers; teacher can consult with and observe itinerant teacher, who is in a disability area, rarely early childhood

Figure 6–1   Levels of Inclusion

4. Necessary follow-up procedures for next steps are available.
5. The condition(s) screened for is relatively prevalent or the consequences of not discovering a rare problem or condition are severe.
6. Measurement procedures for screening are available. (p. 27)

For children who are identified during the screening process as needing follow-up procedures, assessment follows. A problem that can occur as a result of the screening process is false-positives, when a child is identified as exhibiting problems,

– – – – ➤– – – –➤– – – – ➤– – – – ➤– – – – ➤– – – – ➤– – – – ➤– – – – ➤ Least inclusive

Resource room/pull out therapy	Special class/segregated intervention program in regular school	Special school or day setting	Residential school/institution
Children who need therapy (OT, PT, speech, etc.) or help in a subject area (reading, math, etc.)	Children with moderate, severe, or profound impairments	Children with severe or profound impairments	Children with severe/profound impairments and those living where other services are not available
Teach all children, accommodate pull out schedule, consult with specialists, make accommodations for child	Help nondisabled children socialize (playground, lunch); support children mainstreamed for part of the day; support reverse mainstreaming for part of the day; increase awareness of disabities	Increase other children's awareness of disabilities	Increase nondisabled children's awareness of disabilities
Therapist or special education teacher Teaches child part of the day and provides some technical assistance to teacher, writes and implements most of IFSP or IEP	Early childhood special educator Teaches children; writes and implements IFSP, EIP; supports regular or reverse mainstreaming	Early childhood special educator Teaches children; writes and implements IFSP, IEP	Special education teachers, therapists, nurses Teaches child; writes and implements IFSP, IEP; cares for child's needs and educational program
Child is with peers most of the day; a specialist/teacher provides more individualized instruction in a segregated classroom	Child is integrated some of the day	Child is segregated for the school day	Child is segregated all day; has little contact with family

Source: From *Resources for Teaching Children With Diverse Abilities,* (second edition) by P. L. Deiner, 1993, (pp. 30–31). Copyright 1993 by Harcourt Brace & Company. Reprinted by permission of the publisher.

but in reality has no disabilities, and false-negatives, when a child is found to have no problems but in reality does have a disability that would benefit from early intervention. The younger the child, the higher the possibility of error in screening results (Benner, 1992). Follow-up assessment, sometimes described as diagnosis, then provides a more comprehensive evaluation of the child to confirm if a problem exists, to determine the nature of the problem, and to decide what kinds of intervention measures are needed.

Screening and Assessing Infants and Toddlers

As was described in Chapter 2, accurate screening and assessment with infants and toddlers is very difficult. Developmental limitations of children include highly variable behavior, short time frameworks when assessment can take place, and anxious or wary behavior in the presence of strangers when children are between 7 and 18 months (Widerstrom, Mowder, & Sandall, 1991). Moreover, measures of infant development are poor predictors of what the child's ability will be at school age (McCune, Kalamanson, Fleck, Glazewski, & Sillari, 1990). In addition, it is difficult to obtain reliable results.

The use of standardized tests remains one of the primary screening and assessment strategies for the evaluation of infants and toddlers in spite of concerns about the limitations. To overcome the problems with standardized measures, some infant and toddler developmental specialists recommend that more attention be given to the family environment, parent-child interactions, and family assessments. These types of information can be combined with more traditional measures of infant assessment, which include norm-referenced measures that compare a child's performance with a normative population, ordinal scales that assess behavior that is progressively more complex and sequential, and curriculum-based assessment that assesses the child in comparison to the objectives of an intervention program. Nevertheless, these strategies may fail to provide information about the child's social competence, attentional abilities, and correct movement patterns (McCune et al., 1990).

A strategy to improve infant and toddler screening and assessment is to use a multidisciplinary or team approach. Benner (1992) describes this process as arena assessment where one adult interacts with the child and team members record their observations relevant to their specialization or discipline. Individual team members may also request to conduct an activity with the child. In the multidisciplinary team approach, a core assessment instrument such as the *Bayley Scales of Infant Development* (BSID) (Bayley, 1969) is administered by one examiner, while other members of the team observe the infant's behaviors to acquire other data (McCune et al., 1990).

Alternative forms of assessment are also proposed so that information gained is more relevant for intervention strategies. Cicchetti and Wagner (1990) suggest that many of the traditional assessment measures are more meaningful for research rather than practice. They propose alternative forms of assessment because many children do not fit the profile of the normative group, standardized instruments may not measure the type of information needed about an individual child, and problems verified by an instrument were already confirmed when the child was referred for evaluation. Cicchetti and Wagner propose using assessments that measure multiple domains, that use a transactional model of assessment, and that take place in the child's environment. For example, they would use mother-child interactions and observations of the child's play as two of the transactional strategies that would yield a comprehensive picture of the child's abilities and present behaviors.

Infant screening and assessment is complex. Because very early intervention is critical for many developmental problems, highly skilled professionals need to use a bank of strategies and measures to determine the child's developmental progress and weaknesses within the family and cultural framework. Precise diagnosis is elusive, but correct identification and assessment are essential if the child's individual intervention plan is to be effective.

Screening and Assessing Preschool and Primary Age Children

As was explained in Chapter 2, screening of preschool and primary age children often occurs when the child attends an early childhood program for the first time. If the child was not identified and served as an infant and toddler, the first indication of a problem might emerge when the child enters a preschool program and the teacher becomes aware of developmental difficulties. In addition, when children with disabilities are included in programs with children who do not have disabilities, screening and assessment might be needed to determine which children are eligible for special services.

An example is the Head Start program that now includes children with disabilities. Sinclair (1993, p. 186) reports that all Head Start programs must "meet certain requirements or program performance standards in the identification and service to children with disabilities that emphasize the unique needs and potential of each child and his or her family." Head Start programs must make a distinction between children who need additional services and those who do not. In addition, Head Start policy requires that an individual plan for special education and services related to the child's specific disabling condition be planned and implemented. Sinclair proposes that these early intervention measures in Head Start programs in some cases prevent later referrals to special education in elementary school. In all cases, referral information forwarded to public schools enhance the possibility of appropriate services being provided for the child in elementary grades without undue delay.

Wolery (1994a) describes the process of screening and assessment in early childhood programs to (1) determine whether to refer the child for additional assessment, (2) determine whether the child has a developmental delay or disability, and (3) determine whether the child is eligible for special services. Like the screening and assessment process used with infants and toddlers, there is a role for standardized instruments combined with teacher observations, information from the family and about the family, and other sources of information. The strategies that are appropriate for preschool and primary age children are discussed extensively in Chapter 2. It needs to be emphasized here that there are different purposes for assessment depending upon how the results will be used. Assessment that is used with and following initial screening is conducted to determine if the child needs and is eligible for special services. Assessment conducted for diagnosis has as its purpose to specify the child's difficulties and needs. It can also help determine the best type of program for the child. As we will see in following sections, assessment is also conducted to determine the child's individual educational plan. This can require additional and different assessment from that used for initial screening and diagnosis. In each case, assessment activities should fit the type of information that is needed about the child (Wolery, Strain, & Bailey, 1992).

The Role of the Family in Screening and Assessment

When intervention and special education services were initiated for young children, the goal was to help children who had a disability or were at risk for development and learning. Family involvement was a component, but the primary focus was on the needs of the child. Programs took the approach that early intervention could either prevent or reduce developmental delays and learning problems in school.

During the history of early intervention programs, the perspective has gradually changed. Whereas parents were once perceived as a source of the child's problem, families are now viewed as having a primary and essential role in the child's development and intervention (Turnbull & Turnbull, 1986). Currently, the understanding is that working with families is integral in serving young children with disabilities. Moreover, services to the family cannot be separated from services to the child. Bailey (1994) offered the following statements to summarize current thoughts about the role of the family in intervention programs:

1. Family support is a primary goal of any early intervention activity.
2. Each family has its own culture and a unique set of strengths, values, skills, expectations, and service needs.
3. Families have a right and a responsibility to play a primary role in determining the nature and extent of services provided for them and their child.
4. To provide appropriate services for families, a coordinated system of services must be in place. (pp. 27–28)

The dynamics in a family with a child with disabilities affect the early development of the young child. In the family, there is interaction between parents and child; the child's introduction to the world occurs through this transactional relationship. The individual characteristics of the child and the parents determine the type of relationship that develops. During the baby's first year, both infant and parents undergo change as adjustments are made in the interactive relationship.

When a baby with disabilities or at risk is born into a family, the development of the interactive relationship is much more difficult. The infant may not respond to parental cues for communication and nurture. The parents, in turn, may become discouraged and apprehensive about their abilities as parents and their relationship with the infant. Parents go through difficult stages of adapting to the infant. The demands of extensive caregiving routines and of adjusting to medical procedures can be tiring and frustrating to the parents and affect both their perception of themselves as competent parents and their perceptions of the competence of the child (Widerstrom, Mowder, & Sandall, 1991).

While the child is in need of intervention services, the family likewise needs services and support to be able to fulfill their primary role as the significant influence in the young child's development. Because parents also can play a major role in screening, assessment, and intervention, they must be involved in all phases of the intervention process.

The family has two functions in the process of screening and assessment. First, the family can contribute to the information needed to assess and diagnose the condition of the child. Second, the needs of the family can be assessed in order to construct the plan for family services and support.

Because there are limitations on the effectiveness of standardized measures used to screen infants and young children, parents can contribute to the multiple and alternative strategies used for screening and assessment. Information provided by the parents about the child's behavior can be used during the screening process to determine if the child should be referred for further diagnostic assessment. There are also concerns about how objective and reliable parental reporting can be. In support of this source of information, Meisels (1992) reported that accuracy in identifying children who are at risk increases when parental information is combined with results of other screening measures.

Parental participation in the assessment process has other benefits for those who are involved with conducting screening and assessment. Working with the parents to elicit information about the child, they may acquire information about the parents, the family, and parental concerns about the child and desires for the services to be provided (Diamond, 1993).

Parents can also participate as part of a team assessment of the child. In this role, the family members should be accepted as full members of the team. Professionals on the team have the family participate in identifying the purposes of the assessment, the strategies that will be used, and where and how assessments will be conducted. The family should be given the choice of to what extent they will be involved in the assessment process (Widerstrom, Mowder, & Sandall, 1991).

Assessment of the family is also part of the family's role in the child's intervention. Because infant intervention is in reality, family-focused intervention, assessment of the family's needs, concerns, stress, environment, life, and support systems must be conducted to determine the family's ability to cope with the child's needs. Intervention for the family, like intervention for the child, is individual and based on the stress the family is experiencing, the family's social and economic stability, and the family's own resources that provide support.

Bailey (1994) described family assessment and family needs within early intervention as follows:

> *Family assessment:* the ongoing and interactive process by which professionals gather information in order to determine family priorities for goals and services
> *Family need:* a family's expressed desire for services to be obtained or outcomes to be achieved
> *Family strength:* the family's perception of resources that are at its disposal that could be used to meet family needs (p. 34)

Support System for Families of Children With Spina Bifida

Gail is five months old and was born with spina bifida. Her father is in the Air Force and stationed in Florida. During her first four months, a pediatrician at the military base attended Gail, but it is now time for a more extensive evaluation of her physical status and decisions to be made for her further development. This evaluation will have to be conducted by a specialist at an Air Force Base in San Antonio. Gail's parents are very young and separated from their families who live in the northeast. Gail and her mother, Helena, will have to fly to San Antonio alone because Gail's father cannot leave his military duties. Helena is not only apprehensive about having to face her baby's evaluation alone, but is frightened about flying by herself to San Antonio.

Before the date of the flight, Helena is contacted by a Spina Bifida support group that has been established by military families in San Antonio. Her caller is Estelle, the mother of another spina bifida child, Shala, who is almost a year old. Estelle tells her what the process of evaluation will be and how it will be conducted. Further, she will meet her and Gail at the airport and be their sponsor and supporter throughout their stay in San Antonio. When Helena and Gail arrive, Estelle and Shala greet them and take them home until the first appointments the next day. At the end of the evaluation, plans are made for corrective surgery for Gail in the near future. Helena and Gail return to Florida knowing that when they return for the surgery, support will be there for them during and after the surgery.

Steps in Assessment and Placement in an Intervention Program

Placement in an intervention program is based on assessment strategies. As was described earlier, each step in the identification and placement process has a different purpose and requires different strategies for assessment. Linked with each stage are important decisions that are to be made about the child. Here are the steps that are conducted in placing and serving the child in the intervention program:

1. The child is identified for initial screening.
2. The decision is made whether to refer the child for more comprehensive assessment.
3. Diagnostic assessment is conducted to determine if the child has a disability or developmental delay or is at risk for developing a problem in learning.
4. The decision is made whether the child will be placed in an intervention program.
5. An instructional plan is developed for the child based on assessment of the child's strengths and weaknesses (IEP, IFSP).
6. The child is placed in an intervention program. Decisions are made about the services the child will receive.

7. The child's progress in the instructional program is monitored to assess whether he/she is achieving the goals in the individual education plan.
8. Program evaluation is conducted to determine if the outcomes on the IEP or IFSP were achieved (Wolery, 1994).

As we have explained previously, assessment and intervention are linked together in the process of identifying and serving children in an intervention program as well as in the process of providing services for the parents. In the next section, we will discuss the goals of early intervention programs in the services planned for the child and the family.

Goals for Intervention Programs

Bailey and Wolery (1992) suggest seven goals for early intervention programs:

1. to support families in achieving their own goals
2. to promote child engagement, independence, and mastery
3. to promote development in key domains
4. to build and support children's social competence
5. to promote the generalized use of skills
6. to provide and prepare for normalized life experiences
7. to prevent the emergence of future problems or disabilities (p. 35)

The first goal—to support families—reflects the understanding that the family is of primary importance in serving the child. The dynamics of the family are a key to successful intervention. The family's attitudes toward the intervention process can make a difference in whether professionals working with the child exert a positive influence or are a source of additional stress for the family.

The second goal—to promote the child's engagement, independence, and mastery—refers to the child's ability to become involved appropriately within experiences in the intervention program, to be able to function as much as possible without depending on help, and to acquire new skills or knowledge. Children with disabilities tend to become less involved or engaged in activities than children without disabilities. Moreover, they may be engaged in such a way that they are dependent upon others rather than independent. Although the child's disability may require dependence on others for physical mobility, the goal is to find ways that the child can develop some independence, using either current abilities and strengths or ones he or she develops.

The goal of promoting development in all domains incorporates cognitive development, communication skills, social skills, motor skills, and self-care skills. This goal implies practices that are developmentally appropriate and that permit inclusion of children with disabilities with children in regular classroom environments. An additional goal is for the child to develop self-esteem (Bredekamp, 1987). Moreover, the inclusion of children with disabilities into early childhood programs requires collaboration between professionals and reinterpretation of developmentally appropriate practices to incorporate the needs of children with diverse learning abilities and styles (Atwater, Carta, Schwartz, & McConnell, 1994).

The fourth goal is to build and support social competence. Social skills are seen as the primary factor that will expedite later success for children with disabilities (Bailey & Wolery, 1992). Unfortunately children with disabilities tend to have lower levels of social play and have deficits in peer interactions. In addition, research with older children with disabilities suggests that early intervention in this area is important because the deficits do not improve with age. The goal to improve social skills must also include measures that will also facilitate the development of friendships.

Promoting the generalized use of skills refers to the child's ability to use skills that are learned in one context to a different context. Because children with disabilities do not readily apply skills beyond the settings in which they are taught, strategies to promote generalization should be used. These strategies include teaching skills in the natural environment, teaching the skills in a variety of settings, varying the adults and peers who teach and reinforce the skills, and providing an instructional setting that is similar to the generalized setting where the skills will be used in real life (Wolery, Bailey, & Sugai, 1988).

The sixth goal—to provide and prepare for normalized life experiences—relates to the requirements that children be placed in the least restrictive environment in intervention programs. Services provided for children with disabilities should be as normal as possible. The practice of inclusion means that if possible, children with disabilities are placed in environments where they would be placed if they had no disabilities. In addition to environments being as normal as possible, the instructional strategies should be as normal as possible. Again developmentally appropriate practices that are used with children without disabilities should be used as much as possible (Wolery, Strain, & Bailey, 1992).

The final goal is to prevent the emergence of future problems or disabilities. The key to this goal is the effort to prevent problems or disabilities from developing through early intervention. This goal relates to children who are at risk for developing problems at a later date. The prevention perspective is that if early intervention is provided, later school failure or institutionalization can be prevented. This goal also focuses on strengthening the family and child rather than just attending to delays and disabilities (Bailey & Wolery, 1992).

The goals for intervention influence the type of intervention program that is planned for the child and family. There are a variety of approaches or models for intervention proposed by experts in early childhood special education. Some of those models are addressed below.

Models of Early Intervention Programs

The models that are used for early intervention programs take a variety of approaches to deliver services to children and their families. Some of the models focus on the child, while others combine intervention for families and children. Intervention programs can be **categorical**; that is, they serve children with a specific disability such as visual or hearing impairment. Most programs, however, are **noncategorical** in that they serve children with a variety or combinations of special needs (McCollum & Maude, 1993). The settings for intervention may also vary from center-based to home-based services. In the models described, some are focused on infants and toddlers, while others target preschool and primary age children.

Child-Focused Intervention Programs   Child-focused early intervention approaches follow guidelines prescribed by P.L. 94–142. Cases begin with screening, proceed through diagnostic assessment and placement, referral, IEP development, and development of instructional programs. Within this framework, models that focus on the child vary greatly. These programs primarily serve children with developmental disabilities. The child is served with instructional strategies that are ecologically based: that is, the child's intervention is based on interaction with the environment. Instruction is designed to maximize the child's development of functional skills, such as social-communication skills, and caregivers and other family members are included in the instructional programs. Instruction occurs through naturally occurring and child-initiated events. Intervention activities parallel activities thought to promote learning in typical children, with transactions occurring frequently so that generalization of skills can occur (Bricker & Veltman, 1990).

As described in Widerstrom, Mowder, & Sandall (1991), infant-focused intervention uses many approaches including a developmental care model and models that focus on remediating deficits, stimulating sensory modalities, facilitating infant-initiated interactions, and teaching skills. Some programs incorporate strategies based on programmed instruction and use of microcomputers and computer networks. The infant-focused programs can be delivered in center-based programs, home-based programs, and combinations of services that include both settings.

Parent- or Caregiver-Focused Intervention Programs   Parent- and caregiver-focused programs have been developed to work with parents of children with disabilities. The approach recognizes the central importance of the parents for the child's well-being and health. The principle followed is that the child with disabilities benefit when services are provided to parents. The intent is to educate, support, and teach parents how to work with their child. The types of programs that deliver services include counseling programs, parent education programs, and parent interaction skill programs. Some models work only with the parent or concurrently with the parent and the child. In both instances, a working relationship is developed between the caregiver parent and the professional workers delivering services. In some situations, a professional delivers the intervention for the child, while in others the parent is trained to function as the therapist (Seitz & Provence, 1990; Widerstrom, Mowder, & Sandall, 1991).

Whether the involvement occurs with parents as teacher-therapists or as clients of intervention, the participation of the family is an important objective in such programs. In many situations, parents are of a low socioeconomic status and are in need of extensive support and services. The type and extent of family participation vary, but the desired outcomes for intervention are similar (Simeonsson & Bailey, 1990).

Preventive Intervention Programs   Prevention intervention programs seek to fulfill one of the goals of intervention: to prevent developmental delay and disabilities. They seek to prevent a problem that might occur. Prevention programs frequently focus on mothers, but can also include infants. More specifically, such programs provide intervention for mothers who are at risk for delivering an infant with a disability or an infant who will be at risk. Programs designed for these mothers can include prepregnancy counseling, advice on nutrition, and instruction on how they can help their child. Mothers from a low socioeconomic background are one population served by prevention programs.

Pregnant adolescent women are at risk for having babies who themselves are at risk. Programs designed for these women provide child development instruction, parenting skills, childbirth education, and social support services.

Settings for prevention intervention services can include clinics, hospitals, schools, and other locations where mothers are likely to receive services.

A Program for Mothers of Babies at Risk

The medical center in a large city is affiliated with a medical school that conducts research on the development of premature babies that are born to mothers at risk who receive free medical care because of their financial status. The researchers have determined that many of the problems they are seeing with the babies might have been prevented if the mothers had better medical care before the baby's birth. In addition, they have found that many of these mothers lack parenting skills, especially with infants that are very fragile.

A program was established to work with mothers at risk who are addicted to a substance, who are teenaged, and who have had a previous premature infant. The participants for the program are referred by schools, free medical clinics, and community agencies. Participants are provided information on how to provide themselves with appropriate nutrition during the prenatal period and the importance of keeping regular medical appointments throughout their pregnancy. As the time for the child's birth nears, the mothers are given instruction in infant care and the need for regular visits after birth. If the children are born with risk factors or are premature, additional support is given through sessions on the child's individual status and needs.

Throughout the baby's first year, home visitors provide support and information to the mothers. If the child is not thriving or developing normally, the home visitor assists the mother in taking the baby for medical help. The home visitor helps the mother with problem solving and provides continuity for the baby's positive development. Group activities for parents are available to further help the mothers continue a positive parenting role with their child.

Parent-Infant Intervention Programs   Parent-infant intervention programs not only focus on the important role of the family in the infant's health, well-being, and development, but also concentrate on the interactive or transactional relationship between parent and child. Based on research that early mutual bonding and adaptation between parent and child is significant for long-term development and interaction, these programs stress reciprocal behaviors between parents and their children. Programs planned for mothers and children must be individual to maintain the unique relationship between each mother and child. Intervention plans should be collaborative between parents and providers of services and incorporate family assessments and family needs (Widerstrom, Mowder, & Sandall, 1991).

Community-based programs described by Halpern (1990) also fit into the parent-infant intervention approach. Community-based programs work with low-income parents with children under three who are identified as being at risk because of lack of resources, infant health needs, social isolation, or lack of knowledge about child development. Community-based early intervention programs are run by neighborhood-based agencies that provide support in improving family conditions through home visiting, peer support groups, and parent education classes. In addition, these programs can provide services such as screening, health services, toy-lending libraries, child care, and adult education.

Inclusive Models of Early Intervention and Education   Early childhood preschool programs have followed different approaches to education based on theories or combinations of theories of early development and learning. Head Start models developed in the 1960s and 1970s are one source of models that can be classified as maturational, behavioral, cognitive-developmental, and ecological. For children with developmental delays or disabilities, the behavioral model was likely to be the theoretical approach used in the early years of intervention programs, as compared to models used with children with typical development.

Current trends for inclusive early education require reconsideration of how a model for early intervention is developed. Planning programs that integrated children with typical development and children with disabilities requires analyzing how best to educate all children in settings that include diversity. In the light of this information, Mallory (1994) proposes that a convergent theoretical approach be taken for an inclusive model of early education and intervention. He incorporates the concept of developmentally appropriate practices in his convergent paradigm, which includes three models: (1) the biogenetic model, (2) the developmental interactionist model, and (3) the functional model. Three models are nested or sequential in their function within a larger, triangulated model.

The first part of Mallory's approach is the biogenetic model, where the child makes the necessary adaptations to survive and thrive. The first task of the infant is to adapt and respond to environmental stimulation and stabilize basic life patterns such as sleeping, arousal, and social interaction. This model applies particularly to premature infants and to infants and toddlers with developmental difficulties or chronic illness.

The second component of the triangulated model is developmental-interaction-ist. This part of the model stresses internal processes and maturation flowing from both experiences and genetic factors.

The third part of the model is functional. Direct and systematic instruction, instilling appropriate behaviors, and teaching adaptive behaviors are the focus of the functional model. This section of the larger model is the theoretical approach typically used in special education programs.

Mallory suggests that this three-part model provides a better way to understand children's needs beyond the present definitions of developmentally appropriate practice. Such an approach is particularly necessary when including children who are atypical or have a wide range of variability in early childhood settings. Mallory (1994) described the interaction of the three components of the triangulated model to meet the needs of children as follows:

> The models are related in a "nested" fashion to each other. At the first level, the bio-genetic model of growth and maturation articulates necessary prerequisites in terms of the basic ability of the infant and young child to maintain some constitutional stability, stamina, and adaptability to environmental demands. Without these building blocks for later growth, successful development will be retarded. Next, the developmental-interactionist model is concerned with the ways in which the basic biogenetic attributes of a child are expressed in the form of cognitive, communicative, motoric, and psychosocial qualities. The expression of these qualities depends on characteristics of the social and materials environment and the quality of the child's interaction with those characteristics. Finally, the functional model encompasses the specific and discrete behaviors that are expressed as a result of physical, social, and intellectual development. Put simply, biogenetic factors prepare the child for coping with the world, developmental factors mediate the child's understanding of that world, and functional abilities enable the child to succeed in varying and increasingly complex social environments. (pp. 57–58)

PLANNING INTERVENTION FOR INDIVIDUAL CHILDREN

Regardless of the types of programs available to serve children and their families, children cannot be served until an individual plan is developed and written. If the child is four years old or older, an Individualized Education Plan (IEP) is written. If the child is three years old or younger, an Individualized Family Service Plan (IFSP) is developed. There are specific requirements or components for each type of plan. Figure 6–2 identifies and describes the requirements.

The Team Role in Developing the Individual Intervention Plan

Both professionals and parents participate in preparing IEPs and IFSPs. They work through several stages in designing and writing the plan. The team used for each plan will depend upon the child's disabilities and needs for intervention. As a result, members of teams can vary significantly from child to child and family to family. A child who has a motor disability perhaps will have a physical therapist and orthopedic specialist as members of the team. Another child who is emotionally disturbed might have a plan developed by a team that includes a child psychologist. The point is that the team should include specialists who can make recommendations related to the child's disability.

The team is multidisciplinary and includes all who will be concerned with the goals and objectives to be established for the child, the intervention services that will be provided, and the desired outcomes for the child's progress. In the case of a child being served in a public school, the child's teacher or teachers, the building principal, the school counselor, the parents or guardian, and the diagnostician or school psychologist might make up the team with other specialists as needed.

For the IFSP, the focus of the plan will be upon the child within the family context, rather than on the child alone. The family plays a central role in the IFSP, and the family assessment will determine how much of the plan focuses on services to the family and how much on the outcomes for the individual child. The members of the IFSP team will depend upon the type of intervention program where the child will be served. If the child is to enter a program for children with hearing deficits, the team will include hearing specialists, program curriculum specialists, speech therapists, and so on (Deiner, 1993; Spodek & Saracho, 1994).

Steps in Developing the Individual Intervention Plan

The individual plan is written after the child has been screened and diagnosed, and intervention needs have been identified. A form designed for the plan is used and can vary from program to program. The form includes information about the instruments and strategies used for assessment as well as the child's strengths and needs for intervention determined from assessment results. The intervention plan includes the following components, which are consistent with the requirements listed in Figure 6–2:

1.   Annual or long-range goals for the child's progress are developed. The goals are designed from the results of the diagnostic testing and other assessment methods, as well as results of previous intervention services that the child might have had. The goals are general and broad and are further specified through instructional objectives.

2.   Instructional objectives break the annual goals into parts, with specific statements of what will be achieved. The objectives are written in a behavioral form with the specified condition, behavior, and the criterion for evaluation of the outcome. Each goal may have a series of objectives or behaviors that are desired for the child to acquire or master.

Individualized Family Service Plan (IFSP)	Individualized Education Plan (IEP)
1. A statement of the infant's or toddler's present levels of physical development, cognitive development, communication development, social and emotional development, and adaptive skills based on acceptable objective criteria.	1. A statement of the child's present levels of educational performance, including academic achievement, social adaptation, prevocational and vocational skills, psychomotor skills, and self-help skills.
2. A statement of the family's resources, priorities, and concerns relating to enhancing the development of the family's handicapped infant or toddler.	2. A statement of annual goals which describes the educational performance to be achieved by the end of the school year under the child's individualized education program.
3. A statement of the major outcomes expected to be achieved for the infant and toddler and the family, and the criteria, procedures, and timelines used to determine the degree to which progress toward achieving the outcomes are being made and whether modifications or revisions of the outcomes or services are necessary.	3. A statement of short-term instructional objectives, which must be measurable intermediate steps between the present level of educational performance and the annual goals.
4. A statement of specific early intervention services necessary to meet the unique needs of the infant or toddler and the family, including the frequency, intensity, and the method of delivering services.	4. A statement of specific educational services needed by the child (determined without regard to the availability of services), including a description of a. all special education and related services which are needed to meet the unique needs of the child, including the type of physical education program in which the child will participate, and b. any special instructional media and materials which are needed.

Figure 6–2 Requirements for the IEP and IFSP

3. Activities to implement the plan are listed. At this point in the development of the plan, it is important to describe what kinds of activities will be developed for the child. The activities listed will include those to be implemented by the parent, the teacher, the specialist, and the therapist. Design of the activities will also be determined by the type of program where the child will be served and, if the setting is an inclusion model, how activities are integrated into the regular classroom instructional program.

Individualized Family Service Plan (IFSP)	**Individualized Education Plan (IEP)**
5. The projected dates for initiation of services and the anticipated duration of such services.	5. The date when those services will begin and length of time the services will be given.
6. The name of the case manager from the profession most immediately relevant to the infant's and toddler's or family's needs who will be responsible for the implementation of the plan and coordination with other agencies and persons.	6. A description of the extent to which the child will participate in regular education programs.
7. The steps to be taken supporting the transition of the handicapped toddler to services provided under part B to the extent such services are considered appropriate.	7. A justification of the type of educational placement that the child will have.
8. A statement of the extent to which services will be provided in natural environments.	8. A list of the individuals who are responsible for implementation of the individualized education program.
	9. Objective criteria, evaluation procedures, and schedules of determining, on at least an annual basis, whether the short-term instructional objectives are being achieved. (Federal Register, 41[252], p. 5692)

Source: From *Teaching Infants and Preschoolers With Disabilities* (pp. 118–119) by D. B. Bailey and M. Wolery, 1992, Englewood Cliffs, NJ: Prentice Hall. Copyright 1992 by Prentice Hall. Reprinted by permission.

4.   An evaluation plan is developed. The instructional objectives describe how each objective will be assessed. The criteria for how objectives will be assessed following intervention activities are also included in the intervention plan.

5.   Identification of who will provide the services for each objective and activities is the final step in completing the individual intervention plan. This will include parents, if appropriate, teachers, specialists, and therapists.

Figures 6–3 and 6–4 show two examples of IEP forms that can be used with children in the primary grades. They are examples of one school district's format for developing IEPs.

INDIVIDUAL EDUCATION PLAN (IEP)

Name of Student _____ D.O.B. _____

NAME OF SCHOOL: _____

DURATION OF SERVICES: FROM _____ TO _____
MM/DD/YY   MM/YY

PAGE _____ OF _____

_____ DRAFT
_____ ACCEPTED BY ARD COMMITTEE
_____ INSTRUCTIONAL SERVICES

GOALS AND OBJECTIVES	POSITION RESPONSIBLE	CRITERIA AND EVAL. PROCEDURES (INDICATE LEVEL OF MASTERY)	SCHEDULE FOR EVALUATION	IF MET
IMPROVE ACADEMIC SKILLS - The student will: ___ Achieve Mastery of Math Essential Elements at Grade Level with assistance as described on the recommended adaptations by the ARD Committee. ___ Achieve Mastery of Reading Essential Elements at Grade Level with assistance as described on the recommended adaptations by the ARD Committee. ___ Achieve Mastery of English Essential Elements at Grade Level with assistance as described on the recommended adaptations by the ARD Committee. ___ Achieve Mastery of Spelling Essential Elements at Grade Level with assistance as described on the recommended adaptations by the ARD Committee. ___ Achieve Mastery of Science Essential Elements at Grade Level with assistance as described on the recommended adaptations by the ARD committee.				

INDIVIDUAL EDUCATION PLAN (IEP)

PAGE _____ OF _____

Name of Student _____ D.O.B. _____

_____ DRAFT
_____ ACCEPTED BY ARD COMMITTEE
_____ INSTRUCTIONAL SERVICES

NAME OF SCHOOL: _____

DURATION OF SERVICES: FROM _____ TO _____
                            MM/DD/YY   MM/YY

GOALS AND OBJECTIVES	POSITION RESPONSIBLE	CRITERIA AND EVAL. PROCEDURES (INDICATE LEVEL OF MASTERY)	SCHEDULE FOR EVALUATION	IF MET
IMPROVE ACADEMIC SKILLS - The student will:				
____ Achieve Mastery of Health Essential Elements at Grade Level with assistance as described on the recommended adaptations by the ARD Committee.				
____ Achieve Mastery of Social Studies Essential Elements at Grade level with assistance as described on the recommended adaptations by the ARD Committee.				
____ OTHER _____				
____ _____				
____ OTHER _____				
____ _____				

White Copy - C/O   Pink Copy - School
Yellow Copy - PSD   Gold Copy - Parent

Figure 6-3 Example of an IEP Form

INDIVIDUAL EDUCATION PLAN PART II
TEACHING STYLE/LEARNING STYLE ADAPTATIONS/ASSISTIVE TECHNOLOGY RECOMMENDED BY ARD

Name of Student _____ Campus _____ School Year _____

Special Education Contact _____ Date of Birth _____

Modifications needed to assure success in regular, remedial, and supportive programs, including eligibility for participation in extracurricular activities.

ADAPTATION OF MATERIALS: Provide

	Denotes Assistive Technology	Reading	Lang. Arts	Science	Soc. Studies	Math	Electives
1. Peer to read materials							
2. Tape recording of required readings	AT						
3. Highlighted materials for emphasis	AT						
4. Altered format of materials	AT						
5. Study aids/manipulatives	AT						
6. ESL materials							
7. Copy of class notes	AT						
8. Peer tutoring/assistance/notetaking	AT						

MODIFICATION OF INSTRUCTION:

1. Leave class for specialized assistance/CMC							
2. Short instructions (1 or 2 step)							
3. Opportunity to repeat instructions							
4. Opportunity to write instructions							
5. Visual aids (pictures, flash cards, etc.)	AT						
6. Auditory aids (cues, tapes, etc.)	AT						
7. Study sheets/preview/summaries	AT						
8. Multisensory information	AT						
9. Extra time for oral response							
10. Extra time for written response							
11. Exams of reduced length/short answer/ fewer essay responses							
12. Oral exams							
13. Open book exams							
14. Tests to be given by special ed. teacher							
15. Preview to test questions							
16. Frequent and immediate feedback							
17. Check for understanding							
18. Simplify vocabulary							

ALTERATION OF ASSIGNMENTS:

1. Reduced assignments (fewer paragraphs, problems and questions)							
2. Taped assignments / lectures	AT						
3. Extra time for assignments							
4. Opportunity to respond orally							
5. Individual contracts							
6. Emphasis on major points							
7. Assignment notebooks							
8. Exemption from reading before peers							
9. Special projects in lieu of assignments							
10. Calculators	AT						

GRADING

	Denotes Assistive Technology	Reading	Lang. Arts	Science	Soc. Studies	Math	Electives
1. Grade (a) given by regular education teacher							
(b) given by special education teacher							
*2. Modifications:							
(a) Criteria for passing changed to ___% in:	AT						
(b) No penalty for spelling or grammatical errors							
(c) Require fewer correct responses							
(d) Do not count semester tests							
(e) Consider effort as an integral part of grading criteria							

*This will be used to determine a student's eligibility to participate in extracurricular activities and to achieve passing grades in all content areas.

MODIFICATION OF THE ENVIRONMENT

Study carrel							
Preferential seating							
Reduce visual/auditory stimuli							
Small group instruction							
One-to-one instruction							

PHYSICAL/ADAPTED EQUIPMENT AND/OR ASSISTIVE DEVICES REQUIRED:

_____

BEHAVIOR MANAGEMENT

Logical consequences							
Clearly defined/consistent limits							
Frequent reminders of the rules							
In-school timeout							
In-class timeout							
Frequent eye contact/proximity control							
Private discussion regarding behavior							
Opportunity to help teacher							
Supervision-during-transition							
Ignoring of minor infractions							
Implementation of behavior contract							
Promote time on task							
Positive reinforcement							

___ ___ This student is capable of following normal school rules; regular
YES NO displinary methods should be appropriate. If NO, Behavior Management Plan is attached.

___ ___ This student is able to follow the state attendance policy. If NO,
YES NO refer to Campus Attendance Committee.

_____
Principal / Designee

STATE ACADEMIC SKILLS ASSESSMENT
___ Will take all areas
___ Will take mathematics   ___ Will take Science
___ Will take writing   ___ Will take Social
___ Will take reading   Studies
___ Not offered for this student's grade placement
___ Exempt in all areas

MODIFICATIONS IN STANDARDIZED TEST PROCEDURES
___ Use of an interpreter for instruction   AT
___ Allow for oral response
___ Provide additional time
___ Use of braille or large print test   AT
___ Read test to student
___ Dictate written response
___ Small group testing

State law requires that an ARD be held if the student receives Fs for two consecutive grading periods in an academic course. Please contact the Special Ed. contact teacher when this student experiences difficulty

White Copy – C/O	Pink Copy – School
Yellow Copy – Parent	Gold Copy – PSD

Figure 6–4   Example of an IEP Form: Teaching/Learning Adaptations

The Role of the Family in Developing Individual Intervention Plans

It has been stressed throughout this chapter that the family has a significant role in the child's intervention program. The parent or parents are included in screening and assessment before a child is placed into a program. In addition, parents must be informed about each step of the process from initial screening to development of the individual intervention plan and give their approval. Every effort must be made to include parents in the development of the individual plan, and meeting times and places for the team's work on the plan must be convenient for the parents to attend. Parents should be encouraged to participate in the planning and make their wishes for the child's intervention program known. When the individual plan is completed, parents must indicate their approval in writing. Parents can disagree with the plan and appeal. The appeal process can extend from a local appeal to appeals to the state educational agency or state and federal courts (McCollum & Maude, 1993; Spodek & Saracho, 1994).

The role of the family in developing the Individualized Family Service Plan is more extensive than for an Individualized Educational Plan. This is because it includes goals and objectives for the family as well as the child. Because the intent of IFSPs is to focus on the family, the services and instruction to be designed and implemented include competencies for the parents. Therefore, the plan must include what the family desires as outcomes for both parents and the child. The family has the major responsibility in deciding what will be in the intervention plan. The other members of the team have the responsibility to work with family members in developing the activities to accomplish the plan and the evaluation strategies that will be used to determine if goals and objectives have been accomplished. Families need to be informed as to the options they can make decisions on. For example, parents might have several choices as to the type of intervention program where their child can be placed and the location of the program, based on their needs and possibilities for transportation.

With the completion of the IEP or IFSP, the intervention program can be initiated. Chapter 7 discusses implementation of the child's individual intervention plan. This chapter closes with a discussion about the issues concerning inclusion of children with disabilities in programs with children who do not have disabilities.

THE ISSUES OF INTEGRATING CHILDREN WITH SPECIAL NEEDS AND AT RISK

Not everyone agrees that inclusion is the best possible form of early intervention for young children with disabilities or who are at risk for development and learning. Wolery and Wilbers (1994) suggest that the benefits of inclusion are well known. They describe that there are benefits for children with disabilities, children without disabilities, communities, families of children with disabilities, and families of children without disabilities. Figure 6–5 provides descriptions of these benefits as listed by Wolery and Wilbers.

Inclusion programs integrate children with disabilities with their peers.

Regardless of the benefits, there are concerns and differences in views about how effective inclusion practices are for both teachers and children. These issues are discussed in terms of early childhood programs in general and early childhood programs in public schools.

Issues Related to Inclusion in Early Childhood Programs

The issues relating to inclusion discussed in this section arise when regular early childhood teachers and special education early childhood teachers must cooperate and collaborate. The practices used by the two types of teachers and the questions of providing services in all types of early childhood settings are in question.

Differences Between Early Childhood and Early Childhood Special Education Teachers   Typically, preservice training programs for early childhood and early childhood special education teachers are separate. As a result, both categories of teachers are not fully prepared to teach all types of children who attend early childhood programs that practice inclusion. Joint training programs for all teachers of young children are recommended as well as inservice sessions for teachers who are currently working in classrooms that include children with disabilities. As inclusion becomes more widespread in early childhood programs, joint or collaborative training will become more widespread. A barrier to this reform in training in higher education is

Recipient of benefit	Description of benefit
Children with disabilities	1. They are spared the effects of separate, segregated education—including the negative effects of labeling and negative attitudes fostered by lack of contact with them. 2. They are provided with competent models that allow them to learn new adaptive skills and/or learn when and how to use their existing skills through imitation. 3. They are provided with competent peers with whom to interact and thereby learn new social and/or communicative skills. 4. They are provided with realistic life experiences that prepare them to live in the community. 5. They are provided with opportunities to develop friendships with typically developing peers.
Children without disabilities	1. They are provided with opportunities to learn more realistic and accurate views about individuals with disabilities. 2. They are provided with opportunities to develop positive attitudes toward others who are different from themselves. 3. They are provided with opportunities to learn altruistic behaviors and when and how to use such behaviors. 4. They are provided with models of individuals who successfully achieve despite challenges.
Communities	1. They can conserve their early childhood resources by limiting the need for segregated, specialized programs. 2. They can conserve educational resources if children with disabilities who are mainstreamed at the preschool level continue in regular as compared to special education placements during the elementary school years.
Families of children with disabilities	1. They are able to learn about typical development. 2. They may feel less isolated from the remainder of their communities. 3. They may develop relationships with families of typically developing children who can provide them with meaningful support.
Families of children without disabilities	1. They may develop relationships with families who have children with disabilities and thereby make a contribution to them and their communities. 2. They will have opportunities to teach their children about individual differences and about accepting individuals who are different.

Figure 6–5 Benefits of Preschool Inclusion

Source: From *Including Children With Special Needs in Early Childhood Programs* (p. ii) by M. Wolery and S. J. Wilbers (Eds.), 1994, Washington, DC: National Association for the Education of Young Children. Copyright 1994 by the National Association for the Education of Young Children. Reprinted by permission.

the conflict over ownership of programs and the compromises that are necessary to provide the best preparation for both types of early childhood teachers (Wolery & Wilbers, 1994).

More serious is the issue of differing philosophies or perceived differences between the two fields. Although the two early childhood fields have commonalities in their histories, they have diverse origins. Early childhood education is based on a developmental approach to instruction, while early childhood special education takes a preacademic and teacher-directed approach (Johnson & Johnson, 1992). Challenging this position are Carta, Atwater, Schwartz, & McConnell (1993), who argue that it is based on outdated programs or practices in early childhood special education and does not reflect current quality programs. In contrast to the belief that the philosophies are very different are arguments that the two fields have much in common and each has strengths that would be beneficial for the other (Bredekamp, 1993; Carta et al., 1993; Johnson & Johnson, 1993).

Changing Roles for Early Childhood Educators in Inclusion Programs   As programs are restructured to implement inclusion, early childhood teachers are experiencing changing roles and responsibilities. Early childhood special education teachers are adjusting to working more closely with families and collaborating with early childhood teachers in various settings such as child care, preschools, and public schools. They have experienced difficulties in moving from programs where they were the primary instructor to having to "wear many hats" (Buysse & Wesley, 1993). This conflict in roles is made more complex by the lack of training for staff members in settings just beginning to deliver services to children with disabilities and their families. As the practice of inclusion continues to evolve, there are questions about the future roles for early childhood special educators.

Early childhood teachers likewise face changing roles and responsibilities. Many early childhood teachers are not prepared to provide the specialized medical attention required by some of their students. They may also lack other supports that children with disabilities need that should but don't follow the children into the regular classroom. A common concern is the child who is so disruptive or the child who requires so much time-consuming care for personal needs that the education of the other children in the class is affected (Shanker, 1994–1995).

Conflicts in Practices in Early Childhood Education   There has been much dialogue in recent publications concerning the differences in Developmentally Appropriate Practices advocated by the National Association for Young Children and appropriate practices in early childhood special education. A criticism of Developmentally Appropriate Practices has been that the guidelines do not include enough information on serving young children with disabilities. Principles of the education of young children with special needs that are not part of the DAP guidelines are the importance of special intervention objectives; comprehensive, multidisciplinary, outcome-based intervention; and frequent assessment for program monitoring (Carta, Atwater, Schwartz, & McConnell, 1993). However, these authors and Bredekamp (1993) also propose that there is overlap between the two approaches. Johnson & Johnson

(1993) point out that Guidelines for Developmentally Appropriate Practices are general one for practices within a field of education, while early childhood special education is a field of education; therefore, the two cannot be compared accurately. They further suggest that there are differences between the fields on perceptions of the needs and abilities of young children and on the planning of curriculum and instruction.

Perceived or actual conflicts about practices with very young children can be a barrier to inclusion. The issue of what constitute appropriate practices for young children of all abilities and diverse backgrounds must be addressed by all early childhood educators in a collaborative and cooperative manner if this issue is to be resolved.

Questions About Availability of Services in All Early Childhood Settings   Families of children with disabilities often need multiple services for their child and themselves. As inclusion has been implemented in Head Start, child care, and other early childhood settings, there are concerns if needed services will follow families into all of those settings. Because adequate services frequently require a team of individuals, some evidence suggests that programs that include preschool children with disabilities do not employ the people needed to address an individual child's disabilities (Wolery & Wilbers, 1994).

Issues Related to Inclusion in Public Schools

Public school settings have their own set of issues related to inclusion. Not all public school educators agree with the benefits of inclusion; moreover, there is disagreement as to how extensive inclusion should be. Although many of the issues discussed below are relevant to all levels of public schooling, they also apply to early childhood programs in the public school setting.

Differences in Capacities of Schools to Implement Inclusion   There are educators that question schools that move too quickly into inclusion without proper resources, training, and support for the children with disabilities. The argument is made that all school districts are not equal in their ability to restructure appropriately for inclusion. A related argument is that the Congress has underfunded special education programs and inclusion is an unfunded mandate that pressures schools to implement integrated classrooms without the resources to provide training and personnel for students' needs to be met adequately. A counterargument is that schools may use lack of resources to delay inclusion and try to continue with the status quo in services for children with disabilities (O'Neil, 1994–1995; Shanker, 1994–1995).

Differences in Needs of Children With Disabilities   The issue of whether it is feasible or desirable that all children be put into inclusion programs is a major question. Advocates of total inclusion propose that if the school is restructured in an adequate manner, it is possible to provide flexibility of instruction, an appropriate environment, and necessary staff members for all children with disabilities. They likewise believe that inclusion provides necessary social interactions with peers that separate class-rooms deny children with disabilities.

Those who question that inclusion is appropriate for all children with disabilities argue that some children cannot benefit from inclusion and are best served in a sepa-rate setting. They also point out that the massive change needed to restructure schools for total inclusion would interrupt the educational process in schools for a lengthy period of time. Extensive planning and training and gradual implementation of inclusion would be necessary for such a radical change (O'Neil, 1994–1995).

Beyond Inclusion: Reforming Education and Special Education to Include All Children

A final issue pertains to meeting the needs of all children in the schools. It has been suggested that the methods of funding and implementing federal programs not only segregate children with special needs into separate, categorical programs, but they attach unnecessary labels on children as prerequisites to providing services. While many children are served in some type of program, others who need the services do not qualify for special instruction and materials provided to categorical programs.

The argument for broadening the concept and practice of inclusion is to ensure that all children's individual needs are served. Overlapping programs for special edu-cation, Chapter 1, and bilingual education would not serve narrowly defined popula-tions, but all populations would be included: gifted students, students at risk for sus-pension or expulsion, and children with problems not considered serious enough for services and support (Wang, Reynolds, & Walberg, 1994–1995).

There are important issues related to how, where, and by whom young children with disabilities and who are at risk will be served in early childhood programs. Inclu-sion is a new practice that is not without problems and concerns. As the issues and problems are addressed, more will be known about the most effective ways to struc-ture early intervention programs for children with diverse needs in diverse settings. Additional models might emerge from these efforts, but the needs of each individual child and his or her family will remain the central focus for all programs.

✦ SUMMARY

This chapter is about young children who have disabilities and the process used to find out if they need to be placed in an early intervention program to minimize the effects of their disability. It is also about the kinds of programs that are available for these children, beginning with infants and toddlers, including inclusion programs where they are placed in programs with children who do not have disabilities.

We discussed the fact that special education early intervention programs have a similar historical background as early childhood education programs. They have been influenced by some of the same early childhood leaders and affected by the same historical trends and events; nevertheless, different forces and trends affected the evolution of programs for young children with disabilities or at risk for developing a disability. Children with special needs were more likely to be served as a result of improvements in health services or social services such as those resulting from the Social Security Act of 1935. The major step in developing programs for intervention was the civil rights movement, which led to the development of preschool programs such as Head Start and recognition of the rights and needs of citizens with disabilities. Beginning in the 1960s and continuing into the 1990s, legislation has steadily extended and improved services for young children who are disabled and their families.

As a result of the series of laws describing who should be served and how intervention programs should function, there are specific provisions in these areas: (1) how young children with disabilities should be identified, screened, and assessed diagnostically; (2) how it is determined whether they should be placed in an intervention program; and (3) how their intervention program should be planned. Early intervention programs now include infants and toddlers as well as children in the preschool and primary grades. The screening and assessment procedures vary for these two populations, but the overall process is the same. The intervention programs differ in that for infants and toddlers the focus is on providing intervention for the family. Infants and toddlers have an Individualized Family Service Plan, while preschool children and older children have Individualized Education Plans.

Families have an important role in the process of identifying, assessing, placing, and serving their children. Parents must be informed at all stages of the process and are encouraged to be active participants in the process. Families of infants and toddlers participate in the intervention process. Parents must approve the decisions that are made for their child—no matter what their age. Parents can appeal if they feel their desires and the needs of their child are not being met in the individual intervention plan. The family's needs and situation are also part of the intervention plan, and family assessments are conducted for infant and toddler intervention programs.

There are numerous models for intervention programs. Some of the first programs focused on intervention for the child. However, as time passed, it was determined that the family plays a central role in the child's well-being and progress. More and more intervention models have focused on the family or the mother and the child. The newest trend for all ages is to integrate or include the child who is disabled or at risk for developing problems in settings with peers who have no disabilities. The inclusion models have benefits for all involved; however, there are difficulties in implementing inclusion models in all types of early childhood settings at the preschool level. Public schools likewise have difficulties in providing inclusion at all levels because of the need to restructure schools and change the roles of professionals in special education and regular education programs.

Regardless of the types of early intervention that are currently provided for young children and their families, it must be remembered that the history of the field demonstrates that the intervention programs and strategies are not static, but are continually changing and improving. Regardless, the goal is to help every young child reach his or her potential and to prevent children from being at risk for development and learning.

In the next chapter we will address the last steps of the intervention process, implementation of the IEP or IFSP and the teaching and learning strategies that are considered best for young children with disabilities. We will discuss instructional approaches and their usefulness for intervention.

→ STUDY QUESTIONS

1. Describe some of the educational and social events prior to 1960 that paved the way for intervention services for children under the age of six.
2. What factors were responsible for the rapid and broadened approaches to early childhood intervention after 1960?
3. How did parents influence the initiation of intervention programs for their children?
4. Describe and explain the features of, and requirements in, legislation for children with disabilities.
5. What are the requirements regarding the role and rights of parents in the legislation?
6. Why are young children screened as a first step in providing services? Explain the purposes for screening.
7. How is the screening process different for infants and toddlers and for older preschool children? Why are these differences necessary?
8. What strategies are used in the screening process for the infants and toddlers and for preschool children?
9. Explain family assessment and the purposes for family assessment.
10. How can errors be made in interpreting screening results? Explain.
11. Explain the purposes for diagnostic assessment.
12. Why should families be involved in screening and assessment? Why are their contributions significant?
13. Why should families be included in the intervention program? How do their needs affect the needs of the young child with disabilities?
14. Explain the steps in assessment and placement in an intervention program.
15. Describe and explain the seven goals for early intervention programs. What are they trying to accomplish?
16. What are the differences between child-centered intervention approaches and parent-focused intervention approaches? Explain.
17. What does prevention intervention mean? Who is served in this type of program and why?
18. What is the rationale behind parent-infant intervention programs?
19. Define inclusion models of early intervention. What kinds of early childhood settings have inclusion programs for children with disabilities?
20. Explain the triangulated model of inclusion and the three levels of intervention.

21. Discuss the issues surrounding the implementation of inclusion models. Explain your position in regard to this issue.
22. Do the benefits of inclusion outweigh the barriers?
23. Who should be placed in an inclusion program?
24. Explain "least restrictive environment." How is this requirement central to the arguments between advocates and those in opposition to total inclusion?

⇢ KEY TERMS

categorical intervention program
Individualized Family Service Plan (IFSP)

least restrictive environment
noncategorical intervention program

⇢ SUGGESTED ACTIVITIES

Locate two or three sources of curriculum for young children who have disabilities. Try to determine the type of program, including theoretical and program approaches.

7

Linking Curriculum and Instruction for Young Children With Special Needs

→ Chapter Objectives

As a result of reading this chapter, you will be able to

1. Discuss how curriculum and instruction evolve from assessment information in programs for children with special needs
2. Explain how intervention strategies focus on the child's individual disabilities but at the same time include all development domains
3. List and describe different approaches to design of intervention programs for young children with disabilities
4. Explain the role of the teacher in designing curriculum and instruction strategies for intervention with infants, toddlers, and young children
5. Discuss how to modify developmentally appropriate classrooms for children with disabilities
6. Discuss the complexity of assessing and planning instruction for young children who are at risk for development and learning
7. Describe different approaches used in curriculum and instruction with young children who are at risk because of cultural and language differences
8. Discuss concerns about developmentally appropriate practices and young children who are at risk because of cultural and language differences

In Chapter 6, we covered most of the steps in identifying, screening, assessing, and placing children in an early intervention program. We discussed the importance of assessment at each step of the process. We also introduced the types of programs that are available to provide early intervention and compared different views concerning inclusion programs.

In this chapter, we will address the last steps in the intervention process, provision of curriculum and instruction as part of the services that are indicated in the child's Individualized Family Service Plan (IFSP) or Individualized Education Plan (IEP). We will look at how instruction is planned and implemented for children with disabilities or who are at risk for success in school. We will describe models of curriculum and the kinds of strategies that are considered effective in addressing the needs of these populations of young children. And, to continue the interactive relationship between learning and assessment, we will include information on how the child's progress is monitored and how the educational program is evaluated. But first, we will establish the link between assessment and instruction by describing how assessment results reflected in the child's individual intervention plan are used to plan the intervention program for children with disabilities. We will also discuss how assessment results are used to plan the instructional program for children at risk for development and learning and how to plan appropriate strategies for children from diverse cultures or with language differences.

PLANNING INSTRUCTION FOR CHILDREN WITH DISABILITIES

Linking Assessment and Curriculum Planning

After the child's assessment has been completed and the decision is made that he or she is eligible for intervention services, the development of an individual plan provides the direction for the child's instructional program. The appropriate early childhood setting is determined, and the child's plan is consulted for planning intervention activities for the child—and the family if appropriate. The assessment information that was gathered, interpreted, and used to develop the goals and objectives for the IFSP or IEP now becomes the framework for the child's intervention program. The instructional program is based on selection of appropriate intervention strategies (Wolery & Wilbers, 1994a). In the next section, we will address how appropriate curriculum decisions are made for individual early intervention programs.

Using Assessment to Plan Instruction for Infants and Toddlers   Program planning for infants and toddlers is individual and flexible because of sleeping, eating, and caregiving needs. Intervention occurs separately for each child, even if the child is in group care. Activities are planned for several domains that include cognition, motor, communication, and self-help. The child's disability in one or more of the domains guides the curriculum activities that will be planned; nevertheless, the child's curriculum will include activities in all domains for overall developmental progress (Deiner, 1993).

Cognitive Impairments.   During infancy, the child constructs information using physical actions and the senses. Curriculum for the cognitive domain in infant intervention programs follows Piaget's theory of cognitive development. The goals that are selected are intended to assist the child in constructing reality through looking, listening, and actively engaging in activities with objects. Piaget's substages in the sensorimotor period can also be used to assess the cognitive status of infants and toddlers with disabilities. Infants and toddlers with **cognitive impairments** or delay will acquire developmental milestones in cognitive development much more slowly than their peers who do not have a cognitive disability. Once the child is assessed, the intervention program can then be structured to match the hierarchy of skill attainment in the cognitive domain. Activities can be planned during routine caregiving; play activities and interaction with toys can be used to facilitate the child's cognitive development. The environment can be organized to respond to the child's needs through physical arrangement and adult support (Wolery & Wolery, 1992).

Motor Impairments.   **Motor impairments** can result in infants and toddlers being restricted in their physical movements. In infants, the basic locomotor skills of sitting and standing may be delayed or accomplished with great difficulty. Causes of impairments in the motor domain can be abnormal muscle tone, retention of primitive reflexes, delayed development, skeletal deformities, and other problems related to movement (Widerstrom, Mowders, & Sandall, 1991).

When the curriculum for the infant and toddler is planned for intervention in the motor domain, intervention objectives must be related not only to the difficulties that have been identified, but also to the causes or source of the impairment in motor skills. The source of the difficulty has an effect on how much improvement the child can achieve, as well as what kinds of intervention activities are best for the child's condition. The goal of the intervention curriculum is to facilitate the child's ability to move as normally as possible and to gain independence in movement when feasible. A physical therapist will usually be involved in planning and administering therapy with the child. Selection of treatment activities takes into account the child's daily environments and outcomes that have application for those environments (Smith, 1989).

Communication Impairments.   Children who are developing normally acquire the ability to communicate through language. By the age of two years, they are able to use words and combinations of words to express a variety of types of verbalizations. They can express wants and needs and engage in verbal exchanges with others. Children with **communication impairments** are delayed in this ability to communicate, and the delay can be indirectly caused by a speech, hearing, cognitive, or motor impairment.

Planning intervention strategies for children with communication impairments is complex because more than oral language is involved. Nonverbal communication is also a factor, as is the source of the delay. In addition, the conflict among theories of language development results in conflict over the best intervention strategies to be used. Regardless of these complications, planned intervention is needed. Assessment results are used to identify the objectives for development of communication skills. Intervention strategies take into account the child's current level and mode of communication, other disabilities that affect communication, and the best means of helping the child to be able to communicate. The human and physical environment are considered to facilitate communication and to be supportive of the child's efforts. For children who lack the capacity to communicate through oral language, other communication modes are used such as sign language, communication boards, and assistive technology (Holder-Brown & Parette, 1992; Widerstrom, Mowder, & Sandall, 1991).

Self-Help Impairments. Children acquire self-help skills throughout the infant, toddler, and preschool years. Young children develop competence in feeding and eating, dressing, grooming, and toileting. A critical self-help skill in infancy is the ability to feed. Infants and toddlers with disabilities often have difficulty or delay in the development of this skill because of physiological and motor function difficulties. Intervention requires close attention to assessment results and extended time for intervention strategies.

Other self-help skills such as dressing, grooming, and toileting can be affected by motor and cognitive delay or disabilities. Assessment of toddlers can demonstrate delay in acquiring these skills as compared to children with normal development. Intervention strategies will depend upon the developmental source of the difficulty and what developmental domains interact to make the self-help skill possible. A team approach to intervention may be necessary, with a combination of strategies and skills to be used as intermediate steps to acquiring the self-help skill (Widerstrom, Mowder, & Sandall, 1991).

Using Assessment to Plan Instruction for Preschool and Primary Age Children

When children with disabilities enter a program at the preschool level or a primary grade, they will bring information with them about past interventions and progress that was made regarding earlier goals and objectives. Their individual intervention plan will reflect past curriculum and strategies that were used with the child and what kinds of activities were most beneficial. Much information is known about the child including personality, level of impairment, the effect of family dynamics and relationships on the child's progress, and the child's interests and preferences.

Professionals who are planning an intervention program for young children can build on the child's previous intervention experiences and evaluation reports to design the most suitable intervention plan. Wolery (1994a) suggests that information gathered about the child's past experiences, plus ongoing assessment in the new program, provides guidance for planning intervention strategies in four areas: (1) the child's current abilities and needs, (2) instructional strategies that are likely to be effective, (3) the child's environments beyond the program environment, and (4) the nature and organization of the program where the child will be placed.

Program planners will also wish to focus on the child's progress in each developmental domain, particularly the domains where there is a disability. They will plan instructional strategies for all developmental domains and take into consideration the influence of environmental and human organization, support, and interaction with the child.

The instructional practices that result from this study of the child's past experiences and current status should also include personal information about the child's interests and preferences. The planning team should know the child's preferences for toys and activities and how well and how long the child is able to stay engaged in activities. The level of independence and the amount of adult support that the child needs are important to know. How much the child interacts with adults and peers and what kinds of adult-child interactions are most successful can guide intervention strategies as can information about skills the child needs to adapt to the environment both at school and at home.

The family's role in translating the child's individual plan into a plan for curriculum and instruction is also needed. The family can provide input on the child's preferences for play and play materials. They can share the goals that they have for the child. Family members can identify the child's abilities and needs for family activities such as outings and shopping trips, where the child has to function in different environments. Family suggestions about what strategies seem to be helpful to the child also contribute to the child's individualized curriculum.

The child's IEP provides a framework for the goals and objectives that are targeted for intervention; nevertheless, other concurrent assessments and processes for gathering information about the child are needed to plan intervention strategies. Once a comprehensive picture is developed about the child and impairments that are present, curriculum and instruction resources can be marshaled to begin the intervention program.

PLANNING AND MANAGING DIFFERENT APPROACHES TO INSTRUCTION

There are published curriculum resources designed for infants, toddlers, and young children available to intervention programs. Some are based on specific theories of development and learning. They can also be related to the approaches to intervention discussed in Chapter 6. Early childhood special education programs often use strategies from more than one program or resource. In the information that follows, we will discuss the types of published curriculums that are available for early intervention programs. Then we will discuss approaches to intervention strategies that teachers can consider when developing their own activities for their classrooms. The theories that form the foundation for the cognitive and behavioral approaches will be discussed in Chapter 8.

Curriculum Models for Early Intervention Strategies

The manner in which a teacher of young children with disabilities approaches the development of curriculum and instruction depends upon the theoretical approach desired for intervention strategies. All curriculums have the goal of improving the child's development and addressing the needs presented by disabilities; however, the theory that underlies the model determines the organization, content, and methods that are to be used (Bagnato, Neisworth, & Munson, 1989; Widerstrom, Mowder, & Sandall, 1991). The models to be discussed take the following approaches: (1) developmental approach, (2) cognitive approach, (3) transactional approach, (4) behavioral approach, and (5) functional and adaptive approach.

Developmental Approach   The developmental approach is based on the premise that there are predetermined norms of development. It is a research-based approach in that it uses research on child development to describe a hierarchy of developmental tasks that children normally acquire at each chronological age. It presupposes developmental milestones as described by Bagnato, Neisworth, & Munson (1989). Each major milestone or task is supported by a hierarchy of skills that occur before the milestone is reached. The curriculum developed from this model uses the hierarchy of developmental skills or tasks as the framework of the curriculum. There are assessment procedures to determine where the child is developmentally, which activities and interventions are available for skill development, and how to assess when the skills leading to the milestone have been acquired. The *Hawaii Early Learning Profile (HELP) and Activities* (Furone et al., 1979) and *Portage Guide to Early Education* (Bluma, Shearer, Frohman, & Hilliard, 1976) are examples of curriculum models that use the developmental approach.

Cognitive Approach   The curriculums that follow a cognitive approach are based on Piaget's work and stress content in the cognitive, social, and communicative domains. The approach focuses on the child's active interaction with the environment and the child's intrinsic motivation as the mode of learning. Developmental goals and objectives based on Piaget's developmental stages and substages are used as the framework for intervention strategies. Developmental stages rather than chronological age or developmental norms are used as the guidelines for attainment of objectives. The stages are hierarchical, with achievement in one cognitive level necessary to advance to the next level. The cognitive curriculum addresses attainment of concepts and the related areas of language and social development; fine and gross motor, self-help skills, and affective development may not be included. An example of a cognitive-developmental curriculum is *Infant Learning* (Dunst, 1981).

Transactional Approach   The transactional or interactive-transactional approach stems from the importance of the interaction between the caregiver and child. Intervention strategies focus on the mother, who uses ongoing interactions with the child to achieve the desired outcomes. In Chapter 6, this approach to intervention was discussed in relation to the role of the family, particularly the role of the mother and mother-child interactions in promoting the child's well-being, development, and learning. Enhancement of the caregiver's relationship with the child and the caregiver's ability to respond to the child's current abilities and interests in initiating interactions is significant. The environment is also important in nurturing and supporting the child. The transactional approach curriculum is considered to be especially useful for infants and toddlers (Bagnato, Neisworth, & Munson, 1989; Widerstrom, Mowder, & Sandall, 1991).

Behavioral Approach   The behavioral approach arises from B. F. Skinner's (1972) theory of learning. The curriculum based on his theory is designed on Skinner's belief of how children learn, and not on a child's stages of development. The strategies used to guide the child's learning are reinforcement based on a philosophy of extrinsic motivation. The role of the adult is significant in that the adult controls activities, providing direct instruction in the behaviors that are targeted. Instructional objectives are sequential, and they are taught systematically with appropriate rewards or reinforcements to achieve the desired goals. An example of a curriculum using a behavioral approach is *Teaching the Child With Down Syndrome* (Hanson, 1987).

Functional and Adaptive Approach   The approach of the functional and adaptive approach centers on the skills that are needed by the child and that can be used immediately. The goals and objectives of the curriculum are to facilitate the child's ability to function in the environment using his or her developmental strengths. The curriculum is determined by the functions and skills that the child needs to interact with the environment or accomplish daily tasks. Curriculums that are available are designed for specific disabilities such as visual impairments or delayed language. Activities are designed to assist children in acquiring skills to function better in daily life. These skills are related to their particular disability (Bagnato, Neisworth, & Munson, 1989).

Prepared curriculums are a valuable resource to teachers of infants, toddlers, and young children who have disabilities. They typically contain the instructions needed to implement them with young children. They often are targeted for a particular type of disability. They relieve teachers from having to spend large amounts of time designing and collecting a curriculum. Nevertheless, teachers also benefit from understanding how to design and use their own intervention strategies. In the next section, instructional strategies that teachers can use to design curriculum activities will be described.

Instructional Strategies for Early Intervention Programs

In the models for intervention strategies described above, it was pointed out that some of the models were based on a theory of learning and that the strategies in the curriculum based on the models were consistent with the theory. For example, the developmental approach model was organized on the basis of patterns of normal development in young children. Using norms for chronological ages in each of the domains of development, instructional strategies would be planned to help the child advance from one level of functioning to another. Gesell's maturational theory, on which the approach was based, would propose that the child's readiness for a task was based on the child's ability to learn and perform that task. Children with a disability might acquire the ability at a slower rate or at a more limited level because of the impairment. Instructional strategies would be used to develop the child's readiness for the task.

Each of the model curriculums has implicit in it an approach for developing curriculum and instructional activities. The behavioral approach would be structured around teacher-directed instruction, with praise and other reinforcing strategies so that the child will continue to use the desired behavior or persist in acquiring a skill. The Piaget-based programs would structure the environment and teacher behaviors to enable the child to interact with materials and experiences and use intrinsic motivation to learn new information and attempt new behaviors. The goal of the Piaget-based programs is for the child to be able to initiate learning.

Teachers of young children with disabilities, then, have a repertoire of strategies that they can draw upon to use with their students, or they can design their own curriculum. The strategies can range from open-ended, unstructured, child-initiated experiences to carefully sequenced objectives based on a hierarchy of skills, with specific responses recommended to the child's attempts and behaviors. The type of strategies used and frequency of use depend upon the individual child's strengths and needs. The teacher will employ different strategies in different circumstances, depending on the child's abilities and the kinds of activities that are most successful in working with a disability or domain of development. The strategies employed would correspond to the ones for individual situations and the extent of the impairment or disability. Wolery (1994b) organized the range of possible strategies into a continuum with child-initiated strategies at one end of the continuum and specific, structured, teacher-directed strategies at the other end. For children with disabilities, the entire range, from child-initiated to adult-controlled, are needed to order that the most appropriate strategies for individual children can be selected. The teacher chooses and implements the amount of structure that is indicated for the child's ability to respond, the seriousness of the impairment, and the rate of progress that has occurred in the past.

One issue concerning inclusion of young children with disabilities in classrooms discussed in Chapter 6 involved differing philosophies between early childhood teachers and early childhood special education teachers. An argument proposed by some is that early childhood educators base curriculum and instruction on child-initiated experiences following Piaget's work, while early childhood special educators follow behavioral strategies based on Skinner's work. The counterargument was made that the perception of early childhood special education as using mostly behaviorist methods was outdated because early childhood special educators actually use a range of strategies with young children with disabilities. Bredekamp (1993) supported that position by stating that early childhood educators in both fields may prefer one or another theory and the instructional strategies that are consistent with that theory.

Wolery (1994b) has demonstrated through his hierarchy of intervention strategies that programs can incorporate a variety of strategies that do not necessarily follow a single theory. In reality, all early childhood educators vary the amount of structure and child-initiated learning experiences, depending upon the objectives of the program and the purposes of activities, as well as the level of self-directed behavior that children with diverse backgrounds bring to the classroom. This is especially true in classrooms where children with disabilities are included with children who have no disabilities. In the section to follow, we will address this type of setting in terms of how developmentally appropriate practices are modified for inclusion classrooms.

Developmentally Appropriate Instructional Strategies

The curriculum models described earlier in the chapter were originally designed for infant and toddler and early childhood intervention programs that served only children with disabilities. The strategies developed for such programs have relevance in intervention programs, including programs that include or integrate children with disabilities into classrooms with children who do not have disabilities. The philosophy of developmentally appropriate practices used increasingly in early childhood programs must also be considered when attempting to design suitable curriculum and instruction for all children included in the classroom. Although there are some differences between recommended practices in early childhood education and early childhood special education (e.g., children with disabilities are served in a wider range of settings), many of the practices are compatible or overlap (McLean & Odom, 1993).

Although children with disabilities can benefit from inclusion in integrated classrooms, participation is not enough. McLean and Odom (1993) propose that children with disabilities still require direct, individualized interventions; in other words, they suggest that the teacher-directed instruction using didactic techniques (i.e., the behavioral approach) must be included in the instructional strategies used with children with disabilities.

How, then, can teachers in early childhood programs ensure that children will get the most fitting intervention strategies within a classroom environment that is more child-initiated? How can the needs of all children be met within a developmentally appropriate environment that supports exploration and learning through interaction with materials and activities?

Wolery (1994c) recommends that instructional needs for children with disabilities be embedded into the environment and routines of the regular early childhood classroom. One strategy recommended is to help children become independent by

Direct, individualized intervention strategies are important in integrated classrooms.

facilitating skills and behaviors that other children are able to use. Second, an integrated approach should be employed by addressing more than one developmental domain at once. Wolery gives the example of activities in learning centers that provide experiences in several domains. Another strategy suggested is that the school day be approached as a whole, with instruction in needed skills interspersed into ongoing activities and routines. Activities and routines can also be adapted by changing materials or children's behaviors to accommodate the needs of the child with disabilities.

Cavallero, Haney, and Cabello (1993) would make changes in the environment, routines, and activities to meet the needs of the child with disabilities. They recommend arranging the environment including materials, activities, and participants to facilitate the child's engagement in activities and interaction with peers. They would structure activities so that a specific activity matches the objectives written for the child in the IEP. Likewise, choices of activities and materials would be guided by adults through visual and behavioral prompting. These authors propose that their approach maintains a developmentally appropriate environment that permits children to play, initiate activities, and interact with peers, but at the same time provides the structured program with specific goals and strategies to facilitate progress and development of children with disabilities.

Inclusion at Adams Hill Elementary School

The prekindergarten and kindergarten teachers at Adams Hill are very proud of the inclusion process that they have implemented at their school. There are two early childhood special education teachers who work with two prekindergarten teachers and two kindergarten teachers. The teachers plan the curriculum together and plan for gradual integration of children with disabilities into the mainstream classroom during the school year based on the individual needs and abilities of the children.

Early in the prekindergarten year the team of teachers consider which children in the special education program are the best candidates for beginning the inclusion process. Children with speech problems and children with behavior disorders are most likely to go to the regular classroom first. At first, they go only for story time and whole-group time. Later, their time is extended on an individual basis, and children with more extensive disabilities are introduced to the classrooms on an individual basis. Some children go only for socialization, while others participate in the instructional program. Children who are included for socialization participate in the regular classroom during center time. Teacher assistants go with the children as needed. The reverse process also occurs, as children from the regular classrooms go for some of their activities in the early childhood special education classrooms.

There are some factors that have made this program a success. The teachers have been able to attend summer training sessions for early childhood inclusion. During their sessions, they have learned how to plan for diversity in their classrooms, how to implement ideas for activities and materials, and how to function as a team. In addition, they have developed their teaming skills by the process of participating in the training program.

The teachers are enthusiastic about the inclusion process. They have a common curriculum developed around themes. They have the same concepts and the same themes in all of the classrooms. In addition, they have developed similar strategies for group management and learning center management. Thus, the children have consistent guidance in all of the classrooms. Curriculum and instruction plans are modified for the children with disabilities. The curriculum might be experienced in the regular classroom or in the special education classroom. If a child is unable to stay in the regular classroom, the same types of activities are occurring in the home classroom and nothing will be missed.

The teachers are also appreciative of some unexpected benefits of inclusion. They are pleased at the sense of belonging and community that has developed among the children. Children without disabilities have developed positive, empathic behaviors and enjoy helping other children whether they have impairments or not. Children from the early childhood special education classrooms have developed an independence that they did not exhibit prior to inclusion. The special education teachers have found that they have higher expectations for their children as they have seen them progress and participate in the regular classroom. The prekindergarten and kindergarten teachers who teach in the regular program have overcome their hesitation and anxiety about having fragile children in their classrooms. In addition, because of the flexibility in moving children back and forth, the teachers do not feel trapped with a child's extreme behavior and know that the child can go back to the home classroom and return when he or she is better able to cope with the environment in the regular classroom.

It is clear in the recent history of inclusion in early childhood programs that there are no clear answers as to how best meet the needs of all children that are included in the program. Just as many curriculum models were developed for the first early intervention programs, early childhood educators in many settings are working to design and implement integrated programs that include instructional strategies that are effective for diverse needs. A repertoire of possibilities for successful practices will emerge over time as programs are expanded and improved.

PLANNING INSTRUCTION FOR CHILDREN AT RISK

The probability or chance that a poor or detrimental outcome might occur by definition defines a condition known as *at risk*. A child at risk for a poor outcome means a child has not yet manifested a developmental delay or behavioral aberration but has a high probability of doing so because of the risk condition or factors (Dunst, 1993, p. 143).

Throughout this text, we have discussed the characteristics and needs of children who are at risk for development and learning. We also reviewed types of risk: these include children with impairments that could lead to disabilities or delay, children who come from culturally diverse families or who are linguistically different, and those who come from families in stress. We need to be aware of the fact that the numbers of children

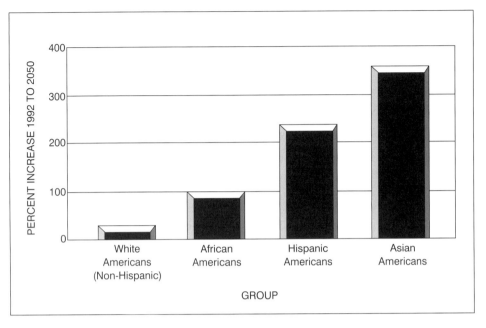

Figure 7–1   Projected Increase of Ethnic Populations
Source: From *U.S. Bureau of Census*, 1992.

from culturally diverse families is rising and will continue to rise at a significant rate in the future. The percentages of Hispanic, African Americans, and Asian Americans are rising faster than white Americans, with Asian Americans the fastest-growing group. Figure 7–1 shows the projected percent of increase between 1992 to 2050.

In Chapter 2, intervention programs for young children who are at risk were identified as including Head Start and other federally funded programs in public schools such as Chapter 1 and bilingual programs. These programs are different from the intervention programs available for infants and young children with disabilities. In Chapter 6, we described how individual plans are designed for young children who have been determined to be eligible for special services in some type of intervention program; and, in the first half of this chapter, we outlined how curriculum and instruction are planned for individual needs as prescribed in an IEP or IFSP. In this part of the chapter, we return to the task of planning curriculum and instruction for children who do not yet have a disability or learning problem, but who might develop a difficulty because of risk factors in their lives. The objective is to identify these children, determine how risk factors might affect them negatively, and plan curriculum and instruction that can have a positive effect to offset the negative influences on their development and learning.

There are many variables that can affect development and learning and put a child at risk for success in school. Dunst (1993, p. 147) has collected a list of variables, the risk factors involved, and opportunity factors that can ameliorate or provide positive conditions for the child. This list is reproduced in Figure 7–2.

Variables	Risk Factors	Opportunity factors
Mother's age	Younger or older than normal childbearing years	Within optimal childbearing years
Parent education	Low educational attainment	High educational attainment
Income	Inadequate income	Adequate income
Occupation status	Low occupation status of head of household	High occupation status for head of household
Socioeconomic status (SES)	Low SES	High SES
Job stability	Repeated job changes or unemployment	Stable job
Pregnancy	Unplanned	Planned
Number of siblings	More than four children	One or two children
Residential stability	Repeated relocations	None or few relocations
Marital status	Absence of spouse or partner	Supportive spouse or partner present
Marital relationship	Conflictive	Harmonious
Marital stability	Repeated changes in a conjugal relationship	Stable conjugal relationship
Child temperament	Avoidant, difficult	Warm, responsive
Infant separation	Prolonged separation in first year	Limited separation in first year
Parental health	Poor physical health	Excellent physical health
Parental mental health	Repeated occurrences of mental health related problem	Stable emotional well-being
Parental self-esteem	Low self-esteem	High self-esteem
Parental locus of control	External	Internal
Parental social skills	Poor	Good
Coping strategies	Reactive	Proactive
Quality of primary caregiver/child interaction	Controlling and emotionally unavailable	Stimulating and warm
Parenting style	Authoritarian/directive	Responsive/facilitative
Toxic substances	High exposure	No exposure
Nutritional intake	Inadequate	Adequate
Accidents	Frequent	Infrequent
Infections/illnesses	Frequent	Infrequent
Alternative caregivers	None	One or more
Presence of extended family	None or few available	Many and supportive
Extrafamily support	Poor/unsupportive	Good/supportive
Life events	Negative life events	Positive life events

Figure 7–2   Possible Risk Factors and Opportunities

Source: From "Implications of Risk and Opportunity Factors for Assessment and Intervention Practices" by C. J. Dunst, 1993, *Topics in Early Childhood Education, 13*, pp. 143–153. Reprinted by permission.

Early childhood programs can also help balance risk factors and produce a more positive outcome. Not included in Dunst's list are cultural and linguistic differences; nevertheless, they too can have a negative effect on the child's later success in school if the teacher and school environment are not responsive to diversity in students. Curriculum and instruction must also address these variables, not only for the children who represent these types of diversity, but also for all children in the early childhood classroom who need to understand how diversity in people enriches our lives.

We are aware, then, of the many factors that can put children at risk for development and learning. Moreover, if there are multiple risk factors, there is increased probability that the child will have difficulties or poor outcomes (Dunst, 1993; Meisels, 1994). On the other hand, if there are multiple opportunities that provide a positive balance in the child's life, the possibility is increased for positive outcomes. Because of the complexity of risk factors that can affect the child, identification and assessment of the child cannot follow the same sequence as for young children with disabilities. Children can be identified as being at risk in several ways.

Some children identified as being at risk could have been screened for intervention services for children with disabilities and not to be found to manifest a disability or significant delay. Although they are not eligible for the intervention program, they do need a program that will address their risk factors so that developmental delay or poor progress in learning will not develop.

Many children are placed into a program designed to prevent negative outcomes in later schooling because of the presence of risk factors described by Dunst in Figure 7–2, particularly if they come from a family with a low income or low socioeconomic status. These children are eligible for services in public preschool intervention programs for children at risk based on income limitations and may or may not be assessed individually before entering a program.

Children who are at risk might also be identified while they are attending a preschool program. Teacher observations of the child's abilities and behaviors may have been followed by assessment procedures to determine if the child had special needs for curriculum and instruction. Language differences, minor speech impairments, inappropriate behaviors, and concerns about nutritional deficits are some of the risk factors that might cause concern about the child and result in curriculum instruction specifically to address that child's needs (Deiner, 1993). (See Figure 10–1 in Chapter 10.)

What kinds of strategies for assessment are most beneficial for use with young children who are at risk? Although they do not undergo the extensive diagnostic testing conducted with children with disabilities, comprehensive information about them is needed if risk factors are to be balanced with positive experiences. In the next section, we will discuss appropriate assessment strategies and how they are linked with curriculum planning and instruction.

Linking Assessment and Curriculum Planning

Assessment information guides curriculum planning for children who are at risk just as it does for all populations of children in early childhood programs. In Chapter 3, vari-

Early childhood programs are planned for children who may be at risk for learning.

ous strategies for appropriate assessment were explained. The nature of assessment for young preschool children was characterized as developmental because information is gathered about progress in motor, social, cognitive, and language development. Observation is a major source of assessment information supported with interviews, performance on developmental tasks provided, portfolio collections, and others. The same types of assessment strategies are used with children in the primary grades, but may also include paper-and-pencil assessments and assessment in content areas. Assessment methods discussed in Chapter 3 apply to the assessment of children at risk.

Assessment information is gathered to make curriculum decisions about each child as follows (Hills, 1992):

> What are this child's strengths, needs, and learning processes?
> How is this child doing?
> How will this child's instruction and guidance be planned?
> What and how can the teacher best communicate with the parents about the status and progress of the child? (p. 45)

These decisions are made for every child in early childhood classrooms; however, they are particularly relevant for children who are at risk. These four questions encapsulate the child's progress toward acquisition of goals and skills. Assessment should include the child's progress as described by Vygotsky's zone of proximal development; that is, what the child cannot do, what the child can do with assistance, and what the child can do alone. This continuum of ability also informs planning for curriculum and instruction (Hills, 1992).

Assessment information for children at risk may also be derived from formal testing. Although there is extensive criticism of the use of standardized tests with young children (Perrone, 1990), such tests are used with young children when they are served in a federal- or state-funded program. Standardized tests generally have poor predictability when used with young children; and it is recommended that they be used only as one of multiple sources of assessment (Meisels, 1994). Nevertheless, selection for programs such as Chapter 1 and bilingual education requires the use of standardized achievement tests. Programs are also required to provide information on effectiveness. Meisels (1994) provided guidelines suitable for assessment of young children who represent diversity or are at risk as follows:

1. Tests, procedures, and processes intended for assessment should be culturally, linguistically, and developmentally sensitive to the child and his or her family.
2. Requirements for norm-referenced measures of such highly inferential constructs such as intelligence or psychomotor competence should meet stringent progressional guidelines for standardization, reliability, and validity. Those administering the test should be well trained.
3. Evaluations of parent-child interaction should be included in developmental assessments. The evaluation process should, whenever possible and appropriate, include observations in the home.
4. Assessors and assessments should actively solicit information about the child from the family, incorporate parent report data into the assessment, and be sensitive to family needs.
5. Assessments should tap multiple sources of information, thus reflecting the complex nature of development and the cumulative nature of early childhood risk.
6. Assessment should focus on those aspects of children's experiences that are central to their development, and should do so, if possible, in a setting that is natural, non-threatening, and familiar to the child and family.
7. Measurement activities should be part of an ongoing, dynamic process taking place over time, with multiple components. (pp. 208–210)

It is clear from Meisels's recommendations that assessment procedures for children at risk are similar to strategies used with children who are not at risk and have much in common with those used with young children who have disabilities.

The initial and ongoing assessment data gathered from all the sources described provide the informational link between assessment and curriculum and instruction.

There are cautions that need to be taken into account in assessing children who are at risk because of cultural, class, or language differences. Some cultural factors can cause differences in how young children learn. Cultural differences can cause teachers to misunderstand young children and misassess their cultural competency (Bowman & Stott, 1994). For example, the assessment of language ability is difficult when children speak a different language or a dialect. When teachers attempt to assess a child who speaks little or no English, it is hard to decide if the child is delayed in understanding concepts because of limited language, immaturity, or socioeconomic problems. Children who speak a dialect are also difficult to understand, and teachers may mistake their linguistic performance as denoting limited cognition (Bowman, 1992; Wolfe, 1992). The implications for cultural and linguistic differences for assessing and planning curriculum and instruction for young children at risk for development and learning are complex. In addition, the socioeconomic and cultural differences between teachers and students may become a problem if teachers use their own background to use assessment results to plan curriculum and instruction. The next section explores how diversity affects development and learning.

Using Assessment to Plan Curriculum and Instruction for Children at Risk

Children who are at risk for development and learning need positive experiences to enhance their potential for success. Their risk factors may be related to cognitive development, social development, language development, and cultural differences. Although physical differences may be present and need to be addressed, in this part of the chapter, we will concentrate on needs for cognitive, language, social, and cultural curriculum and instruction. The significant effect that diversity has on development and learning underlies how curriculum and instruction should be planned for children diverse in language, culture, or class status.

Cognitive Needs of Children at Risk   When young children are assessed for cognitive development, it is frequently found that they are limited in their acquisition of concepts. Children from low socioeconomic homes may come to school with few experiences that prepare them for learning as it is achieved in schools designed for the middle class. The family may not have been able to provide books, take the children to see local museums or on trips, or take advantage of educational events in the community (Davidson & Schniedewind, 1992). For children who are also from a different culture or speak a different language, there is an even wider discrepancy between the home culture and the school culture (Garcia, 1993). In addition, if the parents themselves experienced failure in school, they may feel alienated and have low expectations for their children. They might communicate to their children that school is not important and they do not expect achievement.

Another factor that affects learning in children who are culturally diverse is difference in learning style. Children acquire strategies for thinking and learning from their community, and these strategies may differ from the school culture. For instance, some African American children from poverty homes may have learned to approach a new situation with distrust and caution in their home and community environments and thus may be reluctant to participate in class discussions or respond to questions; moreover, both African American and Mexican American children tend to be field-dependent, intuitive thinkers while schools use teaching methods that reward children who can use field-independent strategies such as analysis and sequencing (Bowman, 1992). However, in spite of these generalizations on learning styles, we need to remember that there are individual differences among children in any population. Instruction should be based on individual rather than perceived group characteristics (Guild, 1994).

Teachers planning cognitive experiences for children at risk for learning need to be aware of the differences that might impede children's successful achievement.

Language Needs of Children at Risk   Children in early childhood programs who have been found to have language limitations are also at risk for learning. The language limitation might be that they speak a language other than English, they speak a dialect, or they have limited ability to use English. Children who speak another language or have limited English proficiency are likely to be served in a bilingual program. Children with dialect differences or who are generally limited in language skills are served in regular classrooms.

Language and culture cannot be separated. For example, the linguistic features of the Hopi language or of Spanish reflect the way those cultures view the world and organize experience. Dialect speakers also reflect the language of their culture. Sensitivity to different ways of thinking, acting, and speaking is essential for teachers working with populations from diverse cultures.

Language development is a slow process. Children who are learning a second language or acquiring Standard English go through similar stages as in acquisition of the first language. Teachers need to understand these developmental stages and build upon them so that the child can develop fluency and vocabulary in English. At the same time, the strategies used to develop English skills should not neglect or demean the child's home language and culture. Valuing the child's home language and culture is essential if positive outcomes are to be accomplished with the child at risk (Byrnes & Cortez, 1992; Wolfe, 1992).

Social Needs of Children at Risk   Children may be at risk for social development as the result of a multiplicity of factors. Children who come from families in stress may present behaviors that affect socialization. The stress can be from numerous sources such as divorce, single-parent homes, poverty, and economic factors. Cultural differences can also have an effect on socialization in the school setting.

The differences in socialization practices in the home and at school make it difficult for many children to make a positive adjustment to the school environment. In low socioeconomic environments in rural settings, children may be socialized to respect others and be interdependent, while in urban settings, children may have socialization experiences that promote competitiveness and reliance on external supports such as social agencies and churches (Garcia, 1993). Cultural differences also result in different socialization practices. Native American cultures promote interdependence and consideration for the needs of the group versus the focus on individual achievement and competition, which is valued in some segments of the American population. Behaviors used to show respect to elders are different between cultural groups (Davidson & Schniedewind, 1992; Guild, 1994; New, 1994). African American children enjoy oral experiences and experiences with physical activity (Guild, 1994).

The teacher's responsibility for positive socialization is to affirm the social characteristics that the child brings from home. It is very important also that the teacher not view socialization from a middle class perspective. The goal for social development in young children is to facilitate positive social interactions in the school setting and to develop every child's self-esteem and a feeling of belonging. At the same time, the teacher needs to facilitate the child's feeling that both the home culture and school culture have value and neither is better than the other. The child needs to learn appropriate school behaviors and social skills; nevertheless, the teacher needs to accept social practices fostered in the home, especially if socialization is culturally or socioeconomically based (Bowman, 1992).

Cultural Needs of Children at Risk   The influence of culture on children who are at risk has been discussed above in relationship to cognitive, language, and social development. The inseparable connection between culture and development has been established. However, it needs to be stressed that cultural difference in itself can cause a child to be at risk. The mismatch between culture of the school and that of the children attending the school can affect school achievement. For example, Native American children are reluctant to participate in teacher-directed instruction, particularly when the teacher calls on individual children for responses. African American children, on the other hand, may respond best in teacher-directed environment (Lubeck, 1994). While the teacher may believe that the children should be self-directed and be able to make choices in the early childhood classroom, the child may feel more comfortable with being told what to do and how to do it (Bowman, 1992).

The perspective of the teacher regarding children who are culturally different affects how curriculum and instruction are designed. There was a time when the perspective of the school was that children who were culturally different were considered deprived or disadvantaged. Teacher expectations from this perspective are that culturally different children are less able to learn and need a lower level of curriculum and instruction. The position taken by some was that culturally different children are biologically inferior.

Children from cultures different from the school culture are at risk. The responsibility is upon the school to bridge the home culture and school culture to ensure that all children succeed. While the school should be sensitive to the differences and diversity that children bring to the school environment, the school must adapt itself to the needs of the children rather than viewing them as lacking in ability, deficient, or disadvantaged. The task of ensuring that all children succeed is complex and difficult; moreover, responses to cultural differences cannot just address group differences. Regardless of the risk factor or factors that may affect the child, planning curriculum and instruction is individual. Stereotyping by culture will not solve the difficulties that the child faces, nor will it result in providing opportunities that the child needs to succeed (Lubeck, 1994; Mallory, 1994).

Planning and Managing Different Approaches to Instruction With Children at Risk

What are the recommended approaches to plan curriculum and instruction for young children who are at risk for development and learning? Understanding diversity and risk factors in young children is one step in planning positive experiences for their educational program. The nature of the diversity and risk factors that affect the child's potential for negative or positive outcomes gives direction for planning the instructional program. The next section discusses approaches to instruction for children who are linguistically and culturally different. The concerns for designing developmentally appropriate practices to include these children with diverse backgrounds will also be analyzed.

Curriculum and Instruction in Bilingual Education   Children who attend school in the United States speak 25 different languages or dialects. Children who speak a language other than English who are enrolled in schools in the United States come from 167 different countries. Although these children have the potential to become **bilingual** and **biliterate**, they are more likely to fail to succeed in school and become dropouts (Bredekamp & Rosegrant, 1992b). Bilingual education programs are provided for young children who speak a language other than English or who have limited use of English when they enter school. Although there is lack of agreement as to the best kind of curriculum and instruction for children who are at risk because of language differences, there are strategies that have been found to be successful.

Bilingual education is defined as instruction in two languages (Wolfe, 1992). Children who are monolingual in a language other than English or have limited facility in English are eligible to be enrolled in bilingual programs. Unfortunately there is disagreement as to the best kind of curriculum and instruction for these children. Two methodologies are currently being practiced in preschools and elementary schools in the United States. One approach is to provide instruction predominantly in English based on the premise that the primary goal is for the child to develop fluency in English. Others propose that instruction for children who speak another language should begin in that language and gradually be replaced with English when the child has developed fluency in English. Proponents of native language instruction suggest that children are able to develop important social and cognitive foundations that promote successful learning. Those who support English as the language of instruction believe that the earlier the child is exposed to English, the greater will be the child's facility in English (Garcia, 1993; Wolfe, 1992).

The debate over methodology has an extensive history and is not likely to be resolved in the near future. In the meantime, some suggestions as to how to plan effective curriculum and instruction to meet language and learning needs can be made. We have discussed previously that language and culture are interrelated; moreover, socialization is part of the learning process. Therefore, it is proposed that curriculum and instruction should be both socioculturally and linguistically meaningful. That is, learning for linguistically and culturally diverse children should occur in a milieu that is meaningful for them. Curriculum and instruction should be responsive to the needs of this population of learners (Byrnes & Cortez, 1992; Garcia, 1993). Teachers need to use strategies that take into account the cognitive, cultural, and social dimensions of learning. This means that the classroom environment, learning experiences, and assessment will reflect knowledge of how linguistically different children acquire knowledge and how they can demonstrate understanding of that knowledge. The important point is that the teacher view the child as competent rather than underprepared and use teaching strategies that complement the child's method of displaying that competence.

For classrooms that have speakers of more than two languages, multicultural education is the mode for delivery of curriculum and instruction. In such classrooms, bilingual education usually is not a possibility, and instruction in the home or native language cannot be implemented. In the case of multilinguistic classes, the teacher needs to understand how children acquire a second language and prepare instructional experiences to reflect stages in second language development (Wolfe, 1992).

Children who are native speakers of another language but have some use of English are described as **Limited English Proficient (LEP).** In some schools, these children are served in bilingual education programs. However, in classrooms where a bilingual teacher is not available or the philosophy of immersion in English predominates, teaching and learning are done in English. There are strategies that teachers can use to minimize difficulties children may have in simultaneously acquiring English and learning new information. Among methods that are recommended are the use of teacher-directed activities so that English can be modeled for the children and consistency in daily routines and patterns so that children can match language with activities. The teacher should encourage participation in class discussions and make sure that activities match the child's language and cognitive abilities. Whenever possible, the teacher should supplement learning resources with native language materials and become knowledgeable about cultural differences that can affect the child's success in the classroom (Byrnes & Cortez, 1992). The teacher needs to be alert to what children do and do not understand and what kinds of visual and verbal clues they need to participate in class activities (Okagaki & Sternberg, 1994).

Finally, Garcia (1993) proposes some principles for curriculum and instruction for children who are linguistically and culturally diverse. He recommends the following:

1. Any curriculum, especially one for "diverse" children, must address all categories of learning goals.
2. The more "diverse" the children are linguistically and culturally, the more content must be related to the child's own environment and experience.
3. The more "diverse" the children are, the more important it is for content, knowledge, and skills to have horizontal relevance. Vertical relevance is preparation for the next stage of life. Horizontal relevance means that the knowledge and skills are relevant to the child's everyday life.
4. The more "diverse" the children are, the more the curriculum should address learning through active endeavors rather than passive ones.
5. The more "diverse" the children are, the more important it is for the curriculum to offer opportunities to apply what they are learning in a meaningful context.
6. The more "diverse" the children are, the more likely it is that excessive "skill" practice and drills will endanger the dispositions to use them.
7. In general, the more the curriculum emphasizes performance goals, the more likely it is that children will distance themselves from the school. Performance goals mean the pressure to get the right answer, as opposed to learning goals that emphasize how much one can learn.
8. The more "diverse" the children are, the larger the proportion of time that should be spent on informal activities, particularly group work on projects.

9. The more "diverse" the children are, the more content integrated the curriculum should be. Children should also have opportunities to study a topic in depth, to apply all kinds of skills they have acquired.

10. The more "diverse" the children are, the larger the variety of instructional strategies that should be used. (pp. 381–382)

Integrating Children and Curriculum at Emma Frey Elementary School

The children who attend Emma Frey Elementary School on the near west side of San Antonio are 98 percent Hispanic. The large majority of these children are in the "at risk" category, and the school is designated as a Chapter 1 school. There are bilingual classrooms at every grade level. They serve children whose language differences range from monolingual (knowing only Spanish), to children who are in the LEP category (that is, with limited proficiency in English), to children who are about ready to transition into an English-only classroom. Children in the bilingual classrooms must be taught by a certified bilingual teacher and generally do not interact with children who are not in the bilingual program.

First grade teachers at Emma Frey plan integrated, thematic curriculum and instruction that is implemented for a block of time in the afternoons. The team identifies curriculum units and plans the activities for a two-week period to accommodate the range of abilities and language proficiency in their students. With the thematic curriculum, teachers select among the possibilities for activities that they would like to have in their classroom. Each teacher on the team might have a different array of unit activities. In an effort for the children to experience different teachers and different children, the children are assigned to a teacher on the team for curriculum activities relating to the theme. Each time a new theme is initiated, the children are redistributed among the classrooms.

Ordinarily, children in the bilingual program would not be able to engage in activities in different classrooms. To solve this problem, the bilingual teachers also mix their children into as many groups as there are bilingual classrooms and the children are able to experience different children and teachers for each unit. The teachers have found that the children enjoy the opportunity to work in another environment from their home room and like exchanging information about the unit activities they conducted with their homeroom classmates, who had different opportunities in other first grade classrooms. The bilingual children especially benefit because they work with children with different language ability levels.

Antibias Curriculum   The antibias curriculum is another approach to meeting the needs of children who are at risk for development and learning because of cultural differences. The antibias curriculum is not just targeted for children who are at risk, but is proposed for all young children, regardless of their background and culture. An antibias curriculum is needed because young children learn prejudice at an early age and need to learn about racial and ethnic differences so that appropriate attitudes can develop (Byrnes, 1992). Antibias, multicultural curriculum is intended to create a nurturing environment for all children and to help children to appreciate differences in people (Derman-Sparks, 1992).

The classroom environment can be planned to facilitate respect and appreciation for differences. Cooperative learning groups where children work together to achieve a common goal permit children of different cultures and abilities to learn about each other in a positive way. Activities that promote self-esteem for all children likewise promote understanding rather than prejudice. Activities that help children understand and respect each other promote empathy and reduce prejudice (Byrnes, 1992).

Derman-Sparks (1992) proposes the following objectives for an antibias, multicultural curriculum:

1. To foster each child's construction of a knowledgeable, confident self-identity
2. To foster each child's comfortable, empathetic interaction with diversity among people
3. To foster each child's critical thinking about bias
4. To foster each child's ability to stand up for herself or himself and for others in the face of bias (pp. 118-121)

Derman-Sparks further recommends that the curriculum be relevant to the diversity reflected in each classroom. Curriculum content should be matched to each child and the child's cultural background. Multicultural curriculum must be adapted to the cultural and individual variations of the group of children.

Children at Risk and Developmentally Appropriate Practices   Developmentally appropriate practices have been proposed as the basis for quality programming for young children. In other chapters in this text, developmentally appropriate practices have been the foundation for assessment and for curriculum and instruction for young children. Discussions of programs for children with disabilities and at differing developmental levels have had the premise that the approach of developmentally appropriate practices is suitable for all young children, especially when children of all backgrounds and abilities are served in an integrated classroom. The principles recommended by Garcia for bilingual education programs above are congruent with developmentally appropriate practices. In spite of the widespread support of the developmental approach by early childhood educators concerned with diverse populations of young children, there are concerns about the applicability of developmentally appropriate practices with young children who are at risk for development and learning.

One concern is that developmentally appropriate practices are designed to teach dominant cultural practices and are problematic for populations that are at risk or that are culturally different. Also the guidelines favor particular practices and propose that these are the best practices for all children (Lubeck, 1994). As a result, developmentally appropriate practices are not broad enough to address the problems faced by culturally diverse children. Mallory (1994) echoed this concern when he proposed that we don't know what works best for all children. There are more questions than answers in what is most effective for young children who are at risk. We still are seeking effective intervention strategies for young children who are at risk for development and learning.

One difficulty with guidelines associated with developmentally appropriate practices is a narrow perspective of what development is. The norms reflected in developmentally appropriate practices do not take into account the variations in development represented by children who have disabilities or by children who are diverse culturally and linguistically. Cross-cultural approaches supported by research need to be utilized when determining educational goals and practices (New, 1994). Williams (1994) proposed that the guidelines for developmental appropriateness be described as age appropriate and individually appropriate. Williams suggests that family background, and children's cultural, religious, and socioeconomic experience also inform what is individually appropriate for young children. Differences in value systems can be a major issue when programs are being developed for some populations of young children.

Efforts are being made to make the developmentally appropriate practices relevant for all young children. The concept of age appropriate and individually appropriate is being expanded to incorporate children with special abilities and with disabilities (Winter, 1994–1995). The needs of culturally diverse children are being addressed in discussions about culturally appropriate programs for minority children and children who speak other languages (Bredekamp & Rosegrant, 1992a). Indeed, Bowman (1992) proposed that developmentally appropriate programs should meet the expectations of different cultures and groups. She proposed additional guidelines for developmentally appropriate practices:

1. Teachers need to know more about the relationship of child development and culture.
2. It is essential to teach teachers not to value some ways of achieving developmental milestones over others, since young children are particularly sensitive to how adults value them and are vulnerable to lowed self-esteem and self-confidence.
3. Learning mediated by teachers who are personally important is more likely to stick than is learning when the adult is socially distant.
4. The assessment of learning outcomes presents a formidable problem for teachers of children outside the economic and cultural mainstream.
5. Schools and centers need people who can mediate between cultures.
6. School learning is most likely to occur when family values reinforce school expectations. (pp. 135–136)

Designing curriculum and instruction in early childhood classrooms to address all types of diversity is a continuing challenge. Teachers of young children now have students with disabilities or who are at risk to develop disabilities. The students represent diversity of income, culture, language, and family structures. Implementing appropriate assessment and curriculum and instruction strategies requires knowledge about the children, their needs, and their potential. In addition, the teacher must be able to evaluate children's progress throughout the year and their accomplishments and achievement at the end of the program year. The program itself must be evaluated when children with disabilities or children at risk are receiving funded services as part of the classroom population. As a final step in this chapter, we will discuss how the assessment and evaluation process is conducted for individual children and for the program.

EVALUATING CURRICULUM AND INSTRUCTION FOR CHILDREN WITH SPECIAL NEEDS AND AT RISK

Continuing the Assessment-Instruction Link

Ongoing monitoring of progress is an essential part of intervention programs for young children with disabilities or who are at risk for successful school achievement. For infants, toddlers, and young children who have disabilities, assessment is specific to the goals and objectives that are written into their IFSP or IEP. The purpose of the monitoring process is to ascertain whether the objectives and goals specified in their plan are being acquired. If they are not, changes need to be made in the intervention curriculum. Collection and recording of progress are ongoing. It can occur daily, weekly, and on a more long-term basis. Parents, teachers, and other adults engaged in working with the child share monitoring and assessment information on a regular basis. Activities are modified when indicated by the monitoring process (Wolery, 1994c).

Assessment strategies discussed in other contexts in this text are appropriate for the monitoring process. Anecdotal records obtained through observation, developmental checklists and rating scales, documentation of performance, and portfolio materials can be used to monitor progress. Widerstrom, Mowder, and Sandall (1991) recommend that audiotapes and videotapes be used to monitor the progress of infants and toddlers. These assessment resources can be used to record and interpret changes in the child's abilities as a result of intervention. The goal of monitoring is to maintain the ongoing relationship or link between assessment and intervention. Intervention plans, activities, and assessment continue in a cyclical manner to be responsive to the child's needs and gains in development and skills.

Although children who are at risk may not have a written plan, monitoring of their progress is related to the factors that cause them to be at risk—whether they relate to motor, social, language, or cognitive development. For example, children in a bilingual program where the native language is used for initial instruction will be monitored for concept development in the first language, while at the same time acquisition of English is also assessed frequently. With children who are linguistically or culturally different, assessment should be conducted with recognition of their individual differences, but not with lowered expectations for their progress and achievement (Howe, 1994). Differences in styles and rates of learning are considered, as well as whether the child has been given the time and appropriate opportunities to acquire the desired development and learning (Wolfe, 1992).

The guidelines for appropriate assessment of young children are summarized in a position statement by the National Association for the Education of Young Children and the National Association of Early Childhood Specialists in State Departments of Education adopted in 1990. Assessment should meet the needs of all young children, including children with individual diversity as follows: "Assessment recognizes individual diversity of learners and allows for differences in styles and rates of learning. Assessment takes into consideration children's ability in English, their stage of language acquisition, and whether they have been given the time and opportunity to develop proficiency in their native language as well as in English" (National Association for the Education of Young Children and National Association of Early Childhood Specialists in State Departments of Education, 1991).

Evaluating Intervention Programs for Children With Disabilities

Program evaluation can refer to the overall evaluation of a single child's intervention program or evaluation of a program that serves a group of children with disabilities. The progress of an individual is part of the evaluation of any program, as are the achievement of goals and objectives for each child and the group as a whole. Other factors of program effectiveness that can be evaluated are the curriculum, parental satisfaction with the program, staff attitudes, and the extent to which the program met community needs (Benner, 1992).

Since the child's progress is a key indicator of program success, program evaluation attempts to determine what features of a program are successful in assisting the child's development. As we have discussed earlier, intervention programs vary widely in theory, philosophy, and pedagogy. Because of these variations, different methods are used to evaluate program effectiveness. Benner (1992) described some factors that are addressed in research about program effectiveness: these include the length of the intervention, the type of intervention used, home-based programs versus center-based programs, levels of severity of disabilities in the children served, characteristics of the child, the family, and provision of support services.

Evaluating Programs for Children at Risk

Like intervention programs for children with disabilities, there are wide variations in programs for children who are at risk for development and learning because of environmental factors, language differences, or cultural differences. The type of evaluation to be conducted depends upon the nature of the program and the source of its funding.

Programs that serve children who are at risk because of socioeconomic or language differences, such as Head Start, Even Start, bilingual education, and public preschool programs, are likely to have federal and state funding. These programs observe government guidelines and requirements that spell out how program effectiveness is determined. One indicator of program success is always if the children made gains in achieving program goals for their development. Frequently standardized tests are one method used to determine program accountability for the child's progress. In addition, evaluation is conducted on appropriate use of the funds that were budgeted, effectiveness for training provided for teachers, success of parent involvement, and success in reaching all types of program goals. In the case of preschool programs seeking to prevent cognitive and language delay, evaluation will be conducted to assess children's progress in those two areas. In the case of bilingual programs, progress in native and English language development is evaluated, as well as the child's progress in other areas of development. The primary focus, however, is on language and cognitive development.

⇒ SUMMARY

In this chapter, we have discussed how curriculum and instruction are designed for young children with disabilities or who are at risk for success in school because of possibilities of developing disabilities. Assessment information guides the construction of learning experiences intended to improve the child's potential for development and learning.

Children who have been identified as having disabilities, determined to be eligible for special services, and have an IEP or IFSP have a prescriptive instructional plan based on specific goals and objectives. There are various models available to teachers, each with teaching strategies consistent with the theoretical base of the model. In addition, teachers can develop their own program, perhaps drawing from commercial programs, but always with the option of designing and constructing their own intervention strategies that are suited to the needs of individual children.

Children who are at risk for developing disabilities or who are at risk because of cultural or linguistic diversity also need intervention services within an early childhood program. These children might be enrolled in a federally funded program such as Head Start, or they might be in a public school program designed for children who are at risk because they need language and cognitive experiences prior to entry into the primary grades. Bilingual programs are one example of this type of preschool program; however, Chapter 1 and other federally and state-funded programs serve children that fit into this category.

Curriculum and instruction for children at risk need to take into account differences in learning styles from one culture to another. The language and culture of the home are important, and services provided should include input and participation of the family, parenting styles, and careful attention to how the child perceives and functions in the school environment.

Ongoing assessment and record keeping are essential elements of the instructional plans for both children with disabilities and children who are at risk for development and learning. Frequent monitoring of the child's progress and new information about the child help to keep curriculum and instruction strategies appropriate and help the teacher make adjustments in the educational program based on the information gathered from current assessments.

Although children with disabilities and children who are at risk need attention to individual needs when curriculum and instruction is designed, the goal is to serve these children in classrooms where they would have been placed if there were no problems or potentials for problems developing. Integration of children with wide ranges of diversity makes the teacher's planning more complex. In addition, because learning styles and rates are so varied, teachers must consider wide variations in developmental levels when planning activities for the children. In the next four chapters, we will discuss how curriculum and instruction is planned for early childhood programs and how it is modified to suit the needs of children with diversities. This is done in the context of specific areas of development—cognitive, language, social, and physical—in an integrated setting.

❖ STUDY QUESTIONS

1. Why does program planning for intervention services for infants and toddlers have to be based on individual schedules?
2. Why are self-help skills significant sources of curriculum and instruction for infants and young children?
3. Describe how curriculum and instruction for children with disabilities in preschool programs can use information from very early intervention programs to plan current interventions.
4. How can parents help design instructional strategies for children with disabilities in preschool and primary classrooms?
5. There are published curriculums available to use with young children with disabilities. From your reading, what do you believe can be the most effective use of these curriculums?
6. Explain the differences between the functional and adaptive models of early intervention and models using the behavioral approach.
7. How does the teacher of children with disabilities make decisions as to the amount of structure that will be present in curriculum and instruction for individual children? Explain some levels of structure.
8. Explain the issues between early childhood educators and early childhood special educators that must be addressed in integrated classrooms. How can they be resolved?
9. Why is it more difficult or complex to determine the effects of risk factors on children as compared with the effects of disabilities?
10. What kinds of assessment information is useful when planning programs for children at risk who are diverse culturally and linguistically?
11. Why is it easy to misunderstand or make a mistake when interpreting assessment data for children who are culturally or linguistically diverse?
12. Why are language, cognitive, and social development particularly significant for young children who are at risk for successful development and learning?

13. Why do we need to understand learning style in culturally diverse children?
14. What is the difference between implementing antibias curriculum in early childhood classrooms and meeting the needs of culturally diverse children?
15. Explain why there are no clear recommendations as to how curriculum and instruction should be designed for young children in bilingual programs.
16. How are bilingual and multicultural education different?
17. How effectively can developmentally appropriate practices be included in programs for bilingual children?
18. Explain some of the concerns about developmentally appropriate practices and curriculum and instruction for children who are at risk because of cultural differences.
19. Why is ongoing assessment and planning needed throughout the year in early childhood intervention programs?
20. Why should teachers be constantly alert to changing instructional plans for young children with disabilities or who are at risk?

⇗ KEY TERMS

bilingual

biliterate

cognitive impairment

communication impairment

Limited English Proficient (LEP)

motor impairment

⇗ SUGGESTED ACTIVITIES

1. Locate and read three current articles with topics related to instruction of bilingual children, children who are culturally diverse, or children with disabilities in early childhood programs. Write a brief paper on current trends in instruction as reported in the articles.
2. Visit a bilingual classroom and a classroom for children who are not served in a bilingual program in the same grade in the same elementary school. Observe how each addresses cultural diversity in visual information in the classroom, curriculum activities, and materials.

 8

Cognitive Development

→ Chapter Objectives

As a result of reading this chapter, you will be able to

1. Describe current trends in curriculum development
2. Define characteristics of a developmental curriculum
3. Explain the theories that underlie understanding of cognitive development and learning
4. Explain cognitive development and its stages
5. Define the teacher's roles in planning instruction for cognitive development
6. Explain how young children acquire concepts in mathematics and science
7. Describe how to organize and design curriculum for cognitive development
8. Describe how to develop assessment strategies for cognitive development
9. Describe how to adapt instruction and assessment in cognitive development for children with disabilities
10. Explain how to evaluate the curriculum for cognitive development

In this and the following three chapters, we will be discussing curriculum and assessment in programs that serve children from ages three to eight: preschool programs for three-, four- and five-year-olds and primary programs for six- to eight-year-olds. In this chapter, we will address cognitive development. Chapters 9, 10, and 11 address language development, social development, and physical development respectively. In this series of chapters, curriculum and assessment are approached from a child development perspective. This means that the curriculum is designed based on knowledge of child development in the early childhood years, rather than from a subject or content area point of view. However, the relationship between development and curriculum content will be described. The emphasis upon the developmental nature of curriculum arises from the importance of child development in preschool programs and its continuing significance in the elementary school, particularly in the primary grades.

Earlier chapters contained discussions about curriculum that is appropriate for the developmental levels of young children. In Chapter 7, we discussed how classrooms based on a developmental approach modify curriculum and instruction to include strategies needed by children with disabilities. Current efforts to broaden the under-standing of developmentally appropriate practices for children with diversity in cul-ture, language, and socioeconomic status were also described. In this chapter, we again add to discussion of how curriculum in early childhood is based on young chil-dren's development, specifically treating curriculum for cognitive development. Theo-ries of cognitive development will be examined, as well as the work of Jean Piaget and Lev Vygotsky as primary theorists that guide the efforts of early childhood educa-tors to provide quality programs for young children.

THE DEVELOPMENTAL BASIS OF CURRICULUM

Understanding Developmental Curriculum

In recent decades, the lines between different types of early childhood programs have become blurred as programs extend and broaden their services to young children. Child care centers have included quality educational programming, while public schools have extended their programs to include younger preschool children, young children with disabilities, and child care services before and after school. In an effort to provide guidance for different settings that serve preschool children, position state-ments and accreditation standards have been developed to describe quality programs for children in the early childhood years from birth to age eight (Bredekamp, 1987; National Association for the Education of Young Children, 1984, 1991; National Asso-ciation of Early Childhood Specialists in State Departments of Education, 1987).

The effort to improve early childhood programs of all types coincided with a national trend in public schools to implement formal, academic instruction with young children. This was described by Shepard and Smith (1988) as downward esca-lation of the curriculum. The efforts in public education to upgrade curriculum and instruction had negative side effects, which included an increase in standardized test-ing, retention, and placement in pre–first grade classrooms. The response to these trends was a major effort to reinstitute curriculum that was appropriate for the devel-opment of young children. The term *developmentally appropriate practice* became the popular descriptor to define quality curriculum based on knowledge of child development in the early childhood years (Bredekamp, 1987). Since the first position statements and guidelines were introduced, public schools and other early childhood settings have become more aware of the significance for using child development as the basis for educational practices implemented with young children; and, as we learned in Chapter 7, this movement has also affected programs for young children with disabilities and those who are at risk for achievement.

Since the late 1980s, there has been an abundant amount of information pub-lished focusing on a developmentally based curriculum for early childhood programs. Although early childhood specialists have a long history of supporting curriculum based on knowledge of child development (Wortham, 1992), the new emphasis has been to counter a trend toward teaching narrowly defined skills, especially in kindergarten and the primary grades. As discussion and efforts have continued to encourage the use of developmentally appropriate practices, textbooks, bulletins, and other published resources have become available for practitioners to use in their own programs. At the same time, clarification about the intent and nature of developmental curriculum have become necessary, particularly regarding the relationship between development and curriculum and assessment (Bredekamp & Rosegrant, 1992b). The inclusion of children with disabilities and the increase in the diversity of children in early childhood programs discussed in Chapters 6 and 7 have also brought new dimensions to the importance of understanding individual development and the resulting implications for early childhood curriculum and instruction. A program that is developmentally based considers individual variations in development and experiences that young children can bring to the early childhood program.

Characteristics of a Developmental Curriculum

How then do we describe a curriculum for preschool children that is developmental? How can theories of development and learning be translated into a curriculum that is appropriate for the young children in a specific classroom in an early childhood center located in a particular area of the country? What characteristics would developmental curriculum have for all early childhood programs, and what characteristics would be unique for each group of children?

First, the developmental curriculum includes all categories of development: cognitive, language, social, and physical. Typically, much more attention is given to cognitive development—and more specifically to cognitive and language development—than to social and physical development. The curriculum should address the developmental abilities and needs of all facets of child development.

Second, curriculum should be specific to the age of the children. Developmentally appropriate curriculum has been described for the entire range of early childhood that includes children from birth to age eight (Bredekamp, 1987). Within a particular classroom or program, developmental curriculum is designed for the age range enrolled in the program. Thus, a curriculum for three- and four-year-old children will reflect different developmental ranges from those in a program for infants and toddlers and those in programs for six- and seven-year-olds. However, whatever the age of the children, individual variation in development implies that every classroom—no matter what age is present—should offer a range of experiences to accommodate differences among the children.

Third, to extend the point made above, the developmental curriculum should be individually appropriate. Children come from different cultures; they come from families that have diverse lifestyles and economic resources. Each child enters school bringing the unique combinations of experiences that he or she encountered in the world. The developmental curriculum designed for a particular class of children complements the backgrounds of the children and takes into account variations in individual children (Bredekamp & Rosegrant, 1992a).

Fourth, the developmental curriculum is group appropriate. Not all classrooms will reflect the same combination of culture and experiential background. Children from the inner city in New York City are very different from children in Salinas, California, even if they share a similar cultural heritage. Children attending a preschool in a wealthy suburb of Dallas, Texas, will have different cultural experiences from children in Ames, Iowa. The point is that the developmental curriculum should address the unique group characteristics represented in a classroom, as well as the uniqueness of the individuals who make up the class.

In the rest of this chapter, the nature of cognitive development and how curriculum and assessment for cognitive development are designed and implemented with young children are examined.

The Nature of Cognitive Development

As we begin the discussion of the curriculum for cognitive development, we will first discuss in more depth how children acquire knowledge and how that process influences instructional practices in the preschool. To accomplish this, we must review the theories of development and learning that inform curriculum practices for young children.

Understanding Cognitive Development

The ability to think is a vehicle by which the young child learns. The acquisition of concepts is the process through which the child uses thinking to expand his or her knowledge of the world. The changes in knowledge and thinking skills and the way they are organized and used in dealing with problems explain cognitive development (Copple, DeLisi, & Sigel, 1982).

Piaget's theory of learning (1952) is divided into two components, **stage dependent** and **stage independent**. In the stage-dependent component, the growth of intelligence from birth through adolescence evolves through a series of three periods and many subperiods. The first period, the sensorimotor stage with its six substages, lasts from birth to approximately eighteen months. During this period, the infant and toddler uses his or her senses and physical actions to learn about the world.

In the second stage, the concrete operations period lasting from about age two to approximately age eleven, the child develops through two subperiods, the preoperational subperiod and the concrete operations subperiod. The preoperational subperiod (about age two to age seven) is of interest because it generally parallels the years of early childhood. During this period, children judge physical characteristics by appearances. That is, they are controlled by their perceptions of physical characteristics. They do not possess the concept of conservation: that the amount or a quantity of a materials stays the same even when the appearance is altered. Likewise, the preoperational child cannot think simultaneously about two physical dimensions. When two sticks of equal length are arranged in a nonparallel position, the child will focus on the position rather than on the length of the sticks and will think that one is longer than the other. The child in the preoperational subperiod is egocentric and therefore unable to appreciate the viewpoint of others or understand causality. Finally, preoperational children cannot understand the relationship between a whole and its parts. They can only think about one characteristic at a time (Sharp, 1969). Piaget divided the preoperational stage into the egocentric period (two to four years) and the intuitive phase (four to seven years).

In the intuitive phase, the child can engage in simple classifying. Reversibility and conservation are not yet achieved because the child centers or focuses on one aspect of a problem at a time. Reversibility means the child understands that what is assembled or arranged can be disassembled or rearranged, while conservation means the child is able to demonstrate an understanding of the constancy of matter when the shape or location of an object is changed. For example, if the child has not achieved reversibility, he or she does not understand that if two numbers such as 3 and 2 are added together to get a total of 5, then 3 can be subtracted to get 2 (Etaugh & Rathus, 1995). The child who has achieved conservation understands that changing the shape of a ball of clay does not change the amount. The preoperational child can, however, discriminate by size. Although the child cannot yet conserve, he or she does understand seriation—where objects are placed in a sequence by some dimension such as tall to short or big to little. The ability to make one-to-one correspondence also develops during this period.

The preoperational child develops concepts through personal action on, interaction with, and reaction to objects, people, events, and ideas; that is, the child is an active learner (Hohmann, Banet, & Weikart, 1979). Further, the child is motivated to learn and understand; intrinsic motivation drives the child to initiate learning. Because the child finds completely familiar events to be uninteresting, children are most likely to learn best when confronted with moderately novel events (Hunt, 1965).

The stage-independent component of Piaget's theory is concerned with the process involved in the child's learning. According to Piaget, intelligence is dependent on adaptive behavior. When encountering new information, the child adapts to the information using **assimilation** and **accommodation**. In assimilation, the child integrates the new information with existing information. Accommodation involves adapting the existing information to include the new input. The mental structure or schema has changed or expanded to incorporate the new information.

The crucial implication of Piaget's theory for early childhood educators is the child's style or mode of learning in the preoperational period. During this period, the child is using real experiences with objects or events to internalize and process the learning of concepts.

There are other important points about Piaget's theory that teachers of young children need to remember. One is that the child does not leave one stage and enter another at a single point in time. The progress is gradual, with the child acquiring characteristics of a new stage at an uneven rate. Some characteristics are acquired before others. More important, since the child develops at his or her own rate, new stages cannot be taught by adults. Children who are provided with stimulating experiences proceed through the stages more rapidly; however, children cannot be pushed into new stages as a result of instruction.

Lev Vygotsky (1978), a Russian contemporary of Piaget, provides further insights into the nature of the acquisition of knowledge. He proposed that the development of higher-order mental functions has its origin in social interactions and that it then is internalized. Vygotsky, like Piaget, included the role of play in intellectual development and, in fact, believed that play was a primary source of development. He perceived teachers and adults as mediators in helping and supporting learners as they attempt to understand the world. The mediating adult assists the process of cognitive development as the child gradually constructs knowledge. Further, he differentiated between spontaneous concepts and school-learned concepts. The child learns some concepts from direct experience without instruction. Other concepts are learned in school and represent a body of knowledge from past generations; this type of knowledge cannot be acquired from individual experience but requires the social context of the school and instruction from the teacher (Strauss, 1987).

Vygotsky used the term **zone of proximal development** to further explain the role of the adult and social interaction in learning. Some information is learned from adults, but more important, the adult provides a support system, or scaffolding, to guide the child's intellectual development. The adult provides assistance to the child to enable him or her to progress to higher levels of functioning. The child enters a zone of proximal development where there is a difference between what the child can understand and demonstrate with assistance and what the child can do alone. The social interaction with teacher and peers allows the child to test mental hypotheses against the thinking of other people, while adult support furthers the child's thinking to an independent level (National Association for the Education of Young Children and National Association of Early Childhood Specialists in State Departments of Education, 1991). Hills (1992) further explains the process:

> Emerging abilities are demonstrated first in an interpersonal context and later independently, according to Vygotsky. Within the boundaries of the zone of proximal development ... , the child can demonstrate abilities with varying amounts of aid. Observing and supporting the child, the teacher integrates instruction and assessment, all the while coming to understand the child's thinking processes more fully. (p. 45)

In their descriptions of cognitive development in preschool children, Piaget and Vygotsky stress the internal nature of learning. Piaget described the developmental nature and stages of learning. Vygotsky added the importance of the social context of peers and adults in mediating and supporting the child's learning. The process of cognitive development can be summarized as follows:

1. Cognitive development is a gradual process that results from the child's interaction with the environment.
2. Children use different levels of understanding at different ages to make sense of the environment or reconstruct knowledge.

The teacher uses a variety of roles to nurture cognitive development.

3. Piaget explained the different levels in terms of stages of cognitive development. The preschool child is in the preoperational stage of development.
4. The process of acquisition of knowledge is the same for different stages of development. The child uses assimilation and accommodation to internalize new information with existing information.
5. Piaget proposed that children learn best when they encounter moderately novel information rather than information that is too familiar or too difficult to incorporate with existing knowledge.
6. Vygotsky proposed that acquisition of knowledge is the result of both direct experience and instruction. Some learning results from the child's encounter with and reaction to experiences. Other knowledge is school-related and requires a social context and an active instructional role on the part of the teacher and peers.

Knowledge of cognitive development in young children forms the foundation for planning curriculum and instruction in preschool and kindergarten classrooms. Once educators understand the nature of development and its implications for program planning, steps can be taken to apply understanding of cognitive development to plan specific strategies and experiences for young children in their particular setting. In the following section, we will discuss the planning process, including the teacher's role, more specific information on how young children learn concepts, how curriculum can be organized, and how to plan and implement curriculum and instruction for all young children, including those with diverse needs and from diverse backgrounds.

PLANNING INSTRUCTION FOR COGNITIVE DEVELOPMENT

Understanding the Teacher's Role

If we understand how young children develop and learn, we perceive that the teacher has various roles. The teacher sets the ambience and tone of the program by designing and organizing the indoor and outdoor environments. Another role is to orient the children as to how to live and learn productively in the environment that has been prepared.

The teacher's role is expanded as the learning program is designed and implemented. Some of the roles are directive, with the teacher using specific behaviors to instruct and guide children during the school day. Other roles are more indirect when the teacher functions as an observer or encourager of children's activities and behaviors. These various roles can be categorized as the teacher as facilitator, the teacher as supporter, and the teacher as instructor.

The Teacher as Facilitator   The role of facilitator evolves as the teacher responds to the needs of children as a group and as individuals. Learning is facilitated when the teachers prepare materials and activities for learning areas in the classroom and outdoors. Teachers function as facilitators when they observe play and work activities and extend them through verbal interaction with children and provision of additional materials to support play themes. Teachers facilitate social development when they provide assistance in clarifying how children can work out social interactions that threaten to become hostile or inappropriate. Whenever the teacher serves a mediating role between children, children and the environment, and children and learning activities in a responsive or indirect manner, the teacher is filling the role of facilitator.

The Teacher as Supporter   The teacher is also responding to children's needs in the role of supporter. Using knowledge of children's developmental differences and individual needs and interests, the teacher supports the individual child's efforts to engage in program activities. The child who is having difficulty pouring juice into a cup can be supported through verbal encouragement and clues on how to hold the pitcher to control the flow of liquid. Likewise, the child who is learning to count can be supported with the teacher's help when the order of numbers becomes difficult. The child who is having difficulty mastering bouncing a ball can be supported when the teacher bounces the ball back and forth to the child. The teacher is alert to ongoing opportunities to provide support when it is needed and to stand back and let the child proceed alone when there is evidence that the child can handle the situation independently.

The Teacher as Instructor   It is important for the teacher to understand when a nondirective role is appropriate to permit the young child to take the lead in conducting an activity and when it is necessary to take the leadership in directive behavior. Teachers are generally more familiar with directive roles; however, in the classroom that follows the theories of Piaget and Vygotsky, a direct role is used only when direct teaching is indicated, and indirect behaviors are frequently used to guide children in their own learning efforts. For example, teachers often model appropriate language and behavior. They are instructing indirectly as they demonstrate behaviors children should emulate. The teacher serves as instructor when conducting small-group instruction activities, large-group instruction, and when teaching an individual child a specific behavior or skill. Actually, the teacher is serving as instructor in every role and behavior, but in this context, the teacher is conducting an activity that has been planned for direct instruction and is intentionally expecting the children to attend to the lesson.

The teacher performs all three roles in the area of cognitive development. Of course, children must develop their own process to develop concepts; nevertheless, the teacher uses all available roles to support and further cognitive development. Rosegrant and Bredekamp (1992) describe the alternating teacher roles in curriculum planning and implementation as "orchestrating": "The teacher coordinates and facilitates numerous activities: she moves around the environment to ensure appropriate use of materials and objects, monitors social and cognitive needs of children, assists when needed, and encourages children's efforts" (p. 82).

Understanding How Young Children Learn

As previously stated, the ability to think is a vehicle by which the young child learns. The acquisition of concepts is the process through which the child uses thinking to expand his or her knowledge of the world. The changes in knowledge and thinking skills and the way they are organized and used in dealing with problems explain cognitive development (Copple, DeLisi, & Sigel, 1982).

Previously, we described this process as the reconstruction of knowledge and characterized the child as an active learner who acts upon the environment to acquire new information. Bredekamp and Rosegrant (1992c) have further explained this process. They discuss the process as a cycle of learning, with levels of child interaction with learning. They propose that children go through a level of awareness with new information, which is followed by exploration as they interact further with the concept. A more complex level of interaction is classified as inquiry: this occurs when the child investigates and examines the information and relates it to prior learning. At the highest level of interaction, utilization, the child is able to use or apply the knowledge and to represent it in various ways. The cycle is repeated as the child develops awareness of new information through the process of interacting with the concept.

Three phases of a learning cycle are described by Barman (1989) and illustrated with concepts in mathematics and science by Charlesworth and Lind (1990). The three phases, which are sequential, are (1) exploration, (2) concept introduction, and (3) concept application. During the exploration phase, young children explore concepts through materials that have been introduced into the environment, while the teacher observes and occasionally guides indirectly. Direct instruction is provided during the concept introduction phase when the teacher builds on the children's explorations and helps children clarify what they found out on their own about the concept. During the application phase, the teacher and children suggest how the information acquired during the first two phases can be used to solve a problem.

Hohmann, Banet, and Weikart (1979) propose three progressions to describe the dimensions of concept acquisition. They explain the cognitive process of acquiring concepts as moving from concrete to abstract, from simple to complex, and from here and now to remote in time and space. They further describe the interaction with information to move from experiencing new information to representing their understanding of that information in diverse ways, including construction of models, dictating stories, drawing pictures, or contributing to the creation of songs to describe and experience.

The examples above and the processes described provide clues for the teacher's role in facilitating and directing cognitive development. The teacher prepares the environment and plans activities that will introduce new concepts and guides the child through the learning cycle with materials of increasing complexity so that children can make sense of, incorporate, and use the new knowledge.

Understanding How Young Children Acquire Concepts in Mathematics and Science

The cognitive processes just described are used by young children to acquire concepts in mathematics and science. Math and science are interrelated in that the processes of comparing, classifying, and measuring are used in both fields and are important in both. Moreover, science process skills such as observing, inferring, and hypothesizing are also used for problem solving in mathematics.

The cognitive processes described above are used by young children as they interact in different contexts in the environment. Some activities are child initiated, while others are teacher directed. Child-initiated activities are engaged in spontaneously as children find interesting ideas to explore in the environment in daily activities. These naturalistic activities occur because the adult has prepared the environment with many types of materials that will attract the child's attention and interest (see exploration phase above). The adult can provide guidance during naturalistic experiences as children are busy with activities. When an opportunity for instruction presents itself, the teacher conducts an impromptu lesson. Teacher-directed activities can be more structured when the teacher preplans and teaches intentionally. Lessons are conducted with small groups or the entire class (Charlesworth & Lind, 1990).

Children use thinking skills to acquire concepts in science. They think, form concepts, and use the thinking process to solve problems. Like scientists, they observe, infer, classify, form hypotheses, and internalize their understanding through communicating with others. As they acquire concepts, they organize them by categorizing them in a meaningful arrangement and storing them. They think further about their store of concepts, draw relationships between them, and consider their common characteristics by making generalizations about them. They learn to group concepts and objects with common characteristics and to use words to associate the concept with language. Once they have acquired language to go with their store of concepts, they can communicate their understanding with others. The process begins with acting on objects using the senses, and it ends with acquiring and using language to communicate knowledge and to acquire new information.

Conservation is the process whereby young children understand concepts in mathematics. Because children in the preoperational period are learning to conserve, they are developing preconcepts and using a semilogical thinking process. They are able to manipulate symbols and representations of the physical world, but are constrained from developing complex problems or tasks (Kamii, 1982). Young children, therefore, are laying the foundation for later, more complex knowledge in mathematics. Gelman and Gallistel (1978) divided number knowledge into two distinct types: number extraction and number reasoning. Preoperational children are able to develop skills in both types of mathematics.

In the first category—number extraction—counting and ordering are the skills acquired by the preschool child. Young children often use unconventional methods of counting. Frequently they skip numbers or change the order of numbers as they count. Although the process may be inaccurate at first, Gelman and Gallistel have pointed out that young children do consistently demonstrate important understanding about numbers. First, children as young as two or three years of age know that every item should be counted just once. Second, although the words used for counting may be inaccurate, the child understands that the words are used in a stable sequence. Finally, young children understand that the proper count of an array of items is not dependent on counting in one particular order. The order of counting may change, but the total counted will be consistent.

Counting is fundamental to more complex mathematical concepts. Wang, Resnick, and Boozer (1971) proposed that numerals are easier to learn once the child has learned to count. Older children use the principles of beginning counting to engage in larger counts. Barr (1978) determined that kindergarten children learn to use two-digit numeration more effectively through counting than by grouping sets by tens and ones. Groen and Resnick (1977) taught four-and-a- half-year-olds to add by counting two small groups of objects, followed by counting the combined set.

Kamii (1982) outlined six principles of teaching that suggest how the teacher can foster the development of logico-mathematical knowledge:

1. The creation of all kinds of relationships. Encourage the child to be alert and to put all kinds of objects, and actions into all kinds of relationships.
2. The quantification of objects
   a. Encourage the child to think about number and quantities of objects when these are meaningful to him.
   b. Encourage the child to quantify objects logically and compare sets (rather than encouraging him to count).
   c. Encourage the child to make sets with movable objects.
3. Social interaction with peers and teacher
   a. Encourage the child to exchange ideas with his peers.
   b. Figure out how the child is thinking, and intervene according to what seems to be going on in his head. (p. 27)

Organizing Curriculum for Cognitive Development

Early childhood teachers have alternatives when determining how they will organize curriculum for cognitive development. One approach to organization is to organize the curriculum by subject areas that are congruent with the subject areas used in the elementary school. Another approach is to organize it by developmental categories. As we learn more about the interrelated nature of learning and the necessity of guiding young children in their understanding of how all types of knowledge are connected, the latter approach is being taken. Thus, in this chapter, curriculum is described within the category of cognitive development rather than as mathematics, science, social studies, and language arts. In this book, language development is also discussed as a separate category, while learning about social science is linked with social development, although it also is part of cognitive development. This example demonstrates the holistic nature of development and the difficulty in thinking of intellectual growth in terms of a category of development. All categories of development—social, physical, and intellectual—are interrelated, and curriculum for young children cannot be organized into discrete groupings.

The integrated nature of development and learning is widely accepted for both preschool and primary children. Appropriate practice for cognitive development in four-year-olds and five-year-olds recommended by the National Association for the Education of Young Children (Bredekamp, 1987) is described as follows:

> Children develop understanding of concepts about themselves, others, and the world around them through observation, interacting with people and real objects, and seeking solutions to concrete problems. Learnings about math, science, social studies, health, and other content areas are all integrated through meaningful activities such as those when children build with blocks; measure sand, water, or ingredients for cooking; observe changes in the environment; work with wood and tools; sort objects for a purpose; explore animals, plants, water wheels and gears; sing and listen to music from various cultures; and draw, paint, and work with clay. . . . (p. 56)

In practice, both approaches—developmental and by subject area—are used in preschool early childhood programs. Therefore, in the next section—where we will discuss the process of developing goals and objectives for cognitive development—both types of organization will be presented.

Designing Goals for Curriculum in Cognitive Development   After the teacher has considered in what manner the curriculum will be designed, it is possible to determine goals. In some settings, teachers must observe required guidelines for curriculum development, which have been determined by an institution, organization, or agency. Some school districts have developed objectives for the early childhood program, which they expect teachers to follow when planning the curriculum. State education agencies may also have defined learning objectives for classrooms on a state-wide basis. Other preschool centers may have a set curriculum or a commercial resource that teachers are expected to consult or follow. The trend in many early childhood programs is to enable teachers to design their own curriculum within some type of framework or goals for the program.

Organizing From a Developmental Approach. When organizing using developmental categories rather than subject areas, teachers can group their curriculum goals in various ways. One possibility is to use categories of types of cognitive experiences. This type of organization has been titled key experiences in the High/Scope cognitive-developmental preschool model (Hohmann, Banet, & Weikart, 1979). Examples of the High/Scope organization of key experiences are the categories of classification, seriation, and number concepts. Descriptions of activities for these key experiences include the following (Hohmann, Banet, & Weikart, 1979, pp. 4-5):

Classification
Investigating and labeling the attributes of things.
Noticing and describing something in several different ways.

Sorting and Matching
Using and describing something in several different ways.
Describing what characteristics something does not possess or what class it does not belong to.
Holding more than one attribute in mind at one time.
Distinguishing between "some" and "all."

Seriation
Comparing: Which one is bigger (smaller), heavier (lighter), rougher (smoother), louder (softer), harder (softer), longer (shorter), taller (shorter), wider (narrower), sharper, darker, etc.
Arranging several things in order along some dimension and describing the relations (the longest one, the shortest one, etc.).

Number Concepts
Comparing number and amount: more/less, same amount; more/fewer, same number.
Comparing the number of items in two sets by matching them up in one-to-one correspondence.
Enumerating (counting) objects, as well as counting by rote.

The Essential Elements developed for prekindergarten education in Texas provide an example of curriculum guidelines described from a developmental perspective. One section of the guidelines for intellectual development is knowledge of integrated content. Figure 8–1 shows the objectives or essential elements for integrated content as follows:

(A) Intellectual development, prekindergarten. Essential elements for intellectual development, prekindergarten, as described in this subsection shall be effective September 1995. Intellectual development, prekindergarten, shall include the following essential elements:

(1) Knowledge of communication. Receptive/expressive language integrated through meaningful listening/speaking and print-related experiences. The essential elements for primary language for bilingual education, prekindergarten, are described in subsection (j) of this section and the essential elements for English as a second language, prekindergarten, are described in subsection (k) of this section. The student shall be provided opportunities to:

(a) focus attention on adult and peer speakers during individual and group interactions;

(b) enjoy repetition, rhyme, and rhythm through poems, chants, and fingerplays individually or with a group;

(c) enjoy daily listening and responding to stories and books;

(d) follow simple oral directions;

(e) recognize voice tone and nonverbal cues to aid in communication;

(f) acquire vocabulary related to concepts in a meaningful context;

(g) engage in conversation to achieve a variety of purposes including getting needs met, requesting, inquiring, sharing information, and playing;

(h) select books for individual needs and interests;

(i) associate print with spoken language;

(j) become familiar with personally meaningful environmental print;

(k) share ideas, feelings, and stories through activities such as dictating stories, conversation, dramatic play; and

(l) recognize that experiences can be written about.

(2) Knowledge of integrated content. Integrated content acquired through processes of identifying, comparing and contrasting, classifying, sequencing and ordering, predicting cause/effect relationships, and exploring. The student shall be provided opportunities to:

(a) Identify:

(i) match objects in one-to-one correspondence;

(ii) become familiar with a variety of geometric shapes in the environment;

(iii) use the senses to gain information about objects from the environment emphasizing color, texture, taste, odor, sound, size, shape, direction, motion, heat/cold, and sink/float;

(iv) celebrate special events (e.g., birthdays, holidays) including those that are culturally related; and

(v) discuss ways people can help and learn from each other.

(b) Compare and contrast:

(i) recognize that there are different types of families, homes, and communities; and

(ii) compare similarities and differences of a variety of objects.

Figure 8–1 Texas Guidelines for Intellectual Development for Kindergarten

(c) Classify:

    (i) a variety of objects by function; and

    (ii) a variety of objects by a single attribute.

(d) Sequence and order:

    (i) repeat and create a simple pattern using concrete objects (e.g., beads, blocks); and

    (ii) describe sequences in basic family and school routines.

(e) Predict cause/effect relationships:

    (i) observe changes in nature and daily events;

    (ii) draw conclusions and predict outcomes based on experience; and

    (iii) assist in setting class rules including rules of safety.

(f) Explore:

    (i) demonstrate creative thinking through fluency, flexibility, elaboration, creation of new ideas, spontaneity;

    (ii) construct structures using blocks and other manipulative materials of different sizes and shapes;

    (iii) explore basic concepts of weight, mass, and volume through water play, sand play, and cooking;

    (iv) explore positional relationships such as in, on, under; and

    (v) interpret simple visuals (e.g., photographs, pictures).

(B) Aesthetic development, prekindergarten. Essential elements for aesthetic development, prekindergarten, as described in this subsection shall be effective September 1995. Aesthetic development, prekindergarten, includes visual arts, music, and theatre arts and shall include the following essential elements:

(1) Visual arts. The student shall be provided opportunities to:

    (a) express individual thoughts, ideas, and feelings through picturemaking, puppetry, modeling, constructing, and printmaking;

    (b) view and talk about different artworks by students and artists; and

    (c) examine and respond to visual and multisensory characteristics in a variety of subjects, objects, and events to develop awareness and sensitivity to natural and human-made environments.

(2) Music. The student shall be provided opportunities to:

    (a) create and imitate sounds;

    (b) sing a variety of songs including those that reflect cultural diversity;

    (c) explore rhythmic sense of steady beat of songs and poems by patting, tapping, and stepping; and

    (d) explore sounds using body percussion and rhythm instruments.

(3) Theatre arts. The students shall be provided opportunities to:

    (a) engage in creative dramatic activities;

Source: Texas Education Agency.

Organizing From a Subject Area Approach.   When curriculum is developed from subject area approach, the arrangement is still based on development. Because of the overlapping nature of the content areas of mathematics and science, Charlesworth and Lind (1990) developed a framework of concepts and skills in mathematics and science by developmental stages in the early childhood years. Figure 8–2 provides their conceptualization of the organization of concepts, which include the primary years in the elementary school.

A more integrated approach to organization of the cognitive curriculum using a subject area structure is through the use of topics. When selecting a topic, the teacher determines the concepts to be developed and plans a series of activities to enable children to explore and interact with materials and to gain experiences related to the topic. All developmental areas are interrelated as children explore a variety of books, pictures, and activities related to the topic. Taylor (1993) developed a series of topics for science education for children three to five years old that included the following: air, animals, body, clothing, color, community, ecology, family, food, health, machines, numbers, plants, safety, senses, shape, size, transportation, water, and weather.

A commercial resource can also provide a framework for cognitive development that use a developmental and subject area approach. *Beginning Milestones Teacher's Guide* (Sheridan, & Murphy, 1986) provides developmental checklists that can be used for assessment as well as guides for developing curriculum. Figure 8–3 is an example of such a checklist that includes objectives for math, social studies, and science, within a checklist for cognitive development.

Each teacher will have or locate resources that provide guidelines for the organization of curriculum for cognitive development. Study of the examples given above will reveal that all of the types of organization of curriculum goals have commonalities and similar topics or categories. They have been developed to reflect stages of cognitive development and provide guidelines for activities that are appropriate for the child's level of development in the preoperational period between the ages of three and eight. Using the guidelines or frameworks for curriculum development, the teacher can now plan specific activities that will encourage the child to engage in many experiences with the concepts that are introduced. When engaging in planning for curriculum for cognitive development, the teacher remembers that all activities should be engaged in within a meaningful context and that opportunities for child-initiated or child-directed activities should be balanced with teacher-initiated activities and direct teaching of concepts.

ASSESSING COGNITIVE DEVELOPMENT

Two types of evaluation are used to assess cognitive development. The teacher is concerned with overall cognitive progress and also with mastery of specific cognitive skills. For example, for determining overall development in a broad cognitive category, the teacher may want to know how the child is progressing toward the ability to classify a group of objects. Is the child attempting to determine a method for group-

Period	Concepts and Skills			
	Section II Fundamental	Section III Applied	Section IV Higher Level	Section V Primary
Sensorimotor (Birth to age two)	Observation Problem-solving One-to-one cor- respondence Number Shape Space			
Preoperational (Two to seven years)	Sets and classifying Comparing Counting Parts and wholes Language	Ordering Informal measurements: Weight Length Temperature Volume Time Sequence	Number symbols Sets and symbols	
Transitional (Five to seven years)		Graphing	Concrete addition and subtraction	
Concrete opera- tions (Seven to eleven years)				Whole number operations Fractions Number facts Place value Geometry Measurement with standard units

Figure 8–2   Developmental Approach to Organizing Concepts in Mathematics and Science

Source: Reproduced by permission. *Math and Science for Young Children.* By R. Charlesworth and K. K. Lind. Delmar Publishers, Albany, New York. Copyright 1990.

STUDENT_____TEACHER _____

UNIT	OBJECTIVE	I	E	M
1M	Sorts concrete objects into groups			
2SS	Identifies acceptable/unacceptable behavior			
	Understands consequences of behavior			
3M	Uses accurate vocabulary to compare sets/groups			
4SS	Identifies potentially dangerous situations			
	Observes safety rules			
5S	Obtains input through sight, smell, taste, sound, feel			
	Describes sensory input			
6M	Sorts and re-sorts objects by different characteristics			
7SS	Uses may I, please, excuse me, thank you appropriately			
8S	Uses sensory input to determine if two stimuli are alike/not alike			
9M	Uses objects to repeat a simple pattern			
10SS	Says name, age, sex			
11S	Labels different types of weather			
	Identifies appropriate clothing for weather conditions			
12SS	Follows school routine			
13M	Matches objects on one-to-one basis			
14SS	Identifies ways people help each other			
	Identifies teacher(s)			
15S	Sorts old/new objects			
	Sorts pictures of past/present events			
	Classifies events based on before/after			
16SS	Identifies family work and play activities			
17M	Uses oral directions to locate an object			
18S	Identifies loud and soft sounds			
	Identifies high and low sounds			
19M	Identifies equal to			
	Identifies as many as			
	Identifies more than			
	Identifies less than			

(M = Math, SS = Social Studies, S = Science)

Figure 8–3   Checklist of Objectives in Cognitive Development

STUDENT_____TEACHER _____

UNIT	OBJECTIVE	I	E	M
20S	Identifies animals that are/are not pets			
	Describes requisites for survival			
21SS	Identifies two special celebrations/parties			
	Demonstrates awareness of at least two traditions			
22M	Compares two objects by weight			
	Labels heaviest and lightest			
23S	Uses sensory input to learn about environment			
	Describes phenomena based on sensory input			
24M	Labels whole			
	Labels part of the whole			
25M	Rote counts up to ten			
	Counts objects up to five			
26SS	Uses oral directions to locate an object			
	Gives accurate oral directions for finding an object			
27SS	Identifies basic survival needs			
28S	Identifies water as basic for survival			
29M	Orders two or more objects by size			
30M	Counts objects through five			
31SS	Identifies ownership			
	Uses his, hers, mine ours appropriately			
32M	Orders two or more objects by size (based on measuring)			
33M	Identifies the empty set			
34M	Groups objects by shape (circle, square, triangle)			
	Names circle, square, triangle			
35M	Uses modified graphs			
36S	Identifies basic needs of plants			
	Plants and cares for a plant			
	Compares plants by size			

(M = Math, SS = Social Studies, S = Science)

Source: From *Beginning Milestones* (pp. 32–33) by S. Sheridan and D. B. Murphy, 1986. Reprinted by permission of McGraw-Hill, Inc.

ing, but is still unclear how to select attributes for grouping? That is, does the child group objects where the decisions for grouping are inconsistent and change? Or does the child have a firm method of deciding how objects are to be grouped, demonstrating consistency in selection and use of attributes in deciding how to arrange the objects?

When the teacher wants to determine if the child has acquired specific skills in cognitive development, assessment is focused on mastery rather than general progress. For example, the teacher may be assessing the child's ability to count. To obtain this type of information, the teacher may want to engage the child in counting activities to make an accurate judgment about whether or not the child has mastered the skill of counting.

The teacher may be interested in assessment for diagnostic purposes. The purpose for assessment may be to determine the child's needs for instruction and experiences or to decide why a child is having difficulty in learning. When using diagnostic assessment, the teacher may be evaluating general cognitive development or specific cognitive skills.

Strategies for Assessing Cognitive Development

Various types of assessment strategies may be used to evaluate cognitive development, as suggested above. These strategies can include observation, interviews, and directed assignments. More important than the type of strategy that is used is the use of meaningful context for assessment. The assessment should be authentic or naturalistic in that it assesses the child's performance in a real-life context (Hills, 1992). This approach to assessment can also be called performance assessment in that children are asked to carry out tasks that represent or replicate problems in real life.

Observation   Assessment to document the child's progress or achievement in cognitive development can be accomplished through teacher observation. Observation permits detached and objective recording of children's cognitive activities. The teacher may use different types of observation such as anecdotal records, running records, or event sampling to obtain the desired information. (See Chapter 3 for a full description of each.) In addition, observation might be used in conjunction with a checklist or rating scale (a specific behavior is selected for observation), as well as to document progress or mastery in cognitive development.

Interviews   Interviews are a dialogue between the teacher and child that permit the teacher to solicit information about the child's understanding of concepts. Interviews can be formal or informal. Informal interviews can be conducted during free play or during learning center activities when the teacher sees an opportunity to determine a child's thinking on a topic or concept. A teacher might question a child building with unit blocks about why the child selected certain blocks for the activity and how the child made decisions while constructing with the blocks.

Formal interviews may also be described as structured interviews. The teacher structures tasks for the child to be able to demonstrate understanding of concepts or skills. For example, the teacher might present the child with an array of pencils of different lengths and ask the child to find the one that is the "shortest" or "longest." Further activities might include asking the child to order the pencils by length and describe how the task was accomplished. The teacher could use questioning to encourage the child to explain his or her thinking in accomplishing the task.

Both informal and structured interviews can be used for diagnostic purposes. The teacher can determine the child's current status in regard to a cognitive development objective and what difficulty is causing the child not to make progress. When the cause of the difficulty is identified, the teacher can decide what might be done to enable the child to move forward.

Directed Assignments   A directed assignment is similar to the structured interview in that the teacher uses a task for the child to perform to enable assessment to be accomplished. The teacher structures a task for the child to carry out to determine if the child demonstrates understanding or mastery of a concept or skill. For example, given an array of red, yellow, and blue objects, the child might be instructed to put all of the blue objects into a basket. This assesses the child's ability to identify the color blue. Another assignment might be to match pairs of pictures. Given a selection of pictures of mother and baby animals, the child might be asked to put the mothers and babies of each type of animal together.

Directed assignments can be combined with the strategy for interviews. They can also be used as a task alone, whereby the child can demonstrate understanding of a concept by carrying out the activity without having to use language to explain how the task was accomplished.

The teacher may use a single approach to assessment or combine strategies to find out what the child understands and can do to demonstrate growth in cognitive development. One element that all strategies have in common is that some type of activity is used to enable the child to perform an action that will indicate how he or she is thinking about concepts. The activity might be placed in a learning center, be part of a teacher-directed lesson, or be specifically constructed for the purpose of assessment. The nature of these activities is that they can be used either as a learning experience or for assessment. The activities relate to the cognitive objectives selected by the teacher for the educational program. Typically objectives were derived from some resource for organizing the curriculum: a checklist, commercial preschool curriculum resource, or other framework used as a guide for designing curriculum for cognitive development in early childhood classrooms.

In the section that follows, examples of teacher-designed activities for cognitive development are given. The activities might be one of a collection of like activities for cognitive development in children ages three to five. They use found or recycled objects and materials and are intended to give young children hands-on experiences with concepts that are common for preschool and kindergarten children in Piaget's preoperational stage of cognitive development. Most can be used as learning center activities for child-initiated experiences or as resources for teacher-directed activities or lessons. And, of course, they can be used for assessment purposes.

ASSESSMENT/LEARNING EXPERIENCES FOR COGNITIVE DEVELOPMENT

Objective: Sorts concrete objects into groups

_____ Source: Figure 8—3, A Checklist of Objectives in Cognitive Development

_____ Materials Needed: An array of two kinds of nuts, such as pecans and walnuts

_____ Activity: Present the array of nuts. Discuss the two kinds of nuts and name them. Ask the child to sort the nuts into two groups so that one group has all of the pecans and the other has all of the walnuts. If the children are unfamiliar with the names of the nuts, ask them to make two groups that have all of one kind of nut.

Objective: Matches objects on a one-to-one basis

_____ Source: Figure 8–3, Checklist of Objectives in Cognitive Development

_____ Materials Needed: Ten plastic drinking cups and ten plastic drinking straws

_____ Activity: Place the paper cups in a row. The child then determines if there are the same number of straws as cups by placing a straw in each cup. The number of cups and straws can then be varied so that the number of items in the two sets are unequal. The child repeats the activity to determine if there is the same number of straws as cups.

Objective: Compares two objects by weight

_____ Source: Figure 8–3, Checklist of Objectives in Cognitive Development

_____ Materials Needed: Plastic fork and metal fork; foam ball and metal ball (ball bearing); a cork and rock of approximately the same size or similar items

_____ Activity: Present a pair of items and ask the child to identify the one that is heavy (or light). Repeat with the other matched items.

Objective: Counts objects up to five

_____ Source: Figure 8–3, Checklist of Objectives in Cognitive Development

_____ Materials Needed: Several groups of objects containing from two to five items. The sets could be composed of crayons, counting bears, stones, milk bottle caps, or other recycled items.

_____ Activity: Present sets of objects for the child to count. Repeat until all sets have been counted.

Objective: Groups objects by shape (circle, square, triangle)

_____ Source: Figure 8–3, Checklist of Objectives in Cognitive Development

____ Materials Needed: Circles, squares, and triangles cut from scraps of fabric, colored construction paper, and glue

____ Activity: Give each child a plastic bag with an assortment of fabric shapes and ask the child to design a picture using the shapes. When the picture is completed, ask the child to identify each shape used in the picture.

Objective: Explores positional relationships such as in, on, and under

____ Source: Figure 8–1, Texas Guidelines for Intellectual Development for Kindergarten

____ Materials Needed: Small counting object or toy such as a counting kitten or other animal; small paper or plastic cup

____ Activity: Present the animal and cup. Demonstrate how the animal can be put in different positions in relation to the cup (e.g., in, on, under, beside). Ask the child to place the animal in different positions.

Objective: Repeats and creates a simple pattern using concrete objects (e.g., beads, blocks)

____ Source: Figure 8–1, Texas Guidelines for Intellectual Development for Kindergarten

____ Materials Needed: Colored one-inch blocks

____ Activity: Make a pattern using the blocks and ask the child to duplicate the pattern. Then ask the child to make and repeat a pattern using the blocks.

Objective: Demonstrates concept of number through 10

____ Source: Figure 8–2, Developmental Approach to Organizing Concepts in Mathematics and Science

____ Materials Needed: An egg carton with egg wells numbered from 1 to 10; dominoes with dots totaling 1 to 10

____ Activity: Place the dominoes in a mixed array. The children are asked to count the dots on each domino and then place the domino in the egg well with the appropriate numeral.

Objective: Orders numerals 1 to 10

____ Source: Figure 8–2, Developmental Approach to Organizing Concepts in Mathematics and Science

____ Materials Needed: Ten clothespins with numerals 1 to 10; small coffee can covered with contact paper

____ Activity: The child empties the can of clothespins onto the desk and then clips the clothespins in correct order on the top of the can.

PLANNING INSTRUCTION IN COGNITIVE DEVELOPMENT FOR CHILDREN WITH DISABILITIES

The extensive use of concrete materials in early childhood classrooms is an advantage when adapting instruction for children who have some type of disability. For some types of disabilities, no modification is needed, while for others, another avenue of learning needs to be included. When studying how to adjust the curriculum for cognitive development, we will discuss meeting the needs of children with communication, hearing, and vision impairments; learning disabilities; and mental retardation.

Children With Communication Disorders

Children who have a disorder that affects their language development may have speech problems and have difficulty in processing information. Because language affects cognitive development, children who have a communication disorder are also likely to have difficulty in learning cognitive skills. Concepts should be introduced to these children through active experiences. A concept should be named, and children should have various experiences with it before they are able to use the appropriate language (Deiner, 1993).

Mathematics and science are enjoyable for children with communication disorders because they can use other avenues besides language to engage in learning experiences. Hands-on experiences with concepts can be successful before verbal communication is attempted. For example, children need opportunities to demonstrate counting abilities with objects rather than oral responses. The focus should be on physical demonstration of number or classification concepts using cutout pictures or drawings made by the child before making verbalizations.

Children With Hearing Impairments

Children who have difficulty hearing learn to rely on vision and touch to learn about the world. Teachers need to be facing them so that the children can use, or learn to use, visual cues and speech reading.

Children with hearing impairments may learn best visually through direct experience; they need many such experiences to acquire concepts. They benefit from activities that incorporate different types of visual media such as television, films, and computer programs. In addition, they need to see many examples of a concept and experience three-dimensional materials before two-dimensional resources such as pictures are used.

In mathematics, three-dimensional objects should be used for number experiences. In both mathematics and science, naturally occurring situations should be used to reinforce concepts that are being learned. Opportunities to count during the day or put language with events and routines help the child use visual clues to learn. In science, particularly, experiences with natural events such as weather changes, experiences with animals, and seeing changes in materials enable the child to understand new information (Deiner, 1993).

Children With Vision Impairments

Children who are visually impaired rely on hearing and touch to explore concepts. They may be delayed in understanding their body and the surrounding environment. Curriculum adaptations depend on how much vision the child has, if any. The more severe the visual impairment, the more the child will need to use hearing and touch to learn.

Children with limited or no sight can use concrete materials to learn concepts in science and math. Familiar objects are the primary source to introduce new concepts. Less familiar and more abstract materials are used when the child has had a substantial number of experiences. Materials that have tactile characteristics are most useful for learning concepts in mathematics. Real objects that are part of the child's everyday experiences should be used for counting activities. Drinking straws, cereal pieces, or buttons are useful for number concepts, while experiences that can be felt in science enable the child to understand scientific phenomena. Hearing rain and feeling wind help the child to understand weather, while smelling foods assists in identifying and labeling differences in taste.

Children With Learning Disabilities

Children with learning disabilities have some type of difficulty in learning that is not related to intelligence or some other disability. They are not able to process and interpret information. Causes of learning disabilities are not known, and in many cases, children with learning disabilities are not identified during the preschool years. Some of the characteristics of learning disabilities are short attention span, inability to follow directions, and hyperactivity and impulsiveness. Children with learning disabilities need consistency in their daily schedule and elimination of environmental distractions that make it difficult for them to concentrate.

Physical involvement with concrete materials helps children with learning disabilities to focus on a learning activity. They benefit from a discovery approach to concept development, where their involvement is required to understand information. Describing the process of problem solving during activities helps the child to learn cause and effect. In directed teaching situations, instructions and questioning should be simple and direct so that the child can attend and not become distracted or confused. Computers can also be helpful in helping the child to complete activities without losing interest or becoming frustrated (Deiner, 1993).

Children With Mental Retardation

Children with mental retardation have fewer intellectual skills than their chronological peers. They are functioning at a lower cognitive developmental level. In addition to needing more time to learn concepts, they must interact with concepts and materials at a very simple level and have many opportunities for repetition. Preschool children need to learn about themselves and depend on sensory experiences to learn. They need to work on a concept for a long period of time and must experience the progression of simple to complex in learning. They learn basic concepts in mathematics and science through real experiences and concrete materials. Integration of more than one sense in learning experiences helps them to process information.

In mathematics, introduction of concepts should be sequential in terms of complexity. One-to-one correspondence is experienced prior to attempts to teach counting. Real objects from the child's daily life should be used for concept development. In science, field trips are essential so that the child is able to use firsthand and relevant information. It is beneficial to incorporate motor skills with learning activities. For example, lacing activities and construction materials provide integrated sensory actions that facilitate learning. Boards with holes for pegs can be used for counting, while a simple shape puzzle can be used to identify shapes.

In each type of disability, the child has some type of difficulty that must be overcome or compensated if learning is to take place. The principles for development and learning for children in the early childhood years is applicable for children with disabilities. In addition, study of the individual child's strengths and interests needs to be done when teachers are adapting materials and activities to meet that child's difficulties and possibilities for cognitive learning.

EVALUATING CURRICULUM AND INSTRUCTION FOR COGNITIVE DEVELOPMENT

A major focus of this book is on the relationship between the assessment of young children's development and learning and the relationship between assessment and planning for curriculum and instruction. In this chapter, we have addressed the relationship between curriculum and instruction in cognitive development and appropriate strategies for evaluation and assessment of cognitive development. However, evaluation extends beyond assessment of the child's progress in cognitive development. There should also be evaluation of the curriculum and instruction in cognitive development, including evaluation of the teacher's effectiveness. This type of evaluation can be ongoing throughout the year, or what is called formative evaluation. In addition, evaluation can be conducted at the end of a period or at the end of the year in the form of summative evaluation.

Formative Evaluation

Formative evaluation of curriculum and instruction is done daily, weekly, and at any time that the teacher needs to reflect upon the effectiveness of the program for cognitive development. Elements of curriculum and instruction for cognitive development that can be addressed in ongoing evaluation can include the environment, materials and activities, and teacher behaviors.

When observing the environment to evaluate how effectively it is organized and furnished for cognitive curriculum, the teacher assesses materials and experiences in the centers over a period of time. Are the materials interesting to the children? Are there enough materials? Can the activities be engaged in without crowding or undue waiting times? Are there enough different activities to provide children with a range of experiences for the concepts being learned? Have children lost interest in some of the opportunities or do they new renewing? Do the children's self-initiated activities indicate a need for more possibilities to enrich their interactions in centers?

Attention to ongoing assessment of the outdoor environment is done in similar fashion. The teacher observes activities that have been located outdoors to determine if they are effective and adequate. A primary question is to ask if enough thought has been given to activities for cognitive development that can be engaged in outdoors. Are there activities for the current curriculum topic or children's interests on the outdoor playscape? Does children's play suggest ideas for activities or props that can be added to the outdoor play area at this time for cognitive development?

Evaluation can also be conducted of learning activities that have been planned by the teacher for individual and small-group or large-group instruction. Daily evaluation of these activities can be conducted to determine if they are appropriate and interesting for the children. The teacher can also reflect on children's progress to decide if more lessons need to be added for some children or if more advanced experiences are needed for those children who are demonstrating understanding of the concepts being studied. Evaluation of individual lessons can be conducted to decide if the best experiences and materials were selected or if changes should be made before additional groups engage in the lesson or before the lesson is used again in the future.

Finally, teachers can assess their effectiveness in teaching the cognitive curriculum. How effective were teacher interactions with children in the centers in dialogues with them about their activities? Were opportunities missed to help children consider additional options for their explorations and investigations of materials available for cognitive development? Were the teacher's instructional strategies effective when direct instruction was used for lessons? Is there a good balance between child-initiated activities and teacher-directed activities and lessons? Is the teacher alert to children's interest and progress in working with materials in centers and prepared to make changes in plans to accommodate children's needs?

Summative Evaluation

Summative evaluation of curriculum and instruction for cognitive development is conducted at the completion of a unit or time period. At this time, the teacher reflects upon the overall effectiveness of the environment, activities, and teaching strategies used for a topic of study. This type of evaluation could be conducted at the end of a week, upon completion of a thematic unit, at the end of a reporting period, and at the end of the year. Summative evaluation of children's progress is broadened to determine effectiveness of curriculum and instruction and to determine how and what improvements are indicated for the future. The overall success of the instructional program and its components are determined. As a part of summative evaluation, the teacher may want to set goals for curriculum and instruction for cognitive development in the future. After the teacher assesses strengths and weaknesses in curriculum and instruction, he or she sets specific objectives for improving and strengthening the program.

To evaluate and plan for improvement in the curriculum for cognitive development, the teacher will want to review goals set for the current year to determine if additions, deletions, or alterations are needed in the primary goals for the program. In respect to planning for curriculum and instruction, assessment results can indicate additional materials that are needed or materials that will be discontinued because they were not effective or interesting. Equipment that will enhance cognitive development might be considered for purchase. For example, the teacher might decide that the science curriculum would be enriched with animal cages and an aquarium. A sand and water table might be ordered to broaden opportunities for exploration and investigation with natural materials in the environment. Games to stimulate thinking skills can be considered for learning centers and teacher-directed activities.

Summative evaluation at the end of the year assists the teacher's reflection about the accomplishments of the current year and projections on the year to come. If the teacher has conducted formative and summative evaluation throughout the year, not only is there information about accomplishments, but there is an ongoing awareness of possibilities that occurred that had not been planned for and opportunities to plan intentionally for such activities with the next group of children.

⇨ SUMMARY

We are in a period where there is much interest in designing curriculum and instruction for preschool children that is compatible with their level of development. To understand developmental curriculum, we have to first review theories of development and learning as they apply to the preschool child.

Our use of development as a base for preschool curriculum is guided by behaviorist and social learning theories, psychosocial theory, and cognitive-developmental theories of development and learning. Although each theory has its own unique perception of the child's development and nature of learning, all have a role in contemporary curriculum and instruction in early childhood. Nevertheless, the cognitive-developmental theories of Jean Piaget and Lev Vygotsky are considered by many early childhood specialists to be the most significant in organizing curriculum that is developmentally appropriate for young children.

The child's style of thinking in cognitive development changes and evolves as the child moves through Piaget's stages of cognitive development. Teachers who have the responsibility for planning learning experiences for young children need to understand the nature of cognitive development and the implications that this knowledge has on how cognitive experiences are planned for young children. With the belief that young children are active learners and interact with the environment to reconstruct knowledge, teachers adapt their roles to complement the child's style of learning. Teachers facilitate and support learning, in addition to the more traditional role of directing instruction or disseminating information.

When determining how to organize cognitive curriculum in the early childhood classroom, early childhood educators choose whether to approach planning from a developmental or content area approach. Both types of organization are commonly used, and result in similar goals and objectives for cognitive curriculum.

Various strategies are used to assess the child's progress in cognitive development. Observation, interviews, and directed assignments are examples of methods of assessment that are appropriate to use with preschool children. A teacher-designed task or activity can be a part of most assessment strategies. When using a task for assessment, the teacher constructs an activity that has a meaningful context for the child and that involves concrete materials when appropriate to permit the child to demonstrate developmental progress or mastery of a skill.

Cognitive curriculum that is planned for children with disabilities must be adapted to the special needs of each child. For different reasons, all children with disabilities benefit from hands-on experiences with concrete materials. Children with hearing impairments must use vision and the sense of touch in cognitive activities, while children with vision impairments use the sense of touch as a primary avenue to learning. Children who have cognitive delay need repeated experiences with real materials that employ the senses, while children with communication impairments benefit from verbal information linked with learning materials.

Evaluating curriculum for cognitive development enables teachers to reflect upon the effectiveness of activities, the environment and teacher behaviors. Information gained from ongoing formative and summative evaluations provide the teacher with feedback that can be used immediately for improvements or for long-range planning that will affect the effectiveness of cognitive curriculum in the future.

✦ STUDY QUESTIONS

1. Explain what is meant by a developmental curriculum in preschool education.
2. Why is there an emphasis on developmentally appropriate practices in preschool programs at this time?
3. Why do preschool teachers need to be aware of the implications of the psychosocial theory of development for their program?
4. How has Vygotsky's theory of development and learning added to our understanding of Piaget's cognitive-developmental theory?
5. Is it possible for a teacher to totally embrace one theory? Explain.
6. Describe the characteristics of a quality developmental curriculum.
7. How are individual differences a key to planning an appropriate preschool curriculum?
8. Explain the implications the characteristics of the preoperational stage of development have for planning cognitive curriculum?
9. Explain how Vygotsky's term *zone of proximal development* can assist teachers in understanding how to assist children in acquiring concepts.

10. How do the teacher's roles as facilitator, supporter, and instructor reflect theories of development and learning?
11. Explain how teachers can establish a process for learning information that is consistent with knowledge of how young children learn.
12. How are science and mathematics similar in cognitive concepts?
13. How does progress in cognitive development affect how children learn concepts in mathematics and science?
14. What are specific strategies teachers can use to facilitate development of concepts in mathematics?
15. How do preschool teachers organize cognitive curriculum? What resources are available to guide them in selecting goals and objectives?
16. When and how does the teacher assess children's progress in cognitive development? Describe at least three strategies.
17. What kinds of information does the preschool teacher need to know to be able to adapt the cognitive curriculum for children with disabilities?
18. Why is it important to conduct formative and summative evaluation of the curriculum for cognitive development?

→ KEY TERMS

accommodation   stage independent
assimilation   zone of proximal development
stage dependent   stage independent

→ SUGGESTED ACTIVITIES

1. Visit a preschool classroom. Observe for about two hours and determine which developmental theories the teacher uses in his or her interactions with children and in the learning activities used with children. Describe behaviors used by the teacher that support your conclusions.
2. Select four objectives for cognitive development from one of the resources in the chapter and design a teaching/learning activity for each objective.
3. Select an objective that can be best assessed through observation. Describe how you would plan an observation to accomplish your objective.
4. Select an objective and describe experiences you could use to follow one of the processes for learning concepts described under the examples for organizing instruction.
5. Select one of the examples for assessment/learning activities and design a plan for modifying the activity for a child with a communication impairment or a visual impairment.

 # 9

Language Development

➔ Chapter Objectives

As a result of reading this chapter, you will be able to

1. Describe how children acquire language
2. Explain the theories of how children acquire language
3. Discuss how to plan instruction for language and literacy development
4. Explain the teacher's role in language and literacy development
5. Describe curriculum for language and literacy for young children
6. Be able to select strategies for assessing development in language and literacy
7. Be able to design curriculum for children with communication impairments and for children from diverse language backgrounds
8. Explain how to evaluate curriculum and instruction for language and literacy development

Language development in the early childhood years incorporates literacy development. An understanding of the nature of language development is basic to understanding how to measure children's progress in literacy development and how to facilitate or complement their development with appropriate experiences in preschool programs.

In this chapter, we will explore how views of language and literacy development influence how teachers construct curriculum for young children. Appropriate methods for assessment of language development will be explored, as well as strategies for promoting language and literacy development. Instruction for children with communication impairments will be addressed, as well as the instructional needs of children from diverse family backgrounds.

THE NATURE OF LANGUAGE DEVELOPMENT

By the time a child enters school at age five or six, he or she has acquired the language spoken at home. During the period from birth to six years of age, the child essentially learns the structure and a substantial part of the vocabulary needed to function in his or her community's language. How the child achieves mastery of language—and further becomes able to read and write—was explored by behaviorist and cognitive-developmental theorists. Their views affect approaches to organizing and evaluating instruction. In the sections that follow, perspectives on language development will be described followed by suggestions for how the language curriculum should be designed.

Understanding Language Development

The ability to speak is a uniquely human characteristic. Although chimpanzees have been taught to use rudimentary verbal language and to communicate through signing or using visual symbols, the human language system is significantly different and more complex (Cole & Cole, 1989).

A necessary requisite for language development is the opportunity to hear and participate in language in the family and community. The young child learning language needs to live in an environment where oral language is part of daily interaction. The nature of the community and culture where the child lives affects the child's style of talking, as does the unique vocabulary that is part of that language community. As part of day-to-day living, the child is likely to be exposed to variations in language, variations that reflect different communication styles in different contexts. Different groups and cultures have their own ways of using language for socialization to enable individuals to be enculturated into the community (Dyson & Genishi, 1993).

Language is part of the child's socialization with peers. As children develop the ability to communicate using language, they are also developing social strategies that allow them to interact with other children through play. When the child engages in initiating and responding to playmates and siblings, language development is enhanced by social interactions.

Language development is part of the ongoing continuum into literacy. The young child not only is exposed to verbal language in the home and community, but written language is also a part of the environment. Parents and adults expose children to writing in different forms as they write checks, make lists, record information, and conduct other writing tasks. Children are also initiated into literacy through opportunities to observe and engage in reading books and storytelling (Dyson & Genishi, 1993).

Components of Language

Language development is divided into four central components: sounds, words, sentences or syntax, and language use. Each component is related to the others as the child engages in the process of acquiring the language or languages of his or her community.

Children acquire the sounds of a language in the first year of life. Beginning a few months after birth and before the age of one, the infant is able to produce the sounds of the home language—even before uttering his or her first words. The sound categories of the language, the phonemes, must be learned by the child in addition to the ability to pronounce them. Infants and toddlers begin the process of developing the ability to pronounce the phonemes of their language as they vocalize the words of their language community. The sounds of the language cannot be separated from the basic units of meaning, morphemes. Morphemes are the smallest unit of meaning in a language. A morpheme may be a whole word or part of a word, such as a prefix or suffix. For example, the word *reteach* has two morphemes, *re* and *teach*. The process of pronouncing sounds and words is interrelated with understanding the meaning of the word (Cole & Cole, 1989).

The process of transitioning from making the sounds of the language to saying words is gradual and sometimes unclear. At about eleven to twelve months of age, the baby begins to use sounds and gestures to communicate with another person. Once babies can use their utterances to enlist the adult's attention, they are able to organize their efforts in an intentional manner. The use of words to communicate opens up the possibility that the very young child can also be influenced by others using words. The first words that are acquired are labeling and action words, whereby babies can identify objects and actions (Nelson, 1986). As children gain experience, their use of words more closely approximates the use of words in their language community.

When children begin to utter two or more words together to communicate, they are beginning to use the syntax of the language. They are learning the process of using sentences. Two-word utterances, called telegraphic speech, are the first step in forming words into sentences. As young speakers continue to practice communicating, they string more and more words together and increase the complexity and variety of words that they use to form sentences. Between the ages of two and six, children use rules of grammar that are different from adult language, but gradually approximate the syntactic constructions used by adults (Chomsky, 1969).

The fourth component in language development is the process of learning how language is used in a language community. The young child must learn to communicate effectively by selecting the correct words and putting them in the right order that is shared by others with whom the child carries on conversations. The young child must be able to ask questions, make statements, and interpret all of the language functions that are part of communicating with others. Subtleties of word order and intonation must be learned to communicate one's full meaning to the language to the listener.

Components of Literacy

Literacy is defined as the ability to read and write. Although much communication is accomplished through oral language, the ability to read and write extends possibilities for transmitting and receiving information. As researchers learn more about how children become literate, it is clear that literacy, like oral language, begins in infancy. Although very young children are unable to interpret words in print and write using adult forms of the alphabet and standard spelling, they become aware of books and written language at a very young age. Like acquisition of oral language, literacy occurs through interaction within the child's language and literacy community. The uses of

Communication is a key to literacy.

literacy that are experienced by the child through day-to-day living are the forces that influence that child's enculturation into reading and writing. The literacy activities within the child's language and cultural community will affect that child's understanding of the purposes and functions of literacy (Dyson & Genishi, 1993).

The basic components of literacy are reading and writing. As young children develop into emergent readers and writers in the preschool years, they need a combination of experiences that enable them to engage in activities that lead to literacy. In preschool settings, play, oral language activities, literature activities, and opportunities to interact with print in books and to write are all components of **emergent literacy** (Fields, Spangler, & Lee, 1991).

Because cognitive, language, physical, and social development cannot be separated in the preschool child's overall development, play is the activity that facilitates the interactive nature of learning. Play, then, enables the child to experience and develop understanding of concepts, interact with others using language, explore books and other written materials, and engage in dramatic play episodes that can include literacy activities. Art activities promote large and fine muscle activities and eye-hand coordination that children use for reading and writing. Physical activities indoors and outdoors also promote the development of skills needed for literacy. For example, playing with small construction toys and manipulating puzzles promote fine motor skills. Sand play outside also facilitates the development of fine motor skills.

Growth in oral language facilitates growth in emergent literacy. Children need many opportunities to engage in conversations, exchange ideas, and listen to the language of others. Engaging in discussions with adults allows children to have more complex forms of language modeled, while group discussions and conversations with peers allow them to listen and respond to all types of verbal expressions and information. Children who come from homes where there are language differences from Standard English are able to hear and experience English or a more standard form of English, which broadens their language milieu.

Reading to children is a powerful influence in teaching them to read. Exposure to books beginning in the home at a very young age and continued in the preschool setting assists children in language acquisition and enables them to experience and construct meaning for print. Exposure to books familiarizes children with language that is used in writing and makes them aware of narratives used in stories and other literature. In addition to reading stories to children, adults can engage in storytelling that can also influence children's use of language and enrich their vocabulary (Cazden, 1981; Durkin, 1980).

Children need their own experiences with books. Through looking at books that are familiar to them, they can learn about the relationship between pictures and the story narrative, the function of pages and the print that accompanies pictures in a book, and how a story is put together on the pages of a book. Behavior that is similar to reading can be observed when a child role-plays reading a book and uses intonation that is familiar from hearing stories and turns pages at regular intervals. Children can engage in these types of experiences with peers or they may sometimes choose to work alone with a book.

Children learn to read by having experiences with hearing stories from books and exploring books. They learn to write by having opportunities to engage in writing activities. In addition to the print that is found in books, exposure to many forms of print around them familiarizes the child with the functions and purposes of writing. Labels in learning centers, as well as other examples of print in the school environment, help children develop awareness of the role of print in daily living. Direct experiences with print in the larger community followed by discussions of how print is used broadens children's awareness of how print affects them and gives them information.

Children need to use written language, as well as observing it around them. They learn to write by trial and error in writing experiences. Many opportunities to write and dictate to the teacher afford children with experiences that help them make sense of the writing process and to gradually move from scribbling and undecipherable communications to written forms that gradually approach the style of writing and spelling used by adults (Fields, Spangler, & Lee, 1991).

Theoretical Bases for Language Development

Theorists have attempted to explain the process of language acquisition for much of the twentieth century. The learning theory or behaviorist theory is in opposition with the innatist position in explaining how children learn language. A third theory, the interactionist theory, offers another basis for explaining language development.

Learning Theory   The view of the learning theory or behaviorist theory is that the child's development of language depends on imitation through operant conditioning. In operant conditioning, learning occurs when a behavior is reinforced. In language acquisition, the parents' reinforcement of the child's utterances would increase the probability that the child would repeat the behavior. Based on B. F. Skinner's theory that learning depends on the environment and the teaching activities and behaviors provided by adults, this approach depends on shaping. According to Skinner, children learn words as parents reinforce them by praising them, smiling at them, and giving them other signals of approval when they pronounce utterances more appropriately. Parents or other adults reward the child's attempts to say words in the initial stages of learning to speak. Improvement in pronunciation and vocabulary occurs through adults' praise for more accurate pronunciation of words. The child is attempting to imitate the language that is heard (Skinner, 1957).

Innatist Theory   Innatist theorists such as linguist Noam Chomsky discount that language is acquired through imitation and conditioning. They point out that young children produce sentences that they have never heard before. Chomsky (1965) believed that the ability to comprehend and use language is innate in humans. He proposed that children are born with a language acquisition device (LAD) that enables children to acquire the language structures used by the adults in the children's language community. Through the inborn tendency to acquire language, children learn the rules of their language. Although children's first attempts to use language are primitive, through practice and maturation, they acquire more complex language structures.

Interactionist Theory   The interactionist approach to language acquisition draws from Piaget's cognitive-developmental theory of development. The view of the interactionist approach is that language develops as a result of the child's innate abilities to interact with the environment. The adult plays a supportive role through language interactions with the child; however, the child plays the dominant role in learning how to use words to communicate. Very early in life, the child is capable of thinking about language and literacy and develops hypotheses about how language is used.

Each of the three theories contributes to an understanding of how children acquire language. Adult praise and reinforcement of the child's efforts to use language can encourage the child; however, encouragement may not have the effect of conditioning what the child will say. Chomsky's innatist theory provides an explanation of how the child develops the syntax of language and focuses on the creative, generative nature of the child's utterances. Nevertheless, the innatist theory does not explain the role of the adult in language development nor how the child acquires word meaning. The interactionist view focuses on the child's initiative and control of the language acquisition process and emphasizes the role of the child's emerging, higher levels of development in understanding and using language (Cole & Cole, 1989).

Implications of Theories for Development of Language and Literacy

Acquisition of language and literacy is a complex process that is not completely understood. Each of the theories cited above provides a partial explanation; as a result, it is important to consider the implications of the theories rather than focus on which one is correct.

Children learn language because they have an inborn mechanism for language acquisition and because they hear and experience language. The adults and older children in the environment play an important role in the language that young children understand and use. The encouragement that young children receive when attempting to communicate verbally is a strong factor in their attempts to use language; likewise, the vocabulary and syntax used in their language community helps form the language that they will use.

The emergence of language in the young child does follow an internal system. Babies and young children use different sentence structures that only gradually approximate adult language as they learn the rules of their language. They use trial and error in their verbalizations and learn from trying out language. The ability to learn to speak does seem to be an innate quality that all children try to acquire in some fashion. Although children with hearing impairments have difficulties in learning to speak, they too can learn the language of their community and culture, but with directed assistance.

Adults in the young child's world have an important role in the child's development of language and literacy. Teachers and parents who understand how theories interact in explaining how children acquire language can provide the type of environment and activities that will facilitate young children's development of language and literacy. The child who lives in a rich language and literacy environment and is surrounded with conversations, books, and experiences with print develops language and literacy as a part of living in that environment.

PLANNING INSTRUCTION FOR LANGUAGE AND LITERACY DEVELOPMENT

When teachers consider how to plan instruction for language and language development, the term instruction is used more broadly than the typical understanding that it implies direct teaching conducted by the teacher. In this context, instruction means all of the experiences provided by the teacher that promote language and literacy development. Planning instruction includes the roles played by the teacher to encourage development in language and literacy; in addition, it includes how the curriculum is organized and what activities are planned for developing receptive language, expressive language, emergent writing, and emergent reading.

Understanding the Teacher's Role

In Chapter 8, we described the teacher as being a facilitator, supporter, and instructor in cognitive development. The teacher has similar roles in language and literacy development. The teacher's perception of how each role will be carried out depends on how he or she perceives that language and literacy develop. The teacher's view of theoretical influences on language development will affect the importance of each role in promoting the child's acquisition of language and literacy.

The Teacher as Facilitator   The teacher begins to serve as a facilitator of language and literacy when planning for the instructional program before the beginning of the school year. Preparing the environment, schedule, and instructional program are vehicles to ensure that language development is an important part of the day for every child.

In setting up the classroom environment, the teacher considers how to include materials and organize space to encourage oral and written language. Centers are organized to stimulate conversation. The dramatic play center is rich with props for fantasy or pretend play experiences. Environmental print is used to make children aware of the role of written language. Centers are labeled, as are bulletin boards, children's cubbies, and storage shelves. Materials in centers promote writing and reading. There is adequate space in the book corner for children to look at books together and to have a variety of books from which to choose. Pencils and paper are available not only in the writing area, but in other centers to encourage the inclusion of writing in play.

The daily schedule is planned to encourage spoken and written language. The teacher makes sure that children have daily opportunities for sharing ideas and discussing important events and activities. Opportunities for using writing are provided through listing information as well through dictated stories, in which children dictate a story to the teacher about a picture they have painted or a group of children dictate contributions to a class story about an event. Times for small- and large-group conversations are part of the everyday routine. Daily opportunities are provided for children to hear stories, both from books and through oral storytelling. Reenactment of stories, for example, with puppets, are planned for children to extend experiences in literacy.

The Teacher as Supporter   The teacher serves as a supporter of language and literacy throughout the day in the preschool classroom and during outdoor play. During play, the teacher interacts with children to extend their language and to make suggestions for when books and writing activities can be used as part of the play activity. Large and small muscles activities are included to support the child's motor development leading to reading and writing. More directly, language and literacy development are supported through oral language activities. Opportunities for children to extend language and develop more descriptive language are planned.

The teacher supports language development through an awareness of individual children's progress in language development and sensitivity to language differences in children from diverse populations in the school community.

Through frequent observations of children's uses of language, the teacher assesses the child's vocabulary, syntax, and other elements of expressive language. The teacher then uses informal intervention and support strategies to extend vocabulary or provide explanations that will help the child to understand and use more "school" language.

The Teacher as Instructor   The teacher serves as an instructor for language and literacy development through modeling and scaffolding. Modeling is conducted when the teacher uses appropriate oral and written language. When engaged in verbal interactions with preschool children, the teacher is careful not to discourage the children's attempts to speak by correcting their mistakes; however, understanding that the child learns by hearing language, the teacher models correct usage in natural interactions that permit children to experience the adult form of the language. Likewise, the teacher includes opportunities for the children to experience adult writing through dictated stories and by writing down and reading information relating to school experiences. The child's attempts at writing are accepted without emphasis on correction, but correct forms are modeled frequently. The preschool teacher's role as instructor is more indirect in this context. The child is receiving information on correct forms of language and literacy, but it is modeled rather than transmitted through direct teaching strategies.

Understanding Language and Literacy Acquisition in Preschool Children

Preschool children from ages three to five are in a rapid stage of language development both in **receptive** and **expressive language**. Receptive language is the language that they understand, while expressive language is the language they are able to use. They have made significant progress in their ability to combine words into sentences and are able to use yes-no questions and questions that begin with a *wh* word. By the age of three, the average length of words children can string together or MLU (mean length of utterance) is 2.50 to 3.00. By the age of four, the MLU has extended to 3.75 to 4.50 (Brown, 1986).

As children construct more complex utterances, they must use the rule systems of the language. They begin using plural and possessive forms of nouns and begin putting endings on verbs such as *s, ed,* and *ing*. However, they frequently overgeneralize the rules in the learning process and may say *goed* instead of *went* when using the past tense. By the age of six, their speaking vocabulary ranges from 8,000 to 14,000 words (Carey, 1977).

In terms of pragmatics, or rules of conversation, preschool children learn to use discourse, or carry on conversations. They learn to relate their discussion to a common topic and to respond to something that has just been said (Vasta, Haith, & Miller, 1992). They also become able to talk about imaginary people and things (Forrester, 1992).

The process of acquiring literacy begins to become evident between the ages of three and five. As a result of experiencing the forms of literacy in their community culture, young children begin to attempt to communicate with others using symbols. Communicating through drawn pictures seems to be a first step as preschool children send letters that are actually drawings (Dyson, 1982). First attempts at using written symbols may take the form of cursivelike script or scribbling to write a letter or a story. Children may also experiment with graphic forms without a communicative purpose (Clay, 1975).

As young children begin to understand that there is a relationship between meaning and print, they become more purposeful in forming letterlike forms. They make lines and letterlike marks. They may incorporate writing into dramatic play or offer their writing to others (Clay, 1975; Schickedanz, 1978).

An important step is taken when the young writer becomes aware that there is a spelling system connected to the use of letters. They become aware of the function of specific letters such as the letters in their name or use a group of letters to represent a word (Ferreiro, 1986). Next, they use characteristics of the sound of the word through invented spelling or use letters to represent sounds.

Through play, children communicate their thoughts orally at first and later through their written communications. At first children use gestures and speech to symbolize ideas and feelings. Later, they include drawings for shared play and expression. With time, writing and dictating are used to describe pictures and share play experiences. Children become more aware of writing and communication efforts used by playmates and use writing to engage friends in play experiences. They have learned that writers interact with words (Dyson & Genishi, 1993).

Extensive research has been conducted regarding emergent literacy. The process of acquiring literacy occurs prior to formal reading instruction and reading, like writing, follows a predictable pattern. Early literacy development related to reading includes knowledge about directionality, reading print in context, using pretend reading, and reading print in context (Mason & Sinha, 1993). Like the process of understanding and using more complex forms of print, the young child acquires the ability to read through an active, constructive role. However, there is an important interaction with adults, wherein adults provide opportunities for the child to engage in reading activities such as story reading or shared reading.

The process of acquisition of reading develops from listening to, telling, and acting out stories. Children become able to recite or retell stories that have been read and reread to them. They acquire information about the nature of literature through storybook reading, shared reading, dictation, and dramatization experiences. Finally, they move into independent reading and writing (Dyson, 1986; Strickland & Morrow, 1989). Each step in the process involves adult-child interaction in that the routines used by adults to read, talk about stories, and talk about books provide a predictable pattern that encourage the child to participate and take over parts of the process. In addition, the adult organizes and assists the child when the task is too difficult, thus providing scaffolding to support the child's development (Sulzby & Teale, 1991). As the child develops more competency, the adult supplies less support until the child begins to interpret text independently. The child depends upon picture props in the first stages of interpreting text, but gradually is able to replace picture understanding with text understanding (Mason & Sinha, 1993).

The process of learning to read and write as described by researchers in emergent literacy evolves from an innatist and constructivist theory of development. Vygotsky's work on language and thought, especially his position that adults play a mediating role in literacy, is significant in describing the process of emergent literacy. Unfortunately, there is still a lack of consensus as to the role of emergent literacy in early childhood programs today. Many settings adhere to the belief that literacy results from early development of reading and writing skills that are taught through formal prereading or reading readiness programs based on a philosophy of transmission of knowledge. Although emergent literacy is gaining in acceptance, especially with the emphasis on developmentally appropriate practices (Bredekamp, 1987), both approaches to literacy are present in preschool programs. Moreover, although emergent literacy practices offer a rational explanation of how the young child learns to write and read, the early childhood teacher is still confronted with the decision of when and if skills instruction should be included in the curriculum for language and literacy.

Organizing Curriculum for Language and Literacy Development

Before deciding how to organize the curriculum for language and literacy development, the teacher needs to understand what approaches to curriculum are available and the theoretical principles upon which they are based. The teacher also needs to be aware of current research related to the acquisition of language and literacy and its implications for the type of program that is to be developed for young children.

Chapter 8 discussed the alternatives for organizing curriculum for cognitive development by developmental categories or by subject area content. In the area of language and literacy, alternatives for curriculum are related to the different approaches to literacy. As for cognitive development, curriculum can be organized by a developmental approach or on a subject area that traditionally focuses on prereading skills.

The emergent literacy approach to acquisition of the ability to read and write is from a developmental perspective. The program for literacy is based on cognitive-developmental theories of how the child develops cognition in language. In relation to the goals for acquisition of literacy from a developmental point of view, the emergent literacy and whole language approaches both fulfill characteristics of a developmentally appropriate curriculum for preschool children. As commercial resources for preschool and primary grades in language arts move to a more developmental approach in curriculum design, teachers are finding these to be helpful resources in developing appropriate language and literacy curriculum and instruction for their children.

Designing Goals for Curriculum in Language Development   All activities that occur in the preschool program are related to language development. Learning centers, the outdoor play area, teacher-directed activities, and child-initiated play involve language. In addition, activities that are specifically designed for literacy also promote language.

The teacher is concerned with two types of language development: receptive language and expressive language. As was mentioned earlier, receptive language is the language that the child is able to understand, while expressive language is the language that the child is able to use in verbalizations. The sequence of acquisition of receptive and expressive language is helpful in organizing curriculum for language development. Figure 9–1 provides guidelines for the process of acquisition of language skills.

What constitutes an appropriate curriculum for language and literacy in early childhood classrooms is a topic of discussion among educators. Because young children enter educational settings from diverse backgrounds and with individual histories of language development, the challenge is to provide an appropriate range of experiences that are suitable for the developmental needs of every child. More specifically, the curriculum should be designed with developmental variation in mind rather than requiring children to be at a certain developmental level in order to participate (Dyson & Genishi, 1993). Whether the curriculum is organized from a developmental or content area approach, accommodation for variations in children's development and background should be part of the organizational plan. Proponents and opponents of the two approaches to curriculum development often disagree on the effectiveness of the other approach; however, the classroom teacher is left with the decision of understanding the two approaches and how to incorporate the best of each approach, if both are to be used.

Organizing From a Developmental Approach.   Proponents of a developmental approach to organizing curriculum for language and literacy base their program on knowledge of child development and the match between literacy development and the experiences that are available for young children. Curriculum organized from a developmental approach supports a holistic or integrated curriculum where all subject matter is learned through meaningful uses of language. The term *whole language,* then, is used to describe the preschool language and literacy curriculum that uses development as the basis for organization. Emergent literacy stresses the stages of development in reading and writing, and curriculum experiences are organized to complement developmental progress within each individual child. When using the whole language or emergent literacy approaches, the teacher focuses on activities that have meaning and purpose for young children. Skills are learned when the child has need of them but are not a prerequisite, nor are they taught in a prescribed hierarchy (Fields, Spangler, & Lee, 1991).

There are variations in how the teacher organizes the curriculum using a developmental approach. One style is to use components of the whole language approach adapted for preschool children. It incorporates six elements of a whole language program as follows:

1.   *Reading aloud to children.* The teacher reads poetry, letters, stories, and so on.

2.   *Shared book experiences.* The teacher and class read and reread big books, songs, poems, stories, and rhymes.

RECEPTIVE LANGUAGE SKILLS

3–4 years

Carries out a sequence of 2–4 directions.

Responds to who, what, where, and when questions.

Follows 2-step verbal commands.

Can give 2 objects on request.

Understands negative forms such as "The baby isn't eating."

Begins to understand sentences involving time concepts such as "Grandmother is coming tomorrow."

Begins to understand sentences involving if, then, or because statements.

Understands concept expressed by "Let's pretend."

Responds to adverbs such as *softly, loudly, quietly.*

Understands comparatives such as *bigger, biggest.*

Understands concept of empty/full.

Understands many plural forms.

Identifies 3 or more colors.

Recognizes colors when used to modify nouns (red bike).

Repeats a sequence of 3 digits.

Repeats 6- to 7-syllable sentences.

Can match animal sound to picture of animal.

Understands concepts such as big/little, fast/slow.

Understands approximately 1,000 words.

4–5 years

Discriminates between real words and similar nonsense words.

Understands simple negation.

Understands a picture story.

Follows 3 unrelated verbal directions in proper sequence.

Listens to longer, more involved stories, but frequently misinterprets the facts.

Incorporates verbal directions in play activities.

Understands sequencing of events such as "First we peel the potatoes, then we cook them, then we eat them."

Is comprehending more comparative forms.

Recognizes basic colors and shapes.

Repeats a series of 4 digits.

Repeats simple nursery rhymes.

Repeats 12- to 13-syllable sentences.

Answers simple questions about a statement or a short story.

Discriminates whether 2 sounds are the same or different.

Imitates sounds of long and short duration.

Imitates fast and slow sounds.

Repeats a sequence of 3 noisemakers.

Understands approximately 1,500–2,000 words.

EXPRESSIVE LANGUAGE SKILLS

3–4 years

Labels his or her own creations.

Questioning is at its peak.

Asks who, what, where, why questions.

Often asks questions to which the answer is already known.

Mean length of utterance is approximately 4.1–5.4 words.

4–5 years

Uses 5- to 8-word sentences with some clauses included.

Average length of response is approximately 5.4–5.7 words.

Usually requests information in sentences that are appropriately constructed.

Figure 9–1   Development in Receptive and Expressive Language, Ages Three to Five

EXPRESSIVE LANGUAGE SKILLS

3–4 years

Says some nursery rhymes and songs.

Uses speech to obtain and hold the attention of others.

Talks about everything and enjoys playing with words.

Begins using language to satisfy needs.

Begins using language to manipulate peers and adults.

Begins using language to express emotions.

Enjoys talking.

Questions activities of others.

Does not like to repeat utterances.

Likes to use inflection and may also use body for emphasis.

Use of pronoun *I* established.

Forms regular plurals by adding *s* and *z*.

Begins to use negation in the form of *can't* and *don't*.

Begins to add ed to indicate past tense.

Refers to self with pronouns *I* or *me*.

Demonstrates decrease in proportion of nouns and increase in use of pronouns and prepositions.

Can sequence a 3-part event.

Repeats a sequence of 3 digits.

Repeats a sentence of 6–7 syllables.

Toward the end of the period begins asking questions to obtain information, not merely to obtain and hold others' attention.

Speech is generally intelligible, even to unfamiliar listeners; however, some articulation errors are still present.

Can name some colors and shapes.

Has a vocabulary of approximately 900 words.

4–5 years

Uses regular past tense of verbs ending in ed.

Questioning is still a major language form; however, questions are now becoming more concise and on target.

Questions are used for obtaining information, not merely as devices for obtaining and holding the listener's attention.

Tag questions such as "The puppy is eating, isn't he?" begin emerging.

Exhibits a marked increase in the number and variety of words used.

Syntax improves markedly.

Continues to increase the number of pronouns and prepositions used.

"I don't know" becomes a frequent expression.

An increase in the usage of comparative and superlative forms such as *bigger-biggest, hotter-hottest*.

Does not always tell the truth, and does not seem to be able to discriminate between what is true and what is not.

Repeats a sequence of 4 digits.

Communicates effectively.

Marked decrease in articulation errors; speech does not sound as infantile.

Counts to 4 by rote.

Requests for actions by others are often stated as imperatives, such as "Give me a cookie" or "Get my ball."

Asks the meanings of words.

Names the basic colors.

Combines color words and nouns (blue ball).

Answers yes/no questions related to color.

Sorts pictures by categories and gives category name—foods, animals, clothing, toys, etc.

Oral vocabulary of approximately 1,000–1,500 words.

Figure 9–1, *continued*

Source: From *Beginning Milestones* by S. Sheridan and D. B. Murphy, 1986. Reprinted by permission of McGraw-Hill, Inc.

3. *Sustained silent reading.* Teacher and children choose books to "read" silently for a prescribed period of time without interruption. Some preschool teachers prefer to encourage children to "read" their book aloud to themselves.

4. *Guided reading.* Teacher and children meet in small groups to discuss a book. The teacher can use this as a time to teach elements of the reading process as books are read together. As individual children become independent readers, sessions can be individualized.

5. *Individualized reading.* Children who are moving toward independent reading meet with the teacher to discuss progress in individually selected books. The teacher monitors progress and provides assistance as needed.

6. *Writing.* Children dictate stories about their experiences. Children are encouraged to write their own stories at individual levels of writing development.

Another method of organizing the curriculum is based on emerging literacy in reading and writing. In addition to story reading and telling and other literacy experiences led by the teacher, the curriculum can be organized around components that foster reading and writing in children (Fields, Spangler, & Lee, 1991):

1. *Book reading.* The child is encouraged to select books for pretend reading. This process is complemented with books read to the child by an adult. From individual and shared reading experiences, the child comes to understand the forms and meaning of print.

Children need many opportunities to express themselves through writing.

2. *Books for beginners.* As children begin to read independently, books with simple text are provided for individual selection. Teacher support is provided when needed and discontinued when independent reading is possible.

3. *Functional print.* A variety of print sources familiar to the child are introduced to the classroom. Commercial advertising, food containers, and other written sources familiar to the child are included. Environmental print related to centers, names, and so on are shared with and by children.

4. *Writing.* Opportunities for individual writing efforts are provided in connection with all classroom activities. Paintings are labeled, drawings are given captions, and stories are written to accompany series of pictures. Children have access to paper, crayons, and pencils for writing experiences. Older children are encouraged to copy letters and words from print in the environment.

5. *Dictation.* Children dictate contributions to group stories about shared experiences. Children dictate for their own individual purposes, to caption pictures, to respond to books, and so on.

Inclusion of Reading Skills in a Developmental Approach.   Proponents of whole language or emergent literacy approaches to curriculum organization oppose teaching reading skills in isolation separate from the reading and writing process. Nevertheless, many advocates of whole language and emergent literacy understand that young readers need to recognize letters and their associated sounds and the functions and conventions of written language. Word awareness is important, as is comprehension of text. Therefore, when appropriate, developmental curriculum for literacy would include the following components:

Sight words
Phonics
Word-analysis activities
Configuration and context clues
Conventions and functions of print
Comprehension

Guidelines for organizing the curriculum from a developmental approach can be derived from developmental checklists. The checklist designed by Morrow (1989) includes language development as well as elements of emergent reading and writing (Figure 9–2).

Organizing From a Subject Area Approach.   When the curriculum is organized using a language arts approach or subject area approach, goals are developed for listening, speaking, reading, and writing. How these components are organized and implemented depends on the teacher or school's philosophy of the nature of learning language and literacy. If the perspective is that there are prerequisite skills that lead to

Checklist for Assessing Early Literacy Development

Child's Name _____

Date _____

Language Development	Always	Sometimes	Never
Makes phoneme sounds			
Speaks in one-word sentences			
Speaks in two-word sentences			
Identifies familiar sounds			
Differentiates similar sounds			
Understands the language of others when spoken to			
Follows verbal directions			
Speaks to others freely			
Pronounces words correctly			
Has appropriate vocabulary for level of maturity			
Speaks in complete sentences			
Uses varied syntactic structures			
Can be understood by others			

The items on this checklist correspond to the stages of language development from birth to 6.

Reading Attitudes and Voluntary Reading Behavior	Always	Sometimes	Never
Voluntarily looks at books			
Asks to be read to			
Listens attentively while being read to			
Responds with questions and comments to stories read to him or her			

Concepts About Books	Always	Sometimes	Never
Knows that a book is for reading			
Can identify the front, back, top, and bottom of a book			
Can turn the pages of a book properly			
Knows the difference between print and pictures			
Knows that the pictures on a page are related to what the print says			
Knows where one begins reading on a page			
Knows what a title of a book is			
Knows what an author is			
Knows what an illustrator is			

Figure 9–2   Checklist for Assessing Early Literacy Development

Comprehension of Story	Always	Sometimes	Never
Retells familiar stories using the pictures in the book to help recall the details			
Retells a story without the help of the book and demonstrates knowledge of details			
Retells stories with readinglike intonation			
Includes elements of story structure in story retellings: setting (beginning, time, place, characters)			
theme (problem or goal of the main character)			
plot episodes (events leading toward the solution of the main character's problem or the attainment of his or her goal)			
resolution (problem solved, goal achieved, story ended)			
Responds to story readings with literal, inferential, and critical questions and comments			
Responds to story readings with inferential and critical questions and comments			
Participates in story-reading behavior by reciting or narrating stories as the teacher is reading them			
When read to, fills in words of a story according to knowledge of syntax and context			

Concepts About Print	Always	Sometimes	Never
Knows that print is read from left to right			
Knows that oral language can be written down, then read			
Knows what a letter is and can point to one on a printed page			
Knows what a word is and can point one out on a printed page			
Is aware of environmental print and can read some signs and logos			
Recognizes some words by sight in book print			
Can identify letters by name			
Associates some sounds with letters			
Asks questions about letter names, words, and sounds			
Attempts reading by attending to pictures			
Attempts reading by attending to print			
Begins to use story context, syntax, and semantics to identify words			

Figure 9–2, *continued*

Writing Development	Always	Sometimes	Never
Independently explores with writing materials			
Attempts writing in order to convey meaning, regardless of writing stage			
Dictates stories or sentences he or she wants written down			
Copies letters or words			
Forms identifiable letters			
Writes from left to right			
Check (✓) the category or categories at which the child seems to be writing:			
_____ uses drawing for writing and drawing			
_____ differentiates between drawing and writing			
_____ scribbles for writing			
_____ uses letterlike forms for writing			
_____ uses learned letters in random fashion for writing			
_____ uses invented spelling for writing			
_____ uses conventional spelling for writing			

General Comments about the Child's Development:

Figure 9–2, *continued*

Source: From *Literacy Development* (2nd ed.) by L. M. Morrow, 1993, Englewood Cliffs, NJ: Prentice Hall. Copyright 1993 by Prentice Hall. Reprinted by permission.

reading and writing, then the teacher is likely to be more involved with teacher-directed activities in prereading and prewriting. Instruction in phonics and reading readiness skills reinforced with workbook or reproduced pages might follow a prescribed language arts program for preschool children. There is teacher-directed instruction in the four components of language arts instruction, which are frequently taught as separate curriculum subjects.

If, however, the teacher and the school believe in an integrated language arts curriculum that is flexible and child-centered, the organization will be similar to a whole language approach, with the four components integrated within the language arts curriculum. The developmental needs and differences of young children are reflected by a wide range of opportunities for children to engage in speaking, listening, reading, and writing activities that incorporate developmental stages in language and literacy. Interactive experiences with peers, adults, and play materials in the environment foster the development of the child's ability to communicate and learn through oral and written language.

Current researchers, while acknowledging the differences between whole language and skills approaches to preschool language and literacy curriculum, warn that there has been little research at the preschool level to support particular types of instruction. Moreover, researchers studying the development of cognitive strategies in young children propose that the limitation of cognitive strategies in preschool children suggests a need for direct teaching of specific knowledge to young children. More specifically, young children need to learn the relationships between letters and corresponding sounds (Seifert, 1993) as part of acquisition of reading.

The implication for teachers of young children is that there should be a balance between child-centered and child-initiated activities and direct and indirect teaching. The emergent literacy or whole language approach is being included in some school districts; nevertheless, the concept of reading readiness and related instructional practices persists in the majority of classrooms (Durkin, 1987). Although we propose the developmental perspective to literacy in this text, the role of the teacher in assisting and supporting children in the developmental process is significant, and purposeful teaching of literacy skills should be part of the balanced language and literacy curriculum. The *Teacher's Guide to Evaluation: Assessment Handbook* (Sulzby, 1993), which accompanies the text *Celebrate Reading* published by Scott, Foresman and Company, includes many guidelines for prereading and reading instruction. Figures 9–3, 9–4, and 9–5 give examples of Sulzby's checklists for emergent literacy, which include skills in alphabet, letter, and word knowledge.

ASSESSING DEVELOPMENT IN LANGUAGE AND LITERACY

The issue of appropriate curriculum and instruction for language and literacy development extends to determining practices to be used for assessment. In the classroom where the program is skills-based, the traditional method for assessment consists of skills worksheets and standardized tests such as reading readiness tests. Standardized test scores can be used to measure achievement and compare children's performance. Developmental curriculum and instruction for language and literacy, on the other hand, is designed to accommodate rather than compare differences in children's development of literacy. Curriculum that is designed to foster literacy in a diverse population of young children leads to assessment of the young child's progress and growth, instead of comparative achievement.

Whole language and emergent literacy advocates recommend evaluation strategies that respond to processes of teaching and learning that are taking place in classrooms. Child-oriented assessment should provide information to the teacher and child about what has been learned and will lead to planning for future activities for the child (Dyson & Genishi, 1993). Two processes for accomplishing this type of

Student_____

General Book-Reading Behaviors	Dates and Comments

General Book-Reading Behaviors

Is attentive and engaged in group reading time

Holds books easily

Turns pages easily

Attempts to read emergently

Is attentive to print as source of reading

Uses patterns (words, familiar phrases, themes, structures)
  from reading in his/her writing

Uses special intonation in reading attempts

    Sounds like a reader

    Sounds like a storyteller

    Uses conversational intonation

Levels of Emergent/Conventional Reading

Reads familiar storybooks emergently

    Level 1   Attending to pictures, not forming stories

    Level 2   Attending to pictures, forming oral stories

    Level 3   Attending to pictures, mixed reading and storytelling

    Level 4   Attending to pictures, forming written stories

    Level 5   Attending to print

        Reads aspectually—word emphasis, letter-sound emphasis,
          comprehension emphasis

        Reads with strategies imbalanced—tracks print but overdepends
          on one or more of the three aspects

        Reads conventionally from familiar material

Reads conventionally from new material

Figure 9–3   Emergent to Conventional Storybook Reading Checklist
Source: From *Teacher's Guide to Evaluation Grade 1* by E. Sulzby, 1993, Glenview, IL:
ScottForesman. Copyright © 1993 by ScottForesman. Reprinted by permission.

child-centered assessment are described as dynamic assessment and situated assessment. Dynamic assessment is information acquired from the child's responses to teacher-child dialogue in context of developmental activities. Situated assessment involves the teacher collecting data about the child's progress and performance while the child is engaged in literacy activities (Fields, Spangler, & Lee, 1991). Strategies for acquiring language development are discussed below.

Student_____

Composes own pieces of writing	Dates and Comments
Uses emergent and conventional forms of writing	
Scribble	
Drawing	
Letterlike forms	
Strings of recognizable letters (nonphonetic)	
Some invented spelling	
Much invented spelling	
Writes readable words (conventionally and with invented spelling)	
Reads emergently from own writing	
Reads conventionally from own writing	
Shows attention to audience needs	
In composing	
During conferencing	
In revising	
In proofreading for publishing	

Figure 9–4   Emergent to Conventional Writing Checklist
Source: From *Teacher's Guide to Evaluation Grade 1* by E. Sulzby, 1993, Glenview, IL:
ScottForesman. Copyright © 1993 by ScottForesman. Reprinted by permission.

Strategies for Assessing Language and Literacy Development

Assessment in the preschool classroom takes place on a daily basis. Because evalua-tion of developmental learning should be consistent with the curriculum and instruc-tion, assessment is conducted in a natural and meaningful context. Three informal strategies that are effective for gathering data about the child's progress in language and literacy development are teacher observation, teacher-student conferences, and portfolios. In addition, the use of checklists as guides to evaluation and record keep-ing assist the teacher in documenting information about the child's work and progress.

Observation   Observation of young children at work and play is the most produc-tive method of assessing their interests and accomplishments. The most natural way to learn about a child's language is to listen to the child's conversations in natural set-tings. The teacher can take notes about the child's verbalizations and determine if more complex forms of syntax are being used or if new words have been added to his or her vocabulary. A whole language teacher describes how she uses blank mailing

Student_____

	Dates and Comments
Sings/recites alphabet	
Names capital letters	
Names lowercase letters	
Recognizes words that begin like a model	
Produces words that begin like a model	
Recognizes words that rhyme	
Produces words that rhyme	
Uses phonograms or rhyming patterns for needed words	
In reading	
In writing	
Sounds out simple words with teacher help	
In reading	
In writing	
Sounds out words independently	
In reading	
In writing	
Sounds out words and cross-checks with meaning when needed	
Is able to sound out nonsense words and/or words not in meaning vocabulary	
Shows evidence of building a sight vocabulary	
In reading	
In writing	
Sight vocabulary includes high-frequency words	
Describes strategies he/she uses in reading and writing	

Figure 9–5   Alphabet, Letter, and Word Knowledge Checklist (Phonemic Awareness)
Source: From *Teacher's Guide to Evaluation Grade 1* by E. Sulzby, 1993, Glenview, IL: ScottForesman. Copyright © 1993 by ScottForesman. Reprinted by permission.

labels to jot down observations as she walks around the room each day working and talking with children. At the end of the day, she places the labels in folders she has prepared for individual children (Pils, 1991).

Observation also permits the teacher to note children's selections from the book center and their writing efforts. Information about difficulties a child is experiencing in writing or retelling a story, or copying written print can be noted for addition to anecdotal records that are kept on the child and that are used for planning instruction for the child.

Teacher-Student Conferences   Many teachers in classrooms using whole language or emergent literacy conduct regular conferences with children to carry out evaluations and obtain feedback on the child's interests and needs. In preschool classrooms, conferences can be incidental in nature as the teacher stops for a minute or two to chat with a child about an activity. The conference can be initiated by a child who has a question or wants to share an idea. The interview techniques discussed in Chapter 8 can also be incorporated into conferences as teacher and students engage in dialogues about ongoing activities and work. Information gained from the conferences give teachers direction for future instructional planning. The teacher can use the conference opportunity to share a book with a child, listen to the child read a story he or she has written, or assist the child in finding information or choose a resource to use in a literacy activity.

Portfolios   Portfolios are a collection of a child's work that can be used for sharing information and for evaluation. There are different types of portfolios and different purposes for using portfolios. Some are organized by the child to share with parents. Others are put together by teachers for assessment purposes. Still other portfolios contain materials selected by both teacher and child.

Portfolios can be any type of envelope, folder, or other container that can be used to house a collection of the child's work. They can be simple in organization with items arranged chronologically, or they can have categories for writing, reading, and work in other subject areas. The portfolio can consist only of samples of the child's work or can also be used for storing checklists or rating scales such as the literacy checklists in Figures 9–3, 9–4, and 9–5, which can be used to track children's progress.

Observation information recorded in anecdotal records or other forms of record keeping can be stored in portfolios as can information gleaned from teacher-child conferences and parent-teacher conferences. The portfolio can serve as the focus for conferences with parents and the child to discuss progress and possible problems. In sum, there is no formula or prescribed format or purpose for portfolios. The portfolio is a flexible evaluation and assessment resource that has as its primary purpose to provide information that will enable the teacher to plan for the child's development and learning.

Checklists and Rating Scales   Checklists were discussed in Chapter 4 and earlier in this chapter as one source for organization of curriculum and instruction in preschool classrooms. They also serve as resources for recording assessments and reporting progress to parents. There has been much criticism of checklists when used as assessment tools for skills related to reading readiness or mathematics. Nevertheless, when used appropriately to record individual progress in literacy or a constructivist approach to cognitive development, they can become valuable resources for teachers. When combined with observation, portfolios, and other assessment strategies, checklists serve as organizers and guides for planning curriculum and instruction. Language and literacy checklists serve as guides to developmental sequences in language, reading, and writing, which are helpful to both teachers and parents in understanding the young child's progress and to guide them in realistic expectations for what the child will be able to do and how to provide for instructional improvement for the child.

ASSESSMENT/LEARNING EXPERIENCES FOR LANGUAGE AND LITERACY DEVELOPMENT

Objective: Understands a picture story

____ Source: Figure 9–1, Development in Receptive and Expressive Language, Ages Three to Five

____ Materials Needed: A picture book or set of pictures depicting a story

____ Activity: Look through the book with the child and discuss the pictures. Ask the child to tell a story using the pictures. If a record of the child's story is desired for a portfolio, individual books can be made with the pictures and blank pages. As the child tells a story, record it in the book. Or the child can use emergent writing skills to tell the story.

Objective: Discriminates whether two sounds are the same or different

____ Source: Figure 9–1, Development in Receptive and Expressive Language, Ages Three to Five

____ Materials Needed: Empty film canisters; foam meat tray; permanent marker; contact paper; assorted objects or material to put into canisters; color dots for coding canisters

____ Instructions for Preparing Activity: Cover six or eight empty film cans with colored contact paper. Trace the shapes of the bottom of film cans on the meat tray to provide a storage tray for the activity. Put matching objects or materials in two separate cans (e.g., beans, salt, safety pins). Code matching pairs with dots on the bottom of the cans. Put the covers back on the cans.

____ Activity: Introduce the activity and model how to shake the cans and listen for the cans that make matching sounds. The child then shakes the cans to find matching pairs. Color-coded dots on the bottom of the cans can be used to check or correct choices.

Objective: Is aware of environmental print and can read some signs and logos

____ Source: Figure 9–2, Checklist for Assessing Early Literacy Development

____ Materials Needed: Used containers of familiar cereals, fast food logos, fruit drinks, cookies, and so on, arranged on a bulletin board

____ Activity: Ask the child to identify as many of the logos or product names as he or she can. As an alternative, ask the child to find the environmental word or logo when it is named.

Objective: Associates sounds with letters

_____ Source: Figure 9–2, Checklist for Assessing Early Literacy Development

_____ Materials Needed: A set of cards with letters that are familiar to the child

_____ Activity: A game similar to Old Maid is played. The cards are dealt. The child draws from another player's hand and identifies the sound that is associated with the letter. If the response is correct, the child keeps the card. If the response is incorrect, the card is returned to the player from which it was drawn and used again.

Objective: Can identify letters by name

_____ Source: Figure 9–2, Checklist for Assessing Early Literacy Development

_____ Materials Needed: Letters of the alphabet are displayed as an array in random order on a sheet of paper

_____ Activity: Ask the child to point to and name the letters that he or she knows. Correct responses are circled. The page is dated and placed in the child's portfolio. The activity can be repeated periodically through the year, with new copies added to the portfolio.

Objective: Recognizes words that begin like a model

_____ Source: Figure 9–5, Alphabet, Letter, and Word Knowledge Checklist

_____ Materials Needed: Big Book storybook and familiar words on cards (e.g., children's names, words with picture labels attached)

_____ Activity: Select a Big Book storybook page that has words that begin with the same letters as the cards to be used. Ask the child to select a word card and name it and the sound it begins with. Then ask the child to find a word or words on the Big Book page that begin with the same letter and sound.

PLANNING INSTRUCTION FOR CHILDREN WITH COMMUNICATION IMPAIRMENTS

Children with communication disorders have a condition that affects their ability to acquire concepts and to follow directions. Disorders can include speechlessness, speech confusion, and poor word comprehension. They have a difficulty in understanding language or expressing themselves through language. Many factors can affect a child's speech and language development, including a sensory deprivation, difficulties in processing information, a poor language environment, and brain damage (Deiner, 1993). The results of a communication disorder can be delayed language; difficulty in production of speech sounds or articulation; voice disorders that affect the pitch, volume, or voice quality of speech; and delayed cognitive development.

Although many of the instructional strategies recommended for children without impairments are also helpful for children with communication disorders, teachers need to be aware of some special characteristics for which they can provide help for improvement. First, young children with communication impairments are frequently reluctant to speak and need opportunities to practice in situations that are comfortable and nonthreatening. Fingerplays, puppets, and organized activities that involve verbalizations in a playlike setting encourage these children to work on speech.

Listening to and reading stories aloud can benefit children with communication disorders, affording them opportunities to hear and practice sounds. Stories and fingerplays that rhyme assist children in hearing and using sounds, while stories that emphasize a single sound help children focus on individual letter sounds.

Traditionally, a reading readiness approach has been used to help young children with communication disorders acquire literacy skills. An obvious reason is that emphasis on letter sounds and pronunciation of letters can be practiced. Visual and auditory strategies are recommended for teaching letter recognition and letter memory through perceptual matching and sorting tasks (Deiner, 1993). However, emergent literacy activities are also appropriate for these children, including dictation of language experience stories where they can make relationships between spoken and written language and practice articulating what they have dictated for the teacher to write.

Emergent writing activities are also beneficial for these children as are shared reading activities and rereading and retelling of familiar stories. Experiencing text in context permits children with communication disorders to use visual and listening activities to support processing communications and using verbal and written language that is difficult for them.

PLANNING INSTRUCTION FOR CHILDREN FROM DIVERSE BACKGROUNDS

The 1990 Census revealed that almost 14 percent of children between the ages of 5 and 17 speak a language other than English at home in the United States, while individual states such as California, Texas, and New Mexico have much higher percentages. Twenty-five different languages were reported by the Census Bureau; and language minority children will become the majority in many school districts in the future (Bredekamp & Rosegrant, 1992a).

Children from linguistically diverse families have traditionally encountered difficulties in academic achievement in elementary schools. Although students in public schools were expected to fit into an "Americanization" model of education in the past (Garcia, 1993), new understandings about language and cultural diversity are enabling educators, particularly early childhood educators, to plan instruction that fosters language and literacy in children from linguistically diverse families in preschool programs.

Children from linguistically diverse families can enter school speaking only the home language, have some facility in a different language as well as English, or speak a dialect that is a variation of Standard English. Whichever, condition the child brings to school, the emergent literacy approach to language and literacy is recommended by many specialists in the education of linguistically diverse children in early childhood programs.

Although there is continuing criticism of bilingual programs in this country, there is strong evidence that these programs can be effective, especially when the language and culture of the child is incorporated into the program along with instruction in English proficiency. Speaking two languages need not be a handicap to academic achievement in bilingual children (Garcia, 1993); nevertheless, educators must accept that the second language develops slowly, and young bilingual children may need several years of schooling before their English skills are on a par with their English-speaking peers (Wolfe, 1992). As more information is acquired on stages of second language acquisition, educators of all types of programs for children of language diversity are becoming aware of the similarities between second language acquisition and first language acquisition.

Young children acquiring English as a second language need modeling and encouragement rather than correcting and drilling, just as is appropriate for first language learners. Children use trial and error to learn the new language vocabulary, syntax, and semantics. Early childhood educators should focus on building children's receptive vocabulary in the early stages and supporting their efforts to verbalize as they start to express themselves in English, even if their first efforts are limited. Children need contextual clues to help them acquire meaning, while concrete materials and real experiences will promote language acquisition and construction of knowledge (Wolfe, 1992).

The constructivist model of literacy or emergent literacy is recommended for children with diversity in language. Au (1993) proposes that the meaningful context of emergent literacy strategies is compatible with the needs of the children from diverse backgrounds. In contrast, the transmission of skills approach, where skills taught in isolation, makes it difficult for children from diverse language backgrounds to understand and process information. An advantage of the constructivist or emergent literacy model is that it draws upon the home and community language of the child in building literacy. The social influences on language and literacy development become a strength rather than a weakness for the young child.

The literacy classroom setting using a whole language or emergent literacy approach that provides for diversity in individual experiences and development is naturally broadened to incorporate cultural and language diversity. The language and culture that the child brings to the educational setting is complemented by the school environment, rather than being dissonant or incompatible with a predetermined expectation of readiness based on established norms of language development.

Learning opportunities and activities are responsive to students' needs and abilities in the emergent literacy environment. Skills instruction is conducted within a meaningful context for the learner, and scaffolding and support are provided to assist the child both in acquisition of the language of the school and in acquisition of literacy.

Children who are from linguistically diverse families need the same kinds of literacy experiences as children who are English speakers. They need to be encouraged to engage in reading and writing activities at whatever level they are comfortable. Children in bilingual programs may learn to read and write first in another language than English. Children who are in multilingual programs, where the first language is not used as a medium of instruction, can work in English at their own level of acquisition. The important element is that the teacher understand the nature of their second language development and provide acceptance and support, using the individual child's interests and strengths. Children from diverse language backgrounds benefit from interacting with children who are English speakers, who can model for them and engage them in conversations that will further their use of English. Children who are limited English speakers or speak a dialect other than Standard English need a classroom that is focused on language development, especially vocabulary expansion through conversations and discussions.

EVALUATING CURRICULUM AND INSTRUCTION FOR LANGUAGE AND LITERACY DEVELOPMENT

The nature of language and literacy development causes teachers of young children to focus on formative evaluation when assessing each child's development. The focus of formative evaluation strategies is on the child's progress in language and literacy. The appropriate strategies for evaluating growth in language and literacy produce data on a child's ongoing progress rather than mastery of specific skills. Evaluation of curriculum and instruction for language and literacy has its strongest emphasis on ongoing or formative evaluation rather than on summative evaluation. This is because the teacher must constantly monitor progress and needs of individual students in language and literacy to obtain input for instructional planning. Nevertheless, summative evaluation has an important function in evaluating overall effectiveness of the language program.

Formative Evaluation

Formative evaluation related to language and literacy development involves all aspects of the program, including the environment, activities, and teacher-directed interactions with the children. Using information from the children's work and information from talks with them, the teacher evaluates the materials and activities used in the classroom. Are there interesting materials in the writing center? Do new books need to be added to the library center? Are the children being provided with adequate time for writing stories or making their own book collections? In other words, are the environment, activities, and schedule appropriate for the emergent literacy program? If changes need to be made, what are the best solutions to making improvements?

The teacher will also want to consult children's portfolios and other assessments to keep appraised of their progress in language and literacy development. Is each child making the kind of progress that is expected or desired? Which children are ready for more shared reading activities? Are there children who need more opportunities for small-group conversations to boost their confidence in using oral language? Are there children who are progressing rapidly in moving into independent reading and who need more challenging books? Which children seem to be moving very slowly and need to be observed for possible clues as to any difficulties or causes of lack of progress? While the teacher is evaluating children on a daily basis, it is also necessary to study overall progress periodically to make appropriate adjustments in plans for children's growth.

The teacher also engages in self-evaluation as part of ongoing or formative evaluation. He or she wants to monitor how time for interacting with children is being scheduled to determine if individual needs are being met. Is the teacher evaluating children's progress on a regular basis and able to manage record keeping so that evaluation information is current? Is teacher-directed instruction conducted regularly and effectively? Does the teacher need to search for new strategies to reach children or engage their interests? Are diagnostic strategies being conducted effectively and results used to assist children in resolving problems they are encountering in their work?

Formative evaluation enables the teacher to take the pulse of the children and the program and to monitor individual and group progress in language and literacy. Much of the success of children's participation in the program depends on the teacher's ability to keep abreast of each child's growth in all components of the program. Each child enters the program with differences in background and development in language and literacy. Throughout the program, these differences, together with the individual child's interests, continue to result in differences in the nature of progress for each child. Ongoing monitoring of that progress enables the teacher to provide encouragement, as well as activities and materials that are engaging and challenging.

Summative Evaluation

Summative evaluation permits the teacher to consider individual accomplishments throughout the year and overall effectiveness of the program. The children's movement toward literacy and growth in language development can be evaluated at the end of the year by interacting with them in literacy activities and studying their portfolios. The teacher compares the child's level of development at the beginning of the program and at the end of the program to evaluate the kind of growth that was made and to synthesize information for final reporting to parents and future teachers.

The teacher also reflects upon the strengths and weaknesses of the program to determine what changes are indicated for the following year and if additional kinds of materials or activities can be incorporated to capture children's interests in engaging in reading and writing activities. How can group activities be personalized to accommodate diversity in children? What new books can be acquired to enrich book reading and sharing experiences? What sorts of integrated curriculum activities can be planned to provide more depth for oral and written language? Should different field trip opportunities be considered to expand language vocabularies and motivation for using oral and written language?

Summative evaluation of the language program enables the teacher to evaluate individual growth and program effectiveness. It closes the work for one year and anticipates interesting possibilities for the year to come. Teachers, parents, and children all derive a sense of satisfaction from reviewing the work of the year that is documented in the work of the children that has been collected and shared.

✦ SUMMARY

The young child's success in school depends partially on the language he or she brings on entering school. Another significant factor is how the school and teacher understand and accept the unique variations in language that children acquire in diverse language communities. Curriculum and instruction for language and literacy are evolving to complement children's language characteristics and need for child-centered teaching strategies. While a skills or transmission of information approach is still practiced in many preschools in an effort to prepare young children for the primary grades, many schools are now moving to an emergent literacy or whole language approach to language curriculum. This approach focuses on young children's natural acquisition of language and literacy. To understand the merits of this approach to curriculum and instruction, the preschool teacher must understand the nature of language and literacy development and its implications for planning experiences for young children.

Children begin to acquire both language and literacy as infants. There are different theories of how young children acquire language, none of which completely explains the process; nevertheless, it is generally accepted that children have an innate or internal process to acquire language that is unique to humans. They initiate efforts to use language and move through stages of development as they acquire language and literacy. Adults model adult forms of the language for the child. They also influence the child's acquisition and use of language in the interactions they have with young children and the encouragement and support or scaffolding they provide for the child's progress in moving to more complex forms of language and literacy.

The ultimate goal for language and literacy development is that beyond being able to communicate through oral language, children will be able to extend communication through reading and writing. It is clear that we are learning more and more that the nature of acquisition of literacy is similar to that of oral language and that the preschool years are significant in the process.

The organization of curriculum and instruction for language and literacy development for preschool children combines support for the development of each individual child. The teacher facilitates the process by organizing the environment to be rich in print examples, materials that motivate attempts to read and write, and activities that support use of oral and written language. Within the classroom and outdoors, the teacher consciously interacts with children through conversations, discussions, reading and sharing books, and questioning children about their work, all with the intent of encouraging the use of language. The teacher also engages in direct teaching activities to provide children with information that will extend and expand their oral, reading, and writing skills in language.

Extensive research on the process of acquiring literacy has implications for curriculum and instruction in preschool classrooms. The environment should be organized so that children have opportunities to use written communication in all types of centers in daily play opportunities. Moreover, many frequent experiences with books, stories, and activities that enable children to retell favorite stories and write or dictate their own stories foster their development into literacy. Skills development in instruction is best taught in meaningful contexts when needed by the child or is indicated by the child's progress.

Evaluation and assessment of children's progress in language and literacy is child centered as is instruction. Assessment strategies must be responsive to the fact that children's progress is individual, gradual, and reflective. Observing children at work, studying their writing and reading efforts, and listening to their natural oral language are the methods teachers use to understand each child's growth and progress. Likewise, collections of children's work and checklists containing documentation of achievements on the path to literacy organized in portfolios provide a means to share the child's progress. At the end of a school year, the portfolios enable the teacher to reflect on the progress of the language and literacy program and to make plans for enriching the program for the year to come.

✦ STUDY QUESTIONS

1. How do explanations of language development also explain literacy development?
2. Explain how both language and literacy follow a predictable pattern of development. Give examples.
3. Why do children come to school with wide diversity in language?
4. Describe some of these possible differences in use of language.
5. Explain the role of play in the child's development of language and literacy.
6. How do adults influence children's language and literacy development?
7. What kinds of experiences do young children need to develop literacy?
8. How do these experiences contrast to more traditional skills approaches to teaching prereading and prewriting skills?
9. Explain how the innatist, interactionist, and learning theory points of view explain how young children learn language.
10. How does the teacher use implications of these theories to design curriculum and instruction for language and literacy development?

11. Why does the teacher serve more of a responsive role in curriculum and instruction for language and literacy than conducting direct instruction with children?
12. Why does language and literacy curriculum need to fit the developmental and cultural needs of the child?
13. How does curriculum designed from a developmental approach fit developmental characteristics of young children?
14. Explain the components of an emergent literacy or whole language approach to the design of curriculum and instruction.
15. What skills for reading are taught to beginning readers? When is it appropriate to teach skills to young children? When is it not appropriate?
16. Describe appropriate strategies to assess progress in language and literacy.
17. What are some possibilities for record keeping or documenting development in language and literacy?
18. Explain some of the unique needs of children with communication disorders for language and literacy curriculum and instruction.
19. What challenges do children from diverse language communities present in preschool classrooms?

➜ KEY TERMS

emergent literacy   receptive language
expressive language

➜ SUGGESTED ACTIVITIES

1. Observe a child three years old and one five years old. Record some of the oral language of each. Identify their language characteristics on the language development profile in Figure 9–1.
2. Observe a child whose first language is not English. Record and analyze the child's verbalizations.
3. Visit a preschool classroom where whole language or emergent literacy activities are implemented. Describe the activities for language and literacy used in the classroom. Do the same type of observation in a classroom that uses a reading readiness program. Compare the types of activities found in the two settings.
4. Observe a group of children engaged in emergent writing activities. Compare how the process is used by individual children.
5. Observe a group of children engaged in a book-sharing or dictated-story activity conducted by the teacher. Describe the activity.

→ 10

Social Development

→ Chapter Objectives

As a result of reading this chapter, you will be able to

1. Describe the nature of social behavior
2. Explain the theoretical bases of social development
3. Discuss the role of play in social development
4. Describe how theories inform practices in early childhood education
5. Explain stages in social and emotional development
6. Discuss how adults can help children develop social competence
7. Describe how the teacher designs and implements instruction for social development
8. Explain roles the teacher uses to promote social development
9. Discuss characteristics of the curriculum for social development
10. Explain how the curriculum for social development addresses the inclusion of children with disabilities and children representing cultural diversity
11. Describe how the early childhood environment affects social interaction
12. Describe how social development is assessed by the teacher

Every child is born into a specific society and must learn the categories and rules pre-scribed by that society. Children must understand, for example, what boys and girls are, what children and adults are, what doctors and patients (or their society's equivalents) are, and how people in each of these categories are supposed to act. Without an understand-ing of these categories and rules, children cannot act competently as members of their society.

The process by which a society teaches children these categories, as well as numer-ous other social rules, are collectively called *socialization*. (Fischer, Hand, Watson, & Tucker, 1984)

The young child's social development and learning is addressed in this chapter. The definition cited above describes one component of social development, socialization, the process through which young children understand and become part of their soci-ety. Nevertheless, social development is more than socialization because the child's individual personality is evolving at the same time. In the early childhood years, children's perception of themselves and their style of interacting with others develop within the process of socialization.

The process that young children use to become socialized into their society can be described more specifically. They must develop social competence, or the skills that they need to be able to have positive social relationships with their peers and adults. Further, moral development is a component of socialization and personality development as children learn the values of their society and the behaviors that are appropriate and inappropriate. Children move through stages of moral development, beginning in early childhood when they first learn to make judgments about right and wrong. According to Piaget (1932), early moral development—which he called moral realism—emerges when children determine that acts are moral when they conform to authority or to rules. While Piaget related moral development to the child's cognitive functioning, Kohlberg's theory (1981) proposed that children's earliest moral behavior is guided by the prospect of punishment.

As young children enter preschool programs, their social development progresses in a group setting. They become socialized into a school community with its expectations and values. Their social development now expands as they learn more about people who live in families and community groups. Part of the young child's socialization and social competence is to understand, appreciate, and interact positively with people from other cultural and language backgrounds. They learn that although there are many differences in people, there are also many similarities: all people have characteristics in common.

This chapter will begin with a discussion of social development, its characteristics and components, as well as theoretical bases that contribute to our understanding of it. The role of play in social development and learning will be described to emphasize play's importance as a natural vehicle for interacting with others and rehearsing and experiencing social roles. The teacher's role in planning instruction includes nurturing the child's socialization leading to competence in peer interactions. The instructional program also includes opportunities for children to appreciate diversity in people in general and specific differences in children within the classroom.

The role of assessment and evaluation in social development will be addressed, followed by how the teacher promotes social development for children with disabilities. The formative and summative evaluation of the program for social development will be described in the final sections of the chapter.

THE NATURE OF SOCIAL DEVELOPMENT

The young child's social development begins in infancy when the newborn establishes a bond with its mother and father and further establishes emotional ties with siblings and other adults and caregivers. The quality of these early attachments affects the baby's responses to new situations and people. Attachment is an affectional bond between babies and their parents that begins at birth and continues through childhood. The child's attachment can be secure or insecure, depending on the pattern of the bonding between child and parent (Ainsworth, 1989). The bonding pattern is affected by child-rearing practices and attitudes.

Early interactions with adults form the first steps in a child's process of socialization. The infant and caregiver are able to establish social interactions. The baby learns the "give and take," or turn taking, that is the basis of all later social interactions. Mother and baby take turns smiling and verbalizing to each other when they socialize.

Infants begin social interactions with their peers at a very young age. By six months, infants can direct smiles and vocalizations to their peers. They use a variety of social behaviors with peers during the first year, and by the second year, they can imitate play partners and perform a variety of social behaviors (Ladd & Coleman, 1993).

The young child's social and emotional development is reflected in the emergence of empathy. Babies tend to respond to the distress of peers by twelve months. This understanding of the distress of others results in attempts to provide comfort by two years of age.

Between the first and second year, toddlers have social signals and gestures they can use in social interactions. Although their play is more likely to be solitary prior to the age of three, some can engage in planned pretend play and are able to sustain play episodes for longer periods of time than children between the ages of one and two (Schickedanz, Schickedanz, Hansen, & Forsyth, 1993).

As early as age two, young children are able to form social relationships as they develop preferences for particular peers and seek to establish play episodes with them. Ladd and Coleman (1993) reported that friendships with a strong emotional component develop in toddlers, an attachment that is similar to the one they form with parents. Some toddler relationships are stable over time (Howes, 1983).

Between the ages of three and five, peer relationships take an increasing amount of time. In addition, social development is molded by other people in the child's social community and is affected by the child's gender. Siblings and the child's birth order in the family are factors that affect social development. Other variations that influence development include parenting styles and cultural and ethnic differences. Factors that can have negative effects on the socialization process include the effects of divorce, child abuse, working mothers, and television (Santrock, 1993). All of these factors affect the child's progress in socialization and personality development. According to Shapiro (1993), nearly three million children are abused or neglected each year. Abused children have a high incidence of social and behavior problems and are likely to be insecurely attached to their parents (Etaugh & Rathus, 1995). Likewise, children from divorced families show more problems than children in non-divorced families (Hetherington et al., 1992).

As children spend more time learning to gain acceptance in a social group, they must also understand the consequences of their behavior related to peer acceptance. They will have to learn how to gain control of their anger and aggression and to place the good of the group before their own desires.

Self-identification is the process whereby the young child develops a sense of who he or she is and wants to be. Part of that identity is developed through the child's participation in his or her family, community, culture, and religious group. Identification of sex or gender is another part of the process. Boys learn that they are boys and girls learn that they are girls through the socialization process that is affected by the child's biology and gender-appropriate behavior nurtured by family, peers, school experiences, and media (Cole & Cole, 1989; Santrock, 1993).

Moral development is the component of social development that enables the child to understand how people should behave in their interactions with other people and how to control their own behavior so that they can interact successfully in social groups. To achieve peer acceptance, they must learn self-control to avoid inappropriate behaviors. More specifically, they learn to control anger, physical aggression, and impulse control. Aggressive behavior is learned through observation, parental discipline styles that include physical punishment, and violence on television.

The positive moral behavior that discourages aggression is the acquisition of **prosocial behavior**. When the young child uses behaviors that involve cooperating, helping, comforting, or sharing with peers and adults, prosocial behaviors are being used. The child learns prosocial behavior through observation, adult modeling, and a nurturing environment (Schickedanz, Schickedanz, Hansen, & Forsyth, 1993).

The socialization process developed in the early childhood years establishes the foundation for more complex social situations that are encountered by school-age children. For example, children who have had parents who nurtured prosocial behavior through their parenting style and expectations for empathy will be more likely to have children with prosocial behaviors. Further, when primary grade children are given responsibilities for household chores and caring for young children, they are more likely to use prosocial skills than those who do not have such responsibilities. Developmental patterns can have negative results. Aggression in preschoolers that is instrumental or possession-oriented can become person-oriented and hostile when children are six or seven years old (Etaugh & Rathus, 1995).

The important social skills required for peer acceptance are acquired between the ages of three and seven or eight. And, because the interactions that promote socialization occur most often with play episodes, the importance of play for social development needs to be discussed.

The Role of Play in Social Development

Mother-infant play that occurs during the child's social interactions early in life establish the role of play. Although mother-infant play is first initiated by the adult, by the first birthday, the baby begins to initiate games. During the second year of life, toddlers increasingly engage in peer games in attempts at socialization. When children play together with toys and materials in the environment, play facilitates socialization. Play activities also increase the probability that children will talk together and share the play experience (Frost, 1992).

There are many types of play. In Chapter 4, we discussed the role of play in early childhood programs. In Chapter 8, we described the role of play for cognitive development. We learned that the level of the child's cognitive development was reflected in the child's style of cognitive play. Likewise, the child's social development is reflected in the child's style of social play.

The classic explanation of the course of development of social play or types of play was developed by Parten (1932). She classified social levels of play as unoccupied play, solitary play, onlooker play, parallel play, associative play, and cooperative play. In each higher level of play, the child is engaging in increasingly complex forms of socialization through play with other children. The very young children play along or observe in solitary or onlooker play; they then play close by peers in parallel play. Increased socialization occurs in associative play as children engage in unstructured social interactions. The most complex form of play, cooperative play, involves social interactions and planning in a group, such as a play episode. There are qualifications to be made about Parten's early research. Toddlers are capable of social play, and children as young as two with play experience can engage in advanced forms of social play. Children who engage in cooperative play may also spend significant amounts of time in parallel play; moreover, a child with advanced social play behaviors may prefer to engage in a solitary play activity (Rubin, 1982).

A similar developmental progression occurs within pretend or symbolic play. The child's ability to engage in pretend or symbolic play is contingent upon cognitive

Group interactions promote important social skills.

development: toddlers need to be able to symbolize objects and substitute one object for another. When the child is able to pretend using an object, he or she can engage in symbolic play. Pretend or make-believe play follows the pattern of levels of social play. At first, the very young child engages in symbolic play alone. With increased socialization, when children are able to engage in group play, sociodramatic play emerges. The preschool years are the most significant for sociodramatic play, since play experts believe that this type of play peaks at around four or five years (Rogers & Sawyers, 1988; Singer & Singer, 1988).

Children's social skills develop as they engaging in dramatic play with peers. To participate in fantasy play, young children must share, develop roles, cooperate with peers, and control their own desires for the benefit of group play. During pretend or fantasy play, they provide feedback and support for other players as they enact the play episode. Frost (1992) reported that frequency of fantasy play affects social competence. Social fantasy play appears to promote social skills and is a predictor of a child's popularity and positive social activity.

The nature of the play environment and availability of toys for play affect social play. The size and arrangement of the space also affects the type and quality of social play. More on these factors will be discussed in later sections of the chapter.

Theoretical Bases for Social Development

Explaining the theoretical bases for social development is difficult, primarily because of its complex nature. There are many facets to social development: one theory might address only one facet, or several theories might address the same elements of social development. Chapters 8 and 9 discussed theories of cognitive and language development to provide a foundation for understanding their role and implications for curriculum and instruction. In this chapter, theories will be discussed in terms of the complex interplay that occurs when children are engaging in socialization. In this discussion, psychosocial theory, social learning theories, and Kohlberg's theories of moral development form a central focus, along with other theories contributing to our understanding of the holistic nature of social development. Additionally, we need to consider the importance of recent research, which provides a more comprehensive picture of the developing young child.

Psychosocial Theory   The psychosocial theory described by Erik Erikson (1963) was based on Sigmund Freud's psychoanalytic theory. Erikson was a student of Freud and derived his basic understanding of socioemotional development from Freud's psychoanalytic theory of development. In addition, Freud's theory is significant in understanding early infant attachment. Freud proposed that the infant becomes attached to the primary caregiver, who provides oral satisfaction or feeds the infant. The significance of attachment was studied by many theorists, especially Bowlby (1969, 1989), who researched its importance for infant development.

Erikson was interested in the child's personality development and believed that personality was strongly influenced by the social contexts, which include the family and school. Erikson extended the concept of early social development and attachment in terms of stages of development. The individual child goes through eight life stages, which resulted his or her personality. He described the infant's development in the first year of life as characterized as trust versus mistrust. The infant with secure attachment and a dependable environment develops a sense of trust. In the second year, the toddler is engaged in developing a sense of self and identity. Erickson's second stage—autonomy versus shame and doubt— engages the young child in developing pride in accomplishments and independence or doubts about his or her ability to become capable. During the early childhood years, the child enters Erikson's third stage, initiative versus guilt. Using their own initiative, young children make serious attempts at becoming part of their social world. Part of the process is the development of conscience that enables them to use self-control and self-guidance. Success in self-initiated activities promotes more initiative, while failure, including social failure, results in guilt and inhibition (Etaugh & Rathus, 1995; Santrock, 1993).

Structural Theory   A newer theory for emotional development has been proposed by Greenspan (Wieder & Greenspan, 1993). Titled the Greenspan Developmental-Structuralist Theory, it focuses on differences in emotional development. Earlier work on emotional and personality differences influenced Greenspan's work for an integrated theory.

Individual differences in emotional and personality development were studied by many researchers. Izard (1991) was one of a group of researchers who studied the emotions and differences in emotional development. Izard (1982) developed a system for decoding emotional expressions of infants, which serve as a form of communication and regulation for infants. Through this type of investigation, Izard and others were able to interpret a whole range of emotions that are communicated by infants and toddlers through facial expressions.

Other investigators have studied differences in temperament. Thomas and Chess (1977) identified differences in temperament using positive and negative characteristics. Jerome Kagan studied consistent temperament differences in young children over time. Kagan (Kagan & Snidman, 1991) believes biological and individual history, which includes attachment, can affect differences in temperament and personality.

Greenspan's structural theory proposes a sequence of psychological stages and uses an integrated approach that includes development, individual differences, and emotional experience. At each stage, new abilities emerge that allow the young child to learn. Cognitive and motor abilities contribute to emotional development as do attachment and psychosocial development. Some children have difficulties in development within Greenspan's stages that account for emotional differences. Greenspan proposes that emotional development is understressed in preschools; moreover, he believes teachers can address emotional differences and difficulties through adult-child interactions, the environment, and nature of activities provided for the child (Wieder & Greenspan, 1993).

Behaviorist and Social Learning Theories   Behaviorism is a theory that proposes that skills and knowledge are learned by children; they are not born knowing them.

The behaviorist theory of learning as described by B. F. Skinner (1953) stemmed from the process of classical conditioning first discovered by the Russian Ivan Pavlov. Pavlov's theory was based on animal studies in which he paired stimuli with responses to shape the animal's behavior. For example, touching a hot stove conditions the child not to repeat the action. Skinner's theory of operant conditioning proposed that children could be taught behaviors through the concept of reinforcement. The frequency of a child's behavior could be increased by the use of reinforcers. Positive reinforcers such as praise or tangible rewards increase the frequency of the desired response.

When applying their theory to parenting and schooling, behaviorists propose that if the environment is arranged to facilitate a desired behavior and adults reward the appropriate, expected behavior, the child will be influenced to use that behavior. Because all behavior is learned according to Skinner, behaviors can be modified if adults use strategies to condition or shape responses. Such strategies can include extinction, which is a decrease and elimination of undesired behaviors in the absence of reinforcers, and punishment, which is an unpleasant stimulus applied after an inappropriate behavior (Etaugh & Rathus, 1995). Behaviorists, who believe social behavior is learned, recommend that adults use strategies to mold the child's appropriate behavior. The adult uses reinforcement, punishment, and extinction to condition the child's social behavior (Schickedanz, Schickedanz, Hansen, & Forsyth, 1993).

Social learning theorists have expanded the work of behaviorists to include imitation and observation. These theorists believe that many behaviors are learned through the individual's reactions to, and interpretation of, situations rather than from shaping alone. Children will respond differently to a stimulus depending upon individual reaction and interpretation (Bandura & Walters, 1963). Adult instruction, together with the child's reaction within a social context, affects the child's behavior. A child can learn through imitation by observing another child being punished for an inappropriate behavior. In a similar fashion, the child can learn by imitating another child's successful behaviors. Although the behaviorist theory stresses the importance of external factors in the child's acquisition of appropriate behaviors, social learning theorists place importance on the social context and the behaviors that children observe and imitate.

The social learning theory seems to have a more significant role in explaining the process of socialization. Social experience is important to social learning theorists, who place more emphasis on the child's role in socialization. Although the adult role of using reinforcement and punishment is considered to be important, this is but one part of the adult-child relationship. The attachment relationship is important, as is the child's perception of self, which is shaped by his or her social experience (Bandura, 1977; Sroufe, 1983, 1988).

Cognitive-Developmental Theories   Cognitive development also has a significant role in social development. Emerging cognitive abilities affect the child's ability to socialize and understand the thoughts of others, as illustrated in the discussion on play earlier in the chapter. Additionally, Piaget described stages of games that approximate stages of intellectual development (Frost, 1992).

In the context of social development, the cognitive-developmental theory of moral development is significant; and the major contributors to these theories are Jean Piaget and Lawrence Kohlberg. Piaget believed that moral reasoning emerged in two stages, the first of which was heteronomous morality wherein the child from about age four to about age seven believes that justice and rules are unchangeable. Piaget believed that social development occurs within peer relations, rather than parent-child relations because parents have the power and determine rules (Santrock, 1993).

Kohlberg's theory of moral development drew a relationship between cognitive development and social behavior. He also described stages of moral development and proposed that young children do not have the cognitive ability to understand adult explanations of right and wrong. Investigators question Kohlberg's stages and contest whether children's development follows the hierarchy of Kohlberg's stages. They likewise question inconsistencies between moral conduct and moral stages (Sunal, 1993).

Implications of Theories for Practices in Early Childhood Education

Much of the literature that one reads related to the implications of theories for social development centers on the relationship between theories and the management or guidance of young children's behavior. More commonly the focus is on the negative aspects of social behavior such as aggression, inappropriate behavior in group settings, and the adult role in managing behavior. In contrast, this chapter focuses on the importance of social development in young children and the role of the theories toward positive outcomes in social development. The theories discussed above provide guidance in understanding the nature of social development and the role that parents and other adults have in the preschool years for helping children to develop socially and morally, within their individual temperament and personalities.

Discussions on the development of young children stress importance of the individual nature of development. In the area of social development, this is particularly important. Whereas it is relatively easy to understand that each child's physical, language, and cognitive development has an individual pattern and pace, it is somehow more difficult to understand that individual children have different patterns for emotional and personality development. Theories provide different clues to how social development progresses and the adult role in responding to individual children.

The psychosocial, social learning, and cognitive-developmental theories all discuss social development as interrelated with other categories of development. The child's social development is dependent upon advances in physical, language, and cognitive development. All of the theories have some role for the adult in the child's development, whether it be to teach the child social roles through mother-infant games, provide instruction on appropriate behavior using behaviorist strategies, or modeling for social learning.

All of the theories stress the importance of very early development during infancy and the toddler years and the cumulative effect on socialization of the child's experiences in the preschool and early elementary years. Positive outcomes from early personality, moral, emotional, and socialization optimize the child's development of social skills and his or her adjustment to group settings in the early childhood years.

The theories provide guidance for adult roles in assisting young children's social development. Behavior management strategies from behaviorist and social learning theories are well established in assisting parents and teachers in helping young children learn self-control and prosocial skills. Erikson's psychosocial stages help adults understand the course of emotional development and the importance of security, stability, and encouragement for the young child's emotional growth. Likewise, the inclusion of cognitive-developmental theories provide understanding of how children's intellectual development affects their understanding of right and wrong and how this affects their behavior and attempts at functioning appropriately in family, community, and group settings. Greenspan's Developmental-Structuralist Theory provides an integrated understanding of individual differences in development with recommendations for how adults can modify their behaviors and activities to complement individual differences in emotional development and temperament.

Implications from research can also provide direction in understanding and facilitating social development. Three important areas of social development to be discussed in this respect are (1) the development of peer relationships and friendships, (2) implications of differences in emotional development, and (3) moral development.

Very young children are able to form social relationships, and Ladd and Coleman (1993) report that early playmate interactions and preferences affect children's later ability to develop friendships and be accepted by peers. Peer status and acceptance in a group setting develop at the beginning of the school year. Even very young children in child care settings establish social relationships in the beginning weeks of school. Moreover, over the course of the year, children become more selective, with popular children more frequently the focus of group interactions (Ladd, Price, & Hart, 1990). Of even more significance is that children who are rejected by the peer group bounce from one playmate to another, and once they become disliked, they are increasingly avoided by peers. Peer rejection becomes more stable and difficult to change as children grow older, thus giving more importance to the development of positive peer relationships in preschool settings.

Children's personal characteristics and behaviors play an important role in peer relationships. Positive social behaviors are related to social success and peer acceptance, while negative, antisocial behaviors lead to rejection. Unfortunately, rejected children seem to take their status from one situation to another (Coie & Kupersmidt, 1983). Characteristics developed in preschool settings tend to be carried forward to kindergarten. Children who used prosocial behaviors in preschool use them in kindergarten, while children who use coercion and aggressive behaviors leading to rejection in preschool experienced the same rejection in kindergarten and the primary grades (Ladd & Price, 1987).

The early stages of emotional development also affect later development and learning. Wieder and Greenspan (1993) explained how individual differences in emotional development cause young children to react differently to experiences in the environment. Some young children have physical hypersensitivities and problems in integrating sensory experiences that may cause them to become anxious, aggressive, withdrawn, or delayed in development. Wieder and Greenspan suggest that teachers can help these children develop the ability to attend and focus by paying attention to what the child is doing and following the child's lead in selection of activities. Opportunities for symbolic and dramatic play also enable children with emotional differences to organize ideas, feelings, and actions. It is important for children with emotional differences to experience pleasure, particularly through play, where they have the opportunity to integrate learning processes and skills.

Sunal (1993) also has suggestions for assisting children to develop social competence and morality. Because sociability remains stable over time, research suggests that intervention should be used with overly shy, uncomfortable, or aggressive children. Teachers should use modeling behaviors and activities that require cooperation. In addition, the teacher can give the child cues for appropriate behavior when interacting with a peer (Bayley & Schaefer, 1960; Bronson, 1978).

Moral reasoning is fostered through adult intervention. Sunal suggests that it is useful for adults to give explanations for required behavior. Pointing out the consequences of a child's behavior or appealing to the child's interest in being mature are constructive adult actions. Using reasoning to prevent children from engaging in a behavior and calling attention to other children's feelings and perspectives can be effective and assist children in developing social competence. Children who become skilled at perspective taking are more likely to reach higher levels of moral reasoning (Selman, 1976; Sunal, 1993).

PLANNING INSTRUCTION FOR SOCIAL DEVELOPMENT

Is there curriculum and instruction for social development? The answer should be a definite yes if curriculum is taken to mean all of the experiences that take place in an early childhood classroom. Some of the curriculum is the setting that is designed for social living, while the nature of play activities are also related to social development. The actions taken by the teacher to intentionally teach rules and skills or indirect behaviors to guide socialization are all part of the instruction for social development. In the following sections, the teacher's role will be discussed first, followed by information about the content of social curriculum and instruction that nurtures the child's understanding about his or her own behavior as well as being perceptive, understanding, and caring about others.

Understanding the Teacher's Role

The teacher has a central role in social development. The role the teacher takes emerges from his or her understanding of social development and the individual characteristics of the children in his or her care. The teacher is concerned with the levels of social development of individual children and the unique emotional characteristics that each brings to the group setting. The teacher understands the need to promote positive socialization of children and the development of friendships. There is also attention to moral development and helping the children understand how to function in the school society. The teacher undertakes these instructional roles as facilitator, supporter, and instructor.

The Teacher as Facilitator   The teacher facilitates prosocial development first by preparing the environment. The indoor classroom is arranged so that children will have opportunities to play and work together. Centers and spaces will be arranged so that there are abundant materials for all, reducing possibilities for conflict and frustration. Center experiences will include activities that require children to work cooperatively with another child or where a small group of children can play in close proximity, thus encouraging interactions.

The outdoor environment is also organized with an eye for socialization. There are spaces where small groups of children can get away from the rest of the group. There are also pieces of equipment that require two or more children to play together. Certain play equipment encourages children to participate in groups. The prime example is complex play structures that accommodate groups of children, as contrasted with swings and slides, which are used by one child at a time.

The teacher facilitates social development both indoors and outdoors by providing materials and props for pretend or fantasy play. Understanding that sociodramatic play has benefits in developing social skills, perspective taking, and integration of cognitive and socioemotional development, the teacher includes an assortment of props indoors and outdoors. These should be changed frequently in response to the topics being studied by the children and interests demonstrated by the children during play.

The Teacher as Supporter   The teacher uses his or her understanding of the social and emotional needs of individual children to support their socialization and successful adaptation to the group environment. To acquire this understanding, the teacher becomes acquainted with the background of the child and the child's cultural and family setting. Knowledge of family background includes circumstances such as divorce, poverty, or abuse and neglect, which might be negative factors in the child's ability to have positive social experiences in school. Likewise, the teacher will also wish to be familiar with cultural and other environmental factors that affect the child's participation in peer relationships and group activities. The teacher supports children during the school year by giving careful attention to children's ability to establish friendships and gain peer acceptance in small and large groups within the class. Children's efforts for positive socialization are guided and supported through the teacher's understanding of the emotional needs of individual children. Children who are popular are guided in using their leadership roles to be perceptive of needs of rejected children and assist in their inclusion in play. Children who are rejected are supported and guided in using strategies for peer acceptance in play.

The Teacher as Instructor   Part of the teacher's role is to provide instruction and intervention when needed for the socialization of individual children and the group. The entire class needs to understand classroom rules for appropriate behavior. Although the children should have a role in the development of rules for behavior, the teacher has the responsibility to ensure that rules are followed and that children understand what conduct is expected from them. Consistent enforcement of expected behaviors throughout the year requires direct action by the teacher.

Direct action is also needed in helping children to develop prosocial skills and to minimize antisocial activities such as aggressiveness. Some of the teacher's efforts may be directed to the large group, while more frequently, the teacher will be working with individual children or a small group of children that is encountering difficulty. The teacher will model prosocial behaviors for children and give suggestions for resolving conflicts when necessary. For example, children who are rejected in group play can be taught how to gain access to a group by the teacher's suggesting a task that they might do or a role that they might play in a group sociodramatic play episode. Part of conflict resolution will include helping children become aware of the feelings of others and be able to take their perspective. They can be taught strategies for resolving problems using verbal communication rather than hitting. Development of empathy and comforting and caring for others will also be modeled and included in direct instruction when indicated.

The teacher will also use direct instructional techniques to develop awareness and understanding of differences in children. Whether the differences be in cultural background, language, emotional characteristics, or a disability, children need instruction that is planned, as well as incidental, in accepting and appreciating differences in children. These curriculum activities can affect children's individual social development and ability to function within the group.

Organizing Curriculum for Social Development

The curriculum for social development in early childhood classrooms for children ages three to eight follows the developmental sequence of the children's understanding of self and their place in the social world. In psychosocial development, the child first has to develop self-identity before he or she is able to become part of a group of peers. Understanding about others then leads to a broader understanding about similarities and differences in individuals and groups of people. The curriculum for social development, therefore, contains the following general components: (1) understanding about self; (2) understanding about others; and (3) understanding about cultures, races, and other differences in people. In the following sections, the curriculum for social development is described in terms of the child's growing ability to move from understanding himself or herself to becoming aware of a wider world. The significant role of play within the curriculum for social development will also be explored further.

Nurturing Socialization and Social Skills Development   One of the primary goals of the curriculum for social development is to help children become accepted socially and to be able to be successful as a part of the peer group. To achieve developmental skills in socialization, the child must understand himself or herself and have a positive self-image. Second, the child must make a positive adjustment to the school environment, and finally, the child must develop an understanding of the characteristics and needs of others.

Understanding About Self.   A child's most basic need in social development is to have a positive perception of self, or a positive self-image. One facet of self-image is to understand one's physical self: what one can do with the body. Another perception is the kinds of emotions that one has. Young children need to be aware of different kinds of feelings and how to express their feelings appropriately. Teachers nurture a positive feeling of self by using children's names, providing a place for each child to store his or her belongings, and other indicators that communicate to the child that he or she is an important individual within the class. Curriculum activities on understanding body parts and feelings contribute to the child's information about self.

Adjusting to School and Group Life.   Young children entering a group setting come with varying backgrounds and experiences that affect their understanding of appropriate social behavior. As they enter a new program, they are at different levels of moral development that affect their perception and understanding of what is right and wrong. As part of their adjustment to the school social group, they must learn the rules and routines and socially appropriate behaviors to function in a positive manner in the classroom. Because young children need time and experience to understand and follow expectations for appropriate behavior, the teacher plans specifically how to nurture behavior that is appropriate. The following suggestions are offered for teachers of young children to nurture socialization into the school and peer group:

1. Acknowledge differing levels of morally relevant abilities and accept them as strengths to build skills in group living.
2. Set clear expectations about standards of behavior and model how positive behaviors are used.
3. Establish environments that will encourage positive individual and group behaviors. Be aware of environmental influences that may be negative as well as positive.
4. Encourage children to be aware of the consequences of their behavior; how their behavior affects the group and classroom routines. (Buzzelli, 1992; Collins & Hatch, 1992)

Understanding About Others.   Part of children's understanding of the effect their behavior has on others involves awareness of the feelings and needs of their peers. If children are to be accepted by the peer group and establish friendships within the group, they have to be able to take the perspectives of others. Prosocial skills must be part of their socialization development if they are to have successful experiences in interacting with others. Children need to understand how their behaviors affect relationship with others. Young children must learn the importance of sharing, cooperating, and using other positive behaviors that facilitate the development of friendships. Teachers can help children make plans for how toys and materials can be shared. The children actively engage in discussing ideas for solving the problem of equitable use of popular play items.

Earlier in the chapter, we discussed research that supports the importance of the early years and beginning weeks of school in establishing peer acceptance and friendships. The social curriculum early in the school year should include measures to establish positive peer relationships and to promote successful attempts at developing friendships. In addition to modeling successful social behaviors and guiding children to be perceptive about the needs and feelings of others, teachers can plan activities that promote socialization (Kemple, 1991). To improve opportunities for peer acceptance, Kemple suggests that teachers organize special play sessions in which socially competent children are grouped with children who are weak in social skills or group a more experienced older child with a younger child who needs help. An older inhibited child might benefit from the leadership role with the younger child. Difficult social situations such as problems in sharing may be improved through planned activities in which the teacher uses puppets or discussions to engage children in discussions about alternative solutions. If a conflict is in progress, the teacher can act as a facilitator in guiding and suggesting to children how to reach a positive resolution to the conflict.

Some children need direct assistance in using prosocial skills. Kemple suggests that some children need help in recognizing when cooperation is indicated or how to decide what prosocial behavior is appropriate. The teacher can use modeling, indirect intervention, or point out an appropriate behavior to the child. Likewise, a child who has trouble gaining access to a play group can be given suggestions as to contributions that can be made to the group. The child can then offer to play a needed role or contribute to the activity.

Throughout all attempts to facilitate peer acceptance and successful play groups, the teacher needs to help children focus on the needs and emotions of others and to understand how their actions affect other children. Both socially successful children and children who are rejected need assistance in becoming aware of how they can affect others and how they can be sensitive to helping others.

Nurturing Understanding About Cultural and Ethnic Differences   The next step beyond awareness of others and their needs is to become aware of cultural and ethnic differences in children. Children become aware of gender, ethnicity, and race at a very young age. Derman-Sparks (1992) reported that four-year-old children see themselves as part of their ethnic group and culture, as well as their individual

family group. They are also sensitive to negative expressions and stereotypes about culture and ethnicity. Young children need to develop understanding and acceptance of cultural and ethnic differences. Derman-Sparks recommends that a multicultural antibias curriculum in early childhood classrooms should be relevant to the children and their families and should represent the groups present in the classroom and community. She further suggests that the curriculum should include the following elements:

> (1) children's culturally relevant needs, experiences, interests, questions, feelings, and behaviors; (2) families' beliefs, concerns, and desires for their children; (3) societal events, messages, and expectations that permeate children's environments; and (4) teachers' knowledge, beliefs, values, and interests. (pp. 123–124)

Nurturing Understanding About Children With Disabilities   Children with disabilities are part of the preschool classroom. Mainstreaming, where children with disabilities spend part of a school day in a regular classroom, is rapidly being replaced by the concept of inclusion where children with disabilities are placed in classrooms with children who are not disabled. Preschool children in child care and private preschool settings are now experiencing the presence of children with disabilities. In addition to the needs of the child with handicaps to feel comfortable and accepted, the normal child needs information about disabilities and how to interact with a child with a disability.

The child with a disability requires adult role models and needs to see people with disabilities pictured in books and other materials and toys in the environment. The child with a disability needs to understand the nature of the disability and be able to discuss it with other children or be able to answer other children's questions. The child who is uncomfortable with discussing the disability requires help in being able to refer the children with questions to an adult. The teacher should be alert to modifications that are needed to assist the child with a disability in becoming independent and able to participate in classroom activities.

Children in the classroom with a child or children with disabilities will have many questions and concerns about disabilities. They may have questions, and perhaps fears about equipment or protheses that may be required by the child. Children's questions about disabilities should be answered accurately and briefly. Children also need information about the similarities they have with children with disabilities. Teachers can facilitate understanding and acceptance of the child with disabilities by guiding the other children in understanding what the child can and cannot do, as well as giving clues as to when the child needs help and when self-help is more important.

Social acceptance of children with disabilities is very important. Because a disability may make it difficult for a child to play or communicate with other children, special attention needs to be given to facilitating peer acceptance and development of friendships. In addition to designing the environment to make it accessible to the child with disabilities, children can be made aware of how their play can be modified to include the child with disabilities without making the child with the disability feel different or inadequate. The teacher can model how nondisabled children can interact with the disabled child or can structure play experiences when disabled and nondisabled children can play together successfully (Derman-Sparks and the A. B. C. Task Force, 1989).

The Social Development Curriculum and the Play Environment   Throughout the chapter, the relationship between social development and play has been stressed. The discussions have focused on how peer interactions emerge through play and the role the teacher has in preparing the play environment and in supporting play and socialization among peers. Because play is so basic and necessary for social development, it can be considered to be the curriculum for young children (Pellegrini & Boyd, 1993). The importance of the environment for play leads play specialists to observe that the play environment is the curriculum in preschool settings (Dempsey & Frost, 1993).

Research on various factors that promote or limit play leading to socialization is extensive. This research can have important implications for how the educator arranges and furnishes the environment for social play. Among the factors that can be considered are (1) density of space, (2) physical arrangement, (3) group size, (4) quantity of play materials, (5) the teacher's influence on social play, and (6) time allotted for play.

The design of the classroom and its size have an effect on preschool play. Children enjoy small, enclosed spaces. Likewise, children have higher levels of interaction when classrooms are arranged into individual learning centers. However, density can have a negative affect on play, in that children can become less focused and irritated. In settings with extreme levels of density, children display lower levels of social interaction and higher levels of aggression (Smith & Connolley, 1980). On the other hand, open classrooms seem to promote positive peer interactions with fewer social isolates and fewer children identified as the most popular or "stars" (Ladd & Coleman, 1993).

The physical arrangement of the outdoor play area also affects levels of social play. As was mentioned earlier, structures that accommodate a group of children promote more social play than equipment and materials intended for a single child. The availability of toys can stimulate peer interactions. Nevertheless, complex play equipment facilitates more peer interaction than play with toys. Dempsey and Frost (1993) recommended that small toys be removed from the outdoor play environment on occasion because children are forced to play together when they are absent.

The teacher's role in children's social play is significant, particularly in modeling prosocial skills and guiding rejected children in developing positive social skills. There are indicators, however, that too much intervention or too much direction in play can be a factor in limiting sociodramatic play. Nurturing caregivers and teachers who are responsive and highly verbal with young children appear to have a more positive influence on social play than those who are directive in guiding play experiences

(Clarke-Stewart, 1989). Dempsey and Frost (1993) suggest that teachers use the least intrusive strategies when participating in children's play.

The size of the peer group has an effect on peer interactions. Very young children benefit from playing within small groups. Toddlers vocalize more and engage in more peer interactions when the play group is small. Older preschool children are able to socialize more successfully in a larger group and may benefit from mixed-age groups, where older children can model positive, successful social behaviors (Ladd & Coleman, 1993).

The time allotted for preschool play is important. Although preschool programs for children ages three and four generally devote generous amounts of time for play, there are concerns about the commitment to play in kindergarten classrooms, particularly in public school settings. With the current emphasis on cognitive development and the trend toward inclusion of an academic approach to instruction in kindergartens, recess and play periods are being reduced or eliminated. The significance of play in kindergarten cannot be underestimated; moreover, adequate lengths of play time are required if children are to enjoy the benefits of play. Children need at least 30 minutes of play if exploratory play is to be completed and enough time is to be available for children to plan and engage in sociodramatic or thematic play. Children need time for physical exercise and other forms of play so that socialization and other forms of peer interaction can develop (Dempsey & Frost, 1993; Pellegrini & Boyd, 1993).

Play Environments and Children With Disabilities.   The Americans With Disabilities Act (ADA) (Stein, 1993), passed in 1990, prohibits discrimination against persons with disabilities. Stated in more positive terms, the act requires that public and private facilities be accessible to people with disabilities. Play environments also need to be accessible to children with disabilities. Because the nature of disabilities are so diverse, it is sometimes necessary to design or modify individual play environments for the unique needs of disabled children using that particular play facility.

When play environments are planned for preschool children, the philosophy of inclusion is followed. There was a time when play environments for disabled children were constructed as an area separate from other play areas. The intention of the Americans With Disabilities Act is to provide play facilities that address the play needs of all children, including children with disabilities.

Many of the disabilities experienced by preschool children are physical in nature, and the suggestions for modifying facilities for accessibility are intended to overcome exclusion from play opportunities because the child is unable to gain access to equipment or activities. Nevertheless, the social component of the play experience is equally significant. If research indicates that children use prosocial skills on complex climbing equipment that accommodates a group of children, then the child with disabilities needs to be able to participate in play activities that take place on climbing structures. Within the individual disabilities present in the preschool environment, adaptations should be made so that children with visual, hearing, emotional, and various types of physical handicaps are able to play with their peers whether the level of social play be solitary, parallel, associative, or cooperative (Wortham, 1993). For specific suggestions for adapting play environments, see *Play For All Guidelines: Planning, Design and Management of Outdoor Play Settings for all Children* (Moore, Goltsman, & Iacofano, 1987) and *Leisure Opportunities for Individuals With Disabilities: Legal Issues* (Grosse & Thompson, 1993).

Designing Goals for Curriculum in Social Development

Much of the curriculum in social development is indirect; that is, social development takes place during the ongoing activities of the classroom and outdoors. The teacher's direct teaching role will include preplanned instruction in some categories, such as appropriate classroom behaviors; nevertheless, much of the teacher's responsibilities for social development will be to respond to emerging needs of individual and groups of children within the program. Much of the curriculum and instruction will be planned as the teacher observes social behaviors, peer interactions, and indicators of success and failure in peer acceptance as children learn and play together.

In preschool classrooms for three- and four-year-olds, the approach to curriculum design is likely to focus on social development. The major goals for social development concentrate on facets of self-image, adjustment to the group setting, and positive peer interactions. It is also possible and appropriate to organize goals from a subject area approach, particularly in kindergarten and primary grade classrooms as children become more group oriented and are able to understand social groups beyond peer and family groups. As kindergarten and primary grade children have more experiences in the community and develop an understanding of diversity of cultural and social groups, they are able to develop a foundation for the subject area approach to social development known as the social studies.

Organizing From a Developmental Approach   When goals for curriculum and instruction in social development are organized from a developmental approach, the social characteristics of the young child are the focus. In simplest terms, the goals may address the development of self-concept and the development of prosocial skills. The development of prosocial skills can also extend to peer acceptance and the development of friendships. Seefeldt (1993) describes social skills development as follows:

1. The self-concept. Children's feelings about themselves are the foundation from which they learn to relate to, and communicate with, others.
2. Prosocial skills. Being able to cooperate and share are necessary for forming solid relationships with others.
3. The making and keeping of friends. Children who relate to, and communicate with, others, sharing and cooperating, are those who receive acceptance from their peers and can make and keep friends. (pp. 233–234)

For the youngest preschool children, the development of these social characteristics can be reflected in social development checklists. Beaty (1992) has developed two social development checklists, a self-concept checklist and a social skills checklist, that can assist the preschool teacher in guiding the social development of individual children. Figure 10–1 lists the social characteristics found in these checklists.

McClellan and Katz (1992) have developed a more extensive checklist to describe preschool social development. Their checklist includes individual characteristics or attributes, social skills attributes, and peer relationship attributes. Their social skills include the child's prosocial abilities to gain access to ongoing groups and understanding cultural diversity in children. It also includes indicators of whether children are experiencing peer acceptance or rejection and if they are forming friendships. Their checklist (Figure 10–2) provides more specific social skills characteristics to guide the teacher.

The Skills-Concepts Checklists for three- and four-year-olds, developed by Coleta and Coleta (1986), organize social development into categories related to self and

Self-Concept Checklist

___ Looks at you without covering face when you speak to child

___ Can identify himself/herself by first and last name

___ Seeks other children to play with or will join when asked

___ Seldom shows fear of new or different things

___ Is seldom destructive of materials or disruptive of activities

___ Smiles, seems happy much of the time

___ Shows pride in his/her accomplishments

___ Stands up for his/her rights

___ Moves confidently, with good motor control

Social Skills Checklist (Pretend Play Groups)

___ Plays in solitary manner away from group

___ Plays parallel to other children but alone

___ Seeks other children to play with or joins group

___ Pretends or takes role that satisfies own needs

___ Adjust actions to satisfy group needs

___ Takes turns with roles or toys

___ Carries on appropriate dialogue with other players

___ Solves interpersonal conflicts without teacher's help

Figure 10–1   Social Development Checklists

Source: From *Skills for Preschool Teacher* by J. L. Beaty, 1992, New York: Merrill. Copyright 1992 by Merrill. Reprinted by permission.

I. Individual Attributes

The child:

1. Is usually in a positive mood
2. Is not excessively dependent on the teacher, assistant, or other adults
3. Usually comes to the program/setting willingly
4. Usually copes with rebuffs and reverses adequately
5. Shows the capacity to empathize
6. Has positive relationships with 1 or 2 peers; shows capacity to really care about them, miss them if absent, etc.
7. Sometimes displays the capacity for humor
8. Does not seem to be acutely lonely

II. Social Skill Attributes

The child usually:

1. Approaches others positively
2. Expresses wishes, preferences clearly; gives reasons for actions/positions
3. Asserts own rights and needs appropriately
4. Is not easily intimidated by bullies
5. Expresses frustrations and anger effectively and without harming others or property
6. Gains access to ongoing groups at play and work
7. Enters ongoing discussion on the subject; makes relevant contributions to ongoing activities
8. Takes turns fairly easily
9. Shows interest in others; exchanges information with and requests information from others appropriately
10. Negotiates and compromises with others appropriately
11. Does not draw attention to self
12. Regularly gains access to ongoing groups at play and work
13. Interacts nonverbally with other children with smiles, waves, nods, etc.
14. Accepts peers and adults of other ethnic groups

III. Peer Relationship Attributes

The child is:

1. Usually accepted versus neglected or rejected by other children
2. Sometimes invited by other children to join them in play, friendship, and work

Figure 10–2 Social Attributes Checklist

Source: From "Assessing the Social Development of Young Children" by D. McClellan and L. Katz, 1992, *Dimensions of Early Childhood, 21*(1), p. 9. Reprinted by permission.

SELF		
31. Points to and names body parts (head, hands, arms, knees, legs, chin, feet, and face parts)		
32. Tells own full name, sex, and age		
33. Feels good about self and abilities		
Comments:		

SOCIAL STUDIES		
Interpersonal		
34. Enjoys being with other children		
35. Begins learning the give and take of play		
36. Begins participation in a group		
Concepts		
37. Begins to understand that self and others change		
38. Understands that parental figures care for home and family		
39. Understands that people are alike and different in how they look and feel (3½ to 4)		

Figure 10–3   Skills-Concept Checklists in Social Development

social studies. The section on social studies is further divided into interpersonal characteristics and concepts. These checklists have less information on the development of prosocial skills and personal growth in social development, but include concepts that lend themselves to content that can be learned with the social development curriculum. Figure 10–3 shows an adaptation of part of the checklists for three- and four-year-olds in social development and preschool curriculum in social studies.

The goals for kindergarten education established through essential elements by the State Board of Education in Texas for public schools is organized from a developmental approach. The essential elements are divided into three categories: emotional development, social development, and social responsibility. The first two categories are related to positive development of self and positive peer relationships. The third category relates to the student's ability to be responsible. Responsibility includes environmental issues, property, and valuing similarities and differences in others. The essential elements provide guidelines for the development of the curriculum for social development, as well as indicators of the child's progress in social development. Figure 10–4, from the Essential Elements for Social/Emotional Development in Kindergarten Education, includes the three major goals with the descriptors or objectives that characterize the goals.

SELF		
43. Touches, names, and tells function of parts of the body (head, eyes, hands, arms, feet, legs, nose, mouth, ears, neck, trunk, ankle, knee, shoulder, wrist, elbow, and heel)		
44. Verbalizes full name, address, age, birthday, and telephone number		
45. Identifies expressions of feelings		
46. Feels good about self and abilities		
Comments:		
SOCIAL STUDIES		
Interpersonal		
47. Shows empathy toward other children		
48. Works cooperatively with adults		
49. Works and plays cooperatively with other children		
Concepts		
50. Begins to understand that problems can be solved by talking and not fighting		
51. Understands that we wear appropriate clothing to protect us from extremes of weather		
52. Understands that families share responsibilities of work and recreation		
53. Begins to understand the importance of keeping the school surroundings clean and free from litter		

Source: From *Year-Round Activities for Three-Year-Old Children* by A. J. Coleta and K. Coleta, 1986, West Nyack, NY: The Center for Applied Research in Education, pp. 237, 242. Copyright 1986 by The Center for Applied Research in Education. Reprinted by permission.

Organizing From a Subject Area Approach   Four- to eight-year-old children are developing an awareness of the world beyond themselves and their immediate environment. As they become cognitively able to take the perspective of others, they are also able to learn about other children and other cultures. Beyond these perspectives, they are able to begin understanding about the world. If this approach is taken, then the subject area approach to organizing curriculum can include developing goals for social studies. The social studies curriculum, however, still begins with the child. Seefeldt and Barbour (1990) suggested the following goals for social studies in the early childhood program:

Find experiences that will foster their sense of self-esteem and worth.
Develop the ability to communicate, share, and cooperate with others.

---

§ 75.22 Kindergarten Education

(a) Social/emotional development, kindergarten. Essential elements for social/emotional development, kindergarten, as described in this subsection shall be effective September 1995.
Social/emotional development, kindergarten, shall include the following essential elements:

   (1) Emotional development (knowledge, understanding, and positive acceptance of self).
The student shall be provided opportunities to:

      (A) recognize successes and feel pride in work;

      (B) recognize and appreciate his or her uniqueness;

      (C) persevere with most self-chosen tasks;

      (D) demonstrate emerging self-discipline and autonomous behaviors through
decision making and self-selected activities; and

      (E) develop an emerging awareness of consequences of behavior.

   (2) Social development (interactions with others). The student shall be provided
opportunities to:

      (A) experience positive, supportive interactions with adults and peers;

      (B) develop a sense of belonging to a group;

      (C) engage in cooperative activities;

      (D) learn how to make and maintain friendships;

      (E) show respect for individuals in the diverse school population;

      (F) accept uniqueness of others; and

      (G) participate in leadership as well as follower roles.

   (3) Social responsibility (behaviors of a socially responsible person). The student shall
be provided opportunities to:

      (A) observe and role-play socially responsible behaviors in a variety of situations;

      (B) develop an emerging awareness of the care of property and materials;

      (C) develop an emerging awareness of environmental issues;

      (D) value and respect individual similarities and differences; and

      (E) value and respect similarities and differences in cultural identities and heritage
including linguistic variations.

Figure 10–4   Essential Elements for Social/Emotional Development in Kindergarten Education

   Increase their knowledge of other cultures, ethnic, and racial groups.
   Learn to recognize the similarities among people everywhere.
   Grow in understanding of the nature of the social world, including concepts from history,
      geography, and economics. (p. 478)

   The last goal moves beyond the goals that were previously described for a
developmental approach to social development. Sunal (1993) reviewed research

(b) Intellectual development, kindergarten. Essential elements for intellectual development, kindergarten, as described in this subsection shall be effective September 1995. Intellectual development, kindergarten, shall include the following essential elements;

(1) Knowledge of communication. Receptive/expressive language integrated through meaningful listening/speaking and print-related experiences. The essential elements for primary language for bilingual education, kindergarten, are described in subsection (e) of this section and the essential elements for English as a second language, kindergarten, are described in subsection (f) of this section. The student shall be provided opportunities to;

(A) focus attention on adult and peer speakers during individual and group interactions;

(B) enjoy repetition, rhyme, and rhythm through poems, chants, and fingerplays individually or with a group;

(C) enjoy daily listening and responding to stories and books;

(D) follow simple oral directions;

(E) recognize voice tone and nonverbal cues to aid in communication;

(F) acquire vocabulary related to concepts in a meaningful context;

(G) engage in conversation to achieve a variety of purposes including getting needs met, requesting, inquiring, sharing information, and playing;

(H) select books for individual needs and interests;

(I) associate print with spoken language;

(J) become familiar with personally meaningful environmental print;

(K) make predications of what will happen next in a story;

(L) share ideas, feelings, and stories through activities such as spontaneous drawing, conversation, dramatic play, and informal experimentation with letterlike forms or invented spellings;

Source: Texas Education Agency.

regarding children's ability to understand concepts in social studies. Although most of the research reported related to elementary school children, there were some topics in history, geography, and economics that related to preschool children. Sunal suggested that young children are able to learn about history as it relates to time that is meaningful to them. They can relate to the passage of time as it relates to their daily living, the repetition of events that happen each day, and some concepts related to clocks and calendars. In geographic learning, they can understand about space as it relates to their position in space. They can understand about their personal space and how their body functions in space, such as directionality and positions in space. In economics, they can begin to understand the purpose of money and how it is used in exchange for goods and services. An outline of concepts related to social studies in preschool programs could include the following:

HISTORY
    Time
        Personal time
        Cycle of daily events
        Clock and calendar skills
GEOGRAPHY
    Understanding space
        Personal space-directionality
        Relationship to space
ECONOMICS
    Money

Both the developmental and content approaches to curriculum and instruction have a place in the early childhood curriculum for social development. There is a role for unstructured, incidental instruction for social development and teacher-planned, intentional activities to facilitate social learning. Unstructured, incidental instruction occurs when the teacher observes a social conflict and responds with guidance in problem solving. Assessment and evaluation are also a part of the curriculum for social development. The role of assessment is addressed in the section that follows.

ASSESSING SOCIAL DEVELOPMENT

A major component of assessing social development is for the teacher to be knowledgeable of the child's self-concept and social skills. Much of the teacher's information is derived from incidental observations throughout the day as children engage in play and classroom activities. Nevertheless, the teacher will also want to use more intentional strategies to assess and record information about children's social development and acquisition of concepts in social studies. Observations in the forms of anecdotal records, running records, and time sampling are particularly useful for recording and analyzing the nature of social interactions and behavior problems that need attention. In addition, observation of play can be conducted with the purpose of evaluating change in social and cognitive development. Checklists are helpful in tracking social development, and interview strategies and portfolios are useful in discussing children's understanding of concepts in social studies and in collecting information about social development.

Observation

Observations can be conducted within normal daily routines or, when the teacher needs to explore a child's social behavior, as a separate assessment activity. Because preschool children are in the process of acquiring socialization skills, teachers frequently observe children in social interactions to understand if the child is able to use positive prosocial behaviors or if there are problems that require intervention or assistance from an adult. Three observation strategies—anecdotal records, running records, and time sampling—are easily learned types of observation that help teachers focus and interpret socialization behaviors.

Anecdotal Records

Anecdotal records are the simplest form of recording an observation. During the course of an observation, if the teacher notices a significant behavior or event that illustrates a child's social behaviors, the event is recorded briefly, with the teacher's comments or explanation of the importance of the event. The notes might include the teacher's suggestions for actions that might be taken to assist a child or group of children.

Running Records

When more than one incident or event in an observation is important to understand children's social interactions, running records can be used. A running record is the same as an anecdotal record except that a series of related events are recorded, with relevant notes and interpretations. This type of recording is especially useful when two or more children are playing and individual reactions and interactions are important to understand a problem or progress in socialization.

Time Sampling

When it is important to know how often or how frequently a behavior occurs, time sampling can be used for an observation. This type of strategy is frequently used when a child is using inappropriate behaviors and the teacher wants to document frequency to determine how serious the behavior is for the child's ability to socialize appropriately. Hitting and biting are inappropriate behaviors in very young children that can be understood using time sampling. In time sampling, the teacher observes the child at regular time intervals and records whether or not the target behavior is occurring. As an alternative, the teacher might observe for the behavior and record the time that it occurs and then determine after several observations the average number of times the behavior occurs during established periods of time.

The ideal times to observe social behaviors are during indoor and outdoor play periods when children are playing in groups. Patterns of play choices and success in acquiring playmates can easily be noted and evaluated. Socialization practices that are not appropriate can be noted, along with causes and effects that affect the child's ability to make friends among peers.

Checklists and Rating Scales

Checklists and rating scales are helpful when teachers want to assess progress in social development. Periodically during the year the teacher wants to be able to evaluate the child's current status in socialization and systematically observes and records individual social characteristics as described on a checklist. The Social Development Checklists (Figure 10–1) and Social Attributes Checklist (Figure 10–2) are examples of checklists that can be used for assessing and reporting social development. The Skills-Concepts Checklists in Social Development (Figure 10–3) also include social studies concepts. Additional social studies objectives from particular study themes can be evaluated with or without a checklist format.

Interviews

Interview strategies may also be used to evaluate social studies objectives. The teacher discusses the social studies concept with an individual child or group of children and draws out verbalization of the content that has been studied. The interview can be unstructured or incidental, with the teacher engaging in the interview while children are working in centers or playing with materials related to the concepts being studied. The teacher might also preplan or structure the interview with specific questions that will be asked to elicit responses related to the child's interpretation about the ideas being explored. For example, if the group is studying families, the teacher might engage in a dialogue about different types of families and encourage the child to describe how families can be different. Pictures might be used to stimulate the conversation as part of the interview.

Interviews might also be used to discuss socialization skills. Children might be engaged in a dialogue to talk about problems that occur during play periods and how they might resolve difficulties that are encountered. Incidental interviews also would occur naturally during play times when the teacher observes children behaving inappropriately and guides them through problem solving, using dialogue and questioning within an unstructured interview.

ASSESSMENT/LEARNING EXPERIENCES FOR SOCIAL DEVELOPMENT

Assessment of social development will usually come from observation of children's social interactions and functioning in the school environment rather than from a task. Occasionally a social skills checklist will include objectives that are measurable such as the one below.

Objective: Points to and names body parts (head, hands, arms, knees, legs, chin, feet, and face parts)

____ Source: Figure 10–3, Skills-Concepts Checklists in Social Development

____ Materials Needed: None

____ Activity: Ask the child to point to a body part as it is named. Next point to the child's body part and ask the child to name it. As an alternative, an adaptation of the game, Simon Says, can be played using directions to point to body parts.

PLANNING INSTRUCTION FOR CHILDREN WITH DISABILITIES

Children with disabilities have the same needs for social development and socialization skills as children who do not have them. Some types of disabilities require minor adaptations to promote socialization. Children with hearing problems will need guidance in how to approach other children to initiate play events. Hearing children will need tips on how to use nonverbal, in addition to verbal, methods to engage in play activities with children who have hearing disabilities. Likewise, children with visual limitations will need auditory or sensory clues to interact with another child. Children with normal vision can be taught to approach children with visual impairments to engage them in play with toys or in conversation. Children with physical limitations can engage in social play and sociodramatic play, with modifications in role-playing. Discussions can be held as to how the child with a disability can be involved or how adults who have the same disability carry out a role. Children without disabilities can help facilitate the role of the child with a disability if prompted by the teacher. The child with the disability may have his or her own idea for the role to be played and how it can be implemented.

The social studies curriculum is also adapted with the child's disability in mind. The teacher can be alert to provisions that need to be made for the child to engage in social studies and social development activities. Children with disabilities especially need to learn about the world and the immediate community that is studied in preschool classrooms. Touching, talking, and other sensory experiences are adapted to help the child with a disability explore new information. It is particularly important for children with physical mobility problems to have the opportunity to go on field trips and engage in firsthand experiences that provide new information about the social environment.

Children with emotional disturbances have particular problems with social development. These children may exhibit a wide range of inappropriate social behaviors that include aggression, attention-seeking behaviors, and withdrawal and crying. Aggression can include hitting, biting, and throwing objects. Children may also use inappropriate language and steal from other children.

These children need extensive attention to develop more appropriate socialization. Adults may need to engage in extensive observation of the child to gather information and plan a strategy to stop aggressive and other inappropriate behavior. Special concern is focused on the children who may be victims of the child's antisocial behavior. The teacher wants to identify the events or situations that trigger or may serve as causes of the antisocial behavior. At the same time that the teacher engages in instructing the child and using behavior management strategies to redirect the child's behavior, other children in the classroom can be challenged and guided in helping encourage the child to use appropriate behavior. The goal is to help the child develop a group of friends that can make the effort to accept the child. However, the teacher needs to use caution so that undue responsibility is not placed on other children and they are not abused or victimized by the child with the emotional disability (Deiner, 1993).

EVALUATING CURRICULUM AND INSTRUCTION FOR SOCIAL DEVELOPMENT

Formative Evaluation

Formative evaluation of the curriculum for social development is an ongoing process throughout the year. The teacher is assessing the children's social interactions, the role of the environment and the teacher's role, and the effectiveness of social development experiences.

As the teacher conducts ongoing evaluations of children's progress in socialization, a simultaneous evaluation is occurring concerning how the program is facilitating or negatively affecting children's social behaviors. While individual children's development and personality are affecting how they interact with others in the school setting, physical factors in the environment may be contributing to problems that are occurring. The teacher monitors how physical arrangement, materials, and activities are affecting social behavior. Transitions from one activity to another are observed to determine if they run smoothly, contributing to positive social relationships or result in negative behaviors. Are children experiencing long periods waiting for turns? Are there too many times during the day when children are not constructively engaged in an activity; for example, while they wait to go outdoors or to use the restroom? Do materials in centers need to be changed to challenge the children or promote group play?

The teacher wants to use ongoing evaluation to assess whether children's social needs are being met. Are intervention strategies to help shy children or aggressive children use more positive socialization strategies working? Do more observations need to be conducted to discover additional information about particular children? Are inappropriate behaviors developing that need to be addressed? Are teacher strategies unwittingly serving as negative rather than positive influences on children's progress in social development?

The social studies curriculum is also evaluated using an ongoing process. The teacher monitors curriculum experiences to determine if they are interesting and effective with the children in the group. Likewise, the teacher desires to maintain awareness of the social and cultural characteristics of the children to see if a good match has been made between curriculum planning and the background of individual children. Is appropriate use being made of community and human resources, particularly of family members of the children? Is enough time and attention being devoted to the social development and social studies curriculum?

The teacher also maintains continuing evaluation of his or her own behaviors and strategies. The goal is to evaluate and improve the teacher's ability to understand the child's social development and facilitate progress in socialization. The teacher assesses whether each child's social needs are understood and complemented with activities and opportunities for play experiences. Are some children being overlooked, particularly shy and well-behaved children? Are a few children dominating the teacher's attention with antisocial behavior? Are leadership skills encouraged? Are children assuming more responsibility as the year progresses? Is there regression in group behavior that needs to be corrected?

Summative Evaluation

At the end of the year, the teacher reflects on the social development curriculum to determine the overall effectiveness and to plan for the year to come. Evaluation can include assessment of the social studies curriculum and effectiveness in promoting socialization in the children.

Of primary interest is reflection upon the social studies curriculum and topics that were explored with the children. The teacher evaluates the themes that were studied and their effectiveness for the children. Were they planned with the needs and interests of the children in mind? Were the activities interesting? Which activities should be eliminated and which ones considered for future use? What possibilities for improvement come to mind during the reflection process?

The teacher also reflects upon the social development curriculum. The teacher evaluates how effectively guidance was provided for individual and group growth in socialization skills. Which children still demonstrated social behavior problems at the end of the year? What could have been done differently to help individual children? What classroom practices need to be examined because of their possible effect on group behavior? How can the next year be begun more positively to establish a better pattern of interactions between children? What kinds of intentional teaching needs to be added to establish positive socialization skills and prevent aggression and social isolation?

Social play is part of the social curriculum. The teacher assesses the play opportunities. How did play promote or interfere with social growth? How engaging were sociodramatic play activities? Were there enough challenging possibilities for sociodramatic play? Were more props or time needed? Did the teacher respond with suggestions and materials that would enrich and extend sociodramatic play?

The effectiveness of addressing individual personalities and social development differences is also evaluated. The teacher reviews the progress made by children in developing social skills during the year and proposes possibilities for more effectively facilitating social development with the next group of children. The teacher examines each aspect of the social development and social studies curriculum to evaluate what went well and what could be improved.

⇢ SUMMARY

Social development in the early childhood years enables young children to interact with others and live within a social group. Social learning involves acquiring knowledge and skills about socialization and awareness that there are many cultures with differences and similarities in how families and communities socialize. This chapter addressed social development and learning, as well as roles for curriculum and instruction and assessment and evaluation.

Social development begins in infancy and gains importance in the preschool years when very young children have more opportunities to participate in play and other group activities. Successful peer relationships and positive socialization skills are important social development tasks between the ages of three and eight. If negative socialization behaviors, such as aggressive and antisocial ones develop, it is important for the teacher and parents to guide the child in acquiring more positive, successful socialization patterns.

Play is important for social development because it is through play that natural unstructured social encounters and interactions can develop. Play events reflect children's social development, at the same time that they nurture socialization through sociodramatic play themes.

There are various theories that assist in understanding the nature of social development and its course in the individual child. These theories provide an understanding of stages of development and its interrelatedness with other types of development. Theories provide guidance for adult roles in the child's socialization, such as for facilitating positive peer relationships in group settings. Individual differences in personality and social background affect teacher-child interactions. The teacher serves as a facilitator, supporter, and instructor in the development of prosocial skills.

Curriculum and instruction for social development has the goal of nurturing socialization and social skills development and understanding about cultural and social differences. For example, children may be guided in understanding and interacting with children with disabilities. The curriculum for social development is implemented through play in the indoor and outdoor environments. It can be organized from a developmental and subject area approach and includes learning concepts, as well as skills. Preschool children can learn concepts about history, geography, and economics that are within their range of development.

Social development in young children is assessed using observation as a primary resource. Developmental checklists, interviews, and portfolios are additional strategies and resources that support the collection of information about the child's progress. Evaluation of the social development curriculum is conducted on an ongoing basis throughout the year for formative purposes and at the end of the year to gather summative information.

STUDY QUESTIONS

1. Why are the early years important for social development?
2. How do preschool programs play a significant role in the young child's socialization?
3. Explain the relationship between moral development and socialization.
4. Why do preschool children need adequate time for play to nurture social development?
5. How does the play environment affect social and sociodramatic play?
6. How does the structural theory of emotional development support an integrated approach to social development?
7. Why does the teacher of very young children need to understand theories of social development? Explain implications of these theories for teachers.
8. Explain the significance of group acceptance at the beginning of a school program. How does rejection affect young children?
9. Why is an important facet of the teacher's role incidental or unstructured when addressing preschool children's social development?
10. Explain how the preschool teacher is more likely to address individual socialization needs than large-group social development.
11. What is the difference between curriculum for social development and curriculum for social studies in the preschool program?
12. Describe the major goals in the curriculum for social development and in the curriculum for social studies.
13. How does the teacher address cultural, ethnic and developmental differences with preschool children?
14. How does the physical arrangement and selection of materials in the play environment affect the socialization of young children?
15. Describe some strategies teachers can use to modify children's play behaviors.
16. How is the outdoor play environment modified for children with disabilities?
17. Define the goals for the curriculum for social development.
18. What are the skills and concepts that children need to develop during the preschool years?
19. Describe the concepts in social studies that are appropriate for preschool children.
20. Why is observation the key to assessing children's social development and the acquisition of positive socialization skills?

⇢ **KEY TERMS**

prosocial behavior

⇢ **SUGGESTED ACTIVITIES**

1. Visit a preschool setting and observe the indoor and outdoor environments. Identify arrangements and materials that affect children's social play. Include a discussion of provisions for sociodramatic play.

2. Observe a group of children in unstructured or free play. Identify a child who seems to be successful in social interactions and a child who is unsuccessful. List the prosocial or antisocial behaviors of each child. Compare the behaviors you observed with social skills characteristics on one of the checklists in the chapter. Write an analysis of your observations and each child's rating on the checklist.

→ 11

Physical Development

→ Chapter Objectives

As a result of reading this chapter, you will be able to

1. Describe the nature of physical development
2. Explain how motor development involves gross and fine motor development
3. List and define the stages in physical development
4. Discuss the relationship between physical development, physical fitness, and health
5. Explain the role of play in physical development
6. Describe the role of the teacher and the environment in physical development
7. Design goals and objectives for physical development
8. Plan curriculum for health, safety, and nutrition
9. Develop strategies to assess physical development
10. Describe how to adapt the environment and curriculum for children with physical disabilities
11. Develop a plan to conduct an evaluation of curriculum and instruction for physical development

There is much concern today regarding the physical fitness of children in the United States (Etaugh & Rathus, 1995). The high fat content of many children's diets because of the popularity of fast food restaurants is one negative factor in children's physical health. Another factor is the increase in sedentary activities, primarily as a result of watching television for extended periods of time. This results in less interest and time spent in outdoor play, which often includes vigorous physical exercise.

A young child's physical health and development influence other areas of development; moreover, the child's development of physical skills influences how successfully the child can engage in social and cognitive activities that require gross or fine motor skills.

In this chapter, we will explore information about the physical development of young children between the ages of three and eight. We will look at the sequence of development of motor skills. We will also consider physical fitness and the child's overall health and need for safety. Although a child's physical development is given less time and attention in some early childhood settings because of the emphasis on cognitive or intellectual development, it is equally important for the child's total progress. The chapter begins with an overview of the process of physical development, followed by how the teacher plans appropriate curriculum and instruction. The role of the environment, especially the outdoor environment for physical development is discussed, as well as how curriculum activities can be organized. How to assess physical development is described with examples of activities for assessment. Planning instruction for children with physical disabilities is addressed, including information about the modification of playscapes for the inclusion of children with special physical needs. The evaluation of the program for physical development includes formative and summative evaluation of curriculum and instruction and of the play environment for physical development.

THE NATURE OF PHYSICAL DEVELOPMENT

Preschool and primary age children are growing rapidly. Although the period of infancy and toddlerhood was the most rapid stage of growth, preschoolers continue to grow at a slower pace as they add height and weight, increase muscle tissue, and lose baby fat. Their appetite decreases, and they are physically very active, especially through play. Physical development includes gross motor and fine motor skills, and perceptual-motor development, which combines perceptual development with motor skills. During the primary grades, children expend large amounts of energy and increase the amount of food that they consume. They make steady gains in weight and height, but boys tend to be slightly taller and heavier than girls (Etaugh & Rathus, 1995).

Understanding Physical Development

Motor Development   The preschool years are the period when young children acquire basic motor skills. The skills fall into two categories: (1) fine motor or manipulative skills and (2) gross motor or locomotor skills. Fine motor skills involve use of the hands and fingers, while gross motor skills are the movements that allow the individual to become mobile and engage in skills requiring body movement.

Fine Motor Development.   Preschool children progress in **fine motor development.** They gain more precision in the use of the hands and fingers between the ages of three and five. They acquire more control of finger movement, which allows them to become proficient in using small materials that require grasping and control, such as materials used in construction. In preschool classrooms, children learn to work with puzzles, cut with scissors, use brushes, pencils, pens, and markers, and manipulate small blocks, counters, and modeling clay. They refine self-help skills used in dressing themselves by learning to button, use zippers and snaps, and tie shoelaces

(Schickedanz, Schickedanz, Hansen, & Forsyth, 1993). In the primary grades, during the latter stages of early childhood, children continue to work on self-help skills and improve their fine motor skills by holding pencils correctly and coordinating the use of knife and fork (Etaugh & Rathus, 1995).

Gross Motor Development.   While toddlers are gaining control over basic movement skills and mobility, preschoolers refine mobility skills through a range of motor activities involving the entire body. **Gross motor development** includes (1) locomotor dexterity, which requires balance and movement, and (2) upper body and arm skills.

Locomotor skills are those movements that permit the child to move about in some manner and include jumping, hopping, running, and climbing. Jambor (1990) extended this basic list to include the following types of locomotion: rolling, creeping, crawling, climbing, stepping up and down, jumping, bouncing, hurdling, hopping, pumping a swing, and pushing or pulling a wagon. Marked-time climbing, or climbing up one step at a time, is mastered by toddlers, but preschoolers can use alternating feet to climb stairs. At the latter stages of locomotor development during the preschool years, children are able to add galloping and skipping to running and jumping. They advance from riding a tricycle to a bicycle, and some older preschoolers are able to roller-skate and kick a soccer ball (Schickedanz et al., 1993).

Two basic upper body and arm skills that are practiced during the preschool years are throwing and catching a ball. Older toddlers throw and catch a ball with both hands. Later they are able to use one hand, but require several years to progress through more sophisticated movements (Gallahue, 1993).

In the primary grades, young children improve body balance and can ride a bicycle. Boys gain over girls in overall strength, while girls show greater limb coordination and flexibility; however, boys and girls demonstrate similar performance on other gross motor activities (Etaugh & Rathus, 1995).

Phases and Stages in Motor Development   Gallahue (1993) proposed that children move through a developmental progression in the acquisition of motor skills, which is similar to stages in cognitive development. However, he cautioned that maturity and physical activity alone do not ensure that children will acquire fundamental movement skills. Children who do not master these skills are frustrated and experience failure later in recreational and sports activities. Knowledge of the process of acquisition of fundamental motor skills can help early childhood educators design appropriate curriculum and activities for young children.

Gallahue has described phases of motor development: the rudimentary movement phase occurs during the infant and toddler years, and the fundamental movement phase encompasses the years from two to six or seven. During the fundamental movement phase, children move beyond acquisition of rudimentary movement and mobility skills and are able to move around freely. They are able to refine and develop movement skills through movement experiences. Fundamental movement skills are first learned in isolation from one another and then are combined with other skills as coordinated movements. The development of these skills are described in stages: initial stage, elementary stage, and mature stage. Preschool children need a variety of movement activities that are developmentally appropriate to move through the successive stages of development within the fundamental movement phase. Figure 11–1 lists Gallahue's phases and stages of motor development.

Perceptual-Motor Development   **Perceptual-motor development** refers to the child's developing ability to interact with the environment, combining use of the senses and motor skills. The developmental process of use of perceptual or sensory skills and motor skills is viewed as a combined process. Perceptual-motor development results from the interaction between sensory perception and motor actions in increasingly complex and skillful behaviors (Jambor, 1990). More specifically, visual, auditory, and tactile sensory abilities are combined with emerging motor skills to develop perceptual-motor abilities. Perceptual-motor skills include body awareness, spatial awareness, directional awareness, and temporal awareness. **Body awareness** refers to the child's developing capacity to understand body parts, what the body parts can do, and how to make the body more efficient. **Spatial awareness** refers to knowledge of how much space the body occupies and how to use the body in space. **Directional awareness** includes understanding of location and direction of the body in space, which extends to understanding directionality and objects in space. **Tempo-**

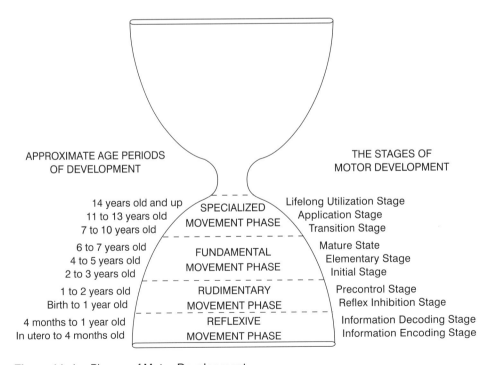

APPROXIMATE AGE PERIODS
OF DEVELOPMENT

THE STAGES OF
MOTOR DEVELOPMENT

14 years old and up
11 to 13 years old
7 to 10 years old

SPECIALIZED
MOVEMENT PHASE

Lifelong Utilization Stage
Application Stage
Transition Stage

6 to 7 years old
4 to 5 years old
2 to 3 years old

FUNDAMENTAL
MOVEMENT PHASE

Mature State
Elementary Stage
Initial Stage

1 to 2 years old
Birth to 1 year old

RUDIMENTARY
MOVEMENT PHASE

Precontrol Stage
Reflex Inhibition Stage

4 months to 1 year old
In utero to 4 months old

REFLEXIVE
MOVEMENT PHASE

Information Decoding Stage
Information Encoding Stage

Figure 11–1   Phases of Motor Development

From David G. Gallahue, *Understanding Motor Development,* 2nd edition. Copyright © 1989 by Wm. C. Brown Communications, Inc., Dubuque, Iowa. Reprinted by permission of Times Mirror Higher Education Group, Inc., Dubuque, Iowa. All rights reserved.

ral awareness is the development of awareness of the relationship between movement and time. Skills involving temporal awareness include rhythm and sequence. The sequence of events using a form of rhythm or pattern reflects temporal awareness (Frost, 1992; Gallahue, 1989; Jambor, 1990).

Health and Physical Fitness   Health is understood as meaning physical well-being, while physical fitness is related to an active, healthful lifestyle that contributes to physical well-being. Proper nutrition, concerns for safety, and daily periods of physical activity that promote motor skills are part of the child's physical development. More about health and physical fitness will be discussed later in the chapter in the topics related to curriculum and instruction for physical development.

The Role of Play in Physical Development

Play, especially outdoor play, is most commonly associated with physical exercise. Parents and teachers are appreciative of the child's need for opportunities for active physical activities. They may not, however, distinguish between free play, teacher-directed motor skills activities, and adult-directed sports. While each type of activity provides opportunities for physical exercise, play is different in that it is child-initiated and directed.

Organized sports for preschool children is gaining in popularity. Four- and five-year-old boys and girls often have the choice of participating on a soccer or T-ball team. Six-year-olds can join a football team. Gymnastic lessons frequently are offered for children as young as three. Children enjoy these group activities and sports, are proud of their uniforms, and look forward to the games and performances. If handled correctly by adults, the sports can have a positive effect, including the social experiences of being a part of a group. Nevertheless, the sports activities are structured and adult-led, and they provide physical activities related to the sport.

Motor skills activities likewise are directed by an adult. They play an important role in large motor development because the teacher can work with children in a variety of activities that ensure that the child will develop the desired physical movements. Children's physical development can be evaluated and attention given to correct inappropriate movements that can be an impediment to the child in later years when participating in sports and recreational physical activities.

Although a full range of motor skills can be nurtured through adult-directed activities, the opportunity for children to engage in physical movements related to spontaneous, natural play is needed as well. Young children need ample time to play. They particularly need to be outdoors where there is space for all kinds of physical movement as they engage in play activities alone or with their friends. Moreover, they need time and opportunity to participate in the social, sociodramatic, and cognitive elements possible in physical play. Since parents feel a need to restrict children's play because of the dangers in contemporary urban and suburban environments and since sports activities may limit time for outdoor play in a neighborhood setting, schools and other preschool centers should be aware of their responsibility in maintaining time for play both indoors and out for the child's physical development.

PLANNING INSTRUCTION FOR PHYSICAL DEVELOPMENT

When considering instruction for physical development, the teacher keeps in mind the importance of providing a balance between unstructured play activities that promote growth in motor skills and more organized motor skill activities. The latter ensure that the child uses locomotor and upper body skills and has opportunities to practice and refine movements that are part of physical development. To plan appropriately, the teacher must understand his or her role and the role of the environment, as well as organize the curriculum for physical development, health, and safety.

Understanding the Teacher's Role

In earlier chapters, we discussed the teacher's role in terms of responsibilities as a facilitator, instructor, and supporter. In terms of physical development, there is also a purpose for each of these roles. As was mentioned earlier, the function of these three roles is to ensure a balance between teacher-directed and structured physical development experiences with unstructured play that promotes physical activity.

The Teacher as Facilitator The teacher serves as a facilitator of physical progress through planning and arranging for possibilities for large motor and fine motor activities in the indoor and outdoor environment. In the classroom, the teacher arranges and equips learning centers with an eye for the fine and gross motor skills that the children will use to engage in the activities. The teacher is concerned that activities involving large and fine motor movement are changed as needed to maintain children's interest in participating in them. The teacher also rotates materials so that a range of fine and gross motor skills are incorporated within the available activities. Attention to self-help and dressing skills are part of the activities provided in the indoor environment.

The outdoors is viewed with the focus on development of gross motor skills. The teacher serves as facilitator by ensuring that permanent and temporary equipment permit both locomotor and upper body exercise. Likewise activities are planned that include fine motor activities, particularly arts and crafts activities that are especially suited to outdoor use.

The Teacher as Instructor Although public schools have specialists in motor development for children at all grade levels, private preschools may not have similar teacher resources. Moreover, because physical education periods may be limited, classroom teachers in all preschool settings need to understand the need for instruction and practice in motor skills. Although there is lack of consensus over the value of perceptual-motor training programs first developed in the 1960s (Chaney & Kephart, 1968; Delacato, 1966; Frostig, 1969), research studies underscoring the importance of guiding children's development of efficient motor skills prior to the age of five (Gallahue, 1993; Hildebrand, 1990) suggests that teachers need to provide direct intervention in motor skills development.

Teachers provide feedback in activities that involve fine motor skills.

The teacher also serves as an instructor in helping children understand and use good health practices, learn good nutrition, and acquire skills in personal safety. Appreciation for physical fitness is also learned through instruction. The teacher includes all of these aspects of physical development, health, and safety in the role of instructor.

The Teacher as Supporter   As is true in all categories of development, children vary in their progress in physical development. They need to be encouraged and challenged in furthering their advancement in fine and gross movement skills. The teacher supports physical development by providing the activities that are needed by individual children and knowing which children need to have movements and skills modeled. He or she also supports the child's participation in motor activities by engaging in the activities with the children. Children who are reluctant to try new physical challenges are given verbal encouragement and praise when they overcome their hesitancy and try to carry out a difficult locomotor or upper body skill or work at using scissors or a pencil correctly. Emphasis is given to play events in encouraging children to try new or physical movements. The teachers participates along with the children to provide the needed support to master the difficult skills.

Understanding the Role of the Environment

The Indoor Environment   The classroom has rich opportunities for the development of physical skills. Fine motor skills are encouraged in the art center through exploration of art media. Painting with a large brush and exploring drawing with markers, pencils, crayons, chalk, and pens provide practice with finger, hand, and arm movements. Finger painting and manipulation of plastic media such as plasticene clay and homemade doughs incorporate sensory experiences and multiple hand and finger movements. Cutting and pasting and other art construction projects such as making collages extend children's fine motor skills and artistic expression.

The manipulative center provides fine motor skill development through materials that encourage children to explore, solve problems, and construct things. Fine motor skills are developed as children work with lacing boards, solve jigsaw puzzles, construct with blocks, and reproduce parquetry patterns by manipulating different-colored wooden shapes. Because most preschool activities are "hands-on" experiences, all centers typically involve some kind of manipulation of materials. Children use fine motor skills as they learn to count using various types of counting materials, compare weights by putting objects on both sides of a balance beam or plant seeds in a small container. Sociodramatic activities in the housekeeping center and puppet play using a theater all engage children in uses of fingers and hands. Emerging writing skills are used in the language arts center as children try expressing themselves and their ideas in writing, using scribbling and evolving letter formations.

Large motor skills are nurtured in the indoor environment at the block and truck center, at the workbench, and through sand and water play activities. Construction with unit and hollow blocks incorporate upper body and arm movement, while play with vehicles incorporates a range of body movements. Sawing and hammering at the workbench develop children's arm and hand dexterity; when children pour, measure, and explore materials in a sand and water table, they are combining fine motor and arm movements. If climbing and other gross motor equipment is available indoors, basic locomotor skills are practiced as children play on the equipment. If such equipment is not available, teachers will want to arrange classroom furniture and portable motor skills equipment from time to time to encourage development of locomotor skills. Furniture can be arranged in an exercise path so that children climb over and under it, step up and down, and engage in other physical movements afforded by such an arrangement. This is particularly important if the climate restricts outdoor play for much of the year.

The Outdoor Environment   The indoor environment promotes fine motor activities more readily, while the outdoor environment encourages gross motor activities more readily. Regardless of the possibilities for gross motor exercise indoors, outdoor play is equally essential for physical development. Outdoor environments generally have more space for children to move about; likewise, in them, children have more possibilities for all types of physical movement.

The quality and range of physical exercise through play depend upon the type of play environment that is available for children to use. Well-equipped preschool playgrounds include complex climbing structures, overhead ladders, tire or net climbers, suspended bridges, and slides. In addition, swings, portable play construction materials, areas and tools for digging soil and playing in sand, carpentry materials, and art materials are needed if children are to engage in a full range of physical play that encourages upper body and locomotor skills as well as fine motor activities. Unfortunately, a national survey of 349 preschool play environments in 31 states revealed that only swings and slides were present on more than 20 percent of the playgrounds. The other types of equipment and materials mentioned above were present on less than 10 percent of the playgrounds surveyed (Bowers, 1990). The limited availability of appropriate equipment for motor skills development on most preschool play-grounds means children have limited opportunities to exercise the upper body and use locomotor skills.

Organizing Curriculum for Physical Development

The curriculum for physical development is organized in a similar fashion as other categories of development. The child's development in motor skills and physical fitness is the primary focus of the curriculum. However, subject area curriculum is used to meet the goals for health, safety, and nutrition, which are also elements of curriculum for physical development. Establishing goals for curriculum and instruction using a developmental and subject area approach is discussed below.

Designing Goals for Curriculum in Physical Development   The goals for the curriculum in physical development provide a structure for planning the environment, teacher instruction, and child-centered activities that take place both indoors and outdoors. The goals are the basis of a curriculum for motor skills and perceptual-motor skills and a curriculum for health, safety, and nutrition.

Goals for Development of Motor Skills.   The curriculum for motor skills includes both gross and fine motor skills. Gross or large motor skills include the fundamental movement skills that are acquired by young children in the preschool years. These include walking, running, jumping, hopping, leaping, galloping, skipping, climbing, and riding a tricycle. In addition large motor manipulation skills include throwing, catching, kicking, striking, bouncing, dribbling with both hand and foot, and rolling. Balance skills include bending, stretching, twisting, swinging, beam walking, and body rolling (Gallahue, 1989; Jambor, 1990; Poest, Williams, Witt, & Atwood, 1990).

Fine motor or small motor skills can include stringing beads, building with small cubes, cutting, turning faucets and knobs, cutting, pounding, rolling and shaping clay, pouring, manipulating writing and art instruments, and using boards with pegs and puzzles as described in Figure 11–2. Self-help skills include using a fork and spoon, washing and drying hands, putting on and removing clothing, brushing teeth, taking care of toileting needs, lacing and tying shoes, zipping and unzipping, buttoning and unbuttoning, and snapping and unsnapping clothing items (Sheridan & Murphy, 1986).

Because the preschool years are the significant time period when children develop and refine gross and fine motor skills, the curriculum goals for gross and fine motor development should include both structured and unstructured activities for children to engage in using the skills. The teacher needs to be aware of the sequence of development of these skills and provide daily activities that will include time for modeling and practice. As was mentioned earlier, free play with equipment and materials is not adequate for motor skills development. Direct instruction and practice will also be necessary if children are to develop the competency that will promote participation in group games, sports, and acceptance by peers (Gallahue, 1993; Poest et al., 1990).

Physical fitness and perceptual-motor development are elements of motor development that are also part of the curriculum. Physical fitness relates to health development and includes cardiovascular fitness. Cardiovascular fitness requires high-intensity physical activities, such as aerobic exercise, which are not a part of most play and sport activities. Perceptual-motor development, which combines movement responses to sensory input, includes body, time, spatial, directional, visual, and auditory awareness. Perceptual-motor development is basic to learning and children's later ability to read and write and integrate learning in all developmental categories.

Goals for Curriculum in Health, Safety, and Nutrition.   Children are in poorer physical condition than they were in the past. In a country where healthful food is abundant, young children and their families are more likely to eat food high in fat content than fresh fruits and vegetables. Children need a curriculum that will help them develop patterns of healthful nutrition. The goals for nutrition education should include instruction on the four food groups and the nutritional qualities of different types of food; information on how food is grown, processed, and prepared affects nutrition, safety, and taste; and the development of healthful and balanced food choices (Seefeldt & Barbour, 1990).

The curriculum for physical health includes goals for physical fitness discussed above. It also includes the ability to take care of body and grooming needs. The curriculum should include routines that promote the ability to wash hands, teeth, and faces; dress; eat using appropriate utensils; and carry out toileting routines. Children need to understand dental hygiene and purposes for physical examinations and inoculations. Some schools are now also introducing antismoking, antialcohol, and antidrug activities in their curriculum for physical health.

Accidents are a common problem for young children. Part of the physical development curriculum should include teaching children skills, attitudes, and knowledge related to their safety. In addition to contributing to the safety curriculum by providing an environment that is safe for children to use, the teacher prepares children to live safely in the environment. The goals for the safety curriculum include topics for traffic safety, fire safety, poison safety, water safety, and playground safety (Frost, 1992; Seefeldt & Barbour, 1990).

Organizing From a Developmental Approach   Curriculum for physical development is related to motor development, perceptual-motor development, physical fitness, and self-help skills that require gross and fine motor actions. Skills that relate to physical development can be organized by category or combined in some fashion. The objectives for physical development goals are described in terms of tasks that children can do or in terms of natural or organized physical activities that permit the child to demonstrate progress in a particular skill. Sheridan and Murphy (1986) described physical development skills in terms of fine motor skills, gross motor skills, and self-help skills. The skills are organized by chronological age. Figure 11–2 incorporates their skills for three-, four-, and five-year-olds.

The Frost-Wortham Developmental Checklist incorporates self-help skills with the categories of fine and gross motor movement. The checklist of motor development skills is organized by developmental levels that approximate the chronological ages of three through five. Figure 11–3 gives the part of the checklist for gross movement.

Organizing From a Subject Area Approach   As was discussed earlier in the chapter, the content of the physical education curriculum is related to nutrition, health, and safety. The subject area curriculum in physical development stresses the concepts and practices preschool children need to understand and be able to do to live a healthful and safe life. The goals for nutrition, health, and safety education can be further described in terms of objectives. The following objectives for the physical development curriculum (Frost, 1992; Seefeldt & Barbour, 1990) begin in the preschool years and continue into the latter stages of early childhood and into middle childhood.

Nutrition Education

1. To develop a positive attitude toward wholesome foods
2. To be aware of individual differences in food likes and dislikes and be willing to try new foods
3. To learn to select a variety and balance of foods from the four food groups
4. To understand how foods are prepared for eating and participate in food preparation activities

Health Education

1. To understand and use personal hygiene practices
2. To understand parts of the body and body functions
3. To develop physical exercise and activity habits that promote physical fitness
4. To develop a willingness to care for one's own physical health
5. To understand purposes for dental and medical care and examinations

Safety Education

Traffic Safety
1. To stop before stepping into the street
2. To listen and look for traffic
3. To understand traffic signals

Fire Safety
1. To understand the dangers of fire
2. To understand and follow fire drills

Water Safety
   To understand safe practices around water

Playground Safety
   To understand safety practices on playgrounds

MOTOR SKILLS—FINE MOTOR

3–4 years

Turns pages in a book 1 at a time.

Traces straight line, going off the line no more than 2 times.

Traces a square and a triangle, not going more than ¼" off the line.

Copies a drawing of a cross (+) with lines intersecting near the center.

Uses a large crayon, pencil, or marker to copy a circle.

Copies models of letters *X, M,* and *N.*

Picks up scissors correctly.

Cuts a piece of paper from one side to the opposite side.

Cuts out a circle, staying within ¼" of the line.

Uses clay to make objects (cookies, snakes, etc).

Winds up a windup toy if given a demonstration.

Hits large pegs with a toy hammer.

Catches a bean bag.

Accurately puts together 4-piece puzzles.

4–5 years

Places 10 candy pellets or small beads in a bottle.

Strings ½" beads.

Uses a pegboard and pegs to copy 4-peg geometric patterns.

Copies a 5-block bridge.

Accurately puts together 8- to 12-piece puzzles.

Will color a circle and will stay within the lines most of the time.

Colors within a 1" area.

Holds paper with free hand when drawing, coloring, or writing.

Is beginning to use pincer grasp to hold pencils, markers, or crayons.

Imitates a drawing of a square.

MOTOR SKILLS—GROSS MOTOR

3–4 years

Throws a ball by rotating shoulder and arm to rear, then following through.

Bounces a large ball (9") to within reach of another person at least 4' away.

Catches a large ball with elbows bent in front of body.

Jumps down from a stable object 24"–30" high.

Walks up 4 steps without support, placing 1 foot on each step (alternating feet).

Walks down 4 steps without support, placing 1 foot on each step.

Runs easily and smoothly.

Stands on 1 foot with free leg bent backward at the knee for 5 seconds.

Stands on 1 foot for 6 seconds, then on the other foot for 6 seconds.

Jumps forward 6" on 1 foot.

Jumps forward for 20"–24", holding both feet together.

Hops forward 5 consecutive times on 1 foot, then at least 3 times on the other.

Balances on tiptoes with hands above head for at least 2 seconds without moving feet.

Rides a tricycle unassisted.

4–5 years

Throws a ball at least 10' forward in a reasonably straight line.

Catches a large ball with elbows at sides.

Bounces and catches a medium-sized ball.

Bounces a medium-sized ball within reach of a person 6' away.

Bounces a large ball 4 times.

Takes 4 steps forward on an 8' x 4" balance beam without falling off.

Walks at least 10' on a 3" taped line without stepping off the line with either foot.

Jumps down from a stable object 32" high with 1 foot leading.

Figure 11–2 Motor and Self-Help Skills for Preschool Children

4–5 years

Copies a triangle.

Will print some uppercase letters such as *H, T, O, V*.

Is learning to copy his or her first name.

Cuts out a square, staying with ¼" of the lines.

Folds paper in half with edges within ⅛" of each other.

Given a model, can fold a square piece of paper diagonally.

Laces a lacing card or shoe in a designated pattern.

Ties shoe laces in a single knot.

Pours from any small container with minimal spilling.

4–5 years

Runs, moving arms and legs reciprocally for at least 10'.

Walks forward full length of 8' x 4" balance beam without falling off.

Walks backward 5 steps of 8' x 4" balance beam without falling off.

Stands on 1 foot with free leg bent backward at the knee for 10 seconds.

Jumps forward 36", using a 2-footed take-off.

From a flat-footed position, jumps at least 3" beyond normal reach.

Stands on tiptoes with hands over head for 8 seconds without losing balance.

SELF-HELP SKILLS

18 months–2 years

Uses a spoon with some spilling.

Holds a cup in one hand and drinks without assistance.

Takes off shoes, socks, pants, and sweater.

Indicates toileting needs.

2–3 years

Feeds self with spoon, unassisted.

Uses a fork to feed himself or herself.

Gets his or her own drink.

Washes hands with assistance.

Dries hands without assistance.

Turns the handle and opens the door.

Puts arms in armholes of shirt when dressing.

Puts on coat with assistance.

3–4 years

Feeds self without assistance, except for cutting.

Uses knife to spread soft butter and/or peanut butter on bread.

Is capable of wiping up spills.

Washes and dries hands unassisted.

Brushes his or her own teeth.

Takes care of toileting needs.

Unbuttons large buttons.

Unzips clothing.

Takes off jacket or coat, unassisted.

Is beginning to lace shoes.

4–5 years

Washes and dries his or her face.

Zips zippers.

Buttons and unbuttons large buttons.

Dresses himself or herself, but usually cannot tie.

Source: From *Beginning Milestones* (pp. 42–44) by S. Sheridan and D. B. Murphy, 1986. Reproduced with permission of McGraw-Hill, Inc.

Motor Development: Preschool (Gross Movement)			
Level III (approx. age 3)	**Introduced**	**Progress**	**Mastery**
1. Catches a ball with both hands against the chest	_____	_____	_____
2. Rides a tricycle	_____	_____	_____
3. Hops on both feet several times without assistance	_____	_____	_____
4. Throws a ball five feet with accuracy	_____	_____	_____
5. Climbs up a slide and comes down	_____	_____	_____
6. Climbs by alternating feet and holding on to a handrail	_____	_____	_____
7. Stand on one foot and balances briefly	_____	_____	_____
8. Pushes a loaded wheelbarrow	_____	_____	_____
9. Runs freely with little stumbling or falling	_____	_____	_____
10. Builds a tower with nine or ten blocks	_____	_____	_____
Level IV (approx. age 4)			
1. Balances on one foot	_____	_____	_____
2. Walks a straight line forward and backward	_____	_____	_____
3. Walks a balance beam	_____	_____	_____
4. Climbs steps with alternate feet without support	_____	_____	_____
5. Climbs on a jungle gym	_____	_____	_____
6. Skips haltingly	_____	_____	_____
7. Throws, catches, and bounces a large ball	_____	_____	_____
8. Stacks blocks vertically and horizontally	_____	_____	_____
9. Creates recognizable block structures	_____	_____	_____
10. Rides a tricycle with speed and skill	_____	_____	_____
Level V (approx. age 5)			
1. Catches and throws a small ball	_____	_____	_____
2. Bounces and catches a small ball	_____	_____	_____
3. Skips on either foot	_____	_____	_____
4. Skips rope	_____	_____	_____
5. Hops on one foot	_____	_____	_____
6. Creates Tinkertoy® and block structures	_____	_____	_____
7. Hammers and saws with some skill	_____	_____	_____
8. Walks a balance beam forward and backward	_____	_____	_____
9. Descends stairs by alternating feet	_____	_____	_____

Figure 11–3   Part of the Frost-Wortham Developmental Checklist

Source: From *Playgrounds for young children: National survey and perspectives* (pp. 5–16) by S. C. Wortham & J. L. Frost (Eds.), 1990, Reston, VA: American Alliance for Health, Physical Education, Recreation, and Dance. Copyright 1990 by American Alliance for Health, Physical Education, Recreation, and Dance. Reprinted by permission.

Home and School Safety
1. To understand causes of injury at home and at school
2. To understand how to prevent accidents and injuries

   The outline for the curriculum for health, safety, and nutrition provides a framework for preschool teachers to use. The teacher has the freedom to develop activities that are appropriate for the group of children in the classroom. The cultural and ethnic differences represented by the group will affect the types of foods, physical activities, and safety and hygiene practices that are unique to lifestyles and living conditions of the families and homes where children live. The teacher will want to use the curriculum for physical development to expand children's knowledge of and appreciation for the concepts and practices that promote a healthful lifestyle within individual family and community groups.

   In the following section, the assessment of physical development is discussed. Because physical development is composed of skills development, assessment strategies focus on observable progress in fine and gross motor development and successful use of self-help skills.

ASSESSING PHYSICAL DEVELOPMENT

Physical development is most readily evaluated by observing the young child. And since almost everything young children do involves some sort of physical activity, adults have multiple opportunities throughout the day to assess a child's ability to use gross and fine motor skills. It is also useful to organize tasks for children to do to determine their progress in developing motor skills.

Observation

While incidental observation of children's play permits the teacher to study the child while the child engages in natural physical activities, the teacher may also need to structure what needs to be observed; therefore, both structured and unstructured observation are used for assessment.

Incidental Observation   Incidental observation occurs when the teacher or parent observes children at play or at work to note the motor skills the child is using. The teacher is looking for skills that are mastered, as well as indications that the child needs assistance in acquiring a gross or fine motor movement. As children are engaged in activities, the teacher makes it a point to observe physical actions so as to be aware of the individual child's abilities and needs in this area. To facilitate assessment, the teacher plans different types of activities and makes a variety of materials available so that children will be engaging in physical actions that require different movements.

Structured Observation   When the teacher desires to collect specific information about developmental progress, structured observations may be planned. In this instance, the teacher has predetermined that all the children will be assessed on physical skills development and arranges a schedule to observe each child during indoor and outdoor play and during a center time. The teacher then looks for as many motor skills as the child demonstrates. As a result of this more systematic study of children's actions, the teacher can make a more comprehensive analysis of the child's progress.

Motor Skills Tasks

Not all motor skills actions take place within natural activities. The teacher will upon occasion need to extend structured observations to more prescribed physical activi-ties. To enable the assessment of specific motor skills, the teacher will need to plan a number of motor skills tasks for the child to perform. Many of the skills objectives described in Figures 11–2 and 11–3 can easily be assessed by planning tasks for chil-dren to do to determine if they have mastered the skill or need activities that provide instruction, modeling, or practice. When systematic assessment is needed during the year, a series of tasks are planned and implemented with individual children or with small groups. The tasks can be organized to be completed during a work or play period or scheduled for a time period when assessment activities are conducted each day.

Checklists

Skills in fine and gross motor development are simple to describe and assess. It would then follow that use of checklists such as the Frost-Wortham Developmental Checklist in Figure 11–3 constitutes an efficient strategy to conduct assessments and keep records on children's progress in physical development. The checklist can be as brief or lengthy as the teacher desires, depending upon how detailed the information desired. If the teacher wishes to have information on a few indicators of fine or gross motor development, a brief checklist can be used. If, however, the teacher has need of more extended information on the child's progress, many indicators can be included on the list, such as are found in Figure 11–2.

The checklist format enables the teacher to select the types of recording infor-mation that will be used. A simple yes or no as to whether the child has mastered a skill can be recorded using two columns for recording the child's status. If the teacher wants information concerning a series of assessment periods, several columns can be designed to record dates of assessment with the child's mastery indicated on the date that mastery was demonstrated. On succeeding assessments, that particular skill is no longer assessed and the teacher moves on to more advanced motor move-ments.

ASSESSMENT/LEARNING EXPERIENCES
FOR PHYSICAL DEVELOPMENT

The following activities are tasks that teachers can use to plan and conduct systematic assessments of physical development. Some of the activities can be used as routine center activities or during play for either practice or assessment of a skill. Many of the activities are self-explanatory, as described in the skills lists and checklists in Figures 11–2 and 11–3; they can be observed in the context of a game or activity.

Objective: Bounces a large ball (9") to within reach of another person at least 4 feet away (gross motor)

_____ Source: Figure 11–2, Motor and Self-Help Skills for Preschool Children, 3–4 years

_____ Materials Needed: Large rubber ball

_____ Activity: Organize a circle game with a small group of children. Place them in a circle 4 feet apart. Show them how to bounce the ball to the next person in the circle. Continue the game for three or four rounds to determine which children have achieved the skill.

Objective: Places 10 candy pellets or small beads in a bottle (fine motor)

_____ Source: Figure 11–2, Motor and Self-Help Skills for Preschool Children, 4–5 years

_____ Materials Needed: Small beans such as split peas, small cups or plastic containers

_____ Activity: Have a small group of children engage in the activity. Give each child a container with the beans inside. Ask the children to put the beans on the table carefully. Then ask them to put the beans back in the container one at a time.

Objective(s): Skips on either foot, hops on one foot, age 5

_____ Source: Figure 11–3, Frost-Wortham Developmental Checklist (Gross Movement)

_____ Materials Needed: None

_____ Activity: Play a hop, skip, and jump game using Follow the Leader. Organize the children in a circle or line. Model how to be the leader. If the leader hops on the right foot, the children follow suit. The leader alternates hopping, skipping, or jumping. As the children take turns being the leader, they can be observed to determine skills ability in hopping and skipping. Hopping should be carried out using alternate feet.

Objective(s): Runs, moving arms and legs reciprocally for at least 10 feet; walks at least 10 feet on a 3-inch taped line without stepping off the line with either foot; walks forward the full length of a 8′ x 4″ balance beam without falling off (gross motor)

_____ Source: Figure 11–2, Motor and Self-Help Skills for Preschool Children, 4-5 years

_____ Materials Needed: 3-inch tape, balance beam

_____ Activity: Organize a simple obstacle course with a starting point. Have the children run a distance to a taped line 10 feet away, which they must walk, and then to the balance beam, where they must walk the full length of the beam. Additional activities can be added to the obstacle course to assess additional large motor skills.

Objective: Copies a 5-block bridge (fine motor)

_____ Source: Figure 11–2, Motor and Self-Help Skills for Preschool Children, 4–5 years

_____ Activity: Provide 5 or more 1-inch cube blocks for each of a small group of children. Model constructions for them to copy, including the 5-block bridge. More complex constructions can also be modeled. As a game activity, the children then can take turns designing constructions for the other children to copy.

PLANNING INSTRUCTION FOR CHILDREN WITH PHYSICAL IMPAIRMENTS

The Nature of Physical Impairments

Children with physical disabilities are also referred to as physically challenged. They are the fastest growing population of children in public schools who are receiving services in special education; however, many of these children may not require special education. Children with physical disabilities have a variety of types of impairments. They can be medically fragile and require life or health support during the school day. They may have limited strength or other health impairments that affect their alertness for educational tasks. Severe chronic illnesses that can cause health impairments include hemophilia, leukemia, sickle-cell anemia, diabetes, asthma, and cystic fibrosis (Knight & Wadsworth, 1993).

Physical disabilities can include cerebral palsy, muscular dystrophy, arthritis, spina bifida, or scoliosis. Correctable orthopedic impairments such as bowlegs, clubfeet, and congenital hip problems can be addressed through surgery, braces or casts, and physical therapy. Because early intervention is important for these conditions, they are frequently corrected during the preschool years, resulting in temporary problems with mobility (Deiner, 1993).

Regardless of the type of physical disability, preschool children who are physically challenged often have difficulties with mobility. They may use some type of equipment to aid them in achieving mobility. Metal or plastic braces may be used to support the child for a physical function such as sitting or walking. Short-distance aids include walkers, scooters, and crutches. Each is designed for the individual physical characteristics and needs of the child for independent mobility. Mobility aids that provide assistance for longer distances include strollers and wheelchairs. Specially designed strollers are helpful for younger children who are too old to be carried, while wheelchairs are introduced as children become larger. These mobility aids are used by children who are physically fragile, have limited strength, or have a physical impairment affecting mobility.

Many children with serious health or physical impairments may be under the care of a school nurse or physical therapist. Teachers should not plan activities for these children without consulting the special education teacher and other professionals who are responsible for the child. Teachers should also be knowledgeable about how and if these children can be moved and routines that must be followed for physically fragile students.

Needs of Children With Physical Disabilities

Young children with physical disabilities need to participate in preschool activities as normally as possible. They should not be excluded from physical activities. If necessary, the activity needs to be adapted for their participation. As was discussed in an earlier chapter, the classroom arrangement may have to be adapted to permit movement for children with wheelchairs and with other short- and long-distance mobility aids. The teacher needs to be informed as to how the child uses the aids and how they function. In addition, the teacher needs to completely understand the child's impairment or health condition and how to pace activities and expectations to meet the child's limitations and potential. While the teacher will want to provide assistance appropriately, the child should be treated as normally as possible and not given unnecessary attention or assistance. Knight and Wadsworth (1993) suggest the teacher should feel "empathy" for the child rather than "sympathy."

Young children who use mobility aids may have to be transferred from one situation to another. Children in wheelchairs must be transferred from the wheelchair to a chair, floor, or toilet. Children who use short-distance aids may need to have braces adjusted or walkers positioned for use. The teacher must work with physical therapists and other specialists to learn how to move the child properly.

Adapting the Preschool Environment for Children With Physical Impairments

The Indoor Environment   Simple modifications to the classroom, in addition to providing extra space where needed, can make activities more accessible and safe for young children. Among the suggestions that Deiner (1993) makes is to check doors and passageways to determine if there is space for wheelchairs to pass. Other considerations for users of wheelchairs are to move tables for such activities as sand and water play away from the wall so that they can be reached from all sides or move such activities to the floor for easier accessibility.

Children who use short-distance mobility aids need nonslip floor coverings. Specially designed chairs or seats with belts may be needed to secure the child who is unable to sit alone. Other suggestions are tables with adjustable legs, baskets on walkers for transporting materials, and temporary ramps if needed to assist mobility impaired children to move from one area to another.

Children with fine motor impairments also need modifications to materials to make them more useable such as shortened handles on paintbrushes and other equipment with handles. Deep-sided bowls instead of plates are helpful for some children as are larger versions of manipulative toys. Special scissors or puzzles with knobs might be needed by children with fine motor disabilities.

The Outdoor Environment   Children who are physically challenged need to engage in outdoor play. Although modifications need to be made for children who have mobility limitations, these young children benefit from exploring and interacting with the world in a play environment. Depending upon the individual child's condition and limitations, some restrictions on physical activities occur; nevertheless, physical accommodation of the playground can broaden the child's access to play experiences and at the same time promote their gross and fine motor development through play activities. Less mobile children can be transferred to a different play experience or the play opportunity can be modified to accommodate to the child's physical limitations and possibilities (Wortham, 1993). Frost (1992) made suggestions for making the playground accessible to children with physical handicaps. Figure 11–4 lists these suggestions.

Planning Learning Experiences for Children With Physical Impairments

Gross Motor Activities   Deiner (1993) suggests that children with physical disabilities be given the opportunity to participate in all physical activities that are possible. Specialists and parents should be consulted when there are questions as to whether a child should be permitted to use some equipment requiring gross motor skills or whether the equipment should be adapted for accessibility by the child. Gross motor strength is important for children with impairments. For some, such as children who use crutches or a wheelchair, upper body strength is particularly important.

Children who are in a wheelchair can readily participate in games that can be done sitting down. They can engage in throwing and catching balls. For tossing games using beanbags or balls, the objects can be attached to the child's chair with a string so that they can be retrieved after they have been thrown.

Children who can stand or use play equipment may have poor muscle control. They must be supervised and assisted, but only when needed. They should be allowed to climb as much as they can and use equipment independently as long as it is within their skill level. Children who are unsteady might need foot straps to hold their feet on tricycles or something to push when walking to increase balance and coordination.

When children are unable to participate in a game, they might serve as score-keepers or play an adapted version of a game. A wheelchair bound child might serve as batter in a baseball game with another child to run the bases.

---

1. The layout of the playground should allow for continuous circulation. A paved path, at least 36 in. wide to accommodate wheelchairs, should wind throughout the entire playground in an intersecting closed loop design.

2. Paths should not exceed a slope of 5 percent (a rise of 1 ft. over a distance of 20 ft.). Best suited to wheelchair travel are walks with slopes of 3 to 4 percent.

3. Ramps one uses to gain access to buildings, play apparatus, hills, bridges, etc., should not exceed a slope of 8.33 percent (a rise of 1 ft. over a distance of 12 ft.). Best suited for wheelchair travel are ramps with slopes of 6 percent (a rise of 1 ft. over a distance of 16.6 ft.).

4. Sand and water play areas should be raised at least 30 in. high on one end with a 36 in. deep by 30 in. wide indentation to allow children in wheelchairs to enjoy and play without removal from chair. However, wheelchair-bound children should be encouraged to leave the chair to play in sand and water, play on slide, or roll down hills.

5. Handrails should be provided on all ramps and play structures.

6. Stairs should be avoided. If stairs are present they should not be recessed.

7. Slides must provide access to all types of handicaps.

   A. No ladders and legs should be used on slides.

   B. Slides should be embedded in a grassy mound. Access to the top of the slide should be a ramp or series of ramps.

   C. Grab bars should be provided along ramps and tops and bottoms of slides to accommodate the semiambulant.

8. Conventional swings are adequate for handicapped children. For severely handicapped children, special swings can be used.

9. Spray pools could be considered for those who cannot be submerged in water. Spray pools should consist of the following:

   A. A jet of water which rises to a height of at least 7 ft. and then falls to a paved basin that has sufficient drainage.

   B. Benches should be provided in the spray area for those with restricted mobility.

   C. A clear area for movement of children in wheelchairs should be provided.

10. Gates and doorways should swing both ways and should be a minimum of 2 ft. 8 in. wide.

11. Drinking and toilet facilities should be made accessible to all children.

Figure 11–4   Suggestions for Playground Accessibility for Children With Physical Impairments

From *Play and Playscapes* (p. 306) by J. L. Frost, 1992, Albany, NY: Delmar. Adapted from "A Playground for All Children: Design Competition, August 1976." U. S. Department of Housing and Urban Development. Used by permission.

Fine Motor Activities   Activities that promote development of fine motor skills and eye-hand coordination are important for all children. For children who are unable to achieve mobility, fine motor skill development is important. Children with poor motor skills may need activities that have been adapted for poor muscle control. Magnets attached to small toys can be used with a cookie sheet or other metal surface to help children to gain muscle control. Lacing cards and boards with pegs can be attached to a holder in a standing-up or vertical position to permit easier use. Manipulatives may need to be larger or made of rubber to allow children with difficulties with motor skills to grasp and manipulate them.

Because children with weaknesses in the hands and fingers need many motor skills activities to develop strength and coordination, a large variety of activities should be available so that children have ample opportunities to practice them in engaging activities (Deiner, 1993). Knight and Wadsworth (1993) provided suggestions to adapt the environment and instructional activities for children with limitations for fine motor skills. Although some of the suggestions may apply to older children who are more likely to be completing written assignments or computations in math, most of the adaptations are useful for young children as well. Figure 11–5 contains Knight and Wadworth's suggestions for adapting instruction.

EVALUATING CURRICULUM AND INSTRUCTION FOR PHYSICAL DEVELOPMENT

Formative Evaluation

Physical development is rapid in children between the ages of three and five. Teachers and parents need to be aware of changes and progress in development, and frequent assessment of gross and fine motor skills provides needed information. Formative evaluation at least once a month allows teachers to maintain awareness of ongoing progress. Children who are lagging behind their peers may need special attention to a specific motor skill, with modeling or instruction to assist the child in acquiring the targeted skill.

Ongoing evaluation of the curriculum for physical development also provides frequent feedback on the appropriateness of the curriculum. The teacher wants to be sure that activities that require motor skills are appropriate for the children in the group. A balance between challenge and mastery is desired so that children are able to engage in the physical activities but are having to reach toward more complex levels of physical skills at the same time. The teacher also wants to evaluate if the curriculum for physical development is given enough priority and is not being neglected in favor of more academic types of activities. The quality curriculum includes experiences for the varied levels of physical development in the classroom, and frequent assessments of individual progress enable the teacher to ensure that curriculum is matched with children's developmental needs.

Instructional Adaptations for Physically Challenged Children

1. Prevent paper and objects from slipping by using pads of paper, tape, clipboards, metal cookie sheets and magnets, photo album pages with sticky backings and plastic cover sheets, dycem (plastic) placed under paper and objects, or plastic photo cubes for displaying and storing materials.

2. Place a rubber strip on the back of a ruler or use a magnetic ruler to measure or draw lines.

3. Use calculators to perform computations.

4. Use felt tip pens and soft lead pencils that require less pressure. Improve grip on writing utensils by placing rubber bands, corrugated rubber or plastic tubing around the shaft. A golf practice ball or a sponge rubber ball may also be used.

5. Permit use of electronic typewriters, word processors, or computers. Typing aids can include a pointer stick attached to a head- or mouth-piece to strike keys, a keyboard guard that prevents striking two keys at once, line spacers that hold written materials while typing and corrective typewriter ribbons that do not require the use of erasers.

6. Use lap desks or a table-top easel with cork that allows work to be attached with push pins.

7. Provide an "able table" that adapts to varying positions and angles and may be attached to a wheelchair or freely stood on a tray (elastic straps hold books/materials in place, while knobs adjust angles).

8. Write or type at tables/desks that adjust to wheelchair heights.

9. Provide two sets of books/workbooks—one for home and one for school use.

10. Tape assignments, lectures, and activities that require extensive writing.

11. Allow a peer to carbon copy or photocopy class notes and provide written copies of board work.

12. Design worksheets/tests that allow students to answer in one of the following modes: one-word answers, lines placed through correct answers, magnetic letters moved on metal cookie sheets to indicate responses, wooden blocks placed on correct answers or containers with different categories in which answers can be dropped.

13. Use color-coded objects that are easy to handle and do not slip to indicate responses to polar questions: true/false, same/different, agree/disagree/don't know.

14. Select materials that are available on talking books or cassette tapes for students unable to hold books.

15. Use communication boards or charts with pictures, symbols, numbers or words to indicate responses.

16. Extend testing/assignment time and/or allow oral responses.

Figure 11–5 Instructional Adaptations for Physically Challenged Children
Source: From "Physically Challenged Students" by D. Knight and D. Wadsworth, 1993, *Childhood Education, 69*, pp. 211–215. Used by permission.

Formative evaluation of the curriculum for health, safety, and nutrition is also conducted throughout the year. The teacher notes health and safety habits that are being used by children as a result of instruction on health and safety topics. Likewise, the teacher notes any changes in eating habits that may have resulted from experiences with foods and information about nutrition. Ongoing evaluation can also pinpoint health and safety concepts that need to be addressed as a result of observing the children. New topics and instruction can be introduced when it is noted that children are playing in an unsafe manner or need information about self-help skills or grooming practices.

Ongoing formative evaluation is appropriate for assessing the teacher's progress concerning physical development. The teacher wants to know if activities and materials for physical development are interesting and motivating for the children. The teacher will want to reflect on his or her own growth in understanding the role of physical development for the child's overall developmental progress. The teacher will want to assess his or her own improvement in designing physical activities that enhance children's progress in cognitive, social, and aesthetic development. The teacher's goal is to be alert to each child and organize physical development activities that are appropriate for all the children. Of particular importance is a curriculum that meets the needs of preoperational children and focuses on developmental progress to discourage premature efforts to have young children compete with one another or participate in sports that are more suitable for older children.

Summative Evaluation

At the end of the school year, the teacher conducts the same types of final assessment as are used for other developmental categories of curriculum and instruction. A final assessment is made of children's physical growth and development of gross and fine motor skills to determine the progress that they made during the year.

The curriculum is evaluated to determine its effectiveness as well. The teacher wishes to understand what was accomplished during the year and develop ideas for continuing to enrich the curriculum the following year. Needed equipment and materials to add to the program are considered. The curriculum is evaluated in both developmental and subject area categories. The teacher needs information about the curriculum for physical development, but also reflects upon the curriculum for health, safety, and nutrition. The evaluation includes curriculum elements that were successful, as well as topics that could have been addressed more effectively.

Finally, the teacher evaluates the indoor and outdoor environments to determine their effectiveness and appropriateness for the physical development of young children. Are their elements that need to be taken out because of lack of interest or because they are unsafe? Are there conditions on the outdoor playground that need to be improved to be more appropriate or modified to improve their safety or interest for the children? Do more goals need to be set related to the existing play equipment to provide more upper body exercises or extend complexity of opportunities for mobility skills? Because equipment can add or detract from the possibilities for play involving physical skills, evaluation of the playground should be included to determine what motor skills need more opportunities for practice during play.

✦ SUMMARY

Physical development in young children includes motor development and physical fitness. During the preschool years, growth is less rapid than during the infant and toddler years; nevertheless, children are adding weight, height, and increasing muscle tissue.

Motor development includes basic skills in fine and gross motor development. Gross motor skills are concerned with locomotor skills and upper body and arm skills. Locomotor skills allow the child to have mobility, while upper body skills permit young children to learn to throw and catch. During the preschool years, children refine and extend movement skills and combine them with other skills into coordinated movements. Fine motor development allows young children to be able to acquire more control of hand and finger movements. Children learn to cut, use art materials, and refine self-help skills.

Perceptual-motor development combines the senses and motor skills. Through the interaction between sensory perception and motor skills, they involve body awareness, spatial awareness, directional awareness, and temporal awareness.

Physical fitness is related to an active, healthful lifestyle. Proper nutrition, physical exercise, attention to safety, and good hygiene habits are conducive to physical fitness.

Play is important for physical fitness and motor development. Young children need opportunities for physical exercise that include periods of free play indoors and outdoors. They need ample time and materials and equipment for play indoors and outdoors where there is ample room for all types of physical movement. Since changing lifestyles tend to limit young children's opportunities to play outdoors in many situations, play at the school setting is even more important for motor development.

Instruction for physical development should include a balance between organized activities that provide opportunities for gross and fine motor skill development and unstructured play activities that allow the child to engage in physical exercise while interacting with peers and the environment in all types of developmental play (as discussed Chapter 4 and Chapters 8 through 10). The teacher has a role in promoting physical development through organizing the environment, indoors and outdoors, to facilitate activities that encourage movements involving fine and gross motor skills. The teacher's role as instructor is to model physical skills and provide direction and practice for children who demonstrate a delay in motor skills or use incorrect locomotor or upper body movements. Teachers also instruct young children about good health practices, good nutrition, and skills for personal safety.

Goals for the curriculum in physical development include activities that promote the fundamental movement skills involved in both gross and fine motor development.

Goals for perceptual-motor development and self-help skills for preschool and primary age children extend motor development to coordinated movements that combine the senses with motor skills and promote the young child's ability to practice care in personal dressing needs. Goals for curriculum in health, safety, and nutrition involve learning the food groups and nutritional qualities of different types of food. Goals for physical health include physical fitness and grooming skills. Goals for the safety curriculum include topics in traffic, fire, poison, water, and playground safety.

Assessment of physical development is most commonly accomplished through observation of young children engaged in physical activities. Observation can be incidental when the teacher studies children during play activities or working in learning centers. Structured observations can be conducted using physical activity tasks. Motor skills can be assessed through planned tasks; and when appropriate, a series of tasks for systematic evaluation can be provided for. Checklists of gross and fine motor skills are useful for recording progress in physical development.

Children with physical disabilities also need experiences in motor development. Physical disabilities can cause children to be medically fragile and may result from chronic illnesses. Some physically challenged children need mobility aids for short distances or longer distances. Regardless of the severity of the physical impairment, young children need to engage in physical activities as much as possible. They should be encouraged to challenge themselves to engage in motor activities within their limitations. If necessary, the teacher will need to adapt activities or equipment to permit the child to participate in the activity.

Evaluation is a part of the curriculum for physical development. During the year, the teacher conducts ongoing evaluation of curriculum and instruction and teacher behaviors. Evaluation is also important for curriculum and instruction for health, safety, and nutrition.

Summative evaluation at the end of the year is used to evaluate the year's accomplishments in the area of physical development. Children's development in motor skills is evaluated, in addition to final evaluation of curriculum and instruction. Strengths and weaknesses in the instructional program are evaluated and desired improvements planned for the next school year.

⇢ STUDY QUESTIONS

1. Why do today's young children especially need a curriculum for physical development?
2. What does the teacher of young children need to know about the development of locomotor and upper body skills? fine motor skills?
3. Why is it important for children to master motor skills during the preschool years?
4. Explain perceptual-motor development and its relationship with coordinated motor skills.
5. How does play facilitate motor development? What is the difference between play and adult-led physical activities?

6. Describe how the teacher's understanding of motor skills development is related to the role of facilitator, instructor, and supporter of the curriculum for physical development.
7. Discuss activities that promote fine and gross motor skills in the indoor environment.
8. How does the outdoor environment promote fine and gross motor skills? Give examples.
9. Why does the teacher need to include structured activities for motor development?
10. What can young children learn about healthful nutrition, safety, and physical fitness?
11. Why is it important that young children understand and practice physical fitness?
12. Why is observation the primary strategy used for assessment of motor development?
13. Why should assessment of physical development be conducted frequently throughout the year?
14. Describe different types of physical impairments and their effects on motor skills development in young children.
15. Explain how the teacher of children with physical disabilities must accommodate the curriculum for physical development for the physical limitations and possibilities of each child. Give examples.
16. What do teachers and children need to understand about mobility aids used by young children with physical impairments?
17. Why is it important that children with physical disabilities be able to participate in physical development activities in the preschool classroom?
18. Explain how formative and summative evaluation contribute to improvement of curriculum and instruction for physical development.

⇒ KEY TERMS

body awareness	locomotor skills
directional awareness	perceptual-motor development
fine motor development	spatial awareness
gross motor development	temporal awareness

⇒ SUGGESTED ACTIVITIES

1. Observe children playing outdoors. Select a boy and girl to observe. List the activities engaged in that use gross motor skills. Compare the play activities of the boy and girl.

2. Observe a group of children engaged in outdoor play. Pick a child that seems to have well-developed gross motor skills and a child that uses limited gross motor skills. Describe the activities engaged in by each child and describe how chosen activities reflect the level of physical development.

3. Observe a preschool classroom. Record the types of fine motor skills used by the children, including the activity and materials involved in the activities.

12

Bringing It All Together

→ Chapter Objectives

As a result of reading this chapter, you will be able to

1. Describe the characteristics of an integrated curriculum
2. Discuss approaches to designing integrated curriculum
3. Explain how integrated curriculum accommodates individual developmental differences
4. Design an integrated curriculum that is group appropriate and individually appropriate
5. Describe how to involve children in all phases of planning for integrated curriculum
6. Design an integrated curriculum that makes connections across developmental domains
7. Describe two models for developing integrated curriculum
8. Explain how to plan for children with cultural diversity and with disabilities in an integrated curriculum
9. Discuss how to apply appropriate assessment and evaluation strategies in an integrated curriculum

In this last chapter, we want to make the final connections between assessment and curriculum with young children by describing a curriculum that is suitable for the development and needs of all children in early childhood classrooms. To accomplish this, we need to discuss in more detail the nature of integrated curriculum and how it relates to the developmental progress of young children. We will describe how an integrated curriculum meets developmental needs, as well as how it can be designed for the diverse characteristics that young children bring to the early childhood program. We will also explore how the integrated curriculum bridges different domains of development and how we evaluate an integrated approach to learning. In short, we will bring together all of the topics that have been discussed in the preceding chapters to explain how all young children, including those with cultural and developmental differences, can be served in early childhood classrooms.

In earlier chapters, we looked at developmental domains, including cognitive, language, social, and physical development, and how appropriate curriculum and instruction are constructed for children in each of the domains. In that context, we presented information on how to adapt the curriculum for children with diversities who might be integrated into the early childhood classroom and how some instruction would need to be individualized to meet the requirements of children's Individualized Education Plan (IEP). We also presented examples of how curriculum and instruction in a particular domain might be assessed using suitable activities.

Now we want to discuss the concept of integration within a broader context. We understand that all young children should be included in the regular classroom; or to say it another way, we want to have an integrated classroom that is appropriate for all populations of young children and includes all young children. In the integrated classroom, none of the children is alike; moreover, their differences might be slight or more pronounced, but all belong equally in the class.

Further, the concept of integration is expanded here to describe the nature of quality programs and instruction in early childhood classrooms. Instead of looking at curriculum in terms of developmental domains or content areas, we will consider the integrated curriculum.

THE INTEGRATED CURRICULUM

Origins of the Integrated Curriculum

Although there has been much attention given to integrated curriculum in recent years (Bredekamp, 1987; Katz & Chard, 1990; Krogh, 1990; Wortham, 1994), the concept is not new. The notion that curriculum should be taught from a holistic perspective with a child-centered approach in contrast to teacher-directed learning had been proposed by some of the pioneers in early childhood education. The original advocate in the United States was John Dewey (1902). Early in this century, Dewey suggested that knowledge be integrated and include child-initiated and self-directed activity. A contemporary of John Dewey's, William Heard Kilpatrick (1941), proposed that curriculum should be designed jointly by teachers and children. Dewey's and Kilpatrick's project approach proposed that the content areas could be learned through theme studies, incorporating real-life activities (Hartman, & Eckerty, 1995; New, 1992). In spite of the popularity of the project approach during the era of progressive education that peaked in the 1930s, it faded with the demise of progressive education.

The influence of Jean Piaget's work, which gained prominence in the 1950s, provided new support for an integrated curriculum, which promoted the child as an active learner who acquired knowledge from interaction with the environment and engaging in hands-on, or concrete, activities. Combined with a new emphasis on early childhood and development of Head Start models, early childhood education continued to focus on child-centered curriculum and instruction. This strategy was reinforced by curriculum and instruction practices in infant schools in Great Britain, which were informal and responsive to student needs and interests (Weber, 1984).

The British Infant School influence was incorporated into Head Start models, but also triggered a move toward open education during the 1970s, including the construction of open schools in all parts of the United States (New, 1992; Weber, 1984). With the advent of a return to an academic approach in the 1980s, open schools also fell from favor. Piaget's influence continued in early childhood education through units of study and through emphasis on child-centered activities, play, and the use of hands-on activities and learning centers.

The current interest in integrated curriculum has come as a reaction to the increased focus on academics in public school early childhood classrooms beginning in the late 1980s and continuing into the 1990s, a trend accompanied by increased testing and retention (Bredekamp, 1987; Shepard & Smith, 1988). Currently the use of thematic, integrated curriculum is gaining widespread use in early childhood and elementary settings as educators seek instructional methods that are developmentally suitable for all types of children with different ability levels and cultural backgrounds.

Integrated Curriculum Today

Integrated curriculum today reflects its accumulated history. The influence of Dewey and Kilpatrick continues with an emphasis upon child-centered and child-initiated curriculum planned together by teachers and children. The curriculum employs integrated studies that include activities that are useful or meaningful to the child. From Piaget (1952) and Vygotsky (1978), we use hands-on learning, play, and the social environment itself to provide a curriculum for the whole child rather than a fragmented curriculum (DeVries & Kohlberg, 1987). Within these guidelines, integrated curriculum has the following characteristics:

1. *Integrated curriculum is contextualized.* Learning needs to be relevant and meaningful to the children. It should have purpose for their lives and be a continuation of their prior experiences. Thus, it has a context for them or is contextualized (New, 1992). Learning activities that permit children to use their own context such as their art or their emergent writing experiences are purposeful because children can relate to their own developmental experience.

Context also means that an activity is purposeful because it permits children to make sense of what they are learning and process how it connects to knowledge they have already acquired. This is in contrast to "mindless" curriculum that fragments learning and consists of a brief exposure to new concepts and ideas (Bredekamp & Rosegrant, 1992b). The mindful curriculum challenges children to solve problems that are real. They engage in encountering cognitive conflict and constructing new concepts to resolve their uncertainty (New, 1992).

2. *Integrated curriculum promotes active learning.* Current literature on developmentally appropriate practice frequently refers to the principle that children must

be actively involved in their learning if it is to be meaningful and individually challenging. Children need to be able to think critically and construct meaning from what they are learning; they need to be able to reflect critically on their learning (O'Neil, 1990). They also need to be actively engaged in activities rather than passive observers of a teacher's or other students' activities. Children construct meaning as they engage in repeated experiences in interacting with materials and other people (Piaget, 1952; Vygotsky, 1978).

3. *Integrated curriculum is designed by children and for children's interests and needs.* A major difference between thematic units as many teachers plan them and the definition here is the involvement of children in the planning process. The planning together by teachers and children incorporates individual backgrounds, abilities, and interests. The connection is made between what is personally meaningful for the child and content that is to be taught. Children actively provide input into the planning process (Katz & Chard, 1990). The teacher considers each child's cultural orientation, developmental abilities, and interests, and provides a variety of activities at different levels using multiple approaches to match the characteristics of children and their preferences for engaging in learning. Moreover, activities account for children's zone of proximal development (Vygotsky, 1978) and facilitates their movement toward complete comprehension.

4. *Integrated curriculum is designed to interrelate development and knowledge.* Educators have discussed the education of the whole child for many decades. Today we discuss the importance of incorporating all categories or domains of development in the learning process. In contrast to the academic approach to instruction, where cognitive development is primary and foremost, integrated curriculum supports all domains of development. Multiple developmental domains are used to strengthen the relevance and motivation of the thematic activities. Intellectual growth is still a significant goal of the curriculum, but the child's social, physical, and language development is also addressed in learning activities.

With this framework and principles of integrated curriculum established, we can now turn to possibilities for curriculum development and processes and approaches in developing curriculum.

UNDERSTANDING INTEGRATED CURRICULUM

What, then, is an integrated curriculum? Is there one format of an integrated curriculum? By definition, an integrated curriculum crosses subject areas, but there are several ways that such combinations can be achieved. In all examples, the intent is to construct meaningful bridges to show connections in development and learning (Katz & Chard, 1990; Krogh, 1990; New, 1992; Wortham, 1994). This is frequently accomplished through the design of integrated thematic units; however, there are multiple possibilities for integration. Among the possibilities are integration initiated from a developmental or subject area, integration through study of a topic, and integration through the early childhood environment.

Integration From a Developmental Domain or Subject Area

Whatever approach to integrated curriculum is used, the intent is to connect some or all curriculum components into a meaningful whole. In the case of a developmental curriculum, different domains of development are incorporated into the curriculum so that all can support and affect the others. If a subject area approach to curriculum development is taken, activities that incorporate more than one curriculum area are included so that they reinforce and support the other.

Because we understand that a child's progress in one domain of development affects progress in others, the developmental integrated curriculum would interrelate developmental domains. For example, we know that the child's acquisition of language affects social development and vice versa. The integrated curriculum with a focus on language development would include experiences where children would play together or work in cooperative groups where both types of development could occur simultaneously. Likewise, if the focus is on motor development, activities to encourage fine and gross motor skills might be combined with objectives for cognitive and language development. In fact, it is almost impossible to have a curriculum that does not cross domains because of the interrelated nature of development.

When the curriculum is integrated by subject area, a similar type of interrelationship between subject areas occurs. Activities from various subject areas are combined to support one another and to make the learning experience more meaningful. Two subject areas might be combined or all subject areas might be incorporated into a more comprehensive form of integrated curriculum. A ready example is restructuring curriculum in mathematics, science, and technology into an integrated approach (O'Neil, 1990).

A popular approach to integration by subject area is in language arts. The primary goals and objectives are to promote progress in the language arts—or reading, writing, speaking, and listening. However, other content areas are also included to support the language arts curriculum. New reading curriculums now are based on children's literature and the whole language approach. Integrated curriculum is developed by using a piece of literature or children's book as the focus, with mathematics, social studies, science, and motor activities that relate to the story, extending and supporting both reading and language and the other subject areas (Raines & Canady, 1989).

The social studies subject area also lends itself easily to integrated curriculum. By nature, social studies is organized on broad topics. Young children might study their school, their community, local geographic characteristics, local cultural observances, and so on. Within these social studies goals, other subject areas can be naturally incorporated. For example, social studies provides connections between humanities and the sciences (O'Neil, 1990). In this approach, two or more distinct disciplines are brought together, using overlapping concepts to organize the integrated curriculum (Fogarty, 1991). Whole language incorporates this perspective since reading, writing, listening, and speaking are learned within overlapping concepts. If the community is studied in social studies, a subtopic might be stores in the immediate area and the kinds of merchandise they sell. Students learn about different types of stores, visit stores, and use reading, writing, language, and mathematics to carry out activities related to their learning.

Integration Through Topics

Topics can be the focus or core of integrated curriculum. A topic similar to the social studies topics described above is chosen. The objectives and activities for the topic are selected so that all categories of the curriculum or developmental domains are included. The topic, which can be very simple, is developed into a comprehensive unit of study. For example, a fruit such as apples or a vegetable such as lettuce might be the topic of study. The children can study different types of apples or lettuce, compare their physical characteristics, study how each grows, read stories about apples, or learn about dishes that use apples or lettuce as ingredients. The nutritional value of the apple or lettuce might be discussed and recipes for each type of food prepared.

Ants might be studied. Children might learn about different types of ants, how they build their homes, what they eat, and so on. An element of local history might be studied or cultural observances of a holiday can be the source of the integrated curriculum. The intent is to develop a topic that will incorporate all components of children's development and learning so that the activities that the children engage in are useful and real.

Integration Through the Early Childhood Environment

In Chapter 4, we learned about different ways to construct curriculum in early childhood programs. The importance of both the indoor and outdoor environments was stressed as supporting the development and learning of young children. Also described was how learning centers or the learning environment could be used as the source of curriculum and instruction.

In this section, we can take that concept further to describe how the integrated curriculum in particular can be facilitated through the indoor and outdoor environments. We understand that play is important and how it promotes development and learning. We described in earlier chapters how it is significant for each developmental domain. It is not difficult, then, to see how integrated curriculum can be initiated and supported by the environment. We can use both the indoor and outdoor environments to make integrated activities possible. For example, by including notepads, newspapers, and books in the housekeeping center, we can promote the integration of emergent literacy and social development. Props in the block center can promote dramatic play related to the study of a storybook, or they can provide opportunities for construction related to a study of different types of homes (Hartman & Eckerty, 1995). Children's interest in butterflies can result in organization of the science center to include activities that integrate reading and social studies into the curriculum.

The outdoor environment can be the focus of integrated curriculum. A study of jump ropes and jump rope games can integrate motor development, language development, and social development with activities to learn how to jump rope, study about jump ropes, learn jump rope rhymes, and create jump rope games and rhymes (Buchoff, 1995).

Integration Through Thematic Units

All of the approaches for developing integrated curriculum and instruction discussed above can be organized into thematic units, although they can be implemented without that type of structure. Thematic units or curriculum projects provide a vehicle for developing integrated curriculum so that long-term and short-term planning can be conducted within a framework of a comprehensive unit.

When units of study are discussed, the reader may have a picture of units that were studied in elementary school, where the teacher chose a topic and selected a collection of activities that would relate to the topic. Everyone in public schools in the United States probably experienced at least one unit on "Indians." In the course of studying the unit, the children made construction paper headdresses and paper tepees decorated with suns and other symbols. Bredekamp and Rosegrant (1992b) call this "mindless" curriculum because not only is it shallow, but the information is stereotyped and portrays Native Americans inaccurately and inappropriately. Derman-Sparks (1989) calls this type of curriculum "tourist curriculum" because a culture is visited only briefly without experiences to understand the culture and its people in depth.

Integrated units discussed here are based on topics that are meaningful to the children. They are designed with the individual group of children in mind. The unit topics and activities are selected with the developmental and cultural characteristics of the children, as well as the children's interests. The intent is to involve the children in preparing for their learning. This contrasts with curriculum based on the teacher's interest or on the teacher's making decisions about children's needs and interests, which may not include the children's ideas. Variations in development within the group of children must also be considered if the unit is to be meaningful. With these requirements in mind, it is difficult to conceive of using commercially prepared thematic units that are developed for normal development and without consideration of the unique social and cultural characteristics of the young children in an individual classroom. The design of integrated units or projects, to be described below, is intended to use knowledge of diversity in young children to develop units rather than use units that might be mindless or unrelated to the interests and experiences of the children studying the unit.

PLANNING INTEGRATED CURRICULUM TO MEET DEVELOPMENTAL NEEDS

Understanding How Development and Learning Are Interrelated

The importance of understanding the child's level of development when planning curriculum and instruction has been a basic premise of this text. In addition, it has been stressed that learning experiences need to take into account the child's level of development and its implications for how the child thinks and interacts with new information.

Children who are progressing through early childhood developmental stages at a normal rate are in Piaget's preoperational stage of cognitive development, which occurs between the ages of two and seven. Curriculum and instruction that is planned for them should be consistent with how the preoperational child thinks and learns. Integrated curriculum should also be congruent with children's levels in all developmental domains. And, because activities in integrated curriculum cut across content areas or developmental domains, the interrelationship between the domains or content must be taken into consideration, particularly when the child's development may be uneven or inconsistent between one domain or another. For example, an objective for children to explore their understanding of creating patterns might include an activity of stringing beads on a shoelace to create or duplicate patterns. A child who does not yet have the motor skills to string beads but understands the concept would not be able to engage in the activity successfully; however, if the activity were changed to using parquetry blocks, the child might be able to participate without difficulty.

Emergent literacy in the first grade can be used as an example. Children will be at different stages of ability to read print. If a group of children is engaged in exploring a topic, an advanced reader might read the material aloud to children who do not yet have that ability. The other children might read along in their books or listen for desired information.

In mathematics, children who are more advanced can be paired with children who are moving more slowly. The advanced children can be used as tutors to work with their partners or as consultants for children who have questions to contact when they have a problem.

In cooperative learning groups, children who have leadership abilities can make efforts to include children who are hesitant or shy in discussing and conducting the activity at hand. Later, children can take turns being in charge of the group so that others can become comfortable in leadership roles.

The importance of matching development with learning activities becomes more significant when children are developmentally different from the norm such as is the case with children with disabilities, or at the other extreme, children who are gifted. Adaptations of integrated curriculum for all variations in development are required if all children in the classroom are to be able to participate fully in the learning experiences.

Planning Integrated Curriculum That Is Group Appropriate

The guidelines for developmentally appropriate practices as originally described (Bredekamp, 1987) proposed that curriculum should be age appropriate and individually appropriate. However, as discussed in Chapter 7, there are concerns about applying those principles to children with disabilities or who are diverse in development beyond normal ranges. Therefore, it is suggested that instead of being age appropriate, integrated curriculum should be group appropriate. Integrated curriculum is designed for the particular developmental characteristics that are represented within the group of learners. Children's chronological age is not as significant, unless the developmental characteristics of the children are similar. If children with disabilities are part of the group, developmental variation will be more important than similarity in age.

Planning Integrated Curriculum That Is Individually Appropriate

The principle that curriculum and instruction should be individually appropriate is a suitable concept to address diversity in young children. Integrated curriculum activities should be designed so that all children will have suitable experiences, regardless of developmental level and cultural background. The activities that are designed should be meaningful for all children. It might be necessary to plan a variety of activities so that they can be matched with individuals or small groups of children. The nature of integrated curriculum is to have multiple opportunities of different types to permit children to actively interact with information in multiple ways; therefore, children who are diverse can also participate in, and benefit from, integrated experiences if adaptations are made for individual differences in each child.

A unit in social studies might be used as an example. After a trip to a store, the teacher arranges the dramatic play center into a store with food containers that can be used for role-playing. While most of the children are able to interact freely, a child with mental delay might need specific instructions on how to engage in the activity. In addition, the teacher might need to explain to the child the roles that are being played so that the child will understand how to participate. Watching the other children role-play also serves as a role model for the child with the developmental disability (Deiner, 1993).

Planning Integrated Curriculum to Meet Cultural Differences

Earlier in the chapter, we discussed integrated curriculum that is contextual; that is, it responds to the backgrounds and experiences of the child. In addition to the contextual relevance of curriculum for individual children, Derman-Sparks (1992) discussed curriculum that is planned for the unique cultural makeup of the children that are in each classroom. It would follow, then, that the cultural context of curriculum would be different for children in one classroom who are ethnically diverse as compared to another classroom where the children are from a single culture or background.

A primary goal of the integrated curriculum would be to include appropriate opportunities for children to learn and appreciate diversity and to become aware and concerned about bias (Byrnes, 1992; Derman-Sparks, 1992). Derman-Sparks proposes that each child should construct a knowledgeable, confident self-identity, appreciate diversity among people, think critically about bias, and be able to respond assertively to bias. Byrnes stresses similar goals in enhancing self-esteem, fostering cooperative interactions, developing cognitive sophistication that will lessen prejudice, and increasing empathy for others. How the integrated curriculum would address these goals would depend upon the context for the children in the classroom. However, it should be remembered that children need also to understand and appreciate diversity of many cultures and languages—whether children in the classroom represent one culture, two or three cultures, or multiple cultures. Children who are from a minority population need to develop self-esteem and confidence from their own cultural perspective, but they also need to have understanding and empathy for children from other cultures.

Integrated curriculum affords the opportunity to weave cultural diversity into the experiences that are planned with and for young children. Some topics or themes such as a topic in science or a theme based on motor development would have fewer possibilities for interrelating cultural diversity. Social studies and language arts or literature themes or topics would include rich opportunities to appreciate diversity. For example, if a second grade class were studying folktales, it would be possible to find folktales from different cultures including cultures represented in the classroom, but not limited to those cultures. Whatever the theme or topic to be addressed through an integrated curriculum, attention is given to the cultural makeup of the children who will engage in the project activities. If the integrated curriculum is to be meaning-

Thematic curriculum should incorporate planning with children.

ful and have relevance for each child, the activities should bridge the child's prior environment and experiences with the knowledge that is to be learned within the integrated curriculum.

PLANNING INTEGRATED CURRICULUM TO RESPOND TO CHILDREN'S INTERESTS

Teacher-Initiated Integrated Curriculum That Includes Input From the Children

The possibility of involving children in the curriculum planning process is uncomfortable for many teachers. All of a teacher's training and experience may have focused on his or her responsibility to plan learning goals, objectives, and activities for the children in the classroom. And further, some teachers may believe that they have child-centered, constructivist classrooms when they provide the environment and activities for the children's active involvement and selection. The perception of some teachers may be that when children are allowed to make choices about their activities during learning center time or select which art materials they will use for a collage, the curriculum is both child centered and child planned.

A step beyond this approach is curriculum planning that actively involves children in the design of what they will be learning as well as during the implementation stage. The teacher may determine the topic or theme based on the school's curriculum guidelines or a subject that is timely and of interest to the children. A first step is to determine how the topic will apply to the individual and group characteristics in the class. As goals and objectives are planned for the topic to be studied, the teacher considers the developmental needs of the children and the relationships between cultural backgrounds of the children and the integrated topic to be studied. However, if the children are to be actively involved in unit planning, the teacher will conduct planning sessions with the children to discuss with them the topic and solicit from them what they would like to learn about it. This can then evolve into combined planning for projects and activities that the children would like to engage in during the implementation process of the unit (Wortham, 1994).

After the unit has been prepared and is ready to be initiated, the teacher will again plan with the children for scheduling and choices they would like to make among activities that will be available. Again, the teacher includes a variety of activities that take into consideration the disabilities that are present in the class as well as diverse cultural factors. Children might plan to work in pairs or small groups to carry out their interests related to the topic to be studied.

Integrated Curriculum That Is Initiated From Children's Interests

A preferred approach to designing integrated curriculum is to begin the planning process with selection of the topic or theme that is based on children's interests. Even young children in preschool and kindergarten classes can help select topics, suggest appropriate activities, and help identify and gather resources that are needed for unit activities. In fact, as children become more experienced, they can assume more roles and responsibilities in the planning process (Barclay & Breheny, 1994).

Another approach to curriculum planning that is more child-centered is for students to engage in topic selection and the projects that they would like to engage to accomplish the learning objectives. Children who are working together on a project develop a plan with the teacher for what they want to accomplish and how they will go about conducting the project. Objectives and project activities can be modified or expanded as children find new avenues that they would like to explore and activities that involve more in-depth investigation or exploration (Katz & Chard, 1990; Wolk, 1994). If children are involved in the planning process from the point of topic selection through activity planning and make choices that are meaningful and purposeful for both individuals and the group of students, children will be motivated to continue working on project activities over a period of time. The children have a personal investment in the topic being studied and are intrinsically motivated because they have chosen what to explore and learn (Barbour & Seefeldt, 1993; Wolk, 1994).

There are options in how to manage the planning of integrated curriculum with children in early childhood programs. With younger children, the teacher initially selects the topics and encourages children to contribute ideas. As more units are planned, children gradually assume a more significant role that reflects their interests. Eventually they will suggest the topics they are interested in planning and studying next (Hartman & Eckerty, 1995). Teachers of older students might have constraints regarding curriculum that is expected to be covered at a primary grade level. The teacher might alternate between topics that are required and those that are chosen by children. Or, part of the day might be spent on individual projects selected and conducted by students based on their interests, and part of the day might be spent in unit activities planned by the teacher and class, focusing on required curriculum topics and objectives (Wolk, 1994; Wortham, 1994).

PLANNING INTEGRATED CURRICULUM TO UNDERSTAND CONNECTIONS IN KNOWLEDGE

Previously in this chapter, we described ways that connections can be made between developmental domains or subject areas. Teachers can design activities that will interrelate domains of development. For example, if young children engage in learning the game of hopscotch or jumping rope games, they are integrating motor development with cognitive development because jumping skills and counting or chanting rhymes both can be used in hopscotch and jumping rope games.

A major purpose of integrated curriculum is to engage children in interrelated learning. The study of concepts such as basic shapes and contrasts in dimension (including heavy versus light, fewer and more, and short and long) overlap cognitive development and language development domains—or mathematics and science, from a subject area viewpoint.

The developmental domain interrelationships described in the examples cited above may be obvious only to the teacher; nevertheless, there is also a purpose for young children to understand connections in knowledge. Food activities always provide a ready example of how children can observe and understand connecting relationships in learning. If children are learning how to make fruit salad, they will use literacy skills as a list is made of the types of fruit that are needs, fine motor skills are involved in preparing the fruit, and health and nutrition concepts are evident when the nutritional value of salad is discussed.

When cooking is part of a food activity, reading, science, and mathematics are added to the knowledge connections. If a soup is to be prepared, a recipe must be read, food ingredients must be counted or measured, and the cooking process changes the form of the food. Children must work in a cooperative manner in cooking activities, adding social skills and understanding of developmental differences, as some children have more advanced motor or reading skills than others. Cultural appreciation can become a knowledge connection if different types of soups are discussed or prepared based on family recipes or recipes from different cultural origins.

Some knowledge connections are readily apparent to young children, while others emerge through the teacher's guidance. For older children, problem solving incorporates understanding of knowledge connections as second graders compile grocery lists and add up costs or hypothesize what will occur to ingredients in a recipe during the cooking process, and then construct a report on the computer to discuss their observations supported with photographs of the cooking project. The students used mathematics and writing skills to prepare a grocery list. The report written at the end of the project enabled students to synthesize what they learned about different content areas during the project activities.

There are multiple ways to help children make connections in knowledge through integrated curriculum. We will now look at two paradigms or models for integrating curriculum with young children. The first focuses on projects that are planned around a topic, concept, or theme. The second, thematic-integrated curriculum, consciously includes the domains of development or subject areas of the curriculum when activities are selected for the unit of study.

MODELS FOR PLANNING INTEGRATED CURRICULUM

The Project Approach to Integrated Curriculum

The project approach to integrated curriculum has is roots in the earlier project curriculum initiated by Dewey (1902) and Kilpatrick (1941), discussed earlier in the chapter. A purpose of the approach is to make it possible for adults and children to experience school as life and to experience the class as a community (Katz & Chard, 1990). It complements the early childhood curriculum, but it is not intended to replace other forms of instruction. It is intended to facilitate the application of concepts and skills in a meaningful context that includes problem solving. Project work permits children's in-depth investigation of topics that interest them. Projects encourage children to make connections in information that is learned over a period of time. The project may be initiated by the teacher or the children; however, the topic should be of interest to the children, rather than significant to the teacher without consideration of the children. An example of the project approach to integrated curriculum is described below.

Jeanette Hartman and Carolyn Eckerty (1995) described a project developed and implemented with four- and five-year-old children. Initiated from interest in a construction site, the project evolved as the "construction site/house project." The project was developed in three phases. Phase One occurred as the children became interested in the construction site next to the school. As the children made comments about the construction and asked questions, the teachers became aware that a project evolving from their interest in the construction was a relevant learning possibility. When the children answered affirmatively when the teachers asked them if they wanted to learn more about construction, the following steps were taken in Phase One (Hartman & Eckerty, 1995):

> The class
> - Agreed on a topic
> - Discussed what the children already knew about construction sites
> - Walked to the construction site
> - Recorded initial impressions about the site in writing and artwork
> - Interviewed a construction worker
> - Read related books
> - Photographed the site and the project planning activities
> - Planned and gathered necessary materials (p. 142)

Additional questions generated during Phase One were sent home in a newsletter to parents and caregivers explaining the project and its purpose.

During Phase Two, the children planned their activities for the project and focused on their goals. The class took the following steps (Hartman & Eckerty, 1995):

> 1. Established specific roles and responsibilities
> 2. Erected a "building" out of boxes
> 3. Read more related books
> 4. Followed through on previously made plans
> 5. Added details (e.g., labeling, painting, cutting out windows and doors)
> 6. Discussed activities that corresponded to content areas (e.g., measuring for windows involved math and making paint involved science)
> 7. Viewed more photographs of their progress
> 8. Shared work samples and stories during group time
> 9. Participated in dramatic play
> 10. Wrote a class story (p. 142)

As the children began to construct a building out of boxes, it began to look more like a house. Therefore, in Phase Three of the project, the building was changed to a house with details such as wallpaper, clotheslines, and carpet squares used for furnishings.

This example of a project fulfills the purposes for the project approach: the project evolved from children's interests; the children experienced school as life; the children experienced the class as a community; the project allowed in-depth investigation; the project facilitated the application of concepts and skills in a meaningful context; and the project encouraged children to make connections in information and use all domains of development.

The Thematic Unit Approach to Integrated Curriculum

The thematic unit approach to integrated curriculum has similar goals and processes as the project approach to integrated curriculum. It should be initiated in response to children's interests or to complement children's interests. It should be relevant and specific to the particular group of children for which it is designed and incorporate their ideas and planning.

However, there are differences in how thematic units are designed. The curriculum planning is approached with the purpose of incorporating all domains of development or subject areas in the unit. The unit can be developed from a topic or concept that is interesting to the children; and the topic, in many cases, is related to curriculum that is expected to be taught at that grade level. During the planning process, the teachers graph or web the activities that are to be incorporated into the unit and determine if there is a balance of experiences for the developmental domains or subject areas. The webbing process can also be used to demonstrate connections among the developmental or content areas. By using this process of analysis and visualization, teachers and children can understand how the unit integrates knowledge (Wortham, 1994). Figures 12–1 and 12–2 show examples of frameworks for webbing.

Another difference between the project approach and unit approach is that the unit approach lends itself to planning that includes goals and objectives and plans for daily implementation of the unit. Teachers do not only design a master plan for the unit, but they can also have daily lessons plans that describe what will take place; and what learning mode is being used, including teacher-directed activities, child-initiated activities; and how the learning environment will be used.

A level team of first grade teachers planned and implemented an integrated unit on spring flowers. Their school was located two blocks away from a major highway that had been seeded with wildflowers for several years. As a result, the flowers not only grew along the highway each spring, but they had spread to fields adjacent to the highway. The children were interested in the multitude of colors displayed by the flowers. The teachers explored with the children what they wanted to learn about the flowers and what kinds of activities they could plan to accomplish that goal. The unit was developed in two stages: the planning stage and the implementation stage.

During the planning stage, the teachers and children took the following steps:

Figure 12–1   Example of a
Topic Web

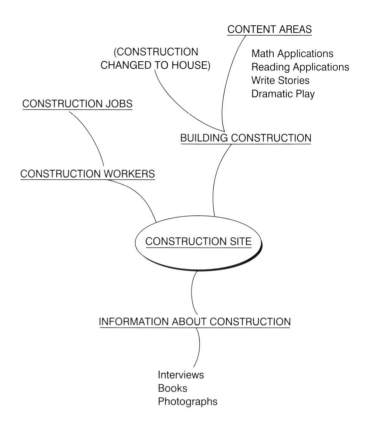

1. The topic was discussed and possibilities for unit activities were listed on the board.
2. The classes took a walking field trip to the field near the school to look at the flowers.
3. The classes brainstormed the kinds of activities they could engage in; these were added to the list on the board.
4. The team of teachers met and compared activity possibilities. They diagrammed the activities that had the most merit into a web of subject areas to determine a balance of curriculum areas. Teachers selected the activities that would be most appropriate for the interests of the children in their classroom.
5. Goals and objectives for the unit were designed by the team of teachers. The activities were analyzed to determine that there was a balance between teacher-directed and child-initiated activities. They were further analyzed to determine if they were a short-term activities or long-term projects. Activities that were suitable for learning centers were so designated. Finally, the teachers wrote goals and objectives for the unit.

During the implementation stage of the unit, the teachers again planned with the children in their individual classroom.

1. Children discussed the activities that the teachers had selected for their room and decided which ones were of interest to them. They selected both short-term activities and long-term projects. In some cases, an activity interested all of the children; in other cases, activities interested smaller groups of children.

2. The teacher discussed the activities with the children, including lessons in which all children would participate. A final list of activities was compiled.

3. The team of teachers met again and wrote their unit and lesson plans. They scheduled the activities and projects into a two-week time frame. In cases where more than one classroom was using an activity, they decided on how to share the resources and make scheduling decisions that were necessary.

4. The team discussed modifications that would have to be made for children with disabilities in their classroom. They brainstormed ways in which all of the children could participate and how that could be accomplished. Individual differences in terms of culture were not addressed because all of the children shared a common background: namely, the presence of the flowers near the school. However, the relationship between home and school could be addressed. That is, children could bring resources concerning flowers from their home to the school. Or parents might participate in unit activities at school.

5. The teachers discussed how the unit would be evaluated.

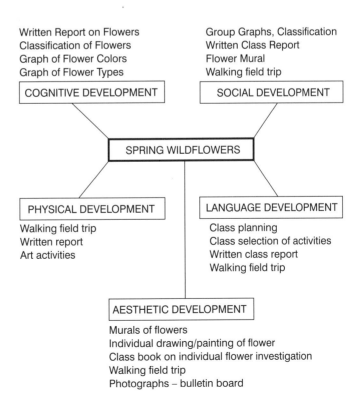

Figure 12–2 Example of an Integrated Curriculum Web

Written Report on Flowers
Classification of Flowers
Graph of Flower Colors
Graph of Flower Types

COGNITIVE DEVELOPMENT

Group Graphs, Classification
Written Class Report
Flower Mural
Walking field trip

SOCIAL DEVELOPMENT

SPRING WILDFLOWERS

PHYSICAL DEVELOPMENT

Walking field trip
Written report
Art activities

LANGUAGE DEVELOPMENT

Class planning
Class selection of activities
Written class report
Walking field trip

AESTHETIC DEVELOPMENT

Murals of flowers
Individual drawing/painting of flower
Class book on individual flower investigation
Walking field trip
Photographs – bulletin board

Some of the activities the teachers and children incorporated into the unit were:

- Constructing murals of flowers from materials in the art centers
- Identifying the names of the flowers
- Charting the colors of the flowers on a graph
- Devising classification schemes for the similarities and differences in the flowers. The children were to determine how many ways the flowers could be grouped based on their characteristics.
- Doing individual reports. Children selected a flower they wished to investigate. They studied their flower, made a drawing or painting of their flower, and wrote a page about the characteristics of their flower on the computer. The individual reports were collected into a class book for the library center.
- Taking photographs of the field for a bulletin board display
- Making a class report of the information learned about wild flowers. This was written as a group and posted along with the photographs.
- Extending the activity. Children looked for wildflowers near their home. If they found any, they brought them to school and compared them with photographs taken of the wildflowers growing in the field.

PLANNING FOR INCLUSION OF DIVERSITY IN THE INTEGRATED CURRICULUM

One step in planning an integrated curriculum project or unit is to look for opportunities to incorporate the individual cultures and backgrounds of young children and plan activities that would help children to appreciate contributions of other cultures. Because the project described above was related to an activity occurring next to the school, all of the children had a common background from which they could explore the topic. If the topic had been "families," the teacher would have had ample opportunity to select activities to incorporate different family structures and lifestyles, as well as the commonalities that all of the children shared.

In the thematic unit in the example above, the children again had a common focus on which to base their learning, which was not related to cultural differences. Nevertheless, their home background was been incorporated by inviting children to bring wildflowers that were blooming inside their home or in the yard, if their home had a yard. They could also bring pictures of flowers that they found in their home, either from photographs, magazines, calendars, or some other source.

Adapting the construction site project for children with disabilities would be a different matter. A blind child would need to have descriptions of the construction site related, and if possible, helped to explore the characteristics of the site. Arrangements would need to be made for wheelchair access to the site if a mobility-impaired child was a member of the class. The same modifications would have to be made for the unit on wildflowers so that all children could participate in the field trips to the field and engage individually in experiencing the flowers.

Modification of project activities would need to be made for children with disabilities. A child with poor fine-motor control would perhaps need adult assistance in cutting and fitting materials in the building. A child with a visual impairment could paint the box surface with guidance from another child. A child with a mental impairment would participate in all activities but might need verbal cues to participate in class discussions and direct instruction in vocabulary related to the topic. Specific planning would have to occur before and during implementation of the project to ensure that each child's developmental needs were considered and planned for to include the entire range of developmental diversity.

The construction project could incorporate cultural diversity in decisions children would make in how the building could be decorated. Children could discuss their preferences for placing materials in the "house" based on discussions of their own homes. The teacher could facilitate and guide discussions to ensure that a multicultural perspective was included.

EVALUATING INTEGRATED CURRICULUM AND INSTRUCTION

As part of the link between assessment and learning, the integrated curriculum is also assessed. Its effectiveness is assessed in terms of (1) children's progress, (2) the effectiveness of the curriculum itself, and (3) evaluation of the teacher's role.

Assessing Children's Progress in Integrated Curriculum

The process of assessment used when implementing integrated curriculum is more likely to be authentic than performance evaluations. Observation of children's activities and behaviors will be ongoing throughout the project or units as children actively participate in the activities they have chosen or have been assigned. There will be many examples of products children have produced for a portfolio. Photographs taken of students engaged in projects and activities can be included as well as reports the children have conducted. Stories written by the children, paintings, and other examples of artwork contribute to sources for assessment.

If unit objectives include specific skills to be acquired, assessment can be more intentional. In the flower unit, the children were to devise strategies to classify the flowers based on the flower's individual and collective characteristics. The teacher could evaluate the child's ability to classify and the thinking strategies the child used to determine classification possibilities. In other activities, the child's acquisition of skills and knowledge might be applicable to checklist assessments. If a young child demonstrated mastery in fine motor skills such as cutting or writing his or her name while engaged in integrated curriculum activities, the teacher could check off the item on a developmental checklist. Likewise, if a child demonstrated understanding of colors or participated in a group activity in a more cooperative manner, developmental progress could be recorded on a checklist.

For children who have disabilities or language differences, assessment might focus on more specific indicators of progress. If an IEP is part of the child's educational program, progress on IEP objectives might be documented as a result of successful accomplishment of activities. In the case of direct instruction with individual children as part of the unit or project experiences, documentation of progress could be accomplished through assessment strategies related to the learning activities.

Some evaluation would be specific in integrated curriculum, and some would be incidental as teachers became aware of improvement in behaviors or skills. This would be true for any child in the classroom.

Assessing Effectiveness of the Integrated Curriculum

Integrated curriculum is planned by teachers and children in contrast to commercial resources available in early childhood programs. During the implementation steps of the curriculum and after the work has been completed, the integrated curriculum is assessed. Teachers and children together determine which activities were successful and which did not turn out as planned or were problematic.

One criterion of effectiveness of integrated curriculum is its flexibility. As was noted in the project curriculum, the project changed as new ideas occurred to the children. Regardless of the origin of the integrated curriculum, it should be possible for children to explore new ideas or conduct different activities as new directions are indicated during the implementation phase. Therefore, assessment of the integrated curriculum should include its flexibility and changes made during the learning process that strengthened the accomplishment of the goals and objectives of the original plan.

The project or unit is also assessed in case it is used again with another group of children. Evaluation of effectiveness of activities and projects as well as problems that might have been encountered is conducted so that future units or the same unit taught in the future can benefit from the lessons learned by teachers and children.

Assessing the Teacher's Role

The teacher will also want to assess her effectiveness during the project or unit. Were effective strategies used when direct teaching activities were used? Was there another way that children could have learned information more successfully?

When functioning as a facilitator rather than instructor, did the teacher use successful behaviors? Were children encouraged to pursue their ideas rather than following the teacher's lead? Did the teacher intervene to help children extend or expand an effort during sociodramatic play or in creating a piece of artwork, or was the teacher's role too intrusive, with the result that the child's responses were negative or resulted in feelings of inadequacy? The teacher will want to look at the various roles engaged in during the integrated curriculum experience to determine when behaviors and strategies were effective, and when another approach might be considered that would be more successful.

A FINAL LOOK AT EARLY CHILDHOOD PROGRAMS

The purpose of this book has been to help teachers and future teachers of young children in preschool through primary grades in early childhood programs understand how to develop programs for all children. In the past, textbooks focused on young children in general. Now we have to be more specific about diversity in children and how early childhood programs can include all of them: they are all members of the classroom community. Inclusion is a fairly new practice when compared to the overall history of early childhood education. As early childhood classrooms in all types of early childhood programs learn how to implement inclusion, teachers need assistance in getting started, and future teachers need to understand the strategies they will need to use to be able to plan curriculum and instruction for children who are diverse in ability, culture, and language.

A major emphasis of this text has been placed on the importance of screening and assessment and its relationship to curriculum and instruction. As we learn to work with children with disabilities and language and cultural differences, it becomes even more important to know the individual developmental levels of young children in all domains of development. We have learned that children with disabilities or development beyond the normal ranges must be assessed very carefully if suitable learning experiences are to be provided for them. Moreover, many of them will require screening early in life followed by diagnostic assessment if they are to receive the early intervention services in programs designed to address their disability and enhance their potential for development. Although early childhood teachers who are not working in special education intervention programs might not directly be involved in screening and assessment, they too need to understand the processes used for children with disabilities in the infant, toddler, and preschool years and how they, too, can best serve the child. In the future, early childhood teachers and early childhood special education teachers will be working together in increasing numbers as children with diverse needs and backgrounds are served in child care settings, private and parochial preschools and primary schools, and in public schools. All will need to know how to evaluate a child's status in order to plan curriculum and instruction. And all will need to know how IFSPs and IEPs are planned, implemented, and evaluated.

Not all early childhood programs currently have children with disabilities or children with language differences enrolled; nevertheless, in the future it will be more and more common to have children with disabilities included in classrooms. We all need to be ready and comfortable with that reality. This text has been developed to help us all understand how to become teachers of all young children. As time goes on, the pioneers in this new world of early childhood programs for all children will show us better ways to plan curriculum and instruction and to assess the needs and accomplishments of each child. We have to view quality early childhood programs with new lenses as we address the needs of children with diverse backgrounds and abilities. We still have the goal of providing programs that celebrate the ways that young children learn; nevertheless, we have to extend and expand our repertoire as to how we best can accomplish the challenge.

⇨ SUMMARY

This chapter has addressed how we provide curriculum and instruction for young children within an integrated curriculum. Throughout the book, we have discussed how to assess young children's development and how we plan curriculum and instruction to meet developmental differences. We first looked at how we plan for individual needs in each developmental domain. We learned how to plan for cognitive, language, social, and motor development.

This chapter discussed how to design curriculum that brings all domains of development together. It explored how to plan and implement integrated curriculum that maximizes children's abilities to learn. Integrated curriculum not only addresses the whole child, but provides learning experiences that address developmental domains in an interrelated fashion, but is designed to be relevant and purposeful for the child. In keeping with what we know about how children acquire new knowledge and skills from intrinsic motivation and through active involvement, we addressed the importance of involving children in planning integrated curriculum and selecting topics, themes, or projects from the point of view of their interests.

We started the first chapters with information on how to assess young children's development so that we would be equipped to provide individually appropriate curriculum and instruction. We then applied that information to how we would plan and adapt curriculum and instruction in the individual developmental domains. Finally in this chapter, we moved to the integrated curriculum, where we considered individual and group needs for an interrelated curriculum that would maximize the potential of all young children to benefit from learning with and from one another in the community of the classroom. We addressed how to pull all of the strategies we have described throughout the text on appropriate assessment of all young children and apply those that are appropriate for integrated instruction to evaluate the children, the curriculum, and the teacher.

⇨ STUDY QUESTIONS

1. How did the idea of integrating curriculum originate?
2. What have been the continuing influences on integrated curriculum?
3. Describe the nature of integrated curriculum today.
4. Discuss some alternatives for integrating curriculum.
5. How can the environment be the focus for integrated curriculum?
6. Why does the teacher need to understand how development and learning are interrelated before designing integrated curriculum?
7. Explain the implications of curriculum being group appropriate when designing integrated curriculum.
8. What kinds of factors must be considered when designing curriculum that is individually appropriate?

9. How do cultural differences affect planning for integrated curriculum?
10. Why are children's interests significant when planning integrated curriculum?
11. How can children select topics to be studied in integrated curriculum?
12. Describe the meaning and importance of connections in knowledge.
13. How are the project approach and unit approach to integrated curriculum alike and different?
14. How do teachers plan for children with disabilities when designing integrated curriculum?
15. Discuss the different types of assessment and evaluation that are conducted with integrated curriculum projects and units.

✦ SUGGESTED ACTIVITIES

1. Study the activities described for the integrated unit on spring flowers. Analyze each activity to determine what developmental or subject areas have been connected in each activity.
2. Select either the project or thematic unit approach to design a unit. Go through the steps for integrated curriculum design to develop your topic or theme. Hypothesize how you would include children in the planning process of your integrated curriculum.

Glossary

Accommodation   The modification of existing schemes in order to incorporate new events or knowledge (Piaget).

Analytical Thinkers   A style of thinking that is characterized by organization or by a step-by-step consideration of parts of information.

Antibias   An active/activist approach to challenging prejudice, stereotyping, bias, and the "isms" (Derman-Sparks and the A.B.C. Task Force, 1989).

Assessment   The process of evaluating an element of development or learning.

Assimilation   The incorporation of new information or knowledge into existing schemes (Piaget).

At Risk   A high probability that a condition affecting development and learning will occur.

Atypical Development   Development that is different from typical patterns or outside the range considered to be normal.

Auditory Learners   Learners whose preference for learning is through listening.

Authentic Assessment   An assessment that uses some type of contextual performance by a child to demonstrate understanding.

Bilingual   The ability to speak in two languages.

Biliterate   The ability to read and write in two languages.

Body Awareness   The child's developing awareness of parts of the body and how the body is oriented in space.

Brain Injury   An injury that affects thought and neural coordination.

Categorical Intervention Programs   Programs for very young children with disabilities that are designed for a specific disability such as vision impairment or physical impairment.

Cognitive Impairment   An impairment that affects mental functions such as intelligence and language.

Communication Impairment   An impairment that affects the child's ability to communicate in an age-appropriate way that can be understood by others.

Compensatory Programs   Programs first implemented in the 1960s and 1970s that were intended to supplement regular education programs to benefit children from disadvantaged environments.

Developmental Delay   A rate of development that is slower than the norms within the average for young children.

Diabetes   An abnormal physical condition characterized by the excessive excretion of urine.

Diagnostic Assessment   An assessment to analyze an individual's areas of weaknesses or strengths and to determine the nature and causes of the weaknesses.

Directional Awareness   The ability to locate oneself in relation to the direction of other people or places in the environment.

Disability   Inability to pursue an activity or occupation because of a physical or mental impairment.

Dyslexia   The partial inability to read or to understand what is read.

Emergent Literacy   The evolution of a child's ability to read and write.

Emotional Disturbance   A disorder in the ability to control emotional states.

Expressive Language   The words and verbal communication that a child can use in social interaction.

Fetal Alcohol Syndrome   A group of symptoms found in children whose mothers drank during pregnancy. These include mental retardation and characteristic facial features.

Field Dependent Learners   Learners who prefer structure in activities, need confidence before beginning tasks, and enjoy working in groups.

Field Independent Learners   Learners who welcome new activities, enjoy working alone, and are confident with open-ended challenges.

Fine Motor Development   The development of skills in small muscles such as in the fingers used in manipulation.

Genetic Disorder   An abnormal mental or physical characteristic that is inherited.

Gross Motor Development   Development of the large muscles used in locomotion.

Handicap   A disadvantage that makes achievement unusually difficult.

Holistic Thinking   Thinking that is characterized by a global view of information rather than focusing on the parts.

Impairment   A condition whereby attainment of an area of development is diminished such as a hearing impairment.

Inclusion   The position that all children belong in the classroom where they would have been assigned if they had no disability.

Individualized Education Plan   A plan for the goals, objectives, and services for a child with disabilities.

Individualized Family Service Plan   An intervention plan for an infant or young child with special needs that includes support needs identified by and for parents.

Integrated Classroom   A classroom where children with disabilities are included as part of the class.

Integrated Learning   Learning that is characterized by an interrelationship between domains or content areas of learning rather than learning that is separated by domains or content areas.

Integrated Curriculum   Curriculum that incorporates the interrelationship or connections between developmental domains or content areas.

Intervention Program   Services provided to infants and young children who have disabilities or are at risk for developing disabilities or learning problems. The services aim at making a difference in the child's developmental outcome.

Kinesthetic Learners   Learners whose preference is to learn through the senses.

Learning Cycles   Sequences of instruction and child-initiated experiences linked with assessment that facilitate the introduction and utilization of new information, concepts, or skills.

Learning Disability   A disorder in the ability to understand and use language to listen, think, speak, read, write, spell, or do mathematical calculations.

Learning Style   The combinations of avenues or strategies that a child utilizes to learn.

Least Restrictive Environment   The provision of services for children with disabilities in as normal an environment as possible.

Limited English Proficient (LEP)   A term used to describe young children who are limited in their receptive and expressive English vocabulary and ability to speak in English.

Locomotor Skills   Motor skills that permit an individual to move from one place to another.

Mainstreaming   The practice of moving children with disabilities from a special education classroom to a regular classroom for part of the school day.

Mental Retardation   A condition where the child's intellectual growth does not keep pace with chronological age and physical development.

Modality of Learning   The sensory or other types of avenues a child prefers for learning.

Motor Impairment   An impairment that affects the capacity for movement.

Multicultural   Related to a combination of distinct cultures.

Noncategorical Intervention Programs Intervention programs that serve children with different disabilities or combinations of disabilities.

Norms Statistics that supply a frame of reference based on the actual performance of test takers in a norm group. A set of scores that represents the distribution of test performance in the norm group.

Perceptual Disability An impairment that prevents the ability to integrate sensory information.

Perceptual-Motor Development The development of the ability to integrate sensory information with motor skills.

Performance-Based Assessment An assessment of development and/or learning that is based on the child's natural performance rather than on contrived tests or tasks.

Progress Evaluation An assessment to determine a child's growth in development or learning.

Prosocial Behavior Behavior that is conducive to positive social interactions.

Readiness Test A test that measures the extent to which a student has the prerequisite skills necessary to be successful in some new learning activity.

Receptive Language The language and vocabulary that a child is able to understand.

Reliability The extent to which a test is consistent in measuring over time what it is designed to measure.

Screening The process of preliminary developmental evaluation of an infant or child to determine if there is a delay or disability.

Self-Help Impairment An impairment that affects the child's ability to feed, dress, and toilet himself or herself and other such daily living skills.

Sensory Delay A delay in the ability to gather information through the senses.

Sensory Impairment An impairment in the ability to use the senses to gather, organize, and interpret information.

Skill Evaluation Assessment with the purpose of determining a child's ability with a specific skill or skills.

Spatial Awareness The ability to identify one's horizontal and vertical location in space.

Spina Bifida A condition in which the bones of the spine allow the nerves of the spinal chord to become tangled and is open or protrudes at birth.

Stage Dependent A characteristic of development that is related to a stage of development in Piaget's cognitive-developmental theory.

Stage Independent A characteristic of development that is unrelated to a stage of development in Piaget's cognitive-developmental theory.

Temperament Individual styles of reaction that are present in infancy.

Temporal Awareness The ability to locate oneself in relation to time; an awareness of time.

Thematic Curriculum Curriculum that incorporates all developmental domains or content areas and that is focused on a topic or theme.

Validity The degree to which a test serves the purpose for which it is to be used.

Visual Learners Learners whose preference is through seeing new information.

Zone of Proximal Development The distance between what a child can do with assistance and what the child can do alone.

References

Abbott, C. F., & Gold, S. (1991). Conferring with parents when you're concerned that their child needs special services. *Young Children, 46,* 10–13.

Ainsworth, M. D. S. (1989). Attachments beyond infancy. *American Psychologist, 44,* 709–716.

Association for Childhood Education International/ Isenberg, J., & Quisenberry, N. L. (1988). Play: A necessity for all children. Position paper. *Childhood Education, 64,* 138–145.

Atwater, J. B., Carta, J. J., Schwartz, I. S., & McConnell, S. R. (1994). Blending developmentally appropriate practice and early childhood special education. In B. L. Mallory & R. S. New (Eds.), *Diversity and developmentally appropriate practices* (pp. 185–201). New York: Teachers College Press.

Au, K. H. (1993). *Literacy instruction in multicultural settings.* Fort Worth: Harcourt Brace Jovanovich.

Bagnato, S. J., Neisworth, J. T., & Munson, S. M. (1989). *Linking developmental assessment and early intervention: Curriculum-based prescriptions.* Rockville, MD: Aspen.

Bailey, D. B., Jr. (1994). Working with families of children with special needs. In M. Wolery and J. S. Wilbers (Eds.), *Including children with special needs in early childhood programs* (pp. 1–22). Washington, DC: National Association for the Education of Young Children.

Bailey, D. B., & Wolery, M. (1992). *Teaching infants and preschoolers with disabilities* (2nd ed.). Englewood Cliffs, NJ: Merrill/Prentice Hall.

Bandura, A. (1977). *Social learning theory.* Englewood Cliffs, NJ: Prentice Hall.

Bandura, A., & Walters, R. (1963). *Social learning and personality development.* New York: Holt, Rinehart & Winston.

Baratta-Lorten, M. (1976). *Mathematics their way.* Menlo Park, CA: Addison-Wesley.

Barbe, W. B., & Swassing, R. H. (1979). *Teaching through modeling strengths: Concepts and practices.* Columbus, OH: Zaner-Bloser.

Barbour, N., & Seefeldt, C. (1993). *Developmental continuity across preschool and primary grades: Implications for teachers.* Wheaton, MD: Association for Childhood Education International.

Barclay, K. H., & Breheny, C. (1994). Letting children take over more of their own learning: Collaborative research in the kindergarten classroom. *Young Children, 49,* 33–39.

Barman, C. R. (1989). An expanded view of the learning cycle: New ideas about an effective teaching strategy. *Council of Elementary Science International Monograph IV.* Indianapolis, IN: Indiana University.

Barnett, S. W., & Escobar, C. M. (1990). Economic costs and benefits of early intervention. In S. J. Meisels & J. P. Shonkoff (Eds.), *Handbook of early childhood intervention* (pp. 560-582). New York: Cambridge University Press.

Barr, D. C. (1978). A comparison of three methods of introducing two-digit numeration. *Journal of Research in Mathematics Education, 9,* 33-43.

Bayley, H., & Schaefer, E. (1960). Relationships between socioeconomic variables and the behavior of mothers toward young children. *Journal of Genetic Psychology, 96,* 61–67.

Bayley, N. (1969). *Bayley Scales of Infant Development.* New York: Psychological Development.

Beaty, J. J. (1992). *Preschool appropriate practices.* Fort Worth: Harcourt Brace Jovanovich.

Benner, S. M. (1992). *Assessing young children with special needs.* New York: Longman.

Bloom, B. (1964). *Stability and change in human characteristics.* New York: John Wiley.

Bloom, B. (1982). The role of gifts and markers in the development of talent. *Exceptional Children, 48,* 510–522.

Bluma, S. M., Shearer, M. S., Frohman, A. H., & Hilliard, J. M. (1976). *Portage guide to early education.* Portage, WI: CESA 5.

Bordner, G. A., & Berkley, M. T. (1992). Educational play: Meeting everyone's needs in mainstreamed classrooms. *Childhood Education, 69,* 38–40, 42.

Bowers, L. (1990). National survey of preschool centers playground equipment. In S. C. Wortham & J. L. Frost (Eds.), *Playgrounds for young children: National survey and perspectives* (pp. 5–16). Reston, VA: American Alliance for Health, Physical Education, Recreation, and Dance.

Bowlby, J. (1969). *Attachment and loss* (Vol. 1). London: Hogarth.

Bowlby, J. (1989). *Secure attachment.* New York: Basic Books.

Bowman, B. T. (1990). Child care: Challenges for the 90s. *Dimensions, 18,* 27–31.

Bowman, B. T. (1992). Reaching potentials of minority children through developmentally and culturally appropriate programs. In S. Bredekamp & T. Rosegrant (Eds.), *Reaching potentials: Appropriate curriculum and assessment for young children* (Vol. I, pp. 128–134). Washington, DC: National Association for the Education of Young Children.

Bowman, B. T., & Stott, F. M. (1994). Understanding development in a cultural context: The challenge for teachers. In B. L. Mallory & R. S. New (Eds.), *Diversity and developmentally appropriate practices* (pp. 119–136). New York: Teachers College Press.

Bredekamp, S. (Ed.). (1987). *Developmentally appropriate practice in early childhood programs serving children from birth through age 8.* Washington, DC: National Association for the Education of Young Children.

Bredekamp, S. (1993). The relationship between early childhood education and early childhood special education: Healthy marriage or family feud? *Topics in Early Childhood Special Education, 13,* 258–273.

Bredekamp, S., & Rosegrant, T. (1992a). Reaching potentials of linguistically diverse children. In S. Bredekamp & T. Rosegrant (Eds.), *Reaching potentials: Appropriate curriculum and assessment for young children* (pp. 137–138). Washington, DC: National Association for the Education of Young Children.

Bredekamp, S., & Rosegrant, T. (1992b). Reaching potentials through appropriate curriculum: Conceptual frameworks for applying the guidelines. In S. Bredekamp and T. Rosegrant (Eds.), *Reaching potentials: Appropriate curriculum and assessment for young children* (Vol. 1, pp. 28–42). Washington, DC: National Association for the Education of Young Children.

Bredekamp, S., & Rosegrant, T. (Eds.). (1992c). *Reaching potentials: Appropriate curriculum and assessment for young children.* Washington, DC: National Association for the Education of Young Children.

Bricker, D., & Veltman, M. (1990). Early intervention programs: Child-focused approaches. In S. J. Meisels & J. P. Shonkoff (Eds.), *Handbook of early childhood intervention* (pp. 373–399). New York: Cambridge University Press.

Brigance, A. (1991). *Brigance Diagnostic Inventory of Early Development* (Rev. ed.). North Billerica, MA: Curriculum Associates, Inc.

Bronson, G. (1978). Aversive reactions to strangers: Adval process interpretation. *Child Development, 49,* 495–499.

Brown, R. (1986). *Social Psychology* (2nd ed.). New York: Free Press.

Bruner, J. (1980). *Under five in Britain.* Ypsilanti, MI: High/Scope.

Buchoff, R. (1995). Jump rope rhymes . . . In the classroom? *Childhood Education, 71,* 149–151.

Burt, M. K., Dulay, H. C., & Hernandes, E. C. (1976). *Bilingual Syntax Measure.* New York: Harcourt Brace Jovanovich.

Buysse, V., & Wesley, P. (1993). Special education: A call for professional role clarification. *Topics in Early Childhood Special Education, 13,* 418–429.

Buzzelli, C. A. (1992). Young children's moral understanding: Learning about right and wrong. *Young Children, 47,* 47–53.

Byrnes, D. A. (1992). Addressing race, ethnicity and culture in the classroom. In D. A. Byrnes & G. Kiger (Eds.), *Common bonds: Anti-bias teaching in a diverse society* (pp. 11–22). Wheaton, MD: Association for Childhood Education International.

Byrnes, D. A., & Cortez, D. (1992). Language and diversity in the classroom. In D. A. Byrnes & G. Kiger (Eds.), *Common bonds: Anti-bias teaching in a diverse society* (pp. 71–86). Wheaton, MD: Association for Childhood Education International.

Byrnes, D. A., & Kiger, G. (1992). Language diversity in the classroom. In D. A. Byrnes & G. Kiger (Eds.), *Common bonds. Anti-bias teaching in a diverse society* (pp. 71–86). Wheaton, MD: Association for Childhood Education International.

Bzoch, K. R., & League, R. (1978). *Receptive Expressive Emergent Language Scale.* Austin, TX: Pro-Ed.

Caplan, J. (1982). *Early Language Milestone Scale.* Austin, TX: Pro-Ed.

Carey, S. (1977). The child as word learner. In M. Halle, J. Bresman, & G. A. Miller (Eds.), *Linguistic theory and psychological reality.* Cambridge, MA: MIT Press.

Carta, J. J., Atwater, J. B., Schwartz, I. S., & McConnell, S. R. (1993). A reaction to Johnson and McChesney Johnson. *Topics in Early Childhood Special Education, 13,* 243–254.

Cattell, P. (1960). *Cattell Infant Intelligence Scale.* San Antonio: The Psychological Corp.

Cavallero, C. C., Haney, M., & Cabello, B. (1993). Developmentally appropriate strategies for promoting full participation in early childhood settings. *Topics in Early Childhood Special Education, 13,* 293–307.

Cazden, C. (Ed.). (1981). *Language and early childhood education.* Washington, DC: National Association for the Education of Young Children.

Chandler, L., Andrews, M., & Swanson, M. (1981). *The movement assessment of infants.* Rolling Bay, WA: Infant Movement Research.

Chaney, C. M., & Kephart, N. C. (1968). *Motoric aids to perceptual training.* Englewood Cliffs, NJ: Merrill/Prentice Hall.

Charlesworth, R., & Lind, K. K. (1990). *Math and science for young children.* Albany, NY: Delmar.

Chess, S., & Thomas, A. (1986). *Temperament in clinical practice.* New York: Guilford.

Children's Defense Fund. (1994). *The state of America's children. Yearbook 1994.* Washington, DC: Children's Defense Fund.

Christie, J. F., & Wardle, F. (1992). How much time is needed for play? *Young Children, 47,* 28–32.

Chomsky, C. (1969). *Acquisition of syntax in children from 5 to 10.* Cambridge, MA: MIT Press.

Chomsky, N. (1965). *Aspects of a theory of syntax.* Cambridge, MA: MIT Press.

Cicchetti, D., & Wagner, S. (1990). Alternative assessment strategies for the evaluation of infants and toddlers: An organizational perspective. In S. J. Meisels & J. P. Shonkoff (Eds.), *Handbook of early childhood intervention* (pp. 246–277). New York: Cambridge University Press.

Clarke-Stewart, A. (1989). Infant day care: Maligned or malignant? *American Psychologist, 44,* 266–273.

Clarke-Stewart, A., & Gruber, C. (1984). Daycare forms and features. In R. C. Ainslie (Ed.), *Quality variations in daycare* (pp. 35–62). New York: Praeger.

Clay, M. (1975). *What did I write?* Auckland, New Zealand: Heinemann.

Coie, J. D., & Kupersmidt, J. B. (1983). A behavioral analysis of emerging social status in boys' groups. *Child Development, 54,* 1400–1416.

Cole, M., & Cole, S. R. (1989). *The development of children.* New York: Scientific American Books.

Coleman, M. (1990). Planning public preschools. *Dimensions, 19,* 7–9.

Collins, T. W., & Hatch, J. A. (1992). Supporting the social-emotional growth of young children. *Dimensions, 21*, 17–21.

Coleta, A. J., & Coleta, K. *Year round activities for three-year-old children.* West Nyaack, NY: The Center for Applied Research in Education, Inc.

Copple, C., DeLisi, R., & Sigel, I. (1982). Cognitive development. In B. Spodek (Ed.), *Handbook of research in early childhood education* (pp. 3–26). New York: Free Press.

Davidson, E., & Schniedewind, N. (1992). Class differences: Economic inequality in the classroom. In D. A. Byrnes & G. Kiger (Eds.), *Common bonds. Anti-bias teaching in a diverse society* (pp. 53–70). Wheaton, MD: Association For Childhood Education International.

DeHaas-Warner, S. (1994). The role of child care professionals in placement and programming decisions for preschoolers with special needs in community-based settings. *Young Children, 49,* 76–78.

Deiner, P. L. (1993). *Resources for teaching children with diverse abilities*. Fort Worth: Harcourt Brace Jovanovich.

Delacato, C. H. (1966). *Neurological organization and reading.* Springfield, IL: Charles C. Thomas.

Dempsey, J. D., & Frost, J. L. (1993). Play environments for early childhood education. In B. Spodek (Ed.), *Handbook of research on the education of young children* (pp. 306–321). New York: Macmillan.

Derman-Sparks, L. (1992). Reaching potentials through antibias, multicultural curriculum. In S. Bredekamp & T. Rosegrant (Eds.), *Reaching potentials: Appropriate curriculum and assessment for young children* (Vol. 1, pp. 114–127). Washington, DC: National Association for the Education of Young Children.

Derman-Sparks, L., & A. B. C. Task Force (1989). *Anti-bias curriculum: Tools for empowering young children*. Washington, DC: National Association for the Education of Young Children.

DeVries, R., & Kohlberg, L. (1987). *Constructivist early education: Overview and comparison with other programs*. Washington, DC: National Association for the Education of Young Children.

Dewey, J. (1902). *The young child and the curriculum.* Chicago: University of Chicago Press.

Diamond, D. E. (1993). The role of parents' observations and concerns in screening for developmental delays in young children. *Topics in Early Childhood Special Education, 13,* 68–81.

Diamond, K. E., Hestenes, L. L., & O'Conner, C. E. (1994). Integrating young children with disabilities in preschool: Problems and promise. *Young Children, 49,* 68–75.

Dunst, C. J. (1981). *Infant learning: A cognitive-linguistic intervention strategy.* Allen, TX: DLM/Teaching Resources.

Dunst, C. J. (1993). Issues related to "at-risk" implications of risk and opportunity factors for assessment and intervention practices. *Topics in Early Childhood Special Education, 13,* 1143–1153.

Durkin, D. (1980). *Teaching young children to read.* Boston: Allyn and Bacon.

Durkin, D. (1987). A classroom-observation study of reading instruction in kindergarten. *Early Childhood Research Quarterly, 2,* 275–300.

Dyson, A. H. (1982). The emergence of visible language: Interrelationships between drawing and early writing. *Visible Language, 6,* 360–381.

Dyson, A. H. (1986). Transitions and tensions: Interrelationships between the drawing, talking, and dictating of young children. *Research in the Teaching of English, 17,* 1–30.

Dyson, A. H., & Genishi, C. (1993). Visions of children as language users: Language and language education in early childhood. In B. Spodek (Ed.), *Handbook of research on the education of young children* (pp. 122–136). New York: Macmillan.

Erikson, E. (1963). *Childhood and society.* New York: Norton.

Esbensen, S. B. (1990). Play environments for young children: Design perspectives. In S. C. Wortham & J. L. Frost, *Playgrounds for young children: National survey and perspectives* (pp. 49–68). Reston, VA: American Alliance for Health, Physical Education, Recreation, and Dance.

Etaugh, C., & Rathus, S. A. (1995). *The world of children*. Fort Worth: Harcourt Brace.

Ferreiro, E. (1986). The interplay between information and assimilation in beginning literacy. In

W. Teale & E. Sulzby (Eds.), *Emergent literacy: Writing and reading* (pp. 15–49). Norwood, NJ: Ablex.

Fewell, R. R. (1991). Trends in the assessment of infants and toddlers with disabilities. *Exceptional Children, 58,* 166–173.

Fewell, R. R., & Langley, M. B. (1984). *Developmental Activities Screening Inventory-II*. Austin, TX: Pro-Ed.

Fields, M. V., Spangler, K., & Lee, D. M. (1991). *Let's begin reading right*. New York: Merrill.

Fischer, K. W., Hand, H. H., Watson, M. M. V. P., & Tucker, J. L. (1984). Putting the child into socialization: The development of social categories in preschool children. In L. G. Katz (Ed.), *Current topics in early childhood education* (Vol. V, pp. 27–72). Norwood NJ: Ablex.

Fogarty, R. (1991). Ten ways to integrate curriculum. *Educational Leadership, 49,* 61–65.

Folio, R., & Fewell, R. R. (1983). *Peabody Developmental Motor Scales and Activity Cards*. Allen, TX: DLM/Teaching Resources.

Forrester, M. A. (1992). *The development of young children's social-cognitive skills*. Hillsdale, NJ: Lawrence Erlbaum.

Frankenburg, W. K., Dodds, J. B., Fandal, A. W., Kajuk, F., & Cohr, M. (1975). *Denver Developmental Screening Test: Revised Reference Manual*. Denver, CO: LADOCA.

Frieman, B. B. (1993). Separation and divorce: Children want their teachers to know. *Young Children, 48,* 58–63.

Frost, J. L. (1992). *Play and playscapes*. Albany, NY: Delmar.

Frostig, R. D. (1967). *Move—grow—learn.* Chicago: Follett.

Furune, S., O'Reilly, K., Hosaka, C., Inatsuka, T., Allman, T., & Jeisloft, B. (1979). *Hawaii Early Learning Profile*. Palo Alto, CA: Vort Corp.

Gallahue, D. L. (1989). *Understanding motor development: Infants, children, adolescents.* Dubuque, IA: Wm. C. Brown & Benchmark.

Gallahue, D. L. (1993). Motor development and movement skill acquisitiion in early childhood education. In B. Spodek (Ed.), *Handbook of research on the education of young children* (pp. 24–41). New York: Macmillan.

Garcia, E. E. (1993). The education of linguistically and culturally diverse children. In B. Spodek (Ed.), *Handbook of reasearch on the education of young children* (pp. 372–384). New York: Macmillan.

Gelman, R., & Gallistel, C. R. (1978). *The child's understanding of number.* Cambridge, MA: Harvard University Press.

Gesell, A. (1925). *The mental growth of the preschool child*. New York: Macmillan.

Glover, M. E., Preminger, J. L., & Sanford, A. R. (1978). *Early Learning Accomplishment Profile*. Winston-Salem, NC: Kaplan.

Gold, S., & Abbott, C. (1989). A dilemma for preschool teachers: When to refer. *Dimensions, 17,* 8–11.

Goodwin, W. L., & Goodwin, L. D. (1993). Young children and measurement: Standardized and nonstandardized instruments in early childhood. In B. Spodek (Ed.), *Handbook of research on the education of young children* (pp. 441–465). New York: Macmillan.

Gordon, A., & Browne, K. W. (1993). *Beginnings and beyond: Foundations in early childhood education* (3rd ed.). Albany, NY: Delmar.

Green, M., & Widoff, E. (1990). Special needs child care: Training is a key issue. *Young Children, 46,* 60–61.

Greenman, J. (1988). *Caring spaces, learning places: Children's environments that work.* Redmond, WA: Exchange Press.

Griffiths, R. (1978). *Griffiths Mental Development Scales*. Sarasota, FL: Test Center.

Groen, C. J., & Resnick, L. B. (1977). Can preschool children invent addition algorithms? *Journal of Educational Psychology, 69,* 645–652.

Grosse, S. J., & Thompson, D. (1993). *Leisure opportunities for individuals with disabilities: Legal issues.* Reston, VA: American Alliance for Health, Physical Education, Recreation, and Dance.

Guild, P. (1994). The culture/learning style connection. *Educational Leadership, 51,* 16–21.

Guralnik, M. J. (1989). Recent developments in early intervention efficacy research: Implications for family involvement in PL 99–457. *Topics In Early Childhood Special Education, 9,* 1–17.

Halpern, R. (1990). Community-based early intervention. In S. J. Meisels & J. P. Shonkoff (Eds.), *Handbook of early childhood intervention* (pp. 469-498). New York: Macmillan.

Hanson, M. J. (1987). *Teaching the child with Down syndrome: A guide for parents and professionals* (2nd ed.). Austin, TX: Pro-Ed.

Hanson, M. J., & Lynch, E. W. (1989). *Early intervention: Implementing child and family services for infants and toddlers who are at-risk or disabled.* Austin, TX: Pro-Ed.

Hartman, J. A., & Eckerty, C. (1995). Projects in the early years. *Childhood Education, 71,* 141–148.

Hedrick, D. L., Prather, E. M., & Tobin, A.R. (1984). *Sequenced Inventory of Communication Development, Revised.* Seattle: University of Washington Press.

Hetherington, E. M., Clingempeel, W. G., Anderson, E. R., Deal, J. E., Hagan, M. S., Hollier, E. R., & Lindner, M. S. (1992). Coping with marital transitions. *Monograph of the Society for Research in Child Development, 57*(2–3, Serial No. 227).

Hetherington, E. M., Stanley-Hagen, M., & Anderson, E. R. (1989). Marital transitions: A child's perspective. *American Psychologist, 44,* 303-312.

Hildebrand, V. (1990). *Guiding young children.* New York: Macmillan.

Hills, T. W. (1992). Reaching potentials through appropriate assessment. In S. Bredekamp & T. Rosegrant (Eds.), *Reaching potentials: Appropriate curriculum and assessment* (pp. 43–63). Washington, DC: National Association for the Education of Young Children.

Hills, T. W. (1993). Assessment in context—Teachers and children at work. *Young Children, 48,* 20–28.

Hohmann, M., Banet, B., & Weikart, D. (1979). *Young children in action: A handbook for preschool educators.* Ypsilanti, MI: High Scope Press.

Holder-Brown, L., & Parette, H. P., Jr. (1992). Children with disabilities who use assistive technology: Ethical considerations. *Young Children, 47,* 73–77.

Honig, A. S., & McCarron, P. A. (1987, April). *Prosocial behaviors of handicapped and typical peers in an integrated preschool.* Paper presented at the Biennial Meeting of the Society for Research in Child Development (ED 281 654).

Howe, C. K. (1994). Improving the achievement of minority students. *Educational Leadership, 51,* 42–44.

Howes, C. (1983). Patterns of friendship. *Child Development, 54,* 1041–1053.

Hunt, J. M. (1961). *Intelligence and experience.* New York: Ronald Press.

Hunt, J. M. (1965). Intrinsic motivation and its role in psychological development. *Nebraska Symposium on Motivation, 13,* 189 282.

Hymes, J. (1991). *Early childhood education. Twenty years in review.* Washington, DC: National Association for the Education of Young Children.

Izard, C. E. (1982). *Measuring emotions in infants and young children.* New York: Cambridge University Press.

Izard, C. E. (1991). Studies of the development of emotion-cognition relations. In C. E. Izard (Ed.), *The development of emotion-cognition relations.* Hillsdale, NJ: Lawrence Erlbaum.

Jambor, T. (1990). Promoting perceptual-motor development in young children's play. In S. C. Wortham & J. L. Frost, *Playgrounds for young children: National survey and perspectives* (pp. 147–166). Reston, Va: American Alliance for Health, Physical Education, Recreation, and Dance.

Johnson, J. E., & Johnson, K. M. (1992). Clarifying the developmental perspective in response to Carta, Schwartz, Atwater, & McConnell. *Topics in Early Childhood Special Education, 12,* 439–457.

Johnson, J. E., Christie, J. F., & Yawkey, T. D. (1987). *Play and early childhood development.* Glenview, IL: ScottForesman.

Johnson, K. M., & Johnson, J. E. (1993). Rejoinder to Carta, Atwater, Schwartz, & McConnell. *Topics in Early Childhood Special Education, 13,* 255–257.

Jones, E., & Prescott, E. (1978). *Dimensions of teaching learning environments.* Pasadena, CA: Pacific Oaks College.

Kagan, J., & Snidman, N. (1991). Temperamental factors in human development. *American Psychologist, 46,* 856–862.

Kamii, C. (1982). *Number in preschool and kindergarten.* Washington, DC: National Association for the Education of Young Children.

Kamii, C., & Kamii, M. (1990). Why achievement testing should stop. In C. Kamii (Ed.), *Achievement testing in the early grades: The games grown-ups play* (pp. 147–162). Washington, DC: National Association for the Education of Young Children.

Kamii, C., & Rosenblum, V. (1990). An approach to assessment in mathematics. In C. Kamii (Ed.), *Achievement testing in the early grades* (pp. 146–162). Washington, DC: National Association for the Education of Young Children.

Katz, L. G., & Chard, S. C. (1990). *Engaging children's minds: The project approach.* Norwood, NJ: Ablex.

Kaufman, A. S., & Kaufman, N. L. (1983). *Kaufman Assessment Battery for Children.* Circle Pines, MN: American Guidance Services.

Kemple, K. M. (1991). Preschool children's peer acceptance and social interaction. *Young Children, 46,* 47–53.

Kilpatrick, W. H. (1941). The case for progressivism in education. *Today's Education: Journal of the National Education Association, 30,* 231–232.

King, E. W., Chipman, M., & Cruz-Janzen, M. (1994). *Educating young children in a diverse society.* Boston: Allyn and Bacon.

Knight, D., & Wadsworth, D. (1993). Physically challenged students: Inclusion classrooms. *Childhood Education, 69,* 211–215.

Knobloch, H., Stevens, F., & Malone, A. F. (1980). *The Revised Developmental Screening Inventory.* Houston, TX: Gesell Developmental Test Materials.

Kohlberg, L. (1981). *The meaning and measurement of moral development.* Worcester, MA: Clark University Press.

Krogh, S. (1990). *The integrated early childhood curriculum.* New York: McGraw-Hill.

Kronowitz, E. L. (1992). *Beyond student teaching.* New York: Longman.

Ladd, G. W., & Coleman, C. C. (1993). Young children's peer relationships: Forms, features, and functions. In B. Spodek (Ed.), *Handbook of research on the education of young children* (pp. 57–76). New York: Macmillan.

Ladd, G. W., & Price, J. M. (1987). Predicting children's social and school adjustment following the transition from preschool to kindergarten. *Child Development, 58,* 1168–1189.

Ladd, G. W., Price, J. M., & Hart, C. H. (1990). Preschoolers' behavioral orientations and patterns of peer contact: Predictive of social status? In S. R. Asher & J. D. Cole (Eds.), *Peer rejection in childhood* (pp. 90–118). New York: Cambridge.

Lazar, I., & Darlington, R. (1982). Lasting effects of early education: A report from the Consortium for Longitudinal Studies. *Monograph of the Society for Research in Child Development, 47*(2–3, Serial No. 195).

Lehr, C. A., Ysseldyke, J. E., & Thurlow, M. L. (1987). Assessment practices in model early childhood special education programs. *Psychology in the Schools, 24,* 390–399.

LeMay, D., Griffin, P., & Sanford, A. (1978). *Learning Accomplishment Profile—Diagnostic Edition (LAP-D).* Winston-Salem, NC: Kaplan School Supply Corporation.

Lubeck, S. (1994). The politics of developmentally appropriate practice: Exploring issues of culture, class, and curriculum. In B. L. Mallory & R. S. New (Eds.), *Diversity and developmentally appropriate practices* (pp. 17–43). New York: Teachers College Press.

Machado, J. M., & Meyer-Botnarescue, H. (1993). *Student teaching: Early childhood practicum guide.* Albany, NY: Delmar.

Mallory, B. L. (1994). Inclusive policy, practice, and theory for young children with developmental differences. In B. L. Mallory & R. S. New (Eds.), *Diversity and developmentally appropriate practices* (pp. 44–61). New York: Teachers College Press.

Malone, D. M., & Stoneman, Z. (1990). Cognitive play of mentally retarded preschoolers: Observation in the home and school. *American Journal on Mental Retardation, 94,* 457–487.

Mardell-Czundowski, C. D., & Goldenberg, D. S. (1983). *Developmental Indicators for the Assessment of Learning-Revised* (DIAL-R). Edison, N. J.: Childcraft Education Corp.

Mason, J. M., & Sinha, S. (1993). Emerging literacy in the early childhood years: Applying a Vygotskian model of learning and development. In B. Spodek (Ed.), *Handbook of research on the education of young children* (pp. 137–150). New York: Macmillan.

McCarthy, D. (1972). *Manual for the McCarthy Scales of Children's Abilities.* New York: Psychological Corp.

McCarthy, M. A., & Houston, J. P. (1980). *Fundamentals of early childhood education*. Cambridge, MA: Winthrop.

McClellan, D., & Katz, L. G. Assessing the social development of young children. *Dimensions of Early Childhood, 21,* 8–9.

McCollum, J. A., & Maude, S. P. (1993). Portrait of a changing field: Policy and practice in early childhood special education. In B. Spodek (Ed.), *Handbook of research on the education of young children* (pp. 352–371). New York: Macmillan.

McCune, L., Kalamanson, B., Fleck, M. B., Glazewski, B., & Sillari, J. (1990). An interdisciplinary model of infant assessment. In S. Meisels & J. P. Shonkoff (Eds.), *Handbook of early childhood intervention* (pp. 219–245). New York: Cambridge University Press.

McLean, M. E., & Odem, S. L. (1993). Practices for young children with and without disabilities: A comparison of DEC and NAEYC identified practices. *Topics In Early Childhood Special Education, 13,* 274–292.

Meisels, S. J. (1989). High-stakes testing. *Educational Leadership, 46,* 16–22.

Meisels, S. J. (1992). Early intervention: A matter of context. *Zero to Three, 12,* 1–6.

Meisels, S. J. (1994). Designing meaningful measurements for early childhood. In B. L. Mallory and R. S. New (Eds.), *Diversity and developmentally appropriate practice* (pp. 202-222). New York: Teachers College Press.

Meisels, S. J., & Shonkoff, J. P. (1990). *Handbook of early childhood intervention.* New York: Cambridge University Press.

Meisels, S. J., Steele, D. M., & Quinn-Leering, K. (1993). Testing, tracking, and retaining young children: An analysis of research and social policy. In B. Spodek (Ed.), *Handbook of research on the education of young children* (pp. 279-292). New York: Macmillan.

Meisels, S. J., & Wiske, M. S. (1983). *The Early Screening Inventory*. New York: Teachers College Press.

Meisels, S. J., Wiske, M. S., & Tivnan, T. (1984). Predicting school performance with the Early Screening Inventory. *Psychology in the Schools, 21,* 25–33.

Mercer, J. (1973). *Labeling the mentally retarded.* Berkeley, CA: University of California Press.

Moore, G. T. (1986). Effects of the spatial definition of behavior settings on children's behavior. *Journal of Environmental Psychology, 6,* 205–231.

Moore, R., Goltsman, S., & Iacofano, D. (1987). *Play for all guidelines: Planning, design, and management of outdoor play settings for all children*. Berkeley, CA: MIG Communications.

Morrow, L. M. (1989). *Literacy development in the early years.* Englewood Cliffs, NJ: Prentice Hall.

National Association for the Education of Young Children. (1984; rev. ed., 1991). *Accreditation criteria and procedures of the National Academy of Early Childhood Programs*. Washington, DC: National Association for the Education of Young Children.

National Association for the Education of Young Children & the National Association of Early Childhood Specialists in State Departments of Education. (1991). Guidelines for appropriate curriculum content and assessment in programs serving children ages 3 through 8. *Young Children, 46,* 21–38.

National Association of Early Childhood Specialists in State Departments of Education. (1987). *Unacceptable trends in kindergarten entry and placement*. Unpublished position paper.

Nelson, K. (1986). *Event knowledge: Structure and function in development*. Hillsdale, NJ: Lawrence Erlbaum.

New, R. S. (1992). The integrated early childhood curriculum: New interpretations based on research and practice. In C. Seefeldt (Ed.), *The early childhood curriculum: A review of current research* (2nd ed.) (pp. 286–324). New York: Teachers College Press.

New, R. S. (1994). Culture, child development, and developmentally appropriate practices: Teachers as collaborative researchers. In B. L. Mallory and R. S. New (Eds.), *Diversity and developmentally appropriate practices* (pp. 65–83). New York: Teachers College Press.

Newborg, J., Stock, J., Wnek, L., Guidubaldi, J., & Svinicki, J. (1984). *Battelle Developmental Inventory (BDI)*. New York: McGraw-Hill.

Okagaki, L., & Sternberg, R. J. (1994). Perspectives on kindergarten. Rafael, Vanessa and Jamlien go to school. *Childhood Education, 71,* 14–19.

Olds, A. R. (1987). Designing space for infants and toddlers. In C. S. Weinstein and T. G. David (Eds.), *Spaces for children: The built environment and child development* (pp. 117–138). New York: Plenum Press.

O'Neil, J. (1990, September). New curriculum agenda emerges for '90s. ASCD Curriculum Update, *1*(8).

O'Neil, J. (1994–1995). Can inclusion work? A conversation with Jim Kauffman and Mara Shapon-Shevin. *Educational Leadership, 52,* 7–11.

Parker, S., & Temple, A. (1925). *Unified kindergarten and first-grade teaching.* New York: Ginn & Company.

Parten, M. (1932). Social play among preschool children. *Journal of Abnormal and Social Psychology, 27,* 243–269.

Pellegrini, A. D., & Boyd, B. (1993). The role of play in early childhood development and education: Issues in definition and function. In B. Spodek (Ed.), *Handbook of Research in the education of young children* (pp. 105–121). New York: Macmillan.

Perreault, J. (1991). Society as extended family: Giving a childhood to every child. *Dimensions, 19,* 3-8, 31.

Perrone, V. (1990). How did we get here? In C. Kamii (Ed.), *Achievement testing in the early grades: The games grown-ups play* (pp. 1–13). Washington, DC: National Association for the Education of Young Children.

Piaget, J. (1932). *The moral judgment of the child.* London: Kegan Paul.

Piaget, J. (1952). *The origins of intelligence in children.* New York: International University Press.

Piaget, J. (1963). *The origins of intelligence in children.* (M. Cook, Trans.). New York: Norton.

Pierson, C. A., & Beck, S. S. (1993). Performance assessment. The realities that will influence the rewards. *Childhood Education, 70,* 29–32.

Pils, L. J. (1991). Soon anofe you tout me: Evaluation in a first-grade whole language classroom. *The Reading Teacher, 45,* 46–50.

Poest, C. A., Williams, J. R., Witt, D. D., & Atwood, M. E. (1990). Challenge me to move: Large muscle development in young children. *Young Children, 45,* 4–10.

Prescott, E. (1987). The environment as organizer of intent in child-care. In C. S. Weinstein & T. G. David (Eds.), *Spaces for children: The built environment and child development* (pp. 73–86). New York: Plenum Press.

Public Health Service (1976). 200 years of child health in America. In E. H. Grotberg (Ed.), *200 years of children* (pp. 61-122). Washington, DC: U.S. Government Printing Office.

Raines, S., & Canady, R. (1989). *Story stretchers.* Mt. Rainier, MD: Gryphon House.

Rogers, C. S., & Sawyers, J. K. (1988). *Play in the lives of children.* Washington, DC: National Association for the Education of Young Children.

Rogers, S. J. (1988). Cognitive characteristics of handicapped children's play: A review. *Journal of the Division for Early Childhood, 12,* 161–168.

Rose, D. F., & Smith, B. J. (1993). Preschool mainstreaming: Attitude barriers and strategies for addressing them. *Young Children, 48,* 59–62.

Rosegrant, T., & Bredekamp, S. (1992). Planning and implementing transformational curriculum. In S. Bredekamp & T. Rosegrant (Eds.), *Reaching potentials: Appropriate curriculum and assessment for young children* (Vol. 1, pp. 74-91). Washington, DC: National Association for the Education of Young Children.

Rubin, K. H. (1982). Nonsocial play in preschoolers: Necessary evil. *Child Development, 53,* 651–657.

Santrock, J. W. (1993). *Children* (3rd ed.). Madison, WI: Brown & Benchmark.

Schickedanz, J. A. (1978). "You be the doctor and I'll be sick." *Language Arts, 55,* 713–718.

Schickedanz, J. A., Schickedanz, D. I., Hansen, K., & Forsyth, P. D. (1993). *Understanding children* (2nd ed.). Mountain View, CA: Mayfield Publishing.

Schweinhart, L., & Weikart, D. (1985, April). Evidence that good early childhood programs work. *Phi Delta Kappan,* 545–553.

Seefeldt, C. (1993). *Social studies for the preschool-primary child* (4th ed.). New York: Merrill/MacMillan.

Seefeldt, C., & Barbour, N. (1990). *Early childhood education* (2nd ed.). Englewood Cliffs, NJ: Merrill/Prentice Hall.

Seifert, K. L. (1993). Cognitive development and early childhood education. In B. Spodek (Ed.), *Handbook of research on the education of young children* (pp. 9–23). New York: Macmillan.

Seitz, V., & Provence, S. (1990). Center-focused models of early intervention. In S. J. Meisels & J. P. Shonkoff (Eds.), *Handbook of early childhood intervention* (pp. 400–427). New York: Cambridge University Press.

Selman, R. (1976). Social-cognitive understanding: A guide to educational and clinical practice. In T. Lickona (Ed.), *Moral development and behavior* (pp. 115–140). New York: Holt, Rinehart, & Winston.

Sexton, D., Aldridge, J., & Snyder, P. Family-driven early intervention. *Dimensions of Early Childhood, 22,* 14–18.

Shanker, A. (1994–1995). Full inclusion is neither free nor appropriate. *Educational Leadership, 52,* 18–21.

Shapiro, L. (1993, April 19). Rush to judgment. *Newsweek,* pp. 54–60.

Sharp, E. (1969). *Thinking is child's play*. New York: Avon Books.

Shepard, L. A. (1989). Why we need better assessments. *Educational Leadership, 46,* 4–9.

Shepard, L. A., & Graue, M. E. (1993). The morass of school readiness screening: Research on test use and test validity. In B. Spodek (Ed.), *Handbook of research on the education of young children* (pp. 293–305). New York: Macmillan.

Shepard, L., & Smith, M. (1988). Escalating academic demand in kindergarten: Some nonsolutions. *Elementary School Journal, 89,* 135–146.

Sheridan, S., & Murphy, D. B. (1986). *Beginning Milestones Teacher's Guide*. Allen, TX: DLM Teaching Resources.

Simeonsson, R. J., & Bailey, D. B., Jr. (1990). Family dimensions in early intervention. In S. J. Meisels & J. P. Shonkoff (Eds.), *Handbook of early childhood intervention* (pp. 428–444). New York: Cambridge University Press.

Simeonsson, R. J., Huntington, G. S., Short, R. J., & Ware, W. B. (1982). The Carolina Record of Individual Behavior: Characteristics of handicapped infants and children. *Topics in Early Childhood Special Education, 2,* 43–55.

Sinclair, E. (1993). Early identification of preschoolers with special needs in Head Start. *Topics in Early Childhood Special Education, 13,* 184–201.

Singer, J. L., & Singer, D. G. (1988). Imaginative play and human development: Schemas, scripts, and possibilities. In D. Bergin (Ed.), *Play as a medium for learning and development*. Portsmouth, NH: Heinemann.

Skinner, B. F. (1953). *Science and human behavior*. New York: Free Press.

Skinner, B. F. (1957). *Verbal behavior*. New York: Appleton-Century-Crofts.

Skinner, B. F. (1972). *Cumulative record: A selection of papers* (3rd ed.). New York: Appleton-Century-Crofts.

Sleeter, C. (1986). Learning disabilities: The social construction of a special education category. *Exceptional Children, 53,* 46–54.

Smith, P. D. (1989). Assessing motor skills. In D. B. Bailey & M. Wolery, (Eds.), *Assessing infants and preschoolers with handicaps* (pp. 301–338). Englewood Cliffs, NJ: Merrill/Prentice Hall.

Smith, P. K., & Connolly, K. J. (1980). *The ecology of preschool behavior*. Cambridge, England: Cambridge University Press.

Sparrow, S. S., Bolla, D. A., & Cicchetti, D. V. (1984). *Vineland Adaptive Behavior Scales*. Circle Pines, MN: American Guidance Service.

Spodek, B., & Saracho, O. N. (1994). *Dealing with individual differences in the early childhood classroom*. New York: Longman.

Sroufe, L. A. (1983). Infant-caregiver attachment and patterns of adaptation in preschool: The roots of maladaptation and competence. In M. Perlmutter (Ed.), *Minnesota symposium in child psychology* (Vol. 16, pp. 41-83). Hillsdale, NJ: Lawrence Erlbaum.

Sroufe, L. A. (1988). The role of infant-caregiver attachment in development. In J. Belsky & T. Nezworksi (Eds.), *Clinical implications of attachment*. Hillsdale, NJ: Lawrence Erlbaum.

Stein, J. U. (1993). The Americans with Disabilities Act: Implications for recreation and leisure. In S. J. Gross & D. Thompson (Eds.), *Leisure opportunities for individuals with disabilities: Legal issues*. Reston, VA: American Alliance for

Health, Physical Education, Recreation, and Dance.

Strauss, S. (1987). Educational-developmental psychology and school learning. In L. Liben (Ed.), *Development and learning: Conflict or congruence?* (pp. 133-157). Hillsdale, NJ: Lawrence Erlbaum.

Strickland, D. S., & Morrow, L. M. (Eds.). (1989). *Emerging literacy: Young children learn to read and write.* Newark, DE: International Reading Association.

Stutsman, R. (1948). *Merrill-Palmer Scale of Mental Tests.* Los Angeles: Western Psychological Services.

Sulzby, E. (1993). *Teacher's guide to evaluation. Assessment handbook.* Glenview, IL: ScottForesman.

Sulzby, E., & Teale, W. (1991). Emergent literacy. In R. Barr, M. Kamil, P. Mosenthal, & P. D. Pearson (Eds.), *Handbook of reading research* (Vol. 2, pp. 727–757). New York: Longman.

Sunal, C. S. (1993). Social studies in early childhood education. In B. Spodek (Ed.), *Handbook of research on the education of young children* (pp. 176–190). New York: Macmillan.

Taylor, B. J. (1993). *Science everywhere. Opportunities for very young children.* Fort Worth: Harcourt Brace Jovanovich.

Tierney, R. J. (1992, September). Setting a new agenda for assessment. *Learning 92,* 62–64.

Thomas, A. T., & Chess, S. (1977). *Foundations of physiological psychology.* New York: Harper & Row.

Trawick-Smith, J. (1992). The classroom environment affects children's play and development. *Dimensions, 20,* 27–30, 40.

Turnbull, A., & Turnbull, H. R. III. (1986). *Families, professionals, and exceptionalities: A special partnership.* Englewood Cliffs, NJ: Merrill/Prentice Hall.

Uzgiris, I., & Hunt, J. M.(1975). *Assessment in infancy: Ordinal Scales of Psychological Development.* Urbana: University of Illinois Press.

Vasta, R., Haith, M. M., & Miller, S. A. (1992). *Child psychology. The modern science.* New York: John Wiley & Sons.

Vygotsky, L. S. (1978). *Mind in society: The development of psychological processes.* Cambridge, MA: Harvard University Press.

Wang, M. C., Resnick, L. B., & Boozer, R. F. (1971). The sequence of development of some early mathematic behavior. *Child Development, 42,* 1767–1778.

Wang, M. C., Reynolds, M. C., & Walberg, H. J. (1994–1995). Serving students at the margins. *Educational Leadership, 52,* 12–17.

Weber, E. (1970). *Early childhood education: Perspectives on change.* Worthington, OH: Charles A. Jones.

Weber, E. (1984). *Ideas influencing early childhood education: A theoretical analysis.* New York: Teachers College Press.

Weinstein, C. S. (1987). Designing preschool classroom to support development: Research and reflection. In C. S. Weinstein & T. G. David, (Eds.), *Spaces for children: The built environment and child development* (pp. 159–181). New York: Plenum Press.

Widerstrom, A. H. (1986). Educating young handicapped children: What can early childhood education contribute? *Childhood Education, 63,* 78-83.

Widerstrom, A. H., Mowder, B. A., & Sandall, S. R. (1991). *At-risk and handicapped newborns and infants: Development, assessment, & intervention.* Englewood Cliffs, NJ: Prentice Hall.

Wieder, S., & Greenspan, S. I. (1993). The emotional basis of learning. In B. Spodek (Ed.), *Handbook of research in the education of young children* (pp. 77–90). New York: Macmillan.

Williams, L. R. (1994). Developmentally appropriate practice and cultural values: A case in point. In B. L. Mallory & R. S. New (Eds.), *Diversity and developmentally appropriate practices* (pp. 155–165). New York: Teachers College Press.

Winter, S. M. (1994–1995). Diversity: A program for all children. *Childhood Education, 71,* 91–95.

Wolery, M. (1994a). Assessing children with special needs. In M. Wolery & S. Wilbers (Eds.), *Including children with special needs in early childhood programs* (pp. 71-96). Washington, DC: National Association for the Education of Young Children.

Wolery, M. (1994b). Designing inclusive environments for young children with special needs. In M. Wolery & J. S. Wilbers (Eds.), *Including childen with special needs in early childhood programs* (pp. 97–118). Washington, DC: National Association for the Education of Young Children.

Wolery, M. (1994c). Implementing instruction for young children with special needs in early childhood classrooms. In M. Wolery & J. S. Wilbers (Eds.), *Including children with special needs in early childhood programs* (pp. 151–166). Washington, DC: National Association for the Education of Young Children.

Wolery, M., Bailey, D. B., & Sugai, G. M. (1988). *Effective teaching: Principles and procedures of applied behavior analysis with exceptional students.* Boston: Allyn and Bacon.

Wolery, M., Strain, P. S., & Bailey, D. B. (1992). *Reaching potentials of children with special needs.* In S. Bredekamp & T. Rosegrant (Eds.), *Reaching potentials: Appropriate curriculum and assessment for young children* (pp. 92–113). Washington, DC: National Association for the Education of Young Children.

Wolery, M., & Wilbers, J. S. (1994a). Introduction to the inclusion of young children with special needs in early childhood education programs. In M. Wolery and J. S. Wilbers (Eds.), *Including children with special needs in early childhood programs* (pp. 1–22). Washington, DC: National Association for the Education of Young Children.

Wolery, M., & Wilbers, J. S. (Eds.). (1994b). *Including children with special needs in early childhood programs.* Washington, DC: National Association for the Education of Young Children.

Wolery, M., & Wolery, R. A. (1992). Promoting functional cognitive skills. In D. B. Bailey & M. Wolery (Eds.), *Teaching infants and preschoolers with disabilities* (2nd ed., pp. 521-572). Englewood Cliffs, NJ: Merrill/Prentice Hall.

Wolfe, L. (1992). Reaching potentials through bilingual education. In S. Bredekamp & T. Rosegrant (Eds.), *Reaching potentials: Appropriate curriculum and assessment for young children* (pp. 139–144). Washington, DC: National Association for the Education of Young Children.

Wolfinger, D. M. (1994). *Science and mathematics in early childhood education.* New York: Harper Collins.

Wolk, S. (1994). Project-based learning: Pursuits with a purpose. *Educational Leadership, 52,* 42–45.

Wortham, S. C. (1992). *Childhood 1892-1992.* Wheaton, MD: Association for Childhood Education International.

Wortham, S. C. (1993). Play in the child care setting: Creating opportunities for preschool children with disabilities. In S. J. Grosse & D. Thompson (Eds.), *Leisure opportunities for individuals with disabilities: Legal issues* (pp. 77–82). Reston, Va: American Alliance for Health, Physical Education, Recreation, and Dance.

Wortham, S. C. (1994). *Early childhood curriculum: Developmental bases for learning and teaching.* Englewood Cliffs, NJ: Merrill/Prentice Hall.

Wortham, S. C. (1995). *Measurement and evaluation in early childhood education.* Englewood Cliffs, NJ: Merrill/Prentice Hall.

Zimmerman, I. L., Steiner, V. G., & Pond, R. (1979). *Preschool Language Scale.* Englewood Cliffs, NJ: Merrill/Prentice Hall.

Author Index

Abbott, C., 36, 37, 38
A. B. C. Task Force, 78, 277
Ainsworth, M. D. S., 263
Aldridge, J., 42
Anderson, E. R., 9
Andrews, M., 39
Association for Childhood Education International, 78
Atwater, J. B., 144, 158
Atwood, M. E., 305
Au, K. H., 254

Bagnato, S. J., 169, 170, 171
Bailey, D. B., 135, 140, 141, 143, 144, 146, 151
Balla, D. A., 39
Bandura A., 268
Banet, B., 199, 204, 207
Baratta-Lorten, M., 91
Barbe, W. B., 53
Barbour, N., 283, 306, 307, 338
Barclay, K. H., 338
Barman, C. R., 203
Barnett, S. W., 27
Barr, D. C., 205
Bayley, H., 271
Bayley, N., 39, 138
Beaty, J. J., 79, 81, 279
Beaty, J. L., 280
Beck, S. S., 54
Benner, S. M., 17, 34, 35, 135, 137, 138, 190

Berkley, 78
Bloom, B., 26, 33, 131
Bluma, S. M., 170
Boozer, R. F., 205
Bordner, G. A., 78
Bowers, L., 305
Bowlby, J., 266
Bowman, B. T., 11, 180, 181, 183
Boyd, B., 277, 278
Bredekamp, S., 4, 78, 90, 107, 143, 158, 172, 184, 188, 196, 197, 203, 206, 237, 253, 328, 329, 333, 335
Breheny, C., 338
Bricker, D., 145
Brigance, A., 91
Bronson, G., 271
Brown, R., 235
Brown, William C., 300
Browne, K. W., 14, 79
Bruner, J., 80
Burt, M. K., 29
Buysse, V., 158
Buzzelli, C. A., 274
Byrnes, D. A., 182, 184, 185, 187, 336
Bzoch, K. R., 39

Cabello, B., 174
Canady, R., 331
Caplan, J., 39
Carey, S., 235

Carta, J. J., 144, 158
Cattell, P., 39
Cavallero, C. C., 174
Cazden, C., 231
Chandler, L., 39
Chaney, C. M., 302
Chard, S. C., 328, 330, 338, 339
Charlesworth, R., 203, 204, 210, 211
Chess, S., 52, 267
Children's Defense Fund, 8
Chipman, M., 27
Chomsky, C., 229
Chomsky, N., 232
Christie, J. F., 76, 78, 83, 85
Cicchetti, D., 39, 138
Clarke-Stewart, A., 80, 278
Clay, M., 236
Cohr, M., 14
Coie, J. D., 270
Cole, M., 228, 229, 232, 264
Cole, S. R., 228, 229, 232, 264
Coleman, C. C., 263, 270, 277, 278
Coleman, M., 9
Coleta, A. J., 280, 283
Coleta, K., 280, 283
Collins, T. W., 274
Connolly, K. J., 80, 277
Copple, C., 198, 203
Cortez, D., 182, 184, 185
Cruz-Janzen, M., 27

Darlington, R., 27
Davidson, E., 181, 182
DeHaas-Warner, S., 7, 11
Deiner, P. L., 6, 27, 31, 32, 100,
  135, 137, 149, 166, 178, 218,
  219, 252, 253, 290, 314, 315,
  316, 318, 335
Delacato, C. H., 302
DeLisi, R., 198, 203
Dempsey, J. D., 277, 278
Derman-Sparks, L., 78, 187, 275,
  276, 277, 333, 335, 336
DeVries, R., 329
Dewey, J., 328, 329, 339
Diamond, D. E., 141
Diamond, K. E., 12
Dodds, J. B., 14, 39
Dulay, H. C., 29
Dunst, C. J., 170, 175, 176, 177,
  178
Durkin, D., 231, 246
Dyson, A. H., 228, 230, 236, 238,
  246

Eckerty, C., 328, 333, 338, 340
Erikson, E., 266–267, 270
Esbensen, S. B., 83, 84, 87
Escobar, C. M., 27
Etaugh, C., 97, 98, 99, 199, 263,
  264, 267, 268, 297, 298, 299

Fandal, A. W., 14, 39
Federal Register, 151
Ferreiro, E., 236
Fewell, R. R., 35, 38, 39
Fields, M. V., 230, 231, 238, 241,
  247
Fischer, K. W., 261
Fleck, M. B., 138
Fogarty, R., 332
Forrester, M. A., 235
Forsyth, P. D., 263, 264, 268, 299
Frankenburg, W. K., 14, 39
Freud, S., 266
Frieman, B. B., 9
Frohman, A. H., 170
Frost, J. L., 75, 76, 77, 83, 84, 85,
  87, 88, 264, 266, 277, 278,
  301, 306, 307, 310, 316, 317

Frostig, R. D., 302
Furone, S., 170

Gallahue, D. L., 299, 300, 301,
  302, 305, 306
Gallistel, C. R., 205
Garcia, E. E., 181, 182, 184, 185,
  187, 253, 254
Gelman, R., 205
Genishi, C., 228, 230, 236, 238,
  246
Gesell, A., 34, 171
Glazewski, B., 138
Glover, M. E., 40
Gold, S., 36, 37, 38
Goldenberg, D. S., 40
Goltsman, S., 279
Goodwin, L. D., 13, 15, 59
Goodwin, W. L., 13, 15, 59
Gordon, A., 14, 79
Graue, M. E., 30, 49
Green, M., 9, 11
Greenman, J., 79, 82
Greenspan, S. I., 267, 271
Griffin, P., 91
Griffiths, R., 39
Groen, C. J., 205
Grosse, S. J., 279
Gruber, C., 80
Guidubaldi, J., 40, 91
Guild, P., 181, 182
Guralnick, M. J., 27

Haith, M. M., 235
Halpern, R., 147
Hand, H. H., 261
Haney, M., 174
Hansen, K. N., 263, 264, 268,
  299
Hanson, M. J., 27, 171
Hart, C. H., 270
Hartman, J. A., 328, 333, 338,
  340
Hatch, J. A., 274
Hedrick, D. L., 39
Hernandes, E. C., 29
Hestenes, L. L., 12
Hetherington, E. M., 9, 263
Hildebrand, V., 302

Hilliard, J. M., 170
Hills, T. W., 49, 54, 179, 200, 214
Hohmann, M., 199, 204, 207
Holder-Brown, L., 167
Honig, A. S., 78
Houston, J. P., 26
Howe, C. K., 189
Howes, C., 263
Hunt, J. M., 39, 131, 199
Huntington, G. S., 39
Hymes, J., 26

Iacofano, D., 279
Isenberg, J., 78
Izard, C. E., 267

Jambor, T., 85, 300, 301, 305
Johnson, J. E., 76, 83, 85, 158,
  158–159
Johnson, K. M., 158, 158–159
Jones, E., 80

Kagan, J., 267
Kajuk, F., 14
Kalamanson, B., 138
Kamii, C., 13, 62, 205
Kamii, M., 13
Katz, L. G., 110, 112, 280, 281,
  328, 330, 338, 339
Kaufman, A. S., 39
Kaufman, N. L., 39
Kemple, K. M., 275
Kephart, N. C., 302
Kilpatrick, W. H., 328, 329, 339
King, E. W., 27
Knight, D., 314, 315, 318, 319
Knobloch, H., 39
Kohlberg, L., 262, 269, 329
Krogh, S., 328, 330
Kronowitz, E. L., 54
Kupersmidt, J. B., 270

Ladd, G. W., 263, 270, 271, 277,
  278
Langley, M. B., 39
Lazar, I., 27
League, R., 39
Lee, D. M., 230, 231, 238, 241,
  247

Lehr, C. A., 14
LeMay, D., 91
Lind, K. K., 203, 204, 210, 211
Lubeck, S., 183, 187
Lynch, E. W., 27

Machado, J. M., 52, 53
Mallory, B. L., 147, 148, 183, 188
Malone, A. F., 39
Malone, D. M., 78
Mardell-Czudnowski, C. D., 40
Mason, J. M., 236
Maude, S. P., 132, 133, 145, 155
McCarron, P. A., 78
McCarthy, D., 39
McCarthy, M. A., 26
McClellan, D., 110, 112, 280, 281
McCollum, J. A., 132, 133, 145, 155
McConnell, S. R., 144, 158
McCune, L., 138
McLean, M. E., 173
Meisels, S. J., 13, 14, 30, 33, 130, 131, 132, 133, 141, 178, 180
Mercer, J., 27
Meyer-Botnarescue, H., 52, 53
Miller, S. A., 235
Moore, G. T., 80
Moore, R., 279
Morrow, L. M., 114, 236, 242, 245
Mowder, B. A., 10, 28, 35, 138, 140, 141, 145, 147, 167, 168, 169, 170, 189
Munson, S. M., 169, 170, 171
Murphy, D. B., 109, 110, 111, 210, 213, 240, 305, 306, 309

National Association for the Education of Young Children, 54, 190, 196, 200
National Association of Early Childhood Specialists in State Departments of Education, 54, 190, 196, 200

Neisworth, J. T., 169, 170, 171
Nelson, K., 229
New, R. S., 182, 188, 328, 329, 330
Newborg, J., 40, 91

O'Conner, C. E., 12
Odom, S. L., 173
Okagaki, L., 185
Olds, A. R., 80
O'Neill, J., 159, 330, 331

Parette, H. P., Jr., 167
Parker, S., 83
Parten, M., 265
Pellegrini, A. D., 277, 278
Perrault, J., 9
Perrone, V., 179
Piaget, J., 4, 26, 34, 131, 170, 171, 172, 196, 198, 199, 202, 232, 262, 269, 328, 329, 330, 334
Pierson, C. A., 54
Pils, L. J., 249
Poest, C. A., 305, 306
Pond, R., 39
Prather, E. M., 39
Preminger, J. L., 40
Prescott, E., 80
Price, J. M., 270, 271
Provence, S., 145
Public Health Service, 131

Quinn-Leering, K., 30
Quisenberry, N. L., 78

Raines, S., 331
Rathus, S. A., 97, 98, 99, 199, 263, 264, 267, 268, 297, 298, 299
Resnick, L. B., 205
Reynolds, M. C., 160
Rogers, C. S., 85, 86, 266
Rogers, S. J., 78
Rose, D. F., 11, 12
Rosegrant, T., 184, 188, 197, 203, 253, 329, 333
Rosenblum, V., 62
Rubin, K. H., 265

Sandall, S. R., 10, 28, 35, 138, 140, 141, 145, 147, 167, 168, 169, 170, 189
Sanford, A., 40, 91
Santrock, J. W., 263, 264, 267, 269
Saracho, O. N., 9, 17, 28, 29, 31, 33, 130, 132, 135, 149, 155
Sawyers, J. K., 85, 86, 266
Schaefer, E., 271
Schickedanz, D. I., 263, 264, 268, 299
Schickedanz, J. A., 236, 263, 264, 268, 299
Schniedewind, N., 181, 182
Schwartz, I. S., 144, 158
Schweinhart, L., 27
Seefeldt, C., 62, 279, 283, 306, 307, 338
Seifert, K. L., 246
Seitz, V., 145
Selman, R., 271
Sexton, D., 42
Shanker, A., 158, 159
Shapiro, L., 263
Sharp, E., 199
Shearer, M. S., 170
Shepard, L., 196, 329
Shepard, L. A., 13, 30, 49
Sheridan, S., 109, 110, 111, 210, 213, 240, 305, 306, 309
Shonkoff, J. P., 130, 131, 132, 133
Short, R. J., 39
Sigel, I., 198, 203
Sillari, J., 138
Simeonsson, R. J., 39, 146
Sinclair, E., 139
Singer, D. G., 266
Singer, J. L., 266
Sinha, S., 236
Skinner, B. F., 4, 34, 170, 172, 232, 268
Sleeter, C., 27
Smith, B. J., 11, 12
Smith, M., 196, 329
Smith, P. D., 28, 167
Smith, P. K., 80, 277
Snidman, N., 267
Snyder, P., 42

Spangler, K., 230, 231, 238, 241, 247
Sparrow, S. S., 39
Spodek, B., 9, 17, 28, 29, 31, 33, 130, 132, 135, 149, 155
Sroufe, L. A., 268
Stanley-Hagen, M., 9
Steele, D. M., 30
Steiner, V. G., 39
Sternberg, R. J., 185
Stevens, F., 39
Stock, J., 40, 91
Stoneman, Z., 78
Stott, F. M., 180
Strain, P. S., 140, 144
Strauss, S., 200
Strickland, D. S., 236
Stutsman, R., 39
Sugai, G. M., 144
Sulzby, E., 64, 67, 236, 246, 247, 248, 249
Sunal, C. S., 269, 271, 284
Svinicki, J., 40, 91
Swanson, M., 39
Swassing, R. H., 53

Taylor, B. J., 210
Teale, W., 236
Temple, A., 83
Texas Education Agency, 209, 235

Thomas, A., 52, 267
Thompson, D., 279
Thurlow, M. L., 14
Tierney, R. J., 66
Tivnan, T., 33
Tobin, A. R., 39
Trawick-Smith, J., 75, 77, 80
Tucker, J. L., 261
Turnbull, A., 140
Turnbull, H. R. III, 140

Uzgiris, I., 39

Vasta, R., 235
Veltman, M., 145
Vygotsky, L. S., 179, 196, 200, 201, 202, 237, 329, 330

Wadsworth, D., 314, 315, 318, 319
Wagner, S., 138
Walbert, H. J., 160
Walters, R., 268
Wang, M. C., 160, 205
Wardle, F., 78
Ware, W. B., 39
Watson, M. M. V. P., 261
Weber, E., 26, 329
Weikart, D., 27, 199, 204, 207
Weinstein, C. S., 80
Wesley, P., 158

Widerstrom, A. H., 10, 28, 32, 35, 78, 138, 140, 141, 145, 147, 167, 168, 169, 170, 189
Widoff, E., 9, 11
Wieder, S., 267, 271
Wilbers, J. S., 132, 133, 135, 157, 158, 159, 166
Williams, J. R., 305
Williams, L. R., 188
Winter, S. M., 188
Wiske, M. S., 33
Witt, D. D., 305
Wnek, L., 40, 91
Wolery, M., 132, 133, 135, 139, 140, 143, 144, 151, 157, 158, 159, 166, 167, 168, 172, 173, 189
Wolery, R. A., 167
Wolfe, L., 180, 182, 184, 185, 189, 254
Wolfinger, D. M., 115
Wolk, S., 338
Wortham, S. C., 13, 14, 26, 30, 36, 38, 54, 61, 63, 66, 131, 132, 133, 196, 278, 310, 316, 328, 330, 337, 338, 341

Yawkey, T. D., 76, 83, 85
Ysseldyke, J. E., 14

Zimmerman, I. L., 39

Subject Index

Academic performance
and 1980s school reform, 3,
107
undue emphasis on, 90
Accommodation (Piaget), 199,
351
Achievement tests, standardized,
3, 20. *See also* Standardized measurement
instruments
Adams Elementary School, as
Chapter 1 school, 19
Adams Hill Elementary School,
inclusion at, 174–175
African Americans
learning style of, 181, 183
projected population increase
of, 176
Alphabet, checklist on, 249
Americans with Disabilities Act
(ADA) (P.L. 101–336),
10–11, 134, 278
Analytical thinkers, 53, 351
Anecdotal records, 59
case study on, 59–60
in social development assessment, 287
Antibias curriculum, 186–187,
276, 351
Antibias environment, 79
Asian Americans, projected popu-
lation increase of, 176

Assessment, 5–6, 14–15, 16–18,
351. *See also* Evaluation;
Tests
appropriate strategies in, 54
authentic (performance-based),
15, 68
for beginning of year (initial),
55–68, 96–100
for children at risk vs. children
not at risk, 47–49
of cognitive development, 50,
97–98, 210, 214–218
and curriculum planning,
47–52, 108–113, 114, 115
for children at risk, 47–48,
178–183
and children not at risk,
48–49
for children with disabilities,
166–168
diagnostic, 48, 64, 351
and diversity, 180, 190
and early intervention programs, 135–137
family role in, 140–142
for infants and toddlers,
138–139, 166–168
for preschool and primary
age children, 139–140,
168–169
steps in, 142–143
federal regulation in, 18–20

in Thelma Goodson's second
grade, 108–109
importance of, 347
and instruction, 17, 189–191
and instruction planning,
17–18, 109–115, 123
balancing teacher-directed
and child-initiated,
117–118
and children with disabilities,
168–169
for grouping, 53–54
in learning centers, 117
and learning (instructional)
cycles, 118–121
teacher-directed, 116–117
of integrated curriculum,
345–346
of language development and
literacy, 50, 52, 98–99,
246–252
checklists on, 243–245,
250–251
in mathematics, 51, 66, 111,
113, 115
ongoing, 123–124
for physical development,
311–314
and progress vs. skill evaluation,
121–123
in reading, 51, 64–65, 111, 113
checklist on, 243

Assessment, *continued*
  and record keeping, 124–125
  and regrouping of children, 124
  of social development, 50,
      96–97, 286–289
  standardized measurement
      instruments for, 12, 180
  teacher-designed, 62–64
  for temperament and learning
      style, 52–53
  trends in, 14–15
  of twins (case study), 55–56
Assimilation (Piaget), 199, 351
At-risk children, 351. *See also* Dis-
      abilities, children with;
      Early intervention pro-
      grams; Impairment; Special
      needs children
  and assessment, 16, 47–48,
      178–183, 189–191
  and developmentally appropri-
      ate strategies, 187–189
  evaluation programs for,
      189–191
  integration of, 155–160 (see
      also Integration)
  objective concerning, 176
  planning instruction for,
      175–178
    approaches in, 183–189
    and assessment-curriculum
      link, 178–183
  programs for mothers of
      (babies), 146
  risk factors and opportunities
      listed, 177
  and screening, 16, 26–30,
      31–33 (see *also* Screening)
  standardized tests for, 13
Atypical development, 32, 351
Auburn School District, screening
      for bilingual classrooms in,
      29
Auditory learners, 53, 351
Authentic assessment, 15, 68, 351

Bathroom use, 93
*Battelle Developmental Inventory,
      The,* 40, 91

*Bayley Scales of Infant Develop-
      ment* (BSID), 39, 138
Beginning of school year, 73–74
  assessment at, 55–68, 96–100
  environment preparation,
      74–75, 92–93
    indoor, 78–83
    outdoor, 83–89
    and play, 75–78
  guiding children's transition,
      94–96
  importance of, 89
  instructional planning, 89–94
Behavioral perspective, 34–35
  and intervention strategies,
      170–171, 173
  on language development, 232
  on social development,
      267–268
Behavior disorders, 4
Behaviors, classroom, 93, 95–96
Bilingual children, 184, 351
Bilingual education, 10, 184–186,
      254, 255. *See also* Diversity
  at Emma Frey Elementary
      School, 186
  evaluation of, 191
  screening for (Auburn School
      District), 29
  and standardized achievement
      tests, 180
Bilingual Education Act (1974),
      26–27, 133
Biliterate children, 184, 351
Biogenetic model, 147
Body awareness, 300, 351
Book-reading behaviors, 241, 247
Books, concepts about, 243
Brain injury, 33, 351
*Brigance Diagnostic Inventory of
      Early Development (Revised
      Edition),* 91
British Infant School, 329

Caregiver-focused intervention
      programs, 145–146
*Caring Spaces, Learning Places:
      Children's Environments
      That Work* (Greenman), 82

*Carolina Record of Individual
      Behavior,* 39
Categorical intervention programs,
      144–145, 351
Chad (case study), 57
Chapter I program, 13, 160
  in Adams Elementary School,
      19
  Emma Frey School as, 186
  and standardized achievement
      tests, 180
Checklists, 66
  alphabet, letter and word
      knowledge, 249
  for cognitive development, 210,
      212–213
  emergent literacy, 67
  for language development and
      literacy, 243–245,
      250–251
  mathematics, 113, 115
  for physical development, 312
  reading, 114, 243, 247
  social attributes, 281
  social development, 112, 280,
      282, 288
  writing, 248
Child care, 7
  in cooperative venture, 11
  and disabilities, 11–12
Child-centered curriculum and
      instruction, 328–329, 337
Child development perspective,
      195. *See also* Develop-
      mental approach
Child Find Mandate, 28
Child-focused intervention pro-
      grams, 145
Child-initiated instruction,
      117–118, 337–338
Children, diversity in, 7–10
Children at risk. *See* At-risk chil-
      dren
Children's Bureau, 131
Children with disabilities. *See*
      Disabilities, children with
Circle time, 93
Civil rights, changing view on,
      132

Civil rights movement, and early childhood education, 26
Classification, 207
Classroom behaviors, 93, 95–96
Classroom design, and preschool play, 277
Cloze tests, 65
Cognitive approach, to intervention strategies, 170
Cognitive development, 198–201
assessment/learning experiences for, 216–218
assessment of, 50, 97–98, 210, 214–216
curriculum for, 206–210, 211, 212–213
evaluation of curriculum and instruction for, 220–222
planning of instruction for, 201–204
for children with disabilities, 218–220
for math and science, 204–205
and play experiences, 76
screening tests for, 39
Cognitive-developmental theories, on social development, 268–269
Cognitive impairments, 166–167, 351
Cognitive needs, of children at risk, 181
Cognitive play, 85–86
and playground zones, 87
Cognitive stages perspective, 34
Communication, in kindergarten goals, 285
Communication disorders, and cognitive development, 218
Communication impairments, 167, 351
planning instruction for children with, 252–253
Compensatory programs, 26, 351
Computer assessment, for reading, 65

Concepts, in cognitive development, 203–204, 206
in mathematics, 205, 211
in science, 204–205, 211
Conferences with parents. See under Parent
Conservation, 205
Constructivist approach, 4, 5
for literacy or emergent literacy, 254
Context, and integrated curriculum, 329, 335
Conversation, rules of, 235
Cooperative learning groups, 54, 334
Creative expression, 77
Creative play, 86
Cultural differences. See Diversity
Cultural needs, of children at risk, 183
Cumulative records, 55
Curriculum. See also Curriculum planning
antibias, 186–187, 276
for cognitive development, 206–210, 211, 212–213, 220–222
developmental basis of, 196–198
evaluation of
for cognitive development, 220–222
for integrated curriculum, 345–346
for language and literacy development, 255–257
for physical development, 318–321
for social development, 290–292
for special-needs and at-risk children, 189–191
for language and literacy development, 237–246, 255–257
for physical development, 305–311, 318–321
for social development, 273–286, 290–292

designing goals for, 279–286
evaluation of, 290–292
and play environment, 277–278
Curriculum continuums, 56
Curriculum models, for early intervention strategies, 169–172
Curriculum planning, 106–108. See also Instruction, planning of
and assessment, 108–113, 114, 115
for children at risk, 47–48, 178–183
for children not at risk, 48–54
for children with disabilities, 166–168
of integrated curriculum, 330
for inclusion of diversity, 335–337, 344–345
to meet developmental needs, 334–337
models for, 339–344
to respond to children's interests, 337–338
to understand connections in knowledge, 338–339
Curriculum resources, published, 169
Curriculum Web, Integrated, 343
Cycle of learning, 203
Cycles, learning (instructional), 118–121

Daily routines, planning of, 93–94
Denver Developmental Screening Test (DDST), 39
Denver Developmental Screening Test-Revised, 14
Denzelle (case study), 61
Development, and learning, 334
Developmental Activities Screening Inventory-II (DASI-II), 39
Developmental approach
and cognitive development, 207–209
and indoor environment, 81

Developmental approach,
continued
   to intervention strategies, 170,
      171
   in language development,
      238–242
   for physical development,
      306–307
   and playground arrangement,
      86–87
   in social development,
      279–283, 284, 285
Developmental basis of curriculum, 196–198
Developmental delay, 28, 351
Developmental domain, integration through, 331–332
*Developmental Indicators for the
   Assessment of Learning—*
   Revised (DIAL-R), 40
Developmental-interactionist
   model, 148
Developmentally appropriate
   curriculum, 106. *See also*
   Curriculum planning
Developmentally appropriate
   instructional strategies,
   172–175
*Developmentally Appropriate Prac-
   tice in Early Childhood Pro-
   grams Serving Children
   from Birth Through Age 8*
   (Bredekamp), 4
Developmentally appropriate
   practices, 187–189, 196
   and integrated curriculum, 335
   and special education,
      158–159
Developmentally appropriate
   programming, 4
Developmental perspective, 34
Developmental profiles. *See* Profiles, student
*Developmental Screening Inven-
   tory-II* (DASI-II), 39
Developmental tasks, as assessment, 63
Development profile, 109–111,
   112

Diabetes, 31, 351
Diagnostic assessment, 48, 64,
   351
Diagnostic tests, published, 65
DIAL-R (*Developmental Indicators
   for the Assessment of
   Learning*—Revised), 40
Didactic techniques, 173
Directed assignments, 215
Directional awareness, 300, 351
Direct testing, 35
Disabilities, children with, 28,
   352. *See also* At-risk children; Early intervention
   programs; Impairment;
   Special needs children
   and Americans with Disabilities
      Act, 10–11, 134, 278
   and child care, 11–12
   curriculum models for, 169–172
   and Developmentally Appropri-
      ate Practices, 158–159
   and developmentally appropri-
      ate strategies, 172–175
   differences in needs of,
      159–160
   in earlier-decades programs, 10
   as future reality, 347
   and Head Start, 7, 134, 139
   historical periods in education
      of, 133
   and initial assessment, 100
   instructional planning for,
      166–169, 314–318
   intervention program for (case
      study), 11
   needs of, 315
   planning instruction for,
      166–169
      in cognitive development,
         218–220
      in physical development,
         314–318
      in social development,
         289–290
   play environments for,
      278–279, 316
   program evaluation for, 190
   and screening, 32–33

   and social development,
      276–277, 289–290
Diversity, 7–10
   and assessment, 180, 190
   attempts to meet, 4
   author's position on, 4–5
   cultural and linguistic, 33
      and antibias curriculum,
         186–187, 276
      and bilingual education, 10,
         29, 180, 184–186, 191,
         254, 255
      and curriculum planning,
         181
      and future increase in ethnic
         populations, 176
      and language development
         planning, 253–255
      and learning style, 181–183
      and social development,
         275–276
      and standardized screening
         measurements, 38
   and developmentally appropri-
      ate practices, 187–188
   evaluation of (beginning of
      year), 94
   and integrated curriculum,
      335–337, 344–345
   at McDougall Elementary
      School, 8
   and play needs, 78
Down's Syndrome children, 32
   curriculum for, 171
Dyslexia, 33, 352

Early childhood, 6, 106
Early childhood environment,
   integration through,
   332–333
Early childhood programs (education), 6–7, 347. *See also*
   Early intervention programs
   assessment in, 16–18 (*see also*
      Assessment)
   current trends in, 3–6
   and developmentally appropri-
      ate practices, 158–159,
      187–189, 335

diversity in, 7–10 (*see also* Diversity)
first examples of, 130
issues and trends in, 10–15
responsibility of, 10
and risk factors, 177–178
screening in, 16–18, 26–42 (*see also* Screening)
and social development theory, 269–271
Early childhood special education. *See* Special education
Early childhood teachers
changing roles for, 158
and special education teachers, 11–12, 156, 158, 172
Early Education Program for Children with Disabilities, 133
Early intervention programs. *See also* Early childhood programs; Head Start programs
background of, 130–135
as cooperative venture, 11
curriculum models for, 169–172
evolution of, 26–27
goals for, 143–144
individual intervention plans, 148–155 (*see also* Individualized Education Plan; Individualized Family Service Plan)
instructional strategies for, 171–175
and integration issues, 155–160
models of, 144–148
and preschool programs, 25
screening and assessment process in, 135–143
Early Language Milestone Scale, 39
Early Learning Accomplishment Profile, 40
Early Screening Inventory, 14
Education, broadening of, 160
Education of All Handicapped Children Act of 1975 (P.L. 94–142), 10, 27, 28, 133, 134, 145

Education of the Handicapped Act amendments of 1986 (P.L. 99–457), 28, 134, 135
Elementary and Secondary Education Act (1965), 27, 133
Emergent literacy, 91, 230–231, 236–237, 241–242, 254, 352
checklist for, 67
development of, 99
and development-learning relation, 334
Emma Frey Elementary School, integrating children and curriculum at, 186
Emotional development
assessment of, 50
as kindergarten element, 284
Emotional disturbances, 33, 352
English as a Second Language (ESL), 10, 30, 33, 254
Environment, 74–75. *See also* Outdoor environment
at beginning of year, 74–75, 92–93
for children with physical impairments (disabilities), 278–279, 315–316
indoor, 75, 78–83, 303–304, 315–316
antibias, 79
integration through, 332–333
least restrictive, 10–11, 133, 135
and physical development, 303–305
and play, 75–78
and social development, 277–279
teaching how to use, 94–95
Evaluation. *See also* Assessment; Screening; Tests
of curriculum and instruction
for cognitive development, 220–222
of integrated curriculum and instruction, 345–346
for language and literacy development, 255–257

for physical development, 318–321
for social development, 290–292
for special-needs and at-risk children, 189–191
of diversity, 94
initial, 16
ongoing, 123–124
progress, 121–122, 123
skill, 121, 122
Event samples, 61
Expressive language, 235, 352
Expressive language skills, 239–240

Facilitator, teacher as, 202, 234, 272, 302
Failure to thrive, 31
Family. *See also* Parent
in assessment process, 140–142
in individual intervention plan development, 155
in screening process, 41–42, 140–142
Federal funding and regulation
and program evaluation, 190–191
in screening and assessment, 18–20
Federal legislation, 21, 131–135. *See also* at P.L.
Federal programs
and screening, 26–27
undue labeling and categorization in, 160
Fetal alcohol syndrome, 9, 352
Field dependent learners, 53, 352
Field independent learners, 53, 352
Fine motor activities, and children with physical impairments, 318
Fine motor development, 298–299, 352. *See also* Motor development
assessment/learning experiences for, 313, 314
assessment of, 49–50, 96, 98

Fine motor skills, 308–309
Formative evaluation
    for cognitive development,
        220–221
    for language and literacy devel-
        opment, 255–256
    for physical development, 318,
        320
    for social development,
        290–291
Froebel, Friedrich, 130
Frost-Wortham Developmental
    Checklist, 307, 310, 313
Functional and adaptive
    approach, to intervention
    strategies, 171
Functional model, 148

Genetic disorder, 31, 352
Gifted and talented children, 33
Goals
    for curriculum
        in cognitive development,
            206–210
        in language development,
            237–238
        in physical development,
            305–306, 307
        in social development,
            279–286
    determining of, 90–92
    for early intervention programs,
        143–144
Graphing, of lunch choices, 62
Greenspan Developmental-Struc-
    turalist Theory, 267, 270
*Griffiths Mental Development
    Scales,* 39
Gross motor activities, and chil-
    dren with physical impair-
    ments, 316–317
Gross motor skills, 308–309
Gross (large) motor skills devel-
    opment, 299, 304, 352.
    See also Motor develop-
    ment
    assessment/learning experiences
        for, 313, 314
    assessment of, 49–50, 96, 97

Group-appropriate integrated
    curriculum, 335
Grouping, instructional
    assessment for, 53–54
    and regrouping, 124
Group life, adjustment to, 274
Group profile, 111
Guidelines for Developmentally
    Appropriate Practices,
    158–159

Handicap, 28, 352
Handicapped Children's Early
    Education Assistance Act
    (P. L. 90–538), 132, 133
Handicapped Children's Early
    Education Program, 133
Hannah (case study of infant),
    31–32
Hard-soft areas, 80
Head Start programs, 7, 26, 27,
    132
    and child-centered curriculum
        and instruction, 328
    and children with disabilities, 7,
        134, 139
    inclusion implemented in, 159
    as models, 147
    selection for, 29
Health, 301
    as curriculum goal, 306, 307
Hearing impairments, and cogni-
    tive development, 218
Hispanic Americans
    learning style of, 181
    projected population increase
        of, 176
Holistic thinkers, 53, 352
Home Start program, 26

IEP. *See* Individualized education
    plan
Impairment, 32, 352. *See also* At-
    risk children; Disabilities,
    children with; Special
    needs children
    cognitive, 166–167, 351
    communication, 167, 252–253,
        351

motor, 167, 352
    physical, 314–315
    self-help, 168, 353
Inclusion, 6–7, 352. *See also* Inte-
    gration
    at Adams Hill Elementary
        School, 174–175
    barriers to, 12
    broadening of, 160
    and instructional strategy, 173
    issues in, 155–160
    levels of, 136–137
    and play environments, 278
    and preschool children, 157,
        276
Inclusive models of early interven-
    tion and education,
    147–148
Individual intervention plans,
    148–155
    and instructional planning, 168
Individualized Education Plan
    (Program) (IEP), 17–18, 74,
    100, 148, 150–151, 352
    and assessment, 189
    forms for, 152–154
    parents' role in, 135
Individualized Family Service Plan
    (IFSP), 100, 134, 148,
    150–151, 352
    family role in, 135, 155
    legislation requiring (P.L.
        99–457), 134
Individuals with Disabilities Edu-
    cation Act (IDEA), 134
Indoor environment, 75, 78–83
    and physical development,
        303–304
    for children with physical
        impairments, 315–316
Infant Intelligence Scale, 39
Infants
    assessment of, 138–139
    and instructional planning,
        166–168
    screening of, 28, 38–40,
        138–139
Initial assessment, 96–100
Initial evaluation, 16–17

Innatist theory, on language development, 232
Inquiry, 203
Instruction
  and assessment, 17, 189–191
  evaluation of, 121–123
    for cognitive development, 220–222
    for integrated instruction, 345–346
    for language and literacy development, 255–257
    for physical development, 318–321
    for social development, 290–292
    for special-needs and at-risk children, 189–191
  and nature of learning, 113, 115
  teacher-directed, 116–118, 173
Instruction, planning of, 89–93.
        See also Curriculum planning
  and assessment, 17–18, 53–54, 109–121, 123, 168–169
  for children at risk, 175–178
    approaches in, 183–189
    and assessment, 178–183
  for children with disabilities, 166–169, 218–220, 289–290, 314–318
  for cognitive development, 201–204
    for children with disabilities, 218–220
    for math and science, 204–205
  and daily routines, 93–94
  for language and literacy development, 233–246
    for children from diverse backgrounds, 253–255
    for children with communication disorders, 252–253
  for physical development, 302–303
    for children with physical impairments, 314–318

curriculum organization, 305–311
  and environment, 303–305
  for social development, 271
    for children with disabilities, 276–277, 289–290
    curriculum goals, 279–286
    curriculum organization, 273–279
    teacher's role, 272–273
Instructional cycles, 118–121
Instructional grouping, assessment for, 53–54
Instructional program, planning of, 89–94
Instructional strategies
  developmentally appropriate, 172–175
  for early intervention programs, 171–172
Instructor, teacher as, 202–203, 235, 273, 302–303
Integrated classroom, 3, 352
Integrated curriculum, 328, 352
  evaluation of, 345–346
  origins of, 328–329
  planning of, 330
    for diversity, 335–337, 344–345
    to meet developmental needs, 334–337
    models of, 339–344
    to respond to children's interests, 337–338
    to understand connections in knowledge, 338–339
  of today, 329–330
  ways of achieving, 330–331
    from developmental domain or subject area, 331–332
    through early childhood environment, 332–333
    through thematic units, 333
    through topics, 332
Integrated Curriculum Web, 343
Integrated language arts curriculum, 245
Integrated learning, 113, 352
Integrated programs, 18

Integration, 6–7, 21, 328. See also Inclusion
  and instructional strategy, 173
  issues in, 155–160
  and P.L. 99–457, 135
Interactionist theory on language development, 232
Interest inventories, 65
Intervention, 6
Intervention programs, 26, 352.
        See also Early intervention programs
Interviews
  in cognitive development assessment, 214–215
  with parents, 56, 57, 41, 125
  for screening, 35, 37
  for social development assessment, 288
  structured, 62
  unstructured, 62
Iowa Test of Basic Skills, 19

Jerome (case study), 59–60
Journaling, 58

Kaufman Assessment Battery for Children, 39
Keryma (case study), 58
Kindergarten
  assessment in, 50–51
  elements for social/emotional development in, 284–285
  establishment of, 130
Kinesthetic learners, 53, 352

Language
  and communication impairments, 167
  components of, 228–229
  difficulties with, 180
Language development, 227–228.
        See also Literacy
  assessment/learning experiences for, 251–252
  assessment of, 50, 52, 98–99, 246–251
  checklists on, 243, 250–251
  curriculum for, 237–246

Language development, *continued*
  evaluation of, 255–257
  planning of instruction for,
    233–246
    for children from diverse
      backgrounds, 253–255
    for children with communica-
      tion impairments, 252–253
    and preschool children,
      235–237
  screening tests for, 39
  theoretical bases for, 231–233
Language needs, of children at
  risk, 182
Language play, 77
Large motor skills. *See* Gross
  motor skills development
Laws, federal, 21, 131–135. *See
  also at* P.L.
Learning. *See also* Cognitive
  development; Learning
  styles
  child's manner of, 113
  cycle of, 203
  and development, 334
  goals and objectives for,
    90–92
  stage dependent and indepen-
    dent, 198
*Learning Accomplishment Profile—
  Diagnostic Edition, The*
  (LAP-D), 91
Learning center activities, timed
  samples of, 60–61
Learning centers
  and curriculum, 81–82
  instruction in, 117
  orienting children to, 95
Learning cycles, 118–121, 352
Learning disability, 4, 33, 219,
    352. *See also* Disabilities,
    children with
Learning environment. *See* Environment
Learning experiences/assessment
  for cognitive development,
    216–218
  for language and literacy devel-
    opment, 251–252

  for physical development,
    313–314
  for social development,
    288–289
Learning styles, 52–53, 352
  and cultural diversity, 181–183
Learning theory, on language
  development, 232
Least restrictive environment
  (LRE), 10–11, 133, 135,
    352
Legislation, federal, 21, 131–135.
  See also at P.L.
Limited English Proficient (LEP)
  children, 185, 352
Literacy, 229–231. *See also* Language; Language
  development
  acquisition of, 233
  assessment/learning experiences
    for, 251–252
  assessment of, 98–99, 246–252
  checklists on, 67, 243–245,
    250–251
  curriculum for, 237–246
    evaluation of, 255–257
  emergent, 67, 91, 230–231,
    236–237, 241–242, 254,
    334
  planning of instruction for,
    233–246
    for children from diverse
      backgrounds, 253–255
    for children with communica-
      tion impairments, 252–253
    and preschool children,
      235–237
Literacy development, emergent,
    99
Locomotor skills, 299, 352. *See
  also at* Motor
Low-income environments, and
  play experience, 78
Lunch choices, graphing of, 62

Mainstreaming, 6, 135, 352
  barriers to, 12
  and preschool children, 276
Materials, instructional, 91–92

Mathematics
  assessment in, 51, 66, 111,
    113, 115
  concept acquisition in, 205
  concept organization in, 211
  and development-learning rela-
    tion, 334
  and mentally retarded students,
    220
Mathematics Their Way (Baratta-
  Lorten), 91
Maturational theory, 171
*McCarthy Scales of Children's Abil-
  ities*, 39
McDougall Elementary School,
  diversity at, 8
Mental retardation, 4, 9, 352
  and cognitive development,
    219–220
*Merrill-Palmer Scale of Mental
  Tests*, 39
Migrant Program, 26
MLU (mean length of utterance),
    235
Modality of learning, 53, 352
Monitoring, of intervention plans,
    189
Montessori, Maria, 130
Montessori schools, 130
Moral development, 262, 264,
    269, 271
Morphemes, 229
Mothers of babies at risk, program
  for, 146
Motor development, 298–300.
  See also Fine motor devel-
  opment; Gross motor skills
  development
  goals for, 305–306
  initial assessment of, 96–97
  screening tests for, 39
Motor impairments, 167, 352
Motor skills, fine and gross,
    308–309
  locomotor skills, 299
Motor skills tasks, 312
*Movement Assessment of Infants,
  The*, 39
Multicultural curriculum, 187

Multicultural perspective, 79, 352
Multidisciplinary or team
    approach
    in individual intervention plan
        development, 148–149
    in screening and assessment,
        138
Multidomain development,
    screening tests for, 39–40
Multilingual programs, 255
Multiple strategies, 15

Native Americans
    learning style of, 183
    "tourist curriculum" on, 333
Naturalistic observation, for
    screening, 35
Noisy-quiet areas, 80
Noncategorical intervention pro-
    grams, 145, 353
Norms, 14, 353
Number concepts, 207, 217
Number extraction, 205
Nutrition, goals for curriculum in,
    306, 307

Objectives, determining of,
    90–92. See also Goals
Observation, 59–61
    case study on, 59–60
    in cognitive development
        assessment, 214
    initial assessment through,
        57–58
    in language and literacy assess-
        ment, 248–249
    naturalistic, 35
    for physical development
        assessment, 311–312
    for screening, 36
    and social development assess-
        ment, 286–287
Opportunity factors, 177
Oral and written language skills
    assessment for, 52
    and emergent literacy, 230–231
Ordinal Scales of Psychological
    Development, 39
Outdoor environment, 75, 83–89

acquainting children with, 95
    assessment of, 221
    for children with physical
        impairments, 316
    and physical development,
        304–305
    for socialization, 272, 277

Parent(s). See also Family
    conference or interview with
        at beginning of year, 56, 57
        records for, 125
        for screening (case study), 41
    and intervention process, 135
Parent-infant intervention pro-
    grams, 147
Parent- or caregiver-focused inter-
    vention programs,
    145–146
Peabody Developmental Motor
    Scales, 39
Peers, and social development,
    263, 264, 266, 270, 275
Perceptual disabilities, 33, 353
Perceptual-motor development,
    300, 353
Performance-based assessment,
    15, 68, 353
Personality differences, 52
Philosophy of learning and devel-
    opment, need to reflect
    on, 89
Phonemes, 228–229
Physical development, 298–301
    assessment/learning experiences
        for, 313–314
    assessment of, 311–312
    evaluation of curriculum and
        instruction for, 318–321
    importance of, 297
    planning instruction for,
        302–303
    for children with physical
        impairments, 314–318
    curriculum organization,
        305–311
    and environment, 303–305
    play in, 301
Physical fitness, 301, 306

and playgrounds, 83
Physical play, 77, 85. See also
    Play
P.L. 88–156 (1963), 132
P.L. 90–538 (1968) (Handicapped
    Children's Early Education
    Assistance Act), 132, 133
P.L. 93–644 (1974), 134
P.L. 94–142 (Education of All
    Handicapped Children Act
    of 1975), 10, 27, 28, 133,
    134, 145
P.L. 94–142 amendments. See P.L.
    99–457
P.L. 98–199 (1983), 134
P.L. 99–457 (Education of the
    Handicapped Act amend-
    ments of 1986), 28, 134,
    135
P.L. 101–336 (1990) (Americans
    with Disabilities Act),
    10–11, 134, 278
P.L. 101–476 (1990), 10
P.L. 101–576 (1990), 134
Planning. See Curriculum plan-
    ning; Instruction, planning
    of
Play, 75–78, 230
    and outdoor environment,
        84–89
    in physical development, 301
    in social development,
        264–266, 277–279
Play and Playscapes (Frost), 85
Playground accessibility, for chil-
    dren with physical impair-
    ments, 317
Playgrounds, 83–89, 304–305.
    See also Outdoor
    environment
Portfolios, 66, 68, 250, 256
Poverty
    in children's environment,
        8–9
    as environmental risk, 31
Pragmatics, 235
Preschool children and programs,
    25. See also Child care
    and assessment, 49, 139–140

Preschool children and programs,
   continued
   and instructional planning,
      168–169
   at-risk identification for, 178
   and children with disabilities,
      276
   curriculum planning for,
      106–108
   inclusion in, 157, 276
   language and literacy acquisi-
      tion in, 235–237
   motor development of,
      299–300, 305
   organized sports for, 301
   and play environment, 277
   screening for, 25, 139–140
      instruments for, 38
      standardized tests for, 13
Preschool Language Scale, 39
Pretend play, 265–266
Preventive intervention programs,
      146
Primary grade children
   assessment ot, 50–51, 139–140
      and instructional planning,
         168–169
      curriculum planning for,
         106–108
      screening of, 139–140
Profiles, student, 100, 109–111,
      112
Program evaluation, 189–191
Progress evaluation, 121–122,
      123, 353
Progressive education, and project
      approach, 328
Progress reports, to parents, 125
Project approach, 328, 339–341
Prosocial behavior, 264, 353
   and environment, 272
Psychosocial theory, 266–267
Public laws. *See at* P.L.
Public schools
   early childhood programs in, 6
   issues related to inclusion in,
      159–160
   state-mandated curriculum for,
      90

Rating scales
   for language development and
      literacy, 250–251
   for social development assess-
      ment, 288
Readiness tests, 13, 353
Reading
   assessments in, 64–65, 111,
      113
      and curriculum planning, 51
      of words with long vowels
         and silent e, 64
   checklists for, 114, 243, 247
   in developmental approach,
      242
   and experiences with books,
      231
   and journaling (case study), 58
Reading to children, 231
*Receptive Expressive Emergent
      Language Scale,* 39
Receptive language, 235, 353
Receptive language skills, 239
Record keeping, 124–125
Records
   anecdotal, 59–60
   cumulative, 55
   running, 60, 287
   and screening, 29, 35, 37
Recycling center, as materials
      source, 92
Regrouping children, 124
Reliability, 14, 353
Risk and opportunity factors,
      177–178
Routines, daily planning of, 93–94
Running records, 60
   in social development assess-
      ment, 287

Safety
   children's understanding of, 95
   goals for curriculum in, 306,
      307
   of outdoor playground, 84–85
Samples
   event, 61
   timed, 60–61, 287
Schedules and routines, 93–94

School life, adjustment to, 274
School reform movement of
      1980s, 3, 107
School year beginning. *See* Begin-
      ning of school year
Science
   concept acquisition in, 204–205
   concept organization in, 211
Screening, 5, 6, 14, 16–18, 25,
      353
   approach for, 34–37
   for bilingual classrooms (Auburn
      School District), 29
   and early intervention pro-
      grams, 135–137
      family role in, 41–42,
         140–142
   for infants and toddlers, 28,
      38–40, 138–139
   for preschool and primary
      age children, 25, 139–140
   steps in, 142–143
   and evolution of early child-
      hood programs, 26–27
   federal regulation in, 18–20
   importance of, 347
   procedures for, 35–37
   scope of, 27–31
   selection of instrument for,
      38–40
   setting up program for, 40–41
   standardized measurement
      instruments for, 12
   target populations for, 31–33
   trends in, 14–15
Second grade, Thelma Goodson's
      (case study), 108–109
Seguin, Edouard, 130
Self-evaluation, by teacher, 256
Self-help impairments, 168, 353
Self-understanding, and social
      development, 274
Sensory delay, 32, 353
Sensory impairment, 353
*Sequenced Inventory of Communi-
      cation Development,
      Revised,* 39
Seriation, 207
Skill evaluation, 121, 122, 353

Social attributes checklist, 281
Social development, 262–264
    assessment/learning experiences
        for, 288–289
    assessment of, 50, 286–288
        initial, 96–97
    checklists on, 112, 280, 282,
        288
    curriculum for
        designing goals of, 279–286
        organizing of, 273–279
        and play environment,
            277–278
    evaluating curriculum and
        instruction for, 290–292
    planning of instruction for, 271
        for children with disabilities,
            276–277, 289–290
        and curriculum, 273–286
        teacher's role, 272–273
    play in, 264–266, 277–279
    screening tests for, 39
    theoretical bases for, 266–271
    and theory-practice connection,
        269–271
Socialization, 261–262, 263
    and play, 277
Social learning theorists, 268
Social needs, of children at risk,
    182–183
Social play, 77, 85, 265. See also
    Play
Social responsibility, as kinder-
    garten element, 284
Social Security Act (1935), 131
Sociodramatic play, 77
Sorting and matching, 207
Spatial awareness, 300, 353
Special education, 11–12
    broadening of, 160
    and Developmentally Appropri-
        ate Practices, 158–159
    and inclusion, 6–7
    and labeling of poor and
        minorities, 27
    screening for, 28–29
Special education teachers, and
    early childhood teachers,
    11–12, 156, 158, 172

Special needs children. See also
    At-risk children; Disabili-
    ties, children with; Early
    intervention programs;
    Impairment
    evaluation programs for,
        189–191
    integration issues on,
        155–160
Speech development, screening
    tests for, 39
Spina bifida, children with, 31,
    353
    support system for families of,
        142
Sports, for preschool children,
    301. See also Physical
    play
Stage dependent learning, 198,
    353
Stage independent learning, 198,
    353
Standardized assessment, and fed-
    eral accountability require-
    ments, 20
Standardized developmental
    inventories, 90–91
Standardized measurement instru-
    ments (tests), 12–14. See
    also Tests
    achievement tests, 3, 20
    in assessment, 12, 179–180
    at Chapter 1 school, 19
    and cultural diversity, 38, 180
    in multiple strategy, 15
    and 1980s teaching focus, 3,
        107
    in program evaluation,
        190–191
State funding, and program evalu-
    ation, 190–191
Statler twins (case study), 55–56
Strategies, instructional. See
    Instructional strategies
Structural theory, on emotional
    development, 267
Student profiles, 100, 109–111,
    112
Subject area approach

    in integration, 331–332
    in language development,
        242–246
    organizing curriculum from,
        210, 211
    for physical development cur-
        riculum, 307
    in social development,
        283–286
Summative evaluation
    for cognitive development,
        221–222
    for language and literacy devel-
        opment, 256–257
    for physical development,
        320–321
    for social development curricu-
        lum and instruction,
        291–292
Supporter, teacher as, 202,
    234–235, 272, 303
Support system(s)
    for families of children with
        spina bifida, 142
    as intervention goal, 143
Survey of records, for screening,
    37. See also Records
Symbolic play, 265–266

Talented children, 33
Tatiana (case study), 58
Teacher(s)
    early childhood and special
        education, 11–12, 156,
        158, 172
    as facilitator, 202, 234, 272,
        302
    as instructor, 202–203, 235,
        273, 302–303
    in physical development,
        302–303
    in social development,
        272–273
    as supporter, 202, 234–235,
        272–273, 303
Teacher-designed assessment,
    62–64
Teacher-directed instruction,
    116–118, 173

Teacher-initiated integrated curriculum, 337

Teacher's role, assessment of (integrated curriculum), 346

Teacher-student conferences, on language development and literacy, 250

Teaching practices
  and 1980s school reform, 3–4, 107
  preschool/kindergarten vs. primary grades, 106

Team approach. *See* Multidisciplinary or team approach

Temperament, 52–53, 353

Temporal awareness, 300–301, 353

Tests. *See also* Assessment; Evaluation
  diagnostic, 65
  direct, 35
  standardized, 12–14, 20, 38, 179–180, 190–191
    in Chapter I school, 19
    in multiple strategy, 15
    and 1980s teaching focus, 3, 107
  written, 63

Texas Guidelines for Intellectual Development for Kindergarten, 208–209

Thematic curriculum, 113, 353
  and cultural diversity, 336
  and progress evaluation, 122

Thematic units, 341–344
  integration through, 333
  and learning cycle, 121

Theoretical influences on screening approach, 34–35

Timed samples, 60
  of learning center activities, 60–61
  in social development assessment, 287

Toddlers
  assessment of, 138–139
    and instructional planning, 166–168
  screening of, 28, 38–40, 138–139

Topics, integration through, 332

Topic web, 341, 342

Toys, and outdoor play environment, 277

Transactional approach, to intervention strategies, 170

Twins, case study on, 55–56

Validity, 14, 353

Vineland Adaptive Behavior Scales, 39

Violence, in children's environment, 8–9

Vision impairments, and cognitive development, 219

Visual learners, 53, 353

Voluntary organizations, 131

War on Poverty, 26, 133

Webbing, 341, 342, 343

Whole language approach, 238, 241

Word knowledge, checklist on, 249

Writing, 231. *See also* Language development; Literacy
  checklists on, 245, 248
  and emerging literacy, 242
  and journaling (case study), 58

Written language skills, assessment for, 52

Written tests, 63

Zigler, Edward, 26

Zone of proximal development, 179, 200, 353

About the Author

Sue Clark Wortham is Professor of Early Childhood and Education at the University of Texas at San Antonio. Prior to beginning a teaching career in higher education in 1979 at UTSA she taught prekindergarten through second grade in the public schools, worked as a school administrator, and was a consultant at an education service center.

In addition to this text she authored *Early Childhood Education: Developmental Bases for Learning and Teaching* and *Measurement and Evaluation in Early Childhood Education* for Merrill/Prentice Hall in 1994. Earlier titles include *Organizing Instruction in Early Childhood* (Allyn & Bacon, 1984) and *Childhood 1892-1992* (Association for Childhood Education International, 1992). In 1990 she coedited *Playgrounds for Young Children: National Survey and Perspectives* with Joe L. Frost (American Alliance for Health, Physical Education, Recreation and Dance).

In 1992 Dr. Wortham served as a Fulbright Scholar in Chile and was elected President Elect of the Association for Childhood Education International in 1994.

She is married to Marshal R. Wortham and has three sons, George, Miles, and Benjamin, and two grandchildren, Elizabeth and Miles Wortham.